Levin Schücking, Eudora Lindsay South

Luther in Rome

Corradina, the last of the Hohenstaufen

Levin Schücking, Eudora Lindsay South

Luther in Rome
Corradino, the last of the Hohenstaufen

ISBN/EAN: 9783337127350

Printed in Europe, USA, Canada, Australia, Japan

Cover: Foto ©ninafisch / pixelio.de

More available books at **www.hansebooks.com**

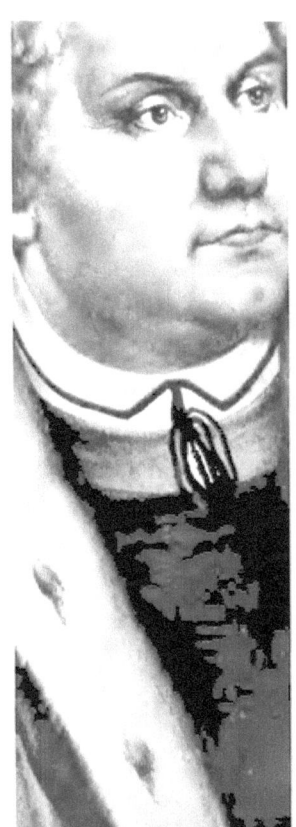

MARTIN LUTHER.

LUTHER IN ROME;

OR,

Corradina, the Last of the Hohenstaufen.

A RELIGIO—HISTORICAL ROMANCE.

TRANSLATED FROM THE GERMAN OF
LEVIN SCHÜCKING
BY
MRS. EUDORA LINDSAY SOUTH,

*Principal of Excelsior Collegiate Institute, Franklin Co., Ky,
and Author of "Wayside Notes and Fireside Thoughts," etc.*

"I would not take a hundred thousand florins not to have seen Rome."
—*Dr. Martin Luther.*

1890:
A. M. THAYER & CO., PUBLISHERS,
BOSTON.

CONTENTS.

VOLUME I. EGINO.

		PAGE
I.	The Bell-founder of Ulm	9
II.	Parva Domus; Magna Quies	18
III.	Irmgard	26
IV.	Notions of a German Girl	33
V.	In the Castle of the Savelli	39
VI.	Wedded to the Dead	52
VII.	Coat of Arms of the Hohenstaufen	56
VIII.	Stanza della Segnatura	60
IX.	A Picture of the Church	75
X.	The Secret of the Handicraft	82
XI.	How the Soul-plant Grows	91
XII.	In the Cloister	95
XIII.	The Exercise-master	106

VOLUME II. THE DAUGHTER OF EMPERORS.

I.	Corradina	119
II.	A Proud Lineage	125
III.	Livio Savelli	130
IV.	In the Studio of Raphael	136
V.	Brother Martin's Resolution	154
VI.	Cinque-Cento	161
VII.	Domestic Life in the House of the Savelli	181
VIII.	The Inquisitor of Heretical Depravity	192
IX.	Thoughts of a German Monk	197
X.	Gossip of an "Artista"	206
XI.	Who Knows?	214
XII.	A Way and a Hope	219
XIII.	Nella Perduta Gente	228

CONTENTS.

VOLUME III. THE DAUGHTER OF EMPERORS (Conclusion).

		PAGE
I.	LIVIO'S STRATAGEM	235
II.	IN THE NIGHT	244
III.	IN THE CHAPEL OF THE IMMURED	253
IV.	BROTHER MARTIN	262
V.	THE INCARNATION OF CHRIST IN THE VATICAN	264
VI.	ALFONSO VON FERRARA	269
VII.	FAITH AND WORKS	274
VIII.	IN THE HOUSE OF GIULIETTA	283
IX.	THE PICTURE OF CHRIST AND THE HEAD OF THE GODDESS	288
X.	THE WATCH-DOG	298
XI.	SAN DOMINICO'S TORCH AND SERPENT	302
XII.	CORRADINA	307
XIII.	A MONOLOGUE OF THE MONK	318
XIV.	THE POPE GOES TO SLEEP	322
XV.	CALLISTO'S NEWS	325
XVI.	THE LAST DROP	335
XVII.	THE BOOK OF FREDERIC II.	341
XVIII.	AT THE COUCH OF IRMGARD	344
XIX.	THROUGH!	354
XX.	THE MORTARA CHILD OF THE WORLD	363
XXI.	THOUGHTS OF THE EMPEROR	370

LIST OF ILLUSTRATIONS.

Portrait, Martin Luther	Frontispiece
Portrait, Mrs. Eudora L. South (Translator)	7
The Roman Forum	39
St. Peter's, Rome, Exterior	60
Portrait, Raphael Santi	68
St. Peter's, Rome, Interior	106
Holy Family	140
Sistine Madonna, Raphael	149
Transfiguration, Raphael	181
Raphael Santi Memorial	206
Madonna, St. Cecelia, Raphael	235
Luther Memorial	262
Portrait, Pope Julius II.	268
Luther, Entry into Erfurth	340
Luther Burning the Pope's Bull	363

PREFACE.

ISTORICAL fiction sustains to history the same relation as the vivid, life-like touch of the artist to a portraiture in words. To most persons, the knowledge of history means but an abstraction of dates and incorporeal facts; but, really, events of history should pass before the mental eye as the moving scenes of a drama, while the main actor in these events should stand out with the distinctness of a life-size portrait. To accomplish this result, several things are needful. In the first place, the period must be one whose events have been world-wide in their influence; one in which all society has become revolutionized; one in which humanity, as upon the lava-streams of some eruption, has been lifted out of darkness into light. Invariably, in such a period, all momentous occurrences seem to center about some one hero; to blend so closely with his personality that we can scarcely decide whether the period made the man, or the man the period. Such a period was the early part of the sixteenth century; such a hero was Martin Luther. "In him," says Schücking, "were blended a gifted intellect, an admirable courage, a deep Christian soul. He demanded for his people, his whole oppressed people, the right to exercise freedom of belief; and this human element in the great contest gave him his success."

But to clothe history with reality the imagination must be aroused. As a rule, however, the historian fails just here; but the sixteenth century with its hero has been unusually fortunate in this respect. As if under the touch of some master artist, the portrait of the stern reformer is evoked by the words of D'Aubigné. He stands out upon the dark background of an age of scholasticism, the figure brought into clear relief by the threatened flames of martyrdom. His attitude is that of fearless, violent assault,— his hand raised as if to hurl some deadly weapon at the hydra-headed form of Error rising out of the Lernean Marshes of his surroundings.

But there is one stage of Luther's life into which history gives us little insight, — the stage of transformation, of mental struggle preceding the resolution to make of himself the reformer he afterward became. "There remains," says Schücking, "ample room for the play of fancy in filling out this gap," and the play of his fancy has resulted in this work, "Luther in Rome." In accordance with history, the time of the narrative is the year 1510. A few years previous, mankind had witnessed the spectacle of the reign of Alexander Borgia; but now, upon the highest throne of Christendom, sat Pope Julius II., whose one aim was to make the whole world but slaves to the Papal Chair. Unwittingly, however, the Pope was nourishing an influence which must ultimately help to defeat his own plans. Classic pagan literature, with Raphael as its exponent, was already doing much to break the shackles Julius was forging; soon, Luther, goaded to this extreme by the evident worldliness and tyranny of Rome, showed men how to become free indeed.

But, suffice it to say, Schücking has furnished, in this volume, the missing views in the panorama of Luther's life. The pleasure derived from the work in the original, the translator now gladly shares with the thousands of those who cannot read German.

If the reader is already familiar with D'Aubigné's "History of the Reformation" and with the "Schönberg-Cotta Family," he will yet derive from the perusal of this volume a far more vivid conception of Luther's character. If, however, this should fall into the hands of one wholly unacquainted with Luther, like the masterpiece of some great artist, he will see in it "a thing of beauty to be a joy forever."

MRS. EUDORA LINDSAY SOUTH,
THE TRANSLATOR.

Yours truly,
    Eudora Lindsay South

VOLUME I.

EGINO.

CHAPTER I.

THE BELL-FOUNDER OF ULM.

N a morning early in the month of May of the year 1510, not far from Rome, on the north side of the city, rode a stately built but youthful personage along a stony path which led between old and broken vineyard walls. It was in the neighborhood of that little, walled-up tunnel which they call the Arco Oscuro.

The rider wore a coat of black, lined with dark-red silk, and from his cap of black velvet depended a long, white ostrich plume. This ornament was attached to the left side, thus marking the wearer as a Ghibelline; for the Guelph wore his on the right. Upon his breast glittered a golden charm, suspended from a chain of gold; and as he seemed too young to have earned such a favor as a princely reward for his services in war or in peace, its possession must have been due to high birth. In his broad, glove-encased right hand he flourished a long, white riding-whip; from his left side hung a long rapier in its great protecting sheath, above which a finely engraved hilt protruded.

This youth, about five and twenty years of age, was the son of a German prince. His name was Egino von Ortenburg. His elder brother was the reigning count in the little German province in which the youthful rider had his home. He had himself been sent to Rome, to carry on a suit in which his house was involved.

The way which he followed on this pleasure ride led over the ridge of the elevation over which his horse was now passing, onward and downward, till it led into an open country,—a bit of the Campagna. Through this, at a distance of five minutes or a little more, one could espy the Tiber, its waters now swollen to the limit of its banks. Still a good stretch before the rider reached the river, he came to a well, all walled up and shaded by lofty, old trees. From its mineral waters, this well bore the name of Aqua Acetosa.

Under the shade of the trees at this well he encountered three living creatures, upon whom he idly let fall his glance,—a glance of that fleeting kind which sees yet does not perceive. While the young man, without interest, rides on, let us give to this group the attention which they failed to win from him. It consisted of a young lad, an old man, and an old donkey,—all on the far side of a wall about three feet high, which surrounded and supported the mouth of the well.

We must first give our attention to the donkey,—for this member of the little family bore a pack-saddle, on each side of which appeared two insecurely over-filled baskets. To the burden-bearer, to the over-laden, to the care-oppressed, to the pack-donkey in a family, should the first rank, in every case, be given.

The donkey was gray, small, and had the soft, mild, and resigned look of one from whom there is always required much action and never any counsel. He saw the steed of the Count of Ortenburg stride past, throwing up his head and snorting upon him, yet by no expression of the countenance did the humble beast betray envy.

The old man was, like the donkey, small and very ugly. Moreover he was very much deformed. He had a nose which seemed to have had the ambition to arrive at a place as quickly as the forward-protruding hump on the breast below it, so it had grown far, far out into the air. This nose (if indeed it was real, and not, as one might have thought, made of pasteboard) expressed a remarkable degree of physical activity, as did also the projecting chin; but the little green-gray eyes disturbed this expression. They had about them something extraordinarily unsteady and shy, thus making more hideous this man with the nut-cracker figure.

The young lad had curly, blonde hair, and a face browned, or rather yellowed, by sun and dust. Perhaps it needed only to be washed to make of it a right-pretty, boyish countenance; although the rather fine-cut features were also irregular, and a little crowded one into another, instead of being disposed in broad, simple lines. He had the hair carefully parted in the middle; and this, together with the drooping, soft, blue eyes, made his appearance somewhat girlish.

As the rider passed by the wall surrounding the well, behind which the group was reposing, the hunchback lying upon the ground, the donkey standing, and the lad resting his elbows upon the wall, his horse shied,— perhaps on account of the man's ugliness. It made a spring to one side, and some object fell clattering to the ground.

Count Egino quieted the animal with his voice, at the same time shortening the reins and bringing him to a halt. Then looking upon the ground, and pointing with his riding-whip, he called to the lad in Italian : —

"You, there,— come and pick that up for me."

It was a little, oblong silver plate toward which he pointed. The bridle of his horse was covered with similar plates, and this one had sprung loose and been hurled to the ground by the movements of the excited animal.

The youth looked at it without moving.

The rider turned his horse close to the wall, and swinging his whip, cried out again : —

"Heh! sluggard, move yourself, and pick up for me that piece of metal."

"I will not," said the lad, angrily knitting his brows, and looking without other motion into the eyes of the rider.

In the same instant fell the riding-whip, the stroke being aimed at the face of the boy; but a sudden movement of the head caused it to strike, instead, the left shoulder.

Up to this time the hunchback had only turned his head with a certain apathy to see what was going on; but now he sprang up with the suddenness of a locust, and swung himself with a wonderful agility upon the back of the wall. With the same agility a fearfully large, powerful, hair-covered fist was thrust into the reins of the horse, and it held them as in an iron grasp. The horse attempted to rise upon its hind feet; the fist held it down as in an iron vise. The rider looked with unconcealed fright upon the face of the hunchbacked creature on the wall before him. The face of this being, transformed by anger and a thirst for revenge, had a somewhat supernatural hideousness; and a supernatural power seemed also, indeed, to lie in the hand which stretched itself out toward the rider, in order to tear him from the horse.

This would probably also have happened, although Egino was on his guard, and was reaching with his right hand for his dagger, if the lad, pressing his right hand upon his wounded shoulder, had not called out : —

"Let him alone, Uncle; let him alone. Do him no harm."

The boy uttered this in the German speech. The enraged monster seemed, however, accustomed to render to him an involuntary obedience. He let the reins loose, and laughed now at the rider, grinning in his face. His laugh had in it something of the insane, if indeed it did not mean to say:—

"See! I could kill you and crush you to atoms if I wished," and it expressed only joy in this superiority of power. Count Egino quieted his horse, then said, likewise in German:—

"You are Germans — fellow-countrymen? Now, then, I am sorry that I have beaten you, my lad, as a good-for-nothing Roman vagabond, for which I mistook you. You might, however, with a little friendliness, and a very little inconvenience, have saved me the trouble of dismounting."

"That would I have done," answered the youth in German, "if you had made the request politely. Now I am glad I didn't do it since you are a German; for your rude behavior shows that you do not deserve the slightest accommodation from your countrymen."

Egino looked upon the boy in surprise; his eye glanced as if inquiringly over the slight, weak form in its simple coat of cloth. Then he replied in a tone of good-humored scolding:—

"Now, now, nothing unkind. If my hand is overhasty, so is your tongue. Let us conclude a peace, and both make it good,— I the stroke with the hand; you your scolding with the tongue. Here is my hand." Stooping over he reached to the boy his right hand. The latter took it, and, appeased, said:—

"I am satisfied, and next time, if you ask me nicely, will pick up what you have lost."

"What I have lost?" rejoined Egino, with a fleeting smile; "of that will you find little to pick up. One loses many a good thing, to be sure, on the way from his twentieth to his thirtieth year, especially if this way leads over Rome. But if they are lost they are not to be found again."

"There is, doubtless, among the things you have lost, either your head, your heart, your calling, or your courage."

"The devil!" said Egino, this time looking with real surprise upon the soft, speaking eyes of the boy. "You have, at least, not lost, on your way from Germany here, a precocious mother-wit. I wonder only that, with it, you have made your journey hither on foot. German mother-wit and German shrewdness stand not at a very high price here, — indeed, German things in general, unless it is German money."

"We come also with German money, even," responded the youth, as with a quiet self-consciousness.

"With German money?"

The hunchback, who, during this conversation, had slipped down from the wall, and propped upon it both elbows, and upon these his head, so that he could stare with still and satisfied grin upon the rider on the other side of the wall, suddenly turned to his young companion.

"Irmgard!" cried he, in a sharp, angry tone of reproof.

"Be still, Uncle; I know what I am saying."

"Irmgard?" said the rider, slowly uttering the name in questioning astonishment.

"That is my name," said Irmgard, candidly.

"That is your name," rejoined Egino, smiling; "and I — well, I name myself a blockhead not to have seen at once that you are a girl. I ought to have known that from your eyes. Now I am doubly sorry that I struck you."

"I am not."

"You are not? Wherefore?"

"Because it was a rude injury you have committed, and because, as an honorable German, you must now seek to make it good. It is but just that you should be of service to poor, stupid, ugly, dear Uncle Kraps and myself. We come unprotected and alone, — my uncle has so willed it, — into this strange land, among a strange people, of whom the more I see the less I like. We should thank Heaven if we find some one who must now advise and help us."

Egino looked upon the maiden awhile in silence, then threw himself from the saddle, fastened his horse to the nearest willow, and seated himself upon the wall. Folding his arms upon his breast, while Irmgard leaned upon the wall from the inner side, he said: —

"You are right about that. I am ready to render you aid and counsel, if you need them. To be sure, I am myself not of much consequence here, as I am a foreigner; but I am Count Egino, of Ortenburg, and having been in the city several weeks, I have, at any rate, more friends than you. So tell me, now, what can I do for you?"

Irmgard did not appear at all excited to learn that the young man was a person of such distinction. Had she inferred as much from his appearance, or had her long journey accustomed her not to manifest surprise at anything? Or did it lie in her character, which showed itself, in general, of a peculiarly quiet and self-possessed kind? She only replied:—

"We are not so distinguished. We are natives of Ulm. My Uncle Kraps is a bell-founder. He is very clever in his art. He can also mould cannon, culverin, falconet, and other tubular pieces of artillery. In this way he has earned much money, which he has saved up, and added to it an inheritance."

"Yes, yes, an inheritance," here interposed Uncle Kraps, with a wonderfully sly laugh, which he still continued to himself long after Irmgard had resumed speaking.

"I am," said she, "an orphan, the daughter of my Uncle's sister. He adopted me; and since I have been large enough I have nursed him and cared for his house. Therefore his talk was always of taking me out into the world as soon as I should be grown up. He talked incessantly of traveling and going out into the world. He did not like to stay in Ulm; for years it had been barely endurable to him. 'If the bells travel so can I,' he would say. On Thursday of the last Passion Week he said: 'To-day the bells I have moulded fly to Rome, where the Pope baptizes them. When the spring comes will I also fly to Rome.'"

"'We will stay there, Irmgard,' he would say; 'I will see what the bells do next Passion Week in Rome. You will go with me. We will buy a donkey,—a donkey and a pack-saddle, with two baskets for carrying. It will carry our clothing and my money. With this money I will in Rome become a lord, as good as the town-clerk or the recorder of Ulm. With money one can become a lord in Rome, and that will I do. They have long enough called me here the crooked silver thief, the spit-devil; long enough has every one who sees me acted as if it cost him the entrance-fee of a jest to dare to look upon me; as if he must make himself even by some new sally of wit, some word of derision or insult at the expense of my appearance. Long enough; Irmgard and I have had enough. Now you are grown large I will set out. I will mould no more bells. Those I have moulded are sufficient to toll them all to the grave, or as poor sinners to the gallows, whither they may be going. I will be a lord! In Rome! There it may come to pass. The city provost has told me so. One receives a great Latin parchment about it, and a title, and a blue hat with a broad silver border on it, or a red one with a gold border. Besides, he receives so much yearly, that he gets richly the desires of his life.' Isn't it true, Uncle, that you have told me all this?"

Uncle Kraps nodded his head with an expression of pleasure.

"Yes, I have said so," he answered. "So it was, Irmgard. But I had rather have the red hat. If my money can bring the red one, I had rather have it red."

Egino shook his head wonderingly over this remarkable pilgrim.

"What, then, do you wish to become?" said he, turning to the bell-founder. "President of the Grain-commission? Secretary of Briefs, or Inspector of Excise? Assessor of the Board of Salt? Doorkeeper? Janizary? Stenographer of the Pope? You could certainly be any one of these, since you are so rich, and there are Germans enough among all these people,— in fact, out of all free lands are they, and especially Germany. Pope Julius has just now begun to appoint one hundred new Writers of the Archives; to obtain that position you need only to pay into the treasury of the Pope seven hundred and fifty *scudi*."

"Do you see, Irmgard — do you see?" and Uncle Kraps turned upon the maiden, his face all laughing. "That is just what the city provost told me; he hasn't lied, as you thought. He has also given me an excellent testimonial of my skill, my good behavior, my honorable calling all my life; and now I will go with it to the — what did you call the man, my lord?"

"The Treasurer of His Holiness."

"I will go to the Treasurer of the Pope. Bridle the donkey, Irmgard. The provost has not lied to me. Bridle the donkey, child; we will now go farther."

"Then I will beg pardon of the provost," said Irmgard, "for I have always had the fear that he was making sport of you, just as the whole city thought they might dare to do."

With that she turned to pick up the bridle, which was lying on the ground, and to put it upon the donkey.

In the meantime Count Egino let his glance pass from the uncle to the niece, and from her back to the uncle. Now his look followed the quiet and graceful movements of the girl, while he said : —

"But you have, as yet, told me only half of your story; and if I am to be your friend and adviser here in Rome, I must know it all. Was it for the sake of safety upon your journey, Irmgard, that you have adopted the garb of a boy?"

"It was not possible to do otherwise," she responded, half turning her back as she busied herself with the donkey. "In order to find safe lodgings we must go always from cloister to cloister. The pious fathers who thus afforded us food and shelter could not have received into their retreat a maiden; and if, on that account, we had knocked for a night's lodging at some nunnery, the nuns would have set up a great cry over the appearance of this poor Uncle, and have driven him away, though he is not at all captivating. It was necessary, you see, that one of us should change sex; and as Uncle Kraps," said Irmgard, with the shadow of a roguish smile, "showed no natural fitness to become a reputable female, I was obliged to become a boy."

"And a very pretty one at that," said Egino, ever more drawn by this apparition, whose simple artlessness and candor had for him something so much the more pleasing the more it stood in contrast with the whole nature of the world in which he had lived for months.

"Will you now, indeed, tear yourself away?" he continued. "Is your Uncle Kraps, then, in such a hurry to see himself in the blue or red hat?"

"You see he is," answered Irmgard, smiling. "We will betake ourselves to the German Wayfarer's Inn. The good monks where we were last night described this place to us, so we can easily search it out. Uncle Kraps finds everywhere the way and path."

"Well, then," responded Egino, "I will come there to look after you; and if you need me, find me at the Albergo del Drago, in the Via della Mercede, by San Silvestro. Can you fix all that in your mind?"

"Oh, yes! Albergo del Drago — Via della Mercede, by San Silvestro," repeated the maiden. "I shall find myself there if anything should happen which would compel us to go to you for advice. On the way hither we have learned to speak Italian, Uncle and I, for which you should rejoice, Count Egon ——"

"Egino — Count Egino, from Ortenburg."

"Count Egino, from Ortenburg. And now farewell. Your horse becomes impatient that you should waste so much time with us humble folk. He is more proud than his master, it seems."

"That is quite likely, when the master is such a modest fellow," laughed Egino, reaching Irmgard again his hand, bowing to the grinning bell-founder, and turning again to remount his horse.

When he had swung himself upon the horse and ridden some distance, he looked back several times upon his new acquaintances, and saw how they started out. Irmgard walked before; the donkey followed; last, with travel-wounded feet, came hunchbacked Uncle Kraps.

"A remarkable pair of clients I have won there," said Count Egino, finally, to himself, — "won through a blow of my riding-whip." "Wonderful," he continued, as they disappeared out of his sight. "I feel, since that occurred, as if the maiden, this free-spoken Irmgard, already stands near me as an old acquaintance; as if, since then, between my soul and hers there were something that binds us closer,— the bond of an obligation toward her; or, indeed, that of an old friendship, — or, — now, let it be what it will, I will do for her what I can. This old bell-founder will buy for himself a title, and a right to go about in stately robes of honor! As if, on that account, the street gamins will any the less cry after him, '*Ecco pasquino*,' or the people the less name him ugly Æsop, although he may have ten times the right to let himself be called Lord Secretary, or Lord Stenographer."

That Uncle Kraps would soon win for himself such a right, Count Egino did not doubt; for in Rome, at that time, such was not difficult to acquire.

The Popes, since the time of Sixtus IV., had adopted a wonderful method of obtaining loans to the state. Our states, when they need money, give bonds with interest coupons. The canonical law, however, forbade the giving or receiving of interest. The Popes gave, instead of a bond, a parchment which conferred a title,— an office with all its privileges. The salary of this office represented the interest of the sum paid to obtain it. So, by the payment of a certain number of *scudi*, one could become, not only, as at present, a creditor, but one of the innumerable, all-important officials and honor-bearers of the state. Let a man even be by birth such an object of ridicule as this bell-founder of Ulm, if it were established that his precious metal consisted of pure stuff, even he could attain to this honor.

CHAPTER II.

PARVA DOMUS; MAGNA QUIES.

COUNT EGINO had taken a course downward along the Tiber; at the foot of precipitous, upheaved heights of tufa on his left, he rode upon his beautiful blooded black steed. On the right, before him, rose the arches of the Milvian bridge, still protected by a strong tower, and extending over the golden flood which swelled and rushed madly roaring beneath. When Egino had reached this, and with it the old Flaminian Way, he followed this road, turning again to the left toward the city. It was alive with pedestrians: with lazy fellows who sat upon donkeys in the shade of a three-cornered roof of old, dirty linen ingeniously attached to the saddle; with women leading children by the hand and carrying great bundles on their heads; with pilgrims, equestrians, and peasants of the Campagna, who led clumsy oxen before heavily laden wagons, urging them on with long goads. All made a great confusion, crying out and raising a cloud of dust, which Egino would not have encountered had it not been his point of destination was on this Flaminian Way. It was the villa of a friend, which arose on the left, behind the endlessly long walls accompanying the Way, and separating from it the vines and gardens by its side. The villa lay about half way between the Ponte Molle and the Flaminian Gate. At the place where it began, a profusion of blooming roses had thrown themselves over the top of the wall. Cypress and laurel reared their dark green behind it, thus making known an asylum of rest and summer retirement. From the hot, deeply dust-covered earth of the sunny, noise-filled street, through the gray, heavy wooden gate on which Egino knocked, one could not enter this circle of green without refreshing his inner being with a deep inhalation, and feeling in all the fibers of sensation an increased delight in the day.

The casino, or dwelling-house of the villa, stood in the background, with its rear moved up close to the steep chain of heights, which here, falling away precipitously, overlooked the valley of the Tiber. It arose three stories above a terrace; from the terrace led to the right a stairway of stone, into a little, open portico, or *pergola*, from which was the entrance to the main story of the building.

It was small,—the whole thing. On the frieze over the upper windows, of which there were four, appeared the inscription, "*Parva domus ; magna quies.*"*

As he entered the villa, admitted by an old gardener, Egino himself led his horse into a stall leaning against the inner side of the wall near the gate,—a narrow place prepared only for two goats. Then he strode to the casino, already waving from a distance at the two persons whom he saw sitting at the breakfast-table under the portico. It was a man and a woman. The former gayly returned his greeting with his hand; the lady stepped to the balustrade of the little hall and cried to him :—

"The cheerful morn brings ever welcome guest."

Egino hastened up the steps of the terrace and the hall, in order to shake the friendly hands stretched out toward him. He was soon seated between them at the table spread with wine, bread, honey and fruits. The hostess tasted for him the Venetian glass which the host had filled with Monte-Pulciano, and soon they were in the midst of a lively conversation, which derived its tenor from what one might have called the mental mirror of their surroundings.

In a portico within whose walls old works of statuary, remnants of classic art, have been built up ; in a villa where the eye rests upon evergreen walls of laurel and cypress, while springing fountains cool the air with their restless play ; upon a height from which one sees the golden Tiber flowing, and looks down upon the ruins of heathen, and basilicas of Christian Rome,— on such a spot, between esteemed and honored persons, whose souls we love because they are kindred souls, can only one kind of interchange of thought exist,— that which mirrors something of the same beauty that has spread its charm over the surroundings.

"'*Magna quies !*'" said Egino. "Have you written that, or some of your predecessors, upon the front of your house, Signor Callisto?"

"I, after I had brought my wife into this house," answered Signor Callisto,—a finely built man in the thirties, with intelligent features, and a mouth around which a mocking smile was ever imminent, if

*Little house; great quiet.

not in actual existence, while his eyes, half shut as in a dream, let his glance wander in the distance.

"Your husband"—Egino turned to the young and beautiful wife, who, in her light morning dress, presented the picture of a stately and distinguished Roman lady, only more tender, smaller, and also sweeter than the usual type of Roman beauty—"your husband speaks for you great praise, Donna Ottavia, if I may be allowed to translate '*quies*' as peace."

"You but poorly comprehend his derisive smile, Signor Conte Gino," answered Donna Ottavia, "if you take it as an expression of praise for me. It is nothing else but an epigram upon me."

"An epigram? And how could that be?" asked Egino.

"He will declare," continued Ottavia, looking roguishly at her husband, "that for a long time I kept him in a sore and stinging pain of the heart, so long as I coquettishly let him sue for me. Now, since I have given him my hand, has he — rest. The heart-flame is extinguished."

She gave him a light tap on the upper part of the arm.

"You women are short-sighted," answered the host; "otherwise would you, in the '*magna quies*,' recognize the greatest compliment, the most brilliant glorification, which a man can inscribe upon a house in which his wife rules——"

"I am of that opinion also," interposed Egino; "for it is next to saying that she rules with quiet sweetness, and makes no noise about it; she is gentle, — she doesn't scold or indulge in anger."

"And, furthermore," said the host, interrupting him, "it says she has given to her husband the blessed rest of the heart, the rest in the beloved, which comes over us only when we have succeeded in winning the full surrender of a wife, — the blissful assurance of possessing her, the affectionate constancy of a true being sacrificing to us her life."

"And I think," continued Egino, "only the woman with a soul, only the great womanly nature, can give this rest. She is simple in her feeling, and in this simplicity strong. Every noble thing is simple, unchangeable, quiet. Therefore is fidelity the most beautiful virtue; it is the highest indication of a character. Only the contracted feminine nature, — you must know, Donna Ottavia, that I divide your whole sex into two classes, ladies and waiting-maids, — only the waiting-maid, with her caprice, her little tricks, her smart play of fickle alluring, then thrusting aside; her alluring, provoking, and growing angry, in order then to soften down again, once more to withdraw, — only she maintains the continual unrest. Especially is this the case when a man has become her sport who himself is a great and simple nature, and who takes such a being, whom he cannot see through, with the full tragic of his own earnest and profound nature. From all this, Donna Ottavia, you see how the inscription of your husband contains a high tribute to your excellence."

Donna Ottavia shook her head.

"You take it as a German, Signor Conte. You interpret it according to your own disposition. I wager my lord and spouse did not think of all this. He is a philosopher, a Stoic, — one of those unfortunately enviable ones to whom the world can give nothing more, and from whom it can take nothing, because they believe themselves to have everything within them, and find in their inner world a full sufficiency. So has he understood the *'magna quies.'*"

"You do me wrong," replied Signor Callisto, laughing. "I have never been a Stoic toward you; when I saw your countenance, there was always as little philosophy in me as in a love ditty that a singer pours forth, accompanied by his lute, under the balcony of his beloved, by the shimmer of the stars of a summer night, by the murmuring of a fountain, and in the fragrance of orange blossoms. Indeed, philosophy was not strong in me in such moments. We men of the south may not be able to know the still, emotion-spinning disposition of the German of which you speak; but there is living in our natures something different, more powerful, more poignant. It is the inextinguishable longing for the wife from whom our whole nature receives tone and tuning, from whom it becomes eternally filled, thus making our natures musical; for only music can express this longing. Wherever one of us strikes a musical tone, there also breaks forth this longing in all its might, and therefore our music has always the same purport."

"Your inscription, then," said Donna Ottavia, interrupting him here, "says nothing more than this: since I have become your wife, this longing no more constrains you to strike the lute, and with a voice of moderate compass and of a culture which leaves much yet to be wished for, to disturb the quiet of the still summer nights."

All laughed, and Count Egino then said: —

"Let us leave the inscription alone; let it mean what it may, it shows, in any case, how rich the world is, and how full of meaning every single thing in it. One needs only to look around him, as here from this portico, in order to discover a thousand objects which captivate our minds, and set our souls to vibrating; one needs only to read two words, as the inscription on your house, to find material for an hour's discussion."

"Until one has learned," interposed Callisto, "to find for the disturbed soul the anchor-ground of such a *quies*, and to let his mind be no more taken captive, but to make himself strong to resist disturbing impressions."

"That is hard to learn," answered Egino. "The wealth of the world, and even of the world which surrounds me here, stirs my soul to its lowest depths, and hurries my mind now to this, now to that form which rises before me here, now in this, now in that realm of thought and feeling. It has about it something distracting. I wish at times to cry out, 'Whence can I go to save myself from this Rome!' There is the Old World, with its monuments, its ruins, its broken columns, its mutilated works of marble; there are the structures of stone reaching high in the air, whose proud outlines fill me with thoughts of the greatness, the mental superiority of the Ancients; there are the dazzling statues of antique art, the marble figures of gods and heroes, from which the conception of the beautiful, I might say, overwhelms me! There are all the creations of Christian Rome, — its basilicas, its graves of the martyrs, its stone and metal wrought traditions of the most sublime mystery, of the deeds of the incarnate God, who now makes gods of men. There is the Holy Father, surrounded by every earthly splendor, — that wonderful man who, in his double nature, belonging half to earth, half to heaven, stands with his feet upon the grave of the Apostles, with his infallible head reaching high above our circle of vision into the clouds of heaven, where the Holy Spirit whispers to him his inspirations. There is the middle point of the world, the point whence the culture of Western humanity goes out, whither their veneration, their thoughts, their cryings for help, flow back. Beneath my steps resound the vaults of the Catacombs, — the mine which, silently dug out under the earth of the heathen world, at last scatters this into the air; beneath my footsteps here rises the dust which perhaps contains the ashes of the Scipios, of the Cæsars. In the storm which rages over my head, I hear now the boisterous shout of the common people at the triumphal procession of their emperors; now the howl of pain from those beaten and dying under the claws of the beasts of the arena; now the shrill outcry of the mob which destroys the golden statues of Nero. I cannot look upon the rolling waves of the Tiber there but, in imagination, I see the statues of gods which rest upon its bottom; I cannot see the Aurelian Wall jutting out, but it places before me the armed pretorian host, as they strode over its battlements, their glance turned to the North, whence the armies of Alaric and Theodoric, the gigantic Goths, threateningly approached. Thus aroused, taken by storm, agitated, yes, often intoxicated, if you would so name it, — whence, then, shall come to the soul this profound quiet, this *magna quies?*"

Donna Ottavia had listened in silence to the young man all aglow with his theme; now she said: —

"You have been thrown a stranger into this world, Signor Conte Gino, and you are young; what so moves you and will not let you rest may have this influence upon your heart, because this heart is free from thoughts of its own existence. As the flood when the sluices are open pours into an empty channel, so the rich world surrounding you here pours its influence into your inner being. When you have grown older, and a life of its own has formed itself in the depths of your soul, filling it full, then the pressure of this flood-tide, finding no longer a deep and empty channel to fill, ceases of itself; and if you are then again at home, some loving hand will surely dare to write upon your German balcony what Signor Callisto inscribed for me upon the frieze of our little dwelling."

"Good Heaven!" exclaimed Egino. "When the heart is so full, do you call it without a life of its own, and altogether empty? A soul which is inflamed with all the beauty of the world; a will which is resolved to weave into its life, as in a garland, only the great and glorious, and a spirit which revels in the blessed foretaste of this greatness and glory, — do you call this still without a life of its own, still empty?"

"Conte Gino," replied Ottavia, "you are to some extent a poet, and therefore can I not make myself intelligible to you with my thought, which will seem to you tame. But there are two kinds of poesy, — one in our breast, the other in our heart; the one belongs to enthusiastic men, the other to more sober-feeling women; the one impels to conquer the great and glorious and makes proud, the other teaches to protect, to foster, to help, and makes humble; the one feeds itself upon the great and powerful, the one agitates, the other quiets; the one looks upon the sun, and with all-controllling hand turns at his will the flame-hoofed span of Phœbus, the other lifts its glance to a beautiful distant star of the night, and, full of renunciation, sees it sink into the dark ocean,—and that is the poesy of which I say, that it will also sometime come to you; for it alone truly fills the heart of man, and brings to him that happiness of rest. You do not understand me, Don Gino? Go fall in love, then — fall a little unfortunately in love, and you will understand me."

"I thank you for your advice, Donna Ottavia," responded Egino, laughing, "but I think I shall not follow it. I am much too busy for that, and a love, at the same time an unfortunate one, might disturb me."

"What can a young son of a prince, like yourself, have so urgent to do?"

"Enough in order for me to see the days rapidly, as the fabric of a dream, fly past me. To-day, for example, I have to go through with your husband the manuscript which Signor Callisto has prepared in the process which I carry on here in the ecclesiastical court; then, after dinner, have I promised to go with some friends to the Colosseum, where a bull-fight is to take place; and in the evening, finally, must I repair to the Albergo dei Pellegrini Tedeschi, in order to look after a remarkable fellow-countryman and his pretty niece, whom I met just now at the Aqua Acetosa, as I was riding by. I promised to render them assistance upon their locating in Rome."

"Because the niece was pretty?" asked Donna Ottavia, smiling.

"Not on that account, but because I struck her, and wish to make amends for the injury."

"You have struck her? Impossible. A man strike a woman!"

"In Italy!" answered Egino. "We Germans are ruder in this respect, I am sorry to say; although I have not acted so ungallantly as my words might make you believe. The maiden, for the sake of safety on her long journey, had clothed herself as a boy. I asked of this fellow a little assistance, and when it was denied me, I in thoughtless anger went at him with my whip — the youngster seemed to me so stiffnecked! I did not know that it was a girl, and that both were German. Am I not right to wish to make it good again?"

"That you are, Don Gino; only don't make it too good," laughed the lady from the house.

"Now to our work," broke in Signor Callisto, rising; "I also have much to do. I have to-day to prepare a marriage contract for a couple out of one of the greatest houses of Rome for a remarkable marriage. I must concentrate my mind very closely upon the matter, in order that I may guard the interests of both clients, and that the stronger of the two may not obtain too fully the lion's share."

"You speak of the Savelli. Will this marriage indeed take place? The poor girl!" exclaimed Donna Ottavia. "I beg of you consider her welfare so as to make her independent as possible; make her remain the mistress of her own fortune, so far as you can accomplish this for her."

"Certainly I will do what I can," responded Signor Callisto. "We jurists, when we forge such bonds, are not so inexorable as the priests, who, because they themselves cannot have a wife, make for others chains of iron which cannot be broken. But now come, Signor Conte, to our business."

With these words the lawyer opened the door leading to the interior of the house, in order to conduct Egino into his study, and there to lay before him what he had written and done as his attorney at the Roman court in the affair which had brought the young German to Rome.

CHAPTER III.

IRMGARD.

N hour before Ave Maria, Egino went to the German Wayfarer's Inn, which lay not far from the Piazza Navona, in a narrow and dirty street where, later, the German Hospital arose. There stood at this time the national church, Santa Maria del Anima, built by the contributions of Germans and Dutch. Begun in the Jubilee year 1500, it now approached completion. Near by lay the inn. In this old, many-storied building Egino had to search long, to grope through dark corridors, till he reached a large but dark chamber with a single window looking out upon the narrow street. In this room, two of the three new acquaintances formed at Aqua Acetosa, Irmgard and Uncle Kraps, had during this interval really found shelter.

Uncle Kraps sat at the window; he had upon a little table near him a straw-covered bottle of the clear wine of Orvieto and a plate with slices of bright yellow anise-bread, and upon his grotesque countenance lay the expression of unspeakable delight and satisfaction.

In spite of the warm weather, Uncle Kraps had the window shut. He saw through the little panes of glass the front of the house on the opposite side of the narrow street; still he had his delight in these panes, through which he could look as if he were a man of rank. In the North, at that time, they were indeed still a costly article; in England, a Duke of Northumberland, when he would leave one of his castles, had his window-panes taken out and packed away, that they might be safer in his absence. At home, in Ulm, Uncle Kraps had not known such a luxury. There, the cathedral and some houses of the richest patricians had glazed windows, but the common citizen had wooden shutters before the cross-bars, which he could open when he wished to have light or to look out.

The German donkey must have found a stall somewhere else, where he, in the companionship of his Roman brethren, could amply enrich his silent meditation. The baskets which he had borne stood in a corner of the room; just as Egino entered, Irmgard shut up a closet in which she had stored a part of their contents.

Irmgard had not yet laid aside her male attire.

"It is kind of you, Count Egino, that you really already to-day come to look after us," said she, coming forward to meet him. "You find us as well fixed as we could expect, and Uncle Kraps is well satisfied that we are at our destination. He has found here in the house a wine, supported by which, even though he must remain during his life a bell-founder, even if they would make nothing else out of him, he — well, the drink rewards him already for his pilgrimage to Rome."

"And you," said Egino, "you have, in the first hours, had so much of the glory of Rome to look upon, you have not found time to change yourself back to a girl."

"That is about so," answered Irmgard, carrying a chair to the window for Egino. "I have wandered a little while through the city, in order to satisfy my curiosity."

"Alone?"

"Alone. Uncle Kraps was too much fatigued. It was unendurable to me, after we for weeks had wandered, wandered day after day without rest, up valleys and down, to be obliged now suddenly to sit still in this room and dream the hours away. I was like the tolling bell, which swings itself out slowly, and cannot suddenly stand still."

"And now, as in a tolling bell, does there not hum within you the noise and bustle of the populous city, and is not your head in a whirl from all that you have seen?"

"The city is populous enough, and a gay crowd upon the streets; at home it is not much worse at the time of a masked procession or at the carnival play. I have seen peasants in divers-colored garb, and beautiful, stately women with ornaments of gold in their ears and around their necks, but with torn skirts, and leading dirty children by the hand. I have seen many kinds of monks and clergymen in different habits, as if they must put to the test what cut or what color is most according to the taste of the beloved God or most conducive to piety; also cardinals, who were all red, and sat upon magnificent steeds, and had marching near them an armed bodyguard,—wild fellows, country summoners, with rifles upon their shoulders and long, clanging swords. I met one procession from which I ran. There were two long rows of men in light-blue linen frocks with capes, which were thrown forward over their heads, and hung down to their breasts; there were holes cut out for the eyes, through which they looked. That frightened me,—I cannot tell you how much; they looked like the loathsomely diseased creatures which, at home, slip around the hospital near our town. So frightful! Why do they disguise themselves so?"

"They are a brotherhood," replied Egino; "they make a united penitential journey, or accompany funeral processions, criminals on the way to execution, or the holy Bambino, the Christ-child, when it is carried to the sick to perform some miracle ——"

"And one time," said Irmgard, interrupting him, "I met a troop of soldiers, who surrounded a long train of many yoke of wild oxen, which were dragging along great heavy cannon upon huge wheels. Then there came to me a thought, Count Egino, which you may know how to explain to me. If our Holy Father now must have cannon, soldiers, a country and subjects, why does he not then rule the whole Christian world? Such an infallible man must understand it still better than all kings; and why not chase away these stupid, fallible kings, and obey only him?"

"You are right, Irmgard," answered Egino, laughing; "he needs only to proclaim it as an article of faith. I fear, however, the princes of the Christian world would not believe in this dogma. Mankind now are in such a state that they yield to dogmas very willingly the price of their understanding, their better judgment, their mother-wit, but not their profits or a productive piece of land."

"Let it be so, and it is not our business to decide it," responded Irmgard, who, while she spoke, had stationed herself with her arms upon the back of the chair in which Uncle Kraps sat, and looked with unembarrassed glance upon Egino, who had taken his place near the uncle's table. "Although," she continued, jestingly, "it would be a good thing for Uncle and his art, for bells would rise in value."

"So they would," replied Egino; "but now tell me further what you have seen. Were you in St. Peter's? Did you not see somewhere a great and beautiful monument of the past? Do you know I find you quite lukewarm, even cool, to have spent your first day in Rome?"

"Does it seem so to you? Perhaps you are right, and I am indeed simple, that I cannot wonder more over all such things. I believe it has been my fault all my life long, that no proper joy comes over me when I see those things over which clever men often break out into great rejoicing that their eyes are permitted to behold them. Uncle Kraps says I would have been the right wife for the strong Michel, who wished to learn fear — though I can fear already, but not wonder. I think if I should be obliged to wonder over something, I should have to begin with the sun, the moon, the stars, with the mountains and the blue heavens stretched above them, and not with the works of men. Where should I there, however, find an end?"

"Does not the work of men, even when it is beautiful and great, make your heart beat faster?" asked Egino.

Irmgard shook her head.

"I am too stupid to decide whether or not it is beautiful or great. My heart beats faster only when I hear of something right, brave, and good a man has done; and most rapidly and joyously when I see I have made this deformed, ugly old Uncle Kraps so thoroughly delighted and at home in these four walls. When I think how mean and heartless men often were toward him, how utterly alone he is in the world, and no one is his friend, and nothing gives to him a proper sense of joy — when I then care for him, and see a smile of happiness spread over the old, ugly, dark-embrowned features, then, indeed, my heart beats higher. Isn't that so, old Uncle?" she continued, smiling and bending over him, and laying her temples upon the gray, shaggy locks of the little monster sitting there with the grin of an idiot upon his visage. "That is the best happiness when we sit at home in quiet contentment! What care we then for men, what mean thing they say to mock us, or what evil they do to harm one another, or even what they build, paint, and bring to perfection of the great or beautiful which we do not understand?"

Egino looked at her a little moved, indeed, but more astonished — it was so far removed from his manner of feeling, so narrow-souled, so contracted. Yet there was something in it for which he dared not condemn it; a something that — Donna Ottavia need only to hear it, and she would, perhaps, have shown him therein a new kind of poesy.

"But now," began Irmgard, again, "I have already spoken too long of myself, and if it is not indeed too bold, I would like to say it is now your time, Count Egino, to tell to your countrymen a little of what leads you to Rome; who are your people at home; whether you intend to remain here long; whether, perhaps, it is your purpose, as a younger son of your house, to dedicate yourself to the church, and ——"

"Dedicate myself to church!" broke in Egino, shaking his head. "Truly that is not my intention; I have not been educated to that. In Bologna I have for three years studied law, along with many others of the German nobility; but when they returned home over the Alps, an elder brother of mine, now ruling, sent me here to Rome to carry on a great, complicated suit which has been brought to the Roman Rota, the highest court of justice in Christendom, if you have ever heard of it in your life before."

Irmgard shook her head. "No," she said; "and on what account is this suit instituted?"

"On account of a contention with the order of Augustines over all kinds of right to an estate bequeathed to the monks, which is put in fee by Belfried of Ortenburg."

"With an order? And do you hope to win it here in Rome?"

"Why not? We believe we are in the right, and always hitherto that is something ——"

"Not much," here put in Uncle Kraps, distorting his face. He had listened very attentively to the conversation during its progress, looking first at Irmgard, then at the young count. "If the monks, who are your opponents, see that you have a right, they will immediately drive it out of the case with their incense."

"Their incense cannot do everything. One of the three holy kings brought to the manger frankincense; another, myrrh; and the third, gold. I do not think St. Joseph looked upon the last most unfavorably."

"Yes, yes, gold — if you have enough of that," nodded Uncle Kraps, grinning. "There is usually none too much of that in the pocket of German princes."

"Uncle Kraps!" exclaimed Irmgard, much shocked.

"Let him talk. What he says is indeed true," said Egino, interrupting her. "But when money must be had, it is always to be found. God be praised! that is not my care, but my brother's. Besides, it is a help to us that our opponents have sent here a fair-thinking, learned, and quite prudent man."

"A member of the order which is your antagonist here?" asked Irmgard.

"A member of the order," answered Egino. "A monk still young; he is from the cloister of Wittenberg, and is called Brother Martin."

"And a learned, intelligent opponent rejoices you?"

"Certainly, for he is an honest German soul, who always contends with an open visor, and from whom I have no Italian artifice to guard against. I shall, I think, immediately come to an agreement with him. The more intelligent and shrewd a man is, so much the better it is to have with him a dispute or contention; only with the stupid and weak-minded must one guard himself against falling into strife. And now farewell. I have now seen that, for the beginning, you are very well provided for. And if Uncle Kraps finds hindrances or difficulties in exchanging his good German coin for a blue or a red official hat, then come to me, and I will take him, if everything else fails, even to that opponent of mine, Brother Martin. He must then help us; and he can, for his order is always the sacristan of the papal chapel, whereby the pastorship in the Vatican is pledged. There we have the most effective tie."

"And you believe, at your wish, this brother, your opponent, would be inclined ——"

"Just because I am his opponent," said Count Egino, laughingly interrupting her. "He is an evangelical man, who has felt the command, 'Love your enemies.' You should only first see what confidential and affectionate enemies we are. Now may God protect you, both of you. Do not let the uncle drink too much; otherwise could his German inoffensiveness be injured by this bright yellow Italian stuff; it is not so harmless as it appears. What were harmless in this beautiful sunny land! Be careful of yourself also, Irmgard."

He nodded to Uncle Kraps with the head, reached Irmgard his hand, and strode with clanging spurs loudly and quickly over the stone floor of the chamber.

Irmgard stood long and listened, as the firm, knightly tread resounded from the walk without.

"Why do you stand there so and listen, Irmgard?" asked Uncle Kraps, looking at her. "That is a fool! Good-natured, but a fool! He praises his opponent, the monk, who will take the advantage of him. He has struck you with his whip, and now he demeans himself in a friendly manner. In this way he means to make good what he has done. He is a fool, Irmgard!"

Irmgard looked at her uncle with a countenance upon which great perplexity displayed itself.

"Are you in earnest?" she exclaimed.

"Do you think otherwise? Can you forget it?"

She was silent.

"Forget?" she answered; then, after a long pause, as if arousing herself out of deep thought: "No! I do not believe a maiden ever forgets such a thing. But by not forgetting, I mean other than what you mean, Uncle."

With that she went into an adjoining room, in order, at last, to lay aside her male attire, which she now suddenly, as if in impatient eagerness, threw from her.

CHAPTER IV.

NOTIONS OF A GERMAN GIRL.

ON the next day, in the afternoon, Egino repaired again to the Albergo dei Pellegrini Tedeschi.

When he entered the room of his German friends, he found Irmgard in her own proper dress. She blushed as she saw him suddenly and unexpectedly enter; and this blush made her very pretty in her dark velvet cap, beneath which her rich blonde hair showed itself in short, curly locks: she had really cut it short for the sake of the journey. A brown bodice, trimmed with narrow black velvet, and a skirt similarly bordered, displayed her form to advantage. It was all very simple, but Egino found her much prettier than he had found her yesterday.

"I come," said the young man, reaching her his hand and nodding to her uncle, "because the thought came to me it would be best to take you to an intelligent and benevolent lady whom I know, and who is certainly in the best condition to give you good advice as to how you shall begin to make yourself safe here, and adapted to your surroundings."

"That is extremely kind in you," responded Irmgard, much rejoiced.

"You have, as yet, rented no dwelling for yourself?"

"No."

"Well, then, come! Donna Ottavia Minucci, to whom we go, is the wife of an attorney, of a prominent lawyer; she is a Roman lady who knows her native city, and will receive you with pleasure. Are you ready?"

"You, sir — and you yourself will conduct me?"

"Would you otherwise find her?"

Joyously excited, Irmgard made herself ready to go out. She brought out a pocket, which she fastened with a silver hook to her girdle; then a pair of gloves; a kerchief, which, on account of the warm day, she did not need, and which the German fashion allowed her to throw over her arm. She then bade Uncle Kraps good-bye.

"Watch yourself well, Uncle," she said, "and do not break any of our things. Don't forget, either, to pour water into your wine, when you drink. May God protect you, and not let the time become long to you."

She started out, and Egino followed her.

On the street she moved along rapidly and in silence. The German maiden was noticed by many men whom she met. The blonde beauty evidently struck them; they stared her boldly in the face; made loud remarks about her; remained standing to gaze after her. Egino was several times on the point of trying to teach these shameless creatures better, but Irmgard, with flying foot, drew him farther on.

When they reached the Porta del Popolo she drew a breath of relief. She let her bright glance sweep over the landscape without.

"The mountains are beautiful. Are those trees palms, there, on that height?" she asked.

"No; they are sweet pines. The palm does not grow in Rome," replied Egino. "As an atonement, however, it has the laurel."

"Out of that they wreathe garlands for victors," responded Irmgard. "That is nothing to girls and women, who can deserve only a palm; for them, indeed, nothing is provided here. Rome appears to me, in no respects, a good place for them," she remarked, perhaps still under the impression of what she had just experienced. "I wished this morning to enter a chapel, but they rudely thrust me back, because I was a woman."

"To that," said Egino, shrugging his shoulders, "you must be reconciled, Irmgard; there are many places here you must not dare to enter, for they are too holy for the foot of a woman."

"Men, then, are purer and more sinless! See here, if I do not wonder over your monuments and great ruins, these are things over which I do wonder. Oh! there are so many things in the faith, over which I wonder. For example, that they always say the Saviour has suffered so infinitely much for us sinners, and taken upon himself almost all the sorrow of the world."

"Doesn't it seem so to you, then?"

"You think, now," said Irmgard, looking timidly at Egino, "that I am a veritable heretic."

"No, no; speak on, Irmgard."

"Well, then, I think one could speak of suffering only when he had suffered deeply in his inner nature; when he had been deceived by a woman whom he loved; when he had been forced to look upon the gradual moral degradation and destruction of an only son, who had been his sole hope; or when he had found his beloved daughter in the arms of vice; or when he, poor and infirm, had been unable to procure bread for a group of hungry children. That would have been the real suffering of the world, an anguish of soul. To be put to death for the sake of convincing men, is a misfortune, a suffering of the body; and who would not take that upon himself, if, thereby, he can redeem all mankind,— pour out an unspeakable happiness upon all present and coming generations,— yes, even make God himself happy, who need no more be angry on account of old, hereditary sin? I mean the Saviour must not have suffered, but have been always very happy in thought over all that he was able to accomplish for man through his dying and remaining dead but the short space of three days. I speak foolishly enough, no doubt; but you yourself, Count Egino, would you not die willingly, not only in appearance, till the third day, but in earnest, forever, if you knew that thereby you could redeem this entire holy Roman kingdom from all its misery? Would you not joyously go to your death, as a true man does for his fatherland?"

"That I would," assented Egino, nodding.

"And then," continued Irmgard, warmly, "the clerical men here, where they must think most of the suffering of the Master, live in such full enjoyment of life. What magnificence is lacking to the Pope —— "

"To be sure, to be sure," put in Egino. "When he, surrounded by his guard, goes in procession through the city, borne aloft on his steed, amid the clangor of bells and the thunder of cannon, there is no one who, in spirit, sees looking over his shoulders the pale, anguish-stricken, sorrow-filled countenance of a sufferer. Also those who have died for father-land or humanity, have always gone to their death rejoicing; and still could no one of them, as did Christ, view with the glance of omniscience what salvation lay in his death for the humanity of all times. Thus," continued he, smiling, "could we explain to ourselves so as to understand it why the Pope lives in such splendor and joy."

"Yes, yes," continued Irmgard; "but one thing is still harder for me to comprehend,— that is, why God has created the lowly and poor.

Here upon the earth is only misery for them, and they cannot come into heaven, because they have not the money and the time to make pilgrimages, to procure masses, to purchase indulgences, to pray the whole day, or to give anything anywhere to the churches for that purpose, and thus win heaven."

"But all these are dangerous thoughts for a girl, Irmgard."

"I know that," said Irmgard, earnestly; "but if they come to me, willing or unwilling, I must think them out."

"And do you also, then, speak them out?"

"No; I keep them to myself."

There lay in this answer an expression of confidence in Egino, of which Irmgard suddenly became conscious, for she blushed and grew silent.

They came to the villa. Donna Ottavia led them to a seat in the shade of a grove.

The young maiden from Germany awakened in her a lively interest. She had Irmgard relate the story of her life as minutely as she was able with what readiness of Italian speech she had acquired upon her journey, but which was even now diminished. Then Irmgard spoke to her of the several points in which she wished advice and information in regard to Roman customs of every-day life, from the chief things of dwelling and washing, down to the preparation of broccoli and artichokes.

"There is, however, nothing in this of interest to you, Conte Gino," said Madame Ottavia, laughing over it. "You see in the Roman earth only the dust of Scipios and Gracchi; for you, there spring forth out of this ground only the shades of Horace and Tacitus. That also cabbage and other vegetables grow out of this soil, that the descendants of the Scipios must trouble themselves with the cleaning of their soiled linen, only destroys for you the illusion."

"Of course," responded Egino, gayly, "to some extent, though not so much now as at first — since you have spoken to me of a poesy which may accompany us even while gathering vegetables or washing soiled clothing. What your lecture did not accomplish, the words of Irmgard have finished. She has given me the example of being astonished at nothing, and thereby has poured water upon my flame. But, while you are conversing together, I will go speak to your husband."

"Do so," said Donna Ottavia; "he wishes to see you, as he has a favor to ask of you, Conte Gino."

Egino left the ladies, and sought Callisto in his study.

"I will not disturb you," said he to the lawyer, who was bent over parchments and papers. "I will go so soon as I have learned from you wherein I may be able to serve you."

"You can, indeed, be of service to me, Count Egino," responded Signor Callisto. "You can do me a favor, in case you are not afraid of a little trouble, and do not object to becoming somewhat acquainted here with a member of the house of Savelli?"

"Neither one nor the other is the case."

"Well, then, to-morrow evening I have to appear before the Duke of Aricia, in order to witness the signature of a marriage contract, which I have prepared at his request. On that occasion I should like to know that at least one of the witnesses is attached to me, and inclined, under all circumstances, to step upon my side. You cannot guess how stormy it often becomes in such scenes, where there is a final decision over the 'mine and thine' to be made — how well it is for the lawyer to have near him a trusted and reliable friend."

"I am ready, with pleasure; but there must be something exceptional about the affair that you do not prefer one of your Roman friends."

"Now, for one time, I prefer such a foreign, unembarrassed, independent friend as yourself; one who has nothing to fear and nothing to expect from the people. Is it agreeable to you?"

"You honor me with the request, and you may depend upon me."

"Can I come to get you to-morrow, an hour before Ave Maria?"

"Certainly; I shall be ready to go any direction with you."

"So be it. I hope it will awaken your interest to cast a glance upon the domestic affairs of the house of Savelli."

"Without doubt! And now you shall not be longer interrupted by me. I know that you wish to work. Also, I shall expect you to-morrow. Shall I," added Egino, smiling, "be mounted on my steed, armed and equipped on account of the scenes to which you refer — at a marriage?"

"No, no; there is no need of that. I have made a wrong impression if you think that. There will be no warfare demanded, only an opportunity where — well, where four eyes can see more than two; where two men can think more conclusively, and better oversee the transaction than one. And in case it should be said to me, 'Change that, or insert this,' I might not be alone when I must say, 'I dare not; it is not possible!' You may take your horse, however; I shall take mine, for the road is long for me."

"Well, then, till to-morrow."

The friends extended to each other the hand, and Egino went to find his protégée in the garden, and accompany her back.

When he came to the two women, Donna Ottavia said:—

"What your countrywoman, Irmgard, needs next, we have, in this interval, fortunately found,—a suitable dwelling with honest people for herself and her uncle. She must only know how to find the way to the Quirinal Hill. There, behind the baths of Constantine, and near to the wall which incloses the garden of the Colonna, lies the little house of a widow named Giulietta. She occupies it with her son Beppo, an excellent young man, who supports himself as an artist. Giulietta, who was once my maid, and then married a mechanic, a dependent of the Colonna, has said to me that she wishes to rent two rooms of her house to well-recommended foreigners. There will your countrymen find the best reception, if they come saying I sent them."

"How thankful I am to you!" exclaimed Irmgard, rising.

"Greet Giulietta for me, and also Beppo, the honest fellow," said Ottavia, extending the hand to her.

With the promise that after some time she would come and report to Donna Ottavia how she had disposed of herself, Irmgard took leave, and Egino accompanied her back to Uncle Kraps, who, fortunately, this time, during their absence, had perpetrated no kind of mischief.

"When he is left alone at home some hours together, he always either breaks some utensil, throws away a lamp, or tears up some article of furniture, in order—well, he is like a bear, so strong and clumsy," said Irmgard, laughing.

Egino left her with the promise that, on the next morning, he would send his servant Götz to guide her to Giulietta's, on the Quirinal.

FORUM, ROME.

CHAPTER V.

IN THE CASTLE OF THE SAVELLI.

T was on the following day, an hour before Ave Maria. The lawyer from the "*Parva domus*" had been punctual. Riding upon a modest, but well-fed pony, he appeared in Via della Mercede in front of the Albergo del Drago.

Here Count Egino's servant led to and fro his master's beautiful German thoroughbred, ready saddled and bridled.

When, now, Egino stepped out at the door of the Dragon Inn, booted, armed with the long dagger, and even then drawing on the long gloves of soft leather, Signor Callisto thus accosted him:—

"Truly it is very foolish in me to start out with such a witness as you."

"Wherefore, Signor Legista? Do you think you will not obtain sufficient honor in such company?" answered Egino, swinging himself into the saddle.

"No," responded the lawyer, setting his horse in motion, while Egino rode at his side; "just the contrary. You are too stately a personage, with your proud and beautiful German head, and your entire self as if you were a prince from the blood of the old Gothic kings, such a grandson of Alaric; and your horse, now, with his trappings all glittering. But you leave your servant at home?" said Callisto, interrupting his speech and looking around as if anxious.

"I leave my excellent Götz at home, as usual," answered Egino, "when he does not thrust himself upon me, because he thinks, without him, I shall be fallen upon, robbed, and carried away by bandits, as a child whom the gypsies steal. To-day, fortunately, I have pacified him in regard to it. He thinks if I ride thus alongside of justice, violence can have no hold upon me. Besides, he is tired since he has assisted my German countrymen to remove from their pilgrim quarter — up on the Quirinal — you know, to that woman Giulietta, whom your lady recommended to us."

"Now, so much the better," said Callisto. "The business is such that I do not wish that my witness attract the attention of the people with whom we have to do. One need not force investigation as to who you are before you have signed the document which we should execute."

"You appear to me to enter upon this business with great distrust, Signor Callisto. Whither, indeed, are you bringing me? Is this the way to Monte Savello?"

"I am bringing you to Santa Sabina."

"On the Aventine? That is far. And what business have we in the cloister?"

"We are not riding to the cloister of Santa Sabina, but to the house of the Savelli, lying adjacent to it."

"But the Savelli live on Montanara, in their palace on the Theatre of Marcellus — on Monte Savello, as they call it."

"That is true; and because they dwell there, it is seldom they have ordered me into their strong castle, which lies alone up there on the Aventine, by Santa Sabina."

"To a marriage?"

"To a marriage. You must confess that the well-arranged dwelling palace would be a better and more commodious stage for such a family event of a joyous kind."

"Perhaps," rejoined Egino, "there is more room in the castle; perhaps the old structure includes the old house chapel, which since the times of their fathers, has always served for such occasions in the house of Savelli; or there is a similarly good reason which urges them to choose it."

Callisto shook his head.

"I think you would yourself not consider it so innocent, if I should relate to you something concerning the bride and bridegroom."

"Well, relate it."

"The bride is a creature over whose beauty those who have seen her seem to be carried away. I have not seen her, and can say nothing about it. But I know she is the last descendant of an old and noble, perhaps even a royal, race. She is descended from the Corrados of Anticoli, out of the Sabine Mountains. She is called Corradina, and her hand controls a large estate."

"And the bridegroom?" asked Egino.

"The bridegroom! That's the thing. The bridegroom is adapted to her about as a boar to a white hind. Not that he has yet much of the boar about him. Alas! no; Luca Savelli is wasted away by his dissolute life,—rotten in all his bones; a fellow such that, when you see him, you will say he appears as if he had been dipped in the poison suds of sin which flows together in the great pool called Rome, and then washed by the Devil with his dirty broth. He was a friend of Cæsar Borgia, till Cæsar Borgia found him too full of vice, and chased him from Rome. Thereupon, with a company of bandits, he has tyrannized a long time over the neighborhood of Nemi and Genzano,—and now we have him here, broken and befouled through and through, and bridegroom of the beautiful Corradina. What do you say to that, Count Egino?"

"That it makes me pity the poor creature from the bottom of my heart."

"You must also know another thing; namely, the Lady of Anticoli is a ward of the Duke of Aricia. You know the Duke of Aricia is the head of the house of Savelli."

"And is it he who compels his ward to marry this monstrous Luca Savelli?"

"I think so," responded Callisto. "Luca Savelli is his second son. The oldest, the heir, is married to a Colonna of Palliano. You see he is already provided for. And for Luca Savelli, who has long ago squandered his paternal inheritance, some provision should now be made."

"I had far rather carry off to some ogre the bride who is to be thus sacrificed," said Egino, "than, as you request me, lend a hand to forging the chains which shall bind her. Why do you lend a hand to such a purpose?"

"I? Am I not the notary and legal adviser of the house? What better would it have been if I had withdrawn my services? Another would have been found to carry out everything according to their desires. But you may be assured I shall do all that I can for the protection of the poor maiden. Into the contract which the Duke of Aricia has bidden me draw up, I have brought seemingly quite harmless expressions and clauses, which yet allow to her the most beautiful play, if she at any time should come before a court of justice and have a clever lawyer point these out. I will keep my eyes open, and if Corradina lets fall a word which betrays want of willingness on her part, it shall not fall to the ground. You see, just for this reason will I not allow any dependent servant or client of the house of Savelli, or yet one of Signor Luca's bandits, or only, perhaps, some corruptible, easily shaken Roman, thrust himself upon me as a witness, I have begged of you to accompany me."

"Truly, you could have asked no one who is more ready and willing to become the saviour of this pitiable Corradina, and to break Luca Savelli's rotten bones for him!" cried Egino, greatly excited.

"I hope you will not fall in love with her, as you seem already far on the road to do," said Callisto, smiling.

"You must at least concede that you have done all you could to lead me to such a step."

"Could you take as a companion for yourself a woman not of your people, — an Italian woman?"

"I seek in a woman, not my blood, but my soul. If I find a soul which is like my own, I care very little whether there exist in her body an Italian, a Turk, or a German."

"But your princely relations by blood there on the other side of the Alps?"

"I think what is good enough for a Savelli is good enough for an Ortenburg," answered Egino, laughing.

"That is a remark more unprejudiced, I must confess, than I should have expected from an offshoot of German nobility. Formerly, they considered the Gothic blood purer and nobler than any other in the world."

"I am not such a fool. I know," continued Egino, "that the Colonna, the Orsini, the Savelli are the greatest names in your history, and that even two Popes, both of the name of Honorius, belonged to this house of Savelli. I know the monument of Luca Savelli in Ara Celi, — a highly artistic work of the time of Cosmo."

"The senator was from Rome as early as the year 1266," broke in Callisto; "but their stock goes even higher yet. That very Aventinus who defended one of the Tiber hills against Æneas, was, according to tradition, one of the Savelli, and the hill, they say, bears its name from him. They are lords of the Castle Savelli bei Albano, lords of the manor of Albano and Aricia, many times united with the Colonna and Ghibellines as they are; they are hereditary marshals of the Holy Chair and warders of the Conclave; they also have such courts of justice of their own as the Corte Savella — so, in fact, we have to do with a people of a moderately respectable extraction. And now, since we are beginning to be beyond the confusion of streets and the stream of human beings, let us put our horses into a trot; we have still a good bit of road before us."

It was indeed a long road; it led over the old Forum, on to the Palatine, and to the valley once encircled by the Circus Maximus, and finally upon the steep declivity of the Aventine, which the horses had to climb slowly, breathing hard. On the right, the two horsemen had soon the mighty substructions of the Castle of the Savelli, with their battlemented walls, their towers and bastions high above them. Higher up, the road turned to the right, southward; they reached an open place, on which some old cypresses stood; farther yet arose to view the Cloister of Santa Sabina, with its church. On this side of the latter, lay, dark, massive, and gloomy, the house of the Savelli.

The open space, covered with short, thin grass, surrounded it as a kind of glacis.

The building was in the style of those castles of which there remain to us as examples the Venetian Palace in Rome, and that of the Signoria, or of the Podesta, in Florence. They have a lower story with almost no openings for the admission of light; a lofty first story; over this a story less lofty with small windows, over which is a row of firm battlements; here and there is a small balcony; over the whole, rising aloft from the middle, is a quadrangular tower, which, above, gives exit from itself to a platform behind the smaller indented battlements. All is ponderous and gloomy in construction, "*alla saracenesca*," out of great blocks of freestone and smaller brickwork in alternate layers. How many of these blocks of stone which now give their support to the stronghold of a Roman baron, may have been torn from demolished monuments of antiquity; may have once served as steps to the Flavian Amphitheatre; as socles for the columns of Jupiter's temple; as sills in the golden house of Nero, or in imperial castles of the Palatine! Truly, the thoughts of our horsemen were not occupied with such reflections; they rode through the open gate into the castle, and dismounted in the court. In this, all around beneath was a row of heavy pillars, which bore an arcade formed of beautiful marble columns running along on the upper story.

In the covered walk beneath and in the yard, all kinds of people were moving about, some of them in festal attire, some — and most of them at that — in a torn and wild condition, with long, uncombed hair and beards, with daggers in their belts, with tied shoes, with skins of goats which served as gaiters, with lean, sun-browned faces and cunning physiognomies, nothing of which marked it as a company invited to a peaceable marriage celebration.

"You are right, Signor Callisto," said Egino, when they had given over their horses to one of the fellows, and now turned toward the interior of the building, "you are right in considering this wedding a little out of the usual way, supposing that these are the wedding-guests."

"We will find the proper guests above," answered the advocate. "That rabble there are the bandits of the Duke and the poorer dependents of the house from the city: these last, you will have observed, have clothed themselves in holiday dress, in honor of the day."

Upon the broad stairway, leading above, servants were found to conduct the new-comers to the great room with the throne-canopy, which adorns the ante-chamber of every Roman prince. In this room were discovered even as few of the guests Callisto had expected to see as on the outside.

Only two men in the black garb of house-officials walked up and down in the room, speaking together in low tones.

"Here I am with my witness, Signor Antonio," said Callisto to one of them, while he bowed to the other. "Have we come at the right time, Signor Giovanni Battista?"

The men bowed, and Sor Antonio, the elder, said:—

"Everything is in readiness for the ceremony, Signor Minucci; we will lead you at once to His Excellency."

The other had already turned to the next door, and opened it, in order to admit Callisto with his companion into a smaller room.

In this room, in a reclining chair at the window, sat the Duke of Aricia,—a small, meager man, clothed in dark-green velvet, with the golden chain of some order on his breast; he had his hands upon the hilt of his dagger, which he held between his knees. Lying upon his hands, and supported by them, was his sharp, projecting chin. The face was that of a bird; but by this crooked nose, these small eyes, lying deep beneath thick, shaggy brows, there was suggested to Egino, not the eagle but the kite.

A younger man in richer attire, with his arms folded over his breast, with his back resting upon the window-casing, stood before the Duke.

"You come at last, Signor Callisto!" said the Duke of Aricia, raising his head. "We are waiting only upon you."

"I come punctually, Your Honor."

"Whom bring you there with you?"

"A young German, who has, in Bologna, studied jurisprudence, and is now learning with me how that law, of which they have told him so much, is really applied in our practice."

"How long have you lawyers been taking pupils as the painters?"

"Wherefore should they not," broke in the younger man, laughing; "even though they paint in only two colors, making the white black and the black white?"

"Yes, yes," said the Duke, nodding his head; "give us, then, what you have painted from white to black."

Callisto drew from his breast-pocket a great, many-folded parchment, and reached it to the Duke.

The latter began to read it attentively, with wrinkled brow. The son had stepped behind him, and looked at it over his shoulder. The twilight began to be observable, appearing after awhile to make it difficult for the old man to read.

"It is growing late," remarked Callisto. "Do you wish, Your Honor, that I call for light?"

"No, no; let it alone — I can see," replied the Duke; and then, after reaching the end, he said, looking at his son: —

"I think it is all as we wish it, Livio?"

Livio Savelli nodded his head.

"Everything is in it as we specified to Signor Callisto, it seems to me," said he; "only a little turned from the speech of the sound human intellect into that of the law; but without that it would never do for Signor Callisto."

"So we can proceed and let the signatures be attached, and then go on with the marriage ceremony," said the Duke, rising. "Signor Callisto, you know that my son Luca is very ill?"

"I knew that he is ailing, Your Honor."

"Ailing — well, yes, so ailing that it is difficult for him to move a member. He had the *perniciosa*, you know. The fever is now overcome, the hot pulse has become stiller, the wild dreams are at an end; but you know such a fever when it subsides leaves behind it in the person a great faintness and debility, and therefore it need not surprise you, Signor Callisto, if during the ceremony the bridegroom seems a little apathetic."

"I only wonder, Your Honor, that you do not await his restoration, in order to have him married then."

"Truly, Signor Callisto, that is very sensible advice which you give, but, alas! Corradina will not listen to it. The maiden, as you know, has been allotted to him for years; for years she has longed for this union with the emotions of a bride. Now the poor thing is uneasy and afraid on account of his illness; she is beside herself with the thought that he may die before he has become her husband, and so we must yield to her desire to marry him. She will at least have the consolation of bearing his name, of being his widow. What is to be done when a woman resolves upon a certain thing?" said the Duke, concluding his speech.

"You will, therefore, also find it natural that we perform the ceremony in the narrowest circle possible," added Livio Savelli. "The marriage ceremony can take place later, when Luca has recovered; to-day, many guests and a noisy feast would not have been suitable. So come, now!"

After these words the two Savelli, father and son, turned to the door of exit from the chamber: on this account the significant glances directed by Callisto to his pupil escaped them. Egino, however, did not understand these glances.

They passed into a great room which, in former times, might well have served as a banquet hall; but now, despoiled of furniture and darkened by the twilight, with its faded frescoes, it appeared very sad and desolate. At the end of the room a door was opened by a servant, who must have heard the steps of those approaching, and the four men stood immediately in a large, occupied chamber more suitably fitted up.

On the left the room had two lofty windows, which opened out on the vacant space and the back of the Aventine. The wall on the right, opposite the windows, ran to only about the middle of the room. Then it sprang back at a right angle, so that one looked there into a second and deeper room adjoining, in the back part of which stood a lofty canopied bed, and in which several strips of carpet covered the floor.

Cushioned reclining-chairs, and curtains before the windows, and bottles with medicine upon the tables, led one to suppose that this room was prepared for the nursing of a sufferer.

Opposite the door through which the Savelli and our friends entered, a broad stairway of eight or nine steps led into a farther room, which lay about a half story higher up; in the background of the same appeared an altar, upon which burned two candles, and upon whose steps knelt two monks, who wore white surplices over their gowns. The elevated room must be the private chapel of the house; the monks must belong to the neighboring cloister of Santa Sabina, they wore the Dominican habit.

Egino's eyes swept over all this with hasty glance, in order, then, to remain fixed upon two groups of persons occupying the chamber in which he found himself.

The first consisted of two women in stately robes of hardly folding material; the one already aged, the other with a beautifully cut face, about thirty years of age, in the transition to that compactness of form and dignified fullness which so often robs Roman women quite early of the gracefulness of their youthful bloom.

They sat talking together in low tones, opposite each other, on the stone seats in the window-niche, and arose now at the entrance of the men.

In the back part of the room, near the entrance to the sick-chamber, stood a table; behind this, in an arm-chair, rested idly, his head sunk upon his breast, his right arm lying upon the table, a man in a waistcoat of dark-red velvet, a hat of the same material encircled with a band of pearls, so placed upon his head that his features were entirely shaded. Also, as the men entered, he lifted not his drooping head; he remained motionless, and as if without interest.

On his left, her right arm supported on the back of his chair, stood a great, tall female form. She was clothed in long, flowing robes of white silk; a wreath of orange blossoms rested upon her head over the rich, dark-blonde hair which fell over her shoulders all unbound. An open-eyed, candid look under the quietly lifted lids met those entering; rested upon none except upon Egino a short while, and then turned again to the motionless bridegroom.

At the sight of this form Egino opened his lips as if he repressed an outcry of surprise, of astonishment.

In all his life he had never seen such a maiden, such a woman,— such an enchanting woman. It was a woman with the appearance of a goddess. It seemed to him she could not wear this wreath for a man — for a dying man; it was impossible that this apparition could have anything in common with the corrupt, half-dead mortal near her, around whose broken limbs the folds of his clothing hung loose. No, no; the wreath upon her golden hair, upon the proud head, was as a wreath of espousal to something infinitely lofty, beautiful, supernatural!

What made the beauty of her features still more captivating for Egino was the great softness, the indistinctness, the halo which the twilight produced. A beautiful face that rises before us in the twilight, receives from it the most dangerous charm. This Egino experienced in this moment; the charm seized him with a force as if from this hour it would never again let him loose. He stood as if rooted to the earth; his arms had gently, involuntarily raised themselves, as they do when something suddenly lays hold upon us,— when out of the dark heaven a meteor suddenly flames forth.

The Duke of Aricia had stepped up to the table; he stood before it, so that he came between the lawyer and the sick bridegroom. Livio drew near at the other side of his brother.

"Here is the contract for which we were waiting," said the Duke, spreading the parchment on the table; "put your names to it, my children,— you first, Luca, and then Corradina, and we others; and then to the chapel. Let us all hasten, that we may shorten the exertion and excitement for Luca as much as possible. Livio, help your brother with the signature; his hand is weak."

Livio had already gently slipped the parchment under his brother's arm, and he now took a reed-pen, which he filled with ink, and forced between the fingers of the sick man, and then took his hand and helped him write the words, "Luca Savelli."

He gave the pen to the bride. Slowly, measuredly, quietly, she received it, and wrote. The Duke followed, then Livio, then the two men clothed in the black garb of higher house servants, whom Callisto had greeted in the ante-chamber as Sor Antonio and Giovanni Battista, and who during the foregoing had softly come out of the sick-chamber. They also wrote their signatures; then both stooped over the chair of the sick man, took him up and bore him to the stairway, up the steps and into the chapel. With peculiar looks Callisto had regarded everything; now, turning to Egino, he said, in a whisper:—

"It appears almost as if our signature will not be desired; we will not urge it upon them. I never did write very willingly in the dark."

It had become (one knows how speedily, in the South, night follows the twilight) so dark that writing was indeed becoming almost difficult; but Egino saw, by a look upon the parchment, in what powerfully firm characters stood the name "Corradina, Countess d'Anticoli," near the almost illegible "Luca Savelli," and over the excitedly, unquietly scribbled "Geronimo Savelli d'Aricia."

Those present had betaken themselves together up the stairs into the chapel; they stood as a guard around the chair of the sick man; near it, upon a cushion on the first step of the altar, knelt the bride.

One of the two monks stood before them, his back turned to the altar, an open book in his hand. The other, as his assistant, stood at one side behind him.

The first began to repeat some form of prayer out of the book. He must have known it by heart, for the light of the two burning wax candles which fell from high above on the little altar, could not be in a position to light up the leaves of his book. The whole chapel room was very low, and must by daylight be already rather dark; now only a few sparing rays penetrated the two lower windows on the left, and fell on the remarkable group,—the sick man in his chair; the woman kneeling near him in dazzling white, and with free-flowing hair; the monks elevated one step higher; and the richly clad men and women around.

Callisto had quickly stepped up into the chapel; Egino, as if drawn by a charm, as if caught in a dream, followed slowly.

Like a dream to him was the whole picture, upon which his eyes fell staring, while he stood immovable on the topmost step of the stair, which was also the threshold of the chapel. One instant he drew himself together shrinkingly. It was when he heard a "Yes" pronounced, the "Yes" of a man,— not loud nor strong, but uttered distinctly and quickly; another "Yes" pure and firm, spoken by a clear feminine voice, followed.

The monk then turned about, by which movement the rays of the tapers lighted up his thin, well-marked face. He turned to the altar, in order to take the ring, then turned back again; and thereupon followed again the mumbling of the monk and the movements of his hands, as if he blessed, then put together hands and blessed again, and then ——

Egino felt a hand upon his arm. It was Callisto's.

"I pray you look closely at the bridegroom when he is carried past you," whispered the advocate.

Egino turned his head slowly to him, as if he did not understand.

Only a few moments longer, and all was over; the group before the altar dissolved; the two men in black lifted up the chair with the sick man and bore him past Egino, down out of the chapel. The bride followed close beside him. Egino did not heed Callisto's admonition; he saw only her. She stepped by him with a carriage proudly erect, with immovable features, like a walking statue; so she descended the stair. As she descended, Egino gazed, from his higher place, upon the wreath of orange blossoms and the golden hair. It was to him as if the vision were sinking before him, — as if she went down, were drawn downward into night and darkness, into the night of her destiny.

And then all disappeared. The little procession, having come to the foot of the stair into the chamber below, turned to the left to the sick chamber. The folds of the trailing garments of the two women in the rear, as they disappeared around the corner of the wall at the stairway below, was the last that Egino saw.

Only the Duke of Aricia remained at the altar. There he spoke in whispers to one of the monks. Now he came with hasty step after the lawyer, who, laying his hand upon Egino's arm, was at this instant descending with him the stairway.

"Signor Legista," he said, "now, since all that is necessary is accomplished, follow me to my chambers above. I think you will take a little recompense for the failure of a marriage banquet, and empty with me a goblet of Montefiascone, to the welfare of the young people, you, and your pupil there."

"No, sir; I cannot do that, if you will not take it as ungracious in me."

"And why not, Signor Minucci?" asked the Duke, throwing back his head.

"As a shrewd jurist not," replied Callisto, with light tone. "If I to-day take the substitute, would I be found absent on the day of the wedding banquet; and to that I will not fool away my right, and will reserve to myself all claims, if you only knew it."

The Duke forced himself to a short laugh.

"Indeed, you are a man of foresight. But now, if I quiet you, and vow — see, there comes Livio back; he will pledge us, as also the monks, as soon as they have laid aside their priestly garments — so follow me."

Callisto felt a heavy pressure from the arm Egino had upon his.

"Excuse us, really," answered, therefore, the lawyer. "You know I live far from the Porta del Popolo; it is growing night, and the night is no one's friend, — or, better, it has in Rome too many friends; therefore do not be angry if we ——"

"Let them go, our legal advisers," here put in Livio. "You see, father, they fear that, while my poor brother is so weak and frail, they would have poor companionship for an evening revel. There may be more cheerful company awaiting them — so *bona sera*, you gentlemen!"

The Duke also now insisted no longer. He reached Callisto his hand, bowed coldly adieu to Egino, and with the words, "Well, then, Livio may be right; farewell, Signor Callisto, and accept first my thanks," he turned away to the room of the invalid.

Livio accompanied Callisto and Egino to the door of the chamber.

When they saw themselves outside, alone, both stepped through the ante-chamber with the haste of a pair pursued, fleeing.

CHAPTER VI.

WEDDED TO THE DEAD.

AVING reached the court below, the two men threw themselves with the same haste upon their horses. In silence they left the Castle of the Savelli.

Outside, Signor Callisto urged his horse close to that of Egino, and whispered: —

"Did you perceive it?"

"Perceive? Perceive what?" exclaimed the German, with a harsh, tempestuous tone. "By God! I have perceived what suffices to make me beside myself. I am deprived of my senses by it; I have no more control of myself; it is to me as if an evil power, a wild demon, had turned my soul round and round. I wish to cry; I wish to weep; I wish to kill somebody, especially all of the name of Savelli. I am no more myself; I am as if lost on this maiden, this marvelous woman; as if enchanted, not merely in my thoughts — no, in my whole inner being, my every muscle, every fiber, every heart-throb, every drop of blood. Callisto, Callisto, what have you done to me, what have you brought upon me in letting me behold this image of a woman, — this image which now possesses me, tears itself away, withdraws into its night and into its horrible misery!"

Shocked, Callisto looked upon the young man uttering these words as if in perfect desperation.

"God help us!" said he; "you hurl disturbing accusation against me, and my soul is, Heaven knows, disturbed enough. You are enchanted, carried away with the beauty of this bride? Your passions are aroused? To the devil! You will not be a fool. You will know how to overcome it."

"I must first have a will to overcome it, and I have. I swear by the blood of Christ only the one will, — that is, to get possession of this woman, — to tear her from the poor, miserable, sickly dog of a bridegroom who could not move a limb! I could murder this Luca Savelli; I could murder his whole kinship, if I, through blood ——"

"Hold, hold, Count Egino!" cried Callisto; "do not utter your madness; and, before all, do not pledge your soul to the Devil, though the Devil has an interest in it. You cannot make this woman free through a murder."

"And why not?"

"Because she is not wedded to a living man, whom you might have put out of the way."

"What do you mean by that?"

"Where did you have your eyes?"

"My eyes? My eyes rested upon her; if I had had a hundred eyes I should have seen only her."

"And did they not rest for a moment upon the — bridegroom?"

"Only long enough to see she was married to a pitiful manikin."

"A manikin? No; a corpse, Count Egino! Corradina was given in marriage to the dead, you could say."

"To the dead?"

"Yes; Count Luca Savelli was dead."

"Dead?" cried Egino, loudly.

"You were blind if you did not see it."

"Righteous Jesus!"

"I knew it very soon," continued Callisto, "in spite of what they did to conceal it from us. Luca Savelli was dead."

"But, for Heaven's sake! for what purpose ——"

"Has it not occurred to you already, then," said Callisto, speaking on without hearing this exclamation, "that the Duke carefully kept away the light even in the first room in which we found him, although it became dark? The whole transaction was appointed for the hour of twilight. Also, upon the altar burned only two poor candles. That I brought with me a stranger might appear disturbing enough; but they had not the conscience sufficiently clear to hazard an objection — and they had no pretext. Didn't you see how they stood all the time around the dead man, in order that our glances should not rest upon him?"

"And the 'Yes' that he spoke?"

"Was Livio's. Don't doubt it; I know the voice."

Egino became speechless with astonishment.

"But the witnesses, — the signatures, — the monk who performed the ceremony!" cried he, then, after a pause.

"My God!" exclaimed Callisto, shrugging his shoulders. "The Duke of Aricia finds tools for every purpose."

"And you,— you yourself, Callisto; for the sake of eternal justice why didn't you tear to pieces your false and lying document, and cast the fragments in the faces of these dreadful people? Why did you not say to me, not with one syllable, what you perceived? I should rather have allowed myself torn in pieces than to have looked in silence upon this sacrilege."

"Thank God I was silent! Of what use would it have been to speak? There would have been enough people there below, under the arcades and in the court, to make us harmless; I saw down there Lanfranco with his sons,— one of the worst cutthroats out of the mountains. Rejoice yourself that we are safe on our way home, and again in the saddle of our horses. By the way, you might shorten the reins of yours a little more upon this steeply descending road. If we had been less quiet spectators, these same horses would now be stepping under a pair of men fast bound, going eastward to the mountains, to some quiet, solitary castle of the Savelli."

"And if also this heavenly woman could have been saved, this terrible thing would not have happened that she should be married to a dead person."

"Do you know that so positively? Was it not her place to speak first? Could she not speak the decisive 'No'? Do you know whether all this did not happen with her consent? Whether she is not proud to be able to wear now the name of this dead Luca? Truly, she appeared as if she gave herself willingly to this atrocious play; her brows were firmly drawn together, and her lips did not tremble."

"Oh, that is impossible, impossible! How could such youth, such beauty, such fullness of life, allow itself to be wedded to the dead,— freely fetter itself to the dead? No, no; horror and despair had turned her to stone."

"It is possible," responded Signor Minucci, reflectively; "it is possible. Who knows? In the first place it is, at least, certain that after some days we shall receive the announcement that Luca Savelli is dead from his illness, and that Rome will have the spectacle of the burial of a Savelli in the old family vault, in Ara Celi. They will be kind enough to invite me to it; if you will accompany me, Count Egino, I will bring you away, as I have done to-day."

"I could hate you, Callisto, for the calmness with which you say all this," rejoined Egino, angrily. "Has it not also changed your heart in your body? Has it —— "

The lawyer again shrugged his shoulders.

"Look around you, Count Egino; it has become very dark; but you can still recognize there to the right the Palatine Hill and the towers to the palaces of the Cæsars; the height there before us is the Capitol. You are in Rome, and do you wonder at anything? You have not forgotten how to be astonished at men and their deeds?"

"You must," he continued, as Egino did not reply, " you must become wiser, and learn that in this world, whose spiritual structure has the miraculous to the lowest foundation, anything becomes possible. In yonder elevated chamber, wherein we assisted at the marriage, the holy Dominicus once slept as the guest of Pope Honorius; for that reason they made of it their private chapel. Why be so horrified if on the altar of such a man the living is sacrificed to the dead! What begins with miracle must end with madness."

CHAPTER VII.

COAT OF ARMS OF THE HOHENSTAUFEN.

THE passionate outburst with which Egino confessed the ineffaceable impression which the bride of the dead Savelli had made upon him, had about it nothing too violent, too fiery, nothing untrue. What he had said to his companion, what he had described, that he felt; he felt it in unconquerable strength during the night, which he passed without sleep; he felt it on the following day, on all the following days, during which he spent the hours alone in his chamber, inactive, dreaming, insensible to everything else, or in slipping around, seeking out solitary roads, avoiding the sight of men, shunning even the voice of men, and wandering around as if lost.

With his clear intellect he had thoroughly turned over and meditated upon all sides of this event; he had penetrated with his sagacity into each of the questions rankling so stormily in his bosom; he had weighed every possibility; he had sifted for himself every interpretation, so far as that was possible without having recourse to some one else, in order thereby to obtain explanations; he feared from Callisto a cold, mocking reception, if he spoke with him in regard to that which lay so heavily upon his soul; he shunned so much as to speak the name of Corradina before any one in the world.

The more he still racked his brain and thought, the more he sank into the helpless despair which had taken possession of him — the despair of the will in the fetters of passion, which runs its brow against the brazen wall of the impossible. Impossible, impossible — it was indeed impossible for him, a foreigner, helpless, to make a way into the castle of the powerful race, and set free the victim who, according to his conception, had no other rescuer, avenger, protector but him. It was a thousand times impossible!

Impossible — even to himself, perhaps especially to himself. Would not another, in his place, have discovered means and ways to make himself known to the Savelli? to win their friendship, their confidence? to have himself invited into their houses, to their villas? to approach, in this way, Corradina, to search into her thoughts, in order to sue for her favor? All this another could have done; but Egino did not think of such a course. To dissemble, to put on a mask, to feign friendship and devotion where he hated — hated even to the death — his honest German nature was not in a condition for that. He had as weapons against a lie, only the truth; against trickery, only anger; against force, only force.

And these weapons — of what avail were they!

Egino felt himself sunken, overcome, lost in this dreadful situation. He could not extricate himself from the narrow circle of thought in which he was entangled, held a prisoner, surrounded as by an iron ring, which robbed him of breath, of the power to live. He could not tear himself loose from the thought of the unhappily wonderful woman and her lot, and the fact that he wished to rescue her, must rescue her, and that he was so powerless against those who were destroying her young life, as a poor bird is powerless to overcome the walls against which he flutters.

The highest blossom into which the life of man may develop has three petals, no more, which stand close together, unfolded from the same bud. They often blend into one — how often! They are love, poesy, and madness. How much of madness is in poesy? how much of poesy in love? how much of poesy and love in madness? Who can say? That, however, could no one say to Egino,— that in his love there was much of madness, that he was sinking into it deeper and deeper. Intellect and passion were in him as if whirling one within the other, and going astray in the immensity of longing, of desire, of burning passion for this unfortunate woman wedded to the dead.

One evening Egino came home tired to death from a long walk. He had been wandering about in the Campagna, among the ruins of old monuments on the "queen of streets." When he entered his dwelling, his servant Götz informed him that Signor Callisto Minucci had been there to take him for a walk to the Capitol.

"And what should I do with him at the Capitol?" asked Egino.

"There is to be some great person buried in the church up there," responded Gotz. "Signor Callisto would have procured for you a good place to witness the solemnities."

"One of the great of Rome is to be buried on the Capitol?" exclaimed Egino. "He is named Luca Savelli, this dead man?"

"I believe it was a name that sounded like that," responded the servant. "Will you follow him, Master?"

Egino threw himself exhausted into his arm-chair.

"No," he said. "I need not see him buried in order to know that he is dead. You go, if it seems enticing to you. Go! Yet hold; give me back my sword and my mantle. I will go, and you follow me."

Egino left the house again in haste. The thought had come to him that at this funeral the women of the house of Savelli might be present, and that it was possible he might see Corradina among the number. He didn't know whether or not the Roman women were wont to appear on such occasions, but it might be.

So, followed by his servant, he walked hastily down the Corso to the Capitol; then up the endless succession of marble steps forming the lofty flight which leads upward to the church of Ara Celi.

The portal was draped with black.

As he stepped into the interior, that was hung with black cloth and lighted with innumerable flaming wax candles and torches, he heard, coming forth from one of the side chapels at the upper end of the church, the sound of a mournful funeral dirge. In the middle of the nave he saw a catafalque surrounded by burning torches. It was empty, the coffin having been removed. They had already deposited the coffin in the vault of the chapel above. When Egino reached the chapel, he saw that the workmen were busy closing up the coping of the vault, while a host of the Franciscan monks of Ara Celi, standing around in a circle, howled in a doleful manner, rather than sang, a funeral song.

A great crowd of spectators were scattered about in all directions; the pall-bearers, a dense crowd of men in mourning garb with prelates clothed in violet or purple between them, were just leaving through the upper side door: the whole thing was at an end. It seemed that no women had taken part except those of the dependents of the house and those of the common people, who now streamed past Egino right and left leaving the church.

Egino also turned to depart. As he again passed through the nave of the church to the catafalque, his eye fell upon the scaffold, adorned with a covering of black velvet and cloth of gold. The ancestral arms of the house of Savelli were displayed upon it, surrounding its base as a wreath; at the head and foot ends was the coat-of-arms of the just-buried dead. The last showed the escutcheons of Luca Savelli and of his wife placed near each other. Upon one were the lions of the Savelli and the swords of the hereditary marshalship; upon the other, the escutcheon of the wife, however —— What did that mean? Upon this coat-of-arms, on which the light of the torches fell red as blood, presented itself, upon a golden ground, a two-headed black eagle, which upon its breast bore a heart-shield with a red lion rampant. That was the shield of the German government, of the German emperor, — as borne by the race of Frederick von Büren, the race of the Hohenstaufens. Wonderful! What had the Countess Corradina von Anticoli to do with the Hohenstaufens?

Egino stood overcome by the sight. Was that pictured coat-of-arms a legendary writing in Runic characters, a charmed circle, which held him bound fast, over which he could not pass? He stood and gazed upon it till the church was entirely deserted, — upon that coat-of-arms of the Hohenstaufens, which suddenly rose before his eyes upon the Capitol, — upon a catafalque!

CHAPTER VIII.

STANZA DELLA SEGNATURA.

THE eminently beautiful and extensive square in front of St. Peter's Church, which, adorned with the obelisk of Pharaoh Rameses VII., overlooked by the dome of Michael Angelo, is to-day the proudest and most imposing expression of the world-swaying church, appeared very wild and desolate in the year 1510. To the mighty church-building, there was still wanting that crowning dome, still the façade of Maderno; there was still lacking those two projecting, semicircular colonnades which, like two giant arms, lie far stretched out around the square. There could not then arise in a sarcastic mind the thought that all of this Vatican basilica lies there like a giant crab, with its two colossal pincers extended for prey. The building was surrounded with scaffolds, the square covered with blocks of travertine, with cutting-blocks and stones of every kind, with rafters and planks, with arrangements for preparing the mortar,— with all that which is wont to accumulate in the neighborhood of a new building for years in process of erection.

And still much more than to-day did the palace of the Vatican present the character of a gigantic, mediæval royal castle, with high towered walls and buttressed pillars, with battlements and defensive stocks. The whole Palazzo Nuovo, now occupied by the Popes, was not standing then. That part of the building, however, into which the admirers of the artistic glories of the Vatican overflow, when they, having come to the Court of San Damaso, turn thence to the left — this old building in which Alexander Borgia, Julius II., and Leo X. dwelt, was even then covered with lofty scaffolds; for, under the direction of Bramante, they had even then begun to add to it the loggias, which to-day surround all three sides of the Court of San Damaso — a structure which, under Leo X.'s pontificate, Raphael pushed to completion, in order then to adorn these loggias

ST. PETER'S, ROME.

with his works, or to have them adorned with the works of his pupils.

Some days after the burial of Luca Savelli, Egino, in his aimless wanderings, fell upon the square in front of St. Peter's. He looked with apathetic glance upon the ant-like movements around the building-site, in whose central space arose the four pillars now supporting the dome. Between these pillars, in the background, appeared the interior of the old St. Peter's Church, the greater part of its walls covered with plank. The separate parts of the old building were borne away and destroyed, only in the proportion in which the necessity to win room for the new made this unavoidable.

Egino stared upon the spectacle, and seated himself then upon a block of marble lying there, without perceiving that he was observed by any one. After awhile a hand was laid upon his shoulder, and, lifting his eyes, he looked into the face of a young monk, who wore an undergarment of white woolen stuff and a white scapulary, over which was a black cape open in front, with wide hanging sleeves. He had removed the leathern girdle which belonged to his costume, and thrown it over his shoulder; because, on this warm day, it might have become too warm for him in his monk's garb.

The young monk appeared quite like a German, with his firm and compact form, his thick blonde hair, his sturdy features, to which a broad, bold chin gave the expression of courage and energy. It was not possible that other than German blood flowed through this powerful, thick-set frame; only what lay in his eyes, looking smilingly down upon Egino, this peculiarly dazzling light, this interchange between the bright beam and the deep glow, which soon manifested itself under the excitement produced by the conversation with Egino, had nothing of the national type; it was a peculiarity, a special characteristic of this young man in the habit of an Augustine monk,—a peculiarity which always exercised a kind of charm over him who looked into this deeply flaming eye of the soul.

"See, see, Count Egino!" said then, in the German speech, the young monk, smiling. "Here sits a young German of princely blood and lets the sun burn his back, in order to observe how the Roman church builds itself anew."

"Brother Martin!" cried Egino, "is it you? Well, yes, I am looking upon and observing all the haste, and see how the ardent Master Bramante manages to keep his host of workmen in breath."

"And what do you think of this sight, you German prince?"

asked Brother Martin, while he familiarly seated himself near Egino, on the broad stone.

"What do I think of it?" continued Egino. "Now, if you wish to know, I think it is an old rule if a man has found happiness and prosperity in a modest and narrow house, he should not leave it to remove into a more showy, larger one; the happiness refuses, indeed, to remove with him into the new one. Who knows whether the future of the church in the new house will be so happy as was the past in the old!"

"You are something of a heretic, Count Egino," answered the monk, shaking his head. "Happiness? What is happiness? Does the church need it?"

"Were I a heretic, I would, on the contrary, say it is good that the church begins to build itself anew; for, as it was, it was even a little worn out and decaying."

"And let that even be heard in preference," responded Brother Martin, nodding. "With everything upon the earth must that which is decaying be renewed; and, alas! there has come into the church, also, as occurs in earthly human phenomena, much, very much of decay and corruption, and new work is necessary to restore the splendor of the temple and the chaste beauty of holiness."

"Do you dare say that, little monk?" asked Egino.

"Wherefore should I not say what lies open to the eyes of all the world? I see here many dirty hands guarding the treasure of the church; the treasure is not, therefore, less if I say, 'Wash your hands.' I see that much moss has formed upon the columns of this tabernacle; the pillars are not, therefore, the less of porphyry and gold if I say, 'Scour this filthy moss and this rust from them.' I see there lies dirt and rubbish on the ground around the altar here; the altar is not, therefore, less a holy place of offering if I say, 'Sweep this trash out.' Am I right, Count Egino of Ortenburg, or not?"

"Such a man as you, Brother Martin, is always right," gave Egino for reply. "You are even a peculiar spirit, and, as a monk, perform already the incredible, if you only perceive and admit the dirt on the hands, the rust on the pillars, the rubbish around the altar."

"Ah, ah! You speak as one who understands nothing about these things," said Brother Martin, interrupting him here. "Should the monk, because he is a monk, be like the humble dog which licks the feet of the great, the high-puissant honor-bearers? I know the world looks upon the poor mendicant monk in this way. But you are mistaken; if he is to you children of the world, even once, an object of ridicule, you would be nearer right to call the poor, begging friar the court-fool of the church — for the court-fool, you know, has the right to speak the truth out plainly."

"The truth! Pilate asked Christ, 'What is truth?' Surely he would not have asked a mendicant monk this question. Perhaps, at the most, he might have asked so learned an Augustine brother as yourself, Brother Martin."

"We, also, are but poor hermit brethren, nothing further, and esteem ourselves no wiser than those in patched, brown capes, with long or short cowls, with long or short beards. And out of the poor cloister has always gone forth opposition to the increasing worldliness of the church; yes, bold, protesting sects, as the Fraticelli and the Umiliati, or whole congregations, as the Minoriten, Celestines, against whom the Inquisition has taken measures sufficiently sharp."

"All that, truly, you know better than I," interposed Egino. "I remain only by my statement in regard to what you asked me, Brother Martin,— that to me the building of new churches is not pleasing. Why be always building greater churches, while the spirit that rules therein always proves itself to be such that it frightens pious men to go in?"

Brother Martin had removed his leathern girdle from his shoulder, and was busying himself with it, clasping and unclasping the buckle. So doing, he said:—

"You talk about this as a German nobleman. The spirit which reigns therein is the same that it was from the beginning, although its form has changed from time to time. Every spirit is a current: upon it the drift of everything that has life goes to a continual production of an ever-improved form."

"Only do not shape and unfold too much, and things which deter men from following you," interposed Egino. "I have learned so much in Bologna, in the college of the learned Greek, Tryphon. The great heresies have always arisen through a protest against your new forms. On account of the new form of the doctrine of the divinity of the Son, the Arians arose and have continued to this day; on account of the unfolding of Papal Infallibility, arose the Waldensians; on account of the dogma which set aside the cup, the Hussites. All these heretics have always declared themselves only against the innovations, and remain by the original Word of God, or wish to return to it; and I fear there will still be many of them, many, remain behind, if this unfolding of new forms, of new extension of power, of new heavenly pardon to be had for money, is continued."

"What do you understand about this, you or your cunning Greek of Bologna, who there leads the German youth astray," answered Brother Martin. "Shall I do you the honor to hold a theological disputation with your young wisdom?"

"Oh, no," responded Egino, smiling; "I grant you my young wisdom is not in condition for that, — never less so than now."

"So come, rather, and follow me; I can help you to a sight which it is, as yet, not allowed to every one to behold."

"And that is?"

"I am going to a brother of my order, the sacristan of the Holy Father. He has bidden me come to the chambers up there"— the monk pointed to the right, where the buildings of the papal residence towered high above them — "which a young, but very celebrated master has adorned with paintings, such that no man has ever in any land beheld finer."

"Oh! I have heard so much of this master, and of his pictures in the Vatican Palace!" here exclaimed Egino. "You confer upon me a great favor, Brother Martin."

"Then come on."

Egino arose, and the two fellow-countrymen turned thence to the right, where they soon found themselves upon a steeply ascending street which led between the substructions of the palace and the lofty, inclosing walls, and up which they slowly walked, with people passing one another in the most various garbs; with men in spiritual and secular costumes, court servants, prelates, Swiss soldiers in the picturesque uniform of their land, Roman grandees, in stately pomp, with armed retinue. It appeared as if there were here a continual ebb and flow in the royal castle of the earthly vicegerent of heavenly power.

Brother Martin seemed to have passed over the road more than once before. When he, with Egino, had reached the Court of San Damaso, he turned to one of the doors, immediately behind which a broad stairway led upward. Upon the first landing stood, leaning motionless upon his halberd, a soldier, who, in an indifferent tone, asked the two men whither they wished to go; and when Brother Martin gave the name of Fra Anselmo, the brother of his order, in the same apathetic manner, with a mere movement of the head, he bade them go farther.

Above, Egino and Martin came to a curtain of green cloth, at which a guardian porter again detained them. Upon Martin's informing him whither he wished to go, he lifted the curtain, and the two Germans entered a room, half hall, half corridor, with vaulted ceilings and walls frescoed with scenes from the Old Testament, with a few high windows, admitting only insufficient light. Seats ran around the walls, with cushions of embroidered stuff placed upon them, and mats of fine hurdle-work covered the stone slabs of the floor. Upon these mats, moving leisurely up and down, stepped several groups of men, two of them in the red robes of a cardinal; others sat talking together upon the seats at the side: men of the most diverse ages, of the most diverse nationalities of the world; the legate of some German order out of the far North, near the long-bearded prior of a Spanish monastery; a Hungarian bishop near a Scotch duke in the costume of his land — men of proud, commanding, and expressive heads and crafty, meagre faces with mobile countenances — all led hither by a common aim. They were led here to this middle point of the spiritual authority of the world, to see fulfilled some desire involving a vital question for themselves; this might be, now, the territory of a sovereign or a bishopric, a verdict or a privilege, a release from some law or absolution from some sin. This Vatican was then, indeed, the heart of a great system of arteries and veins, in which pulsed the religious life of the world; through the arteries flowed out spiritual favors to the world, through the veins flowed back — money.

The two Germans who entered this room let their glance glide inquiringly over the assembly, when, from the other end of the room, where he had been chatting with a man in clerical dress, there came to meet them an elderly monk, bowing familiarly to Brother Martin while yet at a distance. He wore a white habit, like that of Brother Martin, under his black cape.

"That is Brother Anselmo, the sacristan and father confessor of His Holiness," said Martin to his companion.

Then, turning to the one approaching, he continued in the Latin tongue: —

"You see two curious Germans instead of one, worthy father. This is a young count from beyond the Alps, who has come hither in order to carry on a process against me and our cloister. We are still none the less good friends on that account, and we shall soon settle our affairs ourselves, if the Rota doesn't do it."

"Right, just right," answered Fra Anselmo, regarding Egino with a friendly smile; "better that two friends divide a disputed fruit, than that the contention about the fruit divide the friends. You wish to see what our young Urbino is painting in the Sala della Segnatura?"

"Since you promised me to let me see it, worthy father," responded Martin.

"I know, I know; and I was expecting you. Follow me. Only do not let the master know of our presence by talking too loudly; he would then, indeed, be in a condition to send us all three away with a scolding."

Fra Anselmo passed to the other end of the room, and the Germans followed him; through a second curtain they came into a narrow corridor, and then into a vaulted room of more moderate extension.

"Here is what you desired to see," whispered Fra Anselmo, on entering.

The two young men took a few steps, then they both remained standing as if frightened, throwing around them glances of surprise at the splendor of color and form which surrounded them.

The entire frescoing of the room was just finished, the scaffolding had been removed, only a few planks and ropes yet lay on the floor; some workmen were busied in removing these, also, while several young people in light, bright-colored frocks over their garments stood together in a group at the window examining a drawing, which lay spread out before them on the window-sill.

After the two Germans had looked around awhile in silence at that which met their eyes, Egino exclaimed:—

"By my Creator! Brother Martin, if one should threaten to cut out my tongue, I could not remain dumb here, nor could I whisper in a low tone. Something as if overpowering takes possession of me, like the force of an existence which I had never anticipated,—like an intoxication; not because I have drunken wine, but because I have drunken something like the air of Heaven. Brother Martin, Martin, do you not, then, feel as I do? This is beautiful,—beautiful enough to die for, a world of beauty, before which one might throw himself upon his knees in ravished devotion!"

Brother Martin remained silent. He regarded in silence, with a peculiarly glowing look, the picture which they call the "Disputation." Then he raised his head to contemplate the ceiling pictures,— the forms of Theology, Poesy, Philosophy, and Justice; and finally, turning around, he let his eye rest a long time on the wall opposite that on which was the "Disputation," — on the "Parnassus" and "The School of Athens."

"Now, Brother Martin," cried Egino again, "you cannot look mute and silent upon all this?"

Brother Martin passed his hand over his brow and face, as if to collect himself.

"How could one look upon it otherwise than in silence?" said he then, half aloud. "It yields even a world of reflection."

"Of reflection? Aye! who can reflect here? When great pinions are placed upon your shoulders, what do you reflect? Miserable soul to reflect then; one strikes the wings together and soars — up, up, into the morning-glow, into the air of heaven, and into the beam-world of the sun."

"So you feel, Count Egino," replied the German monk, as if in confusion and perplexity. "Here, however, is a celestial atmosphere in which I would tremble to soar and lose myself. In these pictures is much of God; for in beauty is always something of God, and so is beauty also a virtue——"

"But?"

"But," continued Brother Martin, "this virtue is led astray by the serpent, and the Devil stands behind her."

"Oh! now I could laugh if I did not feel so sacredly in earnest."

"Do not laugh! It is so; the race of man, the terrestrial body, our miserable carnality presented in this unfettered beauty, is indeed a deification of the creature, as if it were born without sin! See these forms! Are they earthly creatures, born for pain as we men are, and in need of redemption through the atoning blood of Christ? of pardon in order to live, in order not to be overcome with suffering? Do they not stand there in proud self-sufficiency, and as if they needed not justification, because they are justified through themselves? Does not this new art teach paganism in the house of the Holy Father?"

"Why not paganism," said Egino, "if paganism is so beautiful — as you say, so virtuous?"

Brother Martin regarded him loftily; he answered not; he looked again upon the forms of the pictures and became absorbed in the sight.

In the meantime, out of the group of young people at the window, he who had formed its central figure and led the conversation explaining the drawing, turned around. He was a man of a frame not large, and more elegant than strong, of strikingly beautiful features, with rich brown hair flowing down upon his shoulders. He carried his head a little inclined forward on the long neck; beautiful, wide-open, brown eyes sparkled therein; the skin was overspread with a fine, olive-tinted paleness; he had a thoroughly spiritual appearance, almost imbuing one with melancholy. Coming a step nearer, he fixed his eyes upon the German monk; Fra Anselmo approached him and whispered to him some words as of apology that he had brought the strangers hither. The painter bowed, and then said, smiling, "And what does that brother of your order say to his fellow-countryman? He seems not to be especially pleased with my work?"

Thereupon he threw back his long hair with a motion of the head, which, for a man, had almost too much of grace and something of the effeminate; the voice with which he spoke had about it something clear, silver-toned, which peculiarly penetrated the heart.

The German monk turned from the pictures and advanced a step toward the painter, as if struck and attracted by this appearance.

Egino also could not do otherwise than withdraw his attention from the pictures, in order to direct it toward the two men standing opposite each other; toward the beautiful, soul-lighted countenance of the young painter, out of which looked forth a full, joyous nature, by the side of a remarkable, an almost awe-inspiring earnestness,— toward the firmly chiseled head of the monk, which had about it nothing attractive except the eyes, filled at this moment with an entirely characteristic fire. It was as if out of the four eyes thus encountering each other, intercrossing beams were thrown,— invisible spirit fibers drawn from each toward the other, seeking a union but unable to find it. It was a mutual searching of souls and a daring challenge.

"What a head you have, good brother," then said the painter, smiling with a meditative air; "if I had seen it sooner, I might have used it there among the men of the disputing church."

He pointed to the right at the picture of the "Disputation."

"Perhaps, however," he added, "you would not have consented to that; you put on a very earnest, and as if horrified, face at this picture."

He had said this in tolerably fluent Latin, and Brother Martin replied, in the same tongue:—

RAPHAEL SANTI.

"Horrified, but only at the beauty of your representation, which shows upon its face that you have read more in Plato's Symposium than in the Bible."

The painter nodded, smiling.

"I have read Plato's Symposium, but also the Bible; it has not, as you say yourself, injured my pictures?"

"Not your pictures, but perhaps the souls which become absorbed in these pictures."

"And wherefore?"

"Because they are like an intoxicating magic potion. This fullness of beauty is too great not to take the heart captive, and lull it into a dangerous dream of human grandeur, greatness, and beauty. Grant that you are only the pictures of fully developed mankind, yet you also preach a sermon down from these walls, and you have enough of beauty, of happiness, of inner harmony; you beam forth there as real kings of the world; you have become there the embodiment of eternal ideas, which your Grecian philosophy sends forth out of the lap of the divine Being — you need nothing more."

"And shall I not represent such beings?" said the young painter. "Is the God of the Bible weaker, more powerless, than the eternal Being of Plato? And if this Being creates conceptions which, being embodied, represent themselves as ideals of beautiful forms, shall I then make accusation against them, and annihilate them as heathenish, unchristian, and sinful? Are the creatures of the Christian God weaker, and less perfect? Do you recognize as his children only the deformed, who appear like the long, meager, and wrinkled saints in your German, and, alas! also in our Italian cathedrals?"

"The god of Plato is not our God," responded the German monk, warmly. "The god of Plato is the god of the heathen world. What the Old World represented, what the pagan artists depicted, that is a world of happiness, of heroism, of victory, of physical strength, of self-sufficiency, of present joy. The ancient dispensation was that of earthly happiness; the Christian is that of pain. In former ages man belonged to material nature; in the Christian age, to the spirit. There prevails in Christ a contest between man and nature. Sin has brought this contest about. The contest continues till the entire separation of one from the other,— till death; and thus our whole life is a painful struggle,— a struggle with self up to that dark door into the beyond, on whose threshold we break down, and through which a rescuing arm is extended to snatch us within, into the stronghold of eternal peace. Therefore, Master, you are wrong when you paint men in whom there is no strife; who cannot die, because their harmonious being stands there in a glory of spirit and of form; who have no sin; and who need not struggle until death. We are Christians, and know that we need pardon if we would have life. I have contemplated many an art treasure of antiquity which, here in this ancient city of the world, has been rescued from destruction, and is now freely exposed to the view of foreign visitors. From these I have found that the Egyptians represented best the beauty of the animal; the Greeks, best the beauty of man; the Christian, however, should best represent the beauty of the soul: that should be their art. But you, Master, paint gods incarnate."

While the monk spoke in this way the countenance of the young painter had assumed an expression which strangely transformed it. It was as if the breath of youthful beauty which played upon it had gently withdrawn, in order to make room for an earnest, thoughtful face with wrinkles of pain. The sockets of his eyes had grown deeper; the light tinge of red upon his cheeks had flown.

We possess a little drawing which was prepared by the hand of the engraver Mark Antonio, and which gives to us a portrait of an entirely different Raffaelle Santi from that which stands before the eyes of the world according to the well-known pictures of him. This picture makes a deeply seated and disturbing impression; it shows how even the richest and most happily endowed genius, the most fully inspired soul, is not free from the difficult and painful conditions under which the spirit of man surrounds itself with the most artistic vision of the beautiful. The picture lets us look into a desolate room, wherein stands an easel with an outstretched, empty canvas; upon a seat is the painter, all sunken together, his head bowed under the burden of his thoughts, his deep-set eyes wandering around in uncertain search; it appears to have made him chilly, since he has thrown around him a broad mantle; his form appears emaciated from the exertion of wasting labor.

Something of this Raffaelle of Mark Antonio stood now before the German monk. He crossed his arms upon his breast; he looked upon Brother Martin awhile in silence; then, as if in absent-mindedness, he threw off the restraint of the Latin speech, and answered in Italian:—

"If you should say that in your cell beyond the mountains, German monk, you would be right. Every system is of value so far as it has power over the souls; beyond this limit it becomes folly, and the sport of children. As your system is not in me when I paint, I cannot paint your agonizing men. Look there upon my creations. If there is no sin in them, you see them free from an old curse, whose stamp you imagine burnt upon the brow of all living; now, why do you not say, 'So much the better?' Believe me, if man is born in pain and subject to death, he is, moreover, born to make himself free from pain. Let me show to the world forms in which there is no contest, but a harmony, between the mind and the soul; forms which, with a finer soul in a finer body, have found liberty, and with the liberty happiness, present joy; forms which are not the servants of pain, but its masters. Perhaps, you call it, indeed, a sermon; perhaps this sermon has also its influence for good upon man. Do you understand me?"

"I understand, Signore Raffaelle," answered Brother Martin, in the same tongue; "but let me continue to speak in Latin, as I speak it more fluently than your Italian. I would let you paint your forms as your eye beholds them, your mind creates them, as your marvelously skillful hand knows how to conjure them forth in inimitable perfection, if you did not thus preach too loudly, too pointedly, too movingly. You not only place humanity there as it would be represented by the heathen, you also construct for yourself the world in a manner Christ did not dare to see it built. Upon this wall, here, you place the glorification of religion; upon the opposite wall, where your sages stand assembled, the glorification of philosophy: there, the church with her revelation; here, the self-supporting mind of man and the heroes of searching thought! You give to them, also, an equal right in your world! There, over our heads, in striking beauty, Poesy and Law stand near Theology. Are they the equally strong ground-pillars of your moral world? Art, Law, Philosophy—are they the same to you as Religion? And do you so present them in the house of the Successor of the Apostles—there, the Fathers of the church? here, Apollo and his Muses? Parnassus opposite the Eucharist? The mind which entertains such a view of earthly things can truly also create earthly men as gods, as 'masters of pain.' 'You will be as God,' said the Serpent."

The painter again looked upon the monk earnestly, meditatively, as if lost in thought, and for a long time did not answer. What he heard might not, in the first place, have been understood by him; but, indeed, scarcely had words ever pressed themselves so firmly and plainly over the lips of those who came to admire his works, or to surround him as friends and patrons, and strew upon his life-path, as roses, the homage and glorification which he still found always and everywhere this path led him. And, truly, never had spectator of his works, with such earnest look, recognized and spoken out what was the historical import of his art,—the anomaly of the heathen, human principle in Christian art, and the beauty, attained only at the cost of the most arbitrary union.

"Listen to me, monk," then he said, proudly raising his sunken head: "you preach as you must—that is your calling; but do not let my art disturb you, and I shall not let your preaching disturb me. I place not only 'Law,' and 'Poesy,' and 'Worldly-wisdom' on an equality with your 'Theology'—no, I even place there myself, the living man. I know God has created me as I am, and with power to accomplish what I do; but I have expended a good and hard bit of labor and sour sweat in order, by the help of the beloved God, to become what I am. Now, however, if I have any force in me, it is a good force, to which, when I am in ardor of creating something, I dare to give loose rein, full of confidence that it, having knowledge of the right, will wander in the right ways. And so I do. Do you complain that I paint forms not ecclesiastical? I paint them as proper men are; if they prove not to be ecclesiastic, it must follow that God has not created and appointed the right man for his churchdom. If you wish to see struggling, fettered bodies, which strain their muscles and prop their limbs under sin as under a weight of stone, just go into the chapel beyond, where Michael Angelo is painting. If I were to do so I should commit a crime against myself, and become a hypocrite, for I do not apprehend and see things in that way. The painter's revelation is his eye. If you should command God to color his heavens no longer blue, but green, he would obey you as much as I those who desire of me to paint stiff, bound limbs and lank bodies in the mantle of an ascetic, and no more the nude shoulders of a pure woman like that Muse, there. Let there exist under the mantle of the haggard saint the entire theology of Thomas Aquinas, in the nude shoulders of the Muse is a higher theology, a lesson of divine wisdom preached by beauty, and more of the eternal, perhaps, than in the scholastic 'Summary.' And because you look so clever out of your fiery eyes, German Brother, now take a lesson from me. I have made myself free — and so have found beauty. You go, make yourself free, in order to find truth!"

With that, Master Raffaelle Santi bowed to Brother Martin a cold, proud leave-taking, beckoned to the other young men, and withdrew accompanied by them.

The German monk looked after him with dark and wrinkled brow.

"You are confounded and silenced, Brother Martin?" said Count Egino, after a pause, during which he had been observing his companion.

"Confounded! Yes; that I am," cried the monk; "and I think you ought to be also! There, beyond"— he pointed in the direction of St. Peter's Church — "the Pope is tearing down the sacred dome of Christendom, in which are the graves of the Apostles, and every spot hallowed through the veneration of a thousand years, in order to erect a new work in the pagan style. Here, in his chambers, the first painter of the world paints for him luminous paganism on the walls. Now tell me, Count Egino, what is to become of the church, if those who occupy the highest positions in the world, and if the greatest minds, for the sake of art and beauty, turn their backs upon her?"

"I don't know," answered Egino, shrugging his shoulders. "It appears to me that if the highest minds will no longer come to the church, the church in the end will do well to come to the minds. You know the adage about Mahomet and the mountain; and as you are a learned man, you will best know whether I do right to answer you with it."

Brother Martin made no response. He slowly raised his eyes to the picture of the "Disputation." Egino's looks, however, hung glowing and ravished upon the forms of the other walls.

"The beauty!" at length exclaimed the latter. "Where does it lie here? I believe it lies in the spotless purity of these forms. When this Mester von Urbino paints nude bodies, they stand there as if beings gone forth from the lap of Nature, for which you require a veil as little as for the tree past which your road leads. When you inhale the fragrance of a flower, do you think of its sex? Yes, yes — in his clear purity of soul lies the secret of this painter; his bodies have their beauty, as if they had developed so beautifully through their own inner superiority. Therefore I do not inveigh against his creations. You may call him pagan, if you will; in his chastity lies his Christianity; and if he forces the pagan form to become the living, breathing expression of a pure and ideal soul, you should praise, and not blame him."

"Come, come," said Brother Martin; "let us go; I have seen enough. I have the heart-ache over this place."

CHAPTER IX.

A PICTURE OF THE CHURCH.

HEN Egino again arrived at his dwelling, tired and almost out of breath, he threw aside his dagger and hat, and stretched himself upon his leathern couch; with open eyes he stared long at the opposite wall, a dark-blue, whitewashed surface, with a red finishing-roll and green, interlacing vines, which ran around as a border, and this border soon became for him a confused medley of pictures.

He beheld before him the forms of Raphael as shifting shadows, appearing and again vanishing; upon the blue background they swayed back and forth, coming and going, up and down, as if in a spell of enchantment which would not leave him again, — the Apollo with his viol, the Poesy, the beautiful forms of the Muses, the Poet and the Sage in their commingled glow of colors; and then between them, before them, ruling over them all, and still as if belonging to them, that other form which nevermore left Egino! She was as a being out of this world, as if stepping forth out of it into life, a creation of the most gifted artist, who, in the intoxicating inspiration of beauty, had called her into life — she alone of all to breathe, to live, and thus press back and cast in the shadow, all this lifeless beauty in contrast with her own, warm and living.

And still, even if she lived, was she therefore for him, for Egino, more than a picture? Had he any more claim upon her than upon all these lifeless forms? What was it to him whether she breathed or not? whether or not her lips moved in speech? whether or not her lids rose and fell? A word addressed to him could never come over these lips; in order to throw a glance upon him, these lids could never be lifted; she was nothing, nothing but a picture to him, — a shadowy picture of memory, forever. And on this account the perfect wretchedness of the last few days again seized upon him, though from it the hour just past had a little distracted him. The pictures of the master, which he had just now taken so warmly under his protection, lost for him their enchanting colors; they swam confusedly before him and fled; they lost their power over his soul, into which pain again returned as if into its own exclusive place. A German poet has said: —

> „Daß sie am Schmerz, den sie zu trösten
> Nicht wußte, mild vorüberführt,
> Erkenn ich als der Zauber größten,
> Womit uns die Antike rührt."

Was it not also this which Egino now felt, — that this art was not the comforter of pain; that she only sought mildly to lead one beyond it; and if she failed in this charm, as a strange world thrust the bleeding human heart from herself, and coolly showed it the way out of her elevated, self-sufficient regions. Was it the intention of Brother Martin finally to say this, and to upbraid the painter with it? Had it at once been clear and open to Brother Martin, what Egino now for the first time believed himself to feel, when the forms of the artist paled before him, — that not

> „durch des Schmerzens Gunst
> Sei seinen Blicken aufgegangen
> Die tiefe Welt der Christenkunst, —"

of an art, which must be produced by a different life principle, in order to avail more than the antique — to be able to console, to heal, and to save.

Suffice it to say, Egino forgot the pictures, and gradually all his thoughts drew again into the same channel, toward the same object.

With entirely different thoughts was Brother Martin busy as he wended his way home to his cloister.

All that he had found out and observed in this Roman world, in which he had now tarried some weeks, and which became the more shocking to him the more he became acquainted with the foreign tongue, stood in most direct opposition to his preconceived notions. With his deeply seated religious nature, he had applied to everything the measuring-rod of his theology. And nothing would conform to it! But the appearances which disturbed him, because they seemed to withdraw themselves entirely from his theological measuring-staff, he had gradually submitted to a species of powerful dialectics, and thus gotten rid of them till they no more disturbed his peace, and till the optimism of his faithful soul had become their master.

The church, as he had seen, had a thousand drawbacks. With an open cynicism simony prevailed in it. Worldly and uncultivated men clothed themselves in priests' attire in order to drive bargains with the favors and treasures of the church. And men, as one when a scholar at home took upon himself the vexations which the system of fagging imposed, in order thereafter to be received into a higher schools, took the vexations which the church inflicted upon them. They fasted; they prayed off the whole chaplet; they purchased indulgences, dispensations, masses; they bowed before the priests, who despised them for their conduct; they tortured their mother-wit and their intellect, in order to believe a thousand incredible things, — all this, that they might then be received into heaven. They laid up in a savings-box, in order to receive a great capital of heavenly joy.

That was all shocking! The church had become something of which the miracle-working Mother of God in Sant Agostino presented a striking image. How she sat there! Surrounded with a dazzling light; adorned with garments of silk and cloth-of-gold; a lofty, diamond-sprinkled imperial crown upon her head; strings of diamonds and pearls of inestimable value upon her neck, her arms,—at her feet knelt, in the dust, hundreds of men murmuring prayers!

Upon the lap of the figure, however, there rested a corpse. The Christ, whom this image of the church held upon her knees, was a corpse. The Christ of the gospel, who had uttered the Sermon on the Mount and the words, "You shall pray in spirit and in truth," — he was dead; he had died upon the knees of this woman. Also they did not pray to him; men bestowed their veneration upon the woman in the dress of gold-cloth and strings of pearls.

So sounded forth often Brother Martin's secretly wrathful thoughts, when he looked about him in the holy city of Christendom. But he silenced these thoughts. Did there not lie at hand consolation a hundred-fold? What effect had all this upon the inner being of the church? They were only temporal appearances, which must fall away, like the hull from the kernel when it is ripe. Christ had arisen after three days, and could arise again from the lap of the woman with the imperial crown. The Rock Peter had been established for eternity. The infallibility of doctrine must, by degrees, remove the sores, the excrescences, the diseased material; and the Master must purify his house — it was only a question of time.

And thus had also the General of his order spoken to him when he, sometimes, in the anxiety of his heart, had knocked at the former's cell,— the largest, finest, and most comfortably fitted up of the cloister. This mild and free-thinking man had then received him in a paternal way. Fra Egidius von Viterbo was a man of brilliant attainments, who, in his youth, had distinguished himself as a poet, and who, among the honor-bearers of the church, was prominent for his breadth of spiritual view. That had Brother Martin joyously found out even in the first weeks after he, with his full, piously ardent heart had arrived in the "Eternal City"; and now, out of that which he saw and experienced, the first cold showers poured themselves over this pious flame. He had then, indeed, half indignant and rebellious, half as one pleading for help, fled to this man, and complained to him how the readers of the Mass there below in the church of the order sneered at him because he took it so earnestly, and did it so slowly; and how impatiently they had called out to him, "Go on! go on!"— yes, how he had observed that during the Mass they had uttered blasphemous things; that they had amused themselves with filthy jesting — how he, under the impression of all this, in a puzzled frame of mind had ascended the Holy Stair, and how, suddenly, in the midst of the disagreeable gliding from step to step, a disgust at all works of sanctification had seized him, so that he defiantly arose and walked down. Upon hearing this, Egidius von Viterbo had consoled him with a kind of mild condescension to his childish feelings, to his honest inexperience; then, also, had scolded him, as well, on account of his hypercritical nature, which would not let him take the world as he found it; and, finally, always referred to the unchanging, eternal principle of the church standing high above earthly, mutable forms and human frailties, the Paraclete,— the Spirit remaining with and in it.

With this Brother Martin had consoled himself. But to-day something penetrated his being which would no more be silenced through such a consolation.

For the immoral priesthood, for the thoughtless service of God, for the filth, for the wickedness, for the corruption, there was a consolation; but where was the consolation for that which the beautiful, rising unrestrained in opposition to his holiness, had hurled into his soul? As these thoughts rushed together over his head, a deep anxiety seized upon him. What avail to him then was his trust in the eternity of the Rock of Peter? Did it assure to him the eternity of the mastery of this Rock over the lives of men? Did there not erect itself a new power threateningly before his eyes? Did there not lie in this world of culture a monstrous insurrection, nourishing its growth at the breasts of a classic past, and no longer allowing minds to be guided, or bodies to be mastered, by the church? Did not science already turn itself away from her? Did not art, especially in that which it created, throw to her the gauntlet? Had these Erasmuses, these Reuchlins, these Agricolas, and Heginses so willed to lead men to a culture which then would also despise the voice of the church, when she, sounding forth, called them back under her wings? Had not also the people of the Jews been only a small heap, a narrow island of humanity? Could not the church of the future, with her Rock Peter, become such an insignificant rock-island, on which the waves of life and of history might overflow without noting it?

Like an ice-cold bath these thoughts showered around the German monk. With grievous force there pressed upon his spirit the anxious fear that there could be a "too late" for the reformation of the church, which the previous century had demanded; that there could lie in the infidelity of the cultured men of his time whom the church had offended, not merely a wandering from the right way, from the truth, but also an evolution, a stepping forward of humanity upon another way, in order to seek the truth.

No, no; it must have been a fearful apostasy of the world from Christ! And through Christ alone could it become rectified, could it receive pardon here and become saved hereafter. But, indeed, it was time that from the lap of the diamond-bedizened woman in the dress of gold-cloth, the corpse, newly alive, should arise, and, as master of the world, call man again to himself. It was time. Then, then, too, must the world obey. Brother Martin had been reared in scholasticism; he was a theologian, he was a monk. He was even in this moment hierarch enough to think of the penal power of the church, of compulsion and violence against the insurrection!

Thus had the pictures of Raphael aroused him, alarmed him. He had at home seen many pictures; beautiful delineations by Lucas Sunder from Cronach, who painted such soulful faces of the saints; also some by Albert Dürer and Lucas von Leyden. This had all been perfectly pious and lovely, and had spoken to his soul; when he looked upon their work, it had refreshed his soul as a beautiful chime of bells.

What was all this, however, in comparison with this Raphael? Their work had submitted itself to faithful ecclesiastical representations, as music to the words of a song. Here, however, was the free culture of his age, — the self-sustaining human mind stepping before him in its most beautiful, most refined, most triumphant form,— humanistic culture, the tenor of the century, in its pride, in its triumph.

Must not something lie therein to disturb the compass of the German monk, to make him low-spirited, and then to lay upon the brow of this powerful nature an expression as of challenge, as if an impulse to contest and action flashed up in him?

And still he was very unhappy. Why was there at hand no friend of kindred depth of nature, to whom he might unburden himself? He felt an impulse to speak with a friend. To Fra Egidius he could not betake himself; he was absent on a journey. He would speak to the brethren of his order of the condition of the church and such things. They could not be blind to that which filled his thoughts. So he came home. The brethren were in the garden of the cloister. When he entered the garden he saw his hour had been badly chosen. He saw them in their white habits in a bright heap, moving about in a lively manner, calling, laughing, throwing stones. Brother Martin drew nearer, and perceived what they were doing.

It aroused him; it made his heart bleed. They were having their sport with a poor hare, which, in some manner, had come into the garden. Perhaps a peasant had caught him alive, and brought him to the brother cook for the cloister kitchen. By a long string fastened to his hind leg they had bound him to the stem of an orange tree. Thus they threw at him with stones, and exercised themselves in striking him. Sneers and cries of ridicule became the part of those who missed him; loud laughter and merriment broke out when the poor animal, which dragged behind him the other unbound hind leg, broken and bleeding, became struck in spite of the leaps he made in his agony of fright. The entire heartlessness of the Roman vented itself upon the helpless animal devoted by the church.

With a few hasty strides Brother Martin stood in their midst. With these people could he indeed not speak of that which stirred him so deeply. He said nothing except this: "He who loves the Lord loves also his creatures;" but he said this with pale, trembling lips,—with such a tone that they quietly allowed him, in passing out, to break with strong hand the thread, to hide the poor animal in his black cape, and to carry it to his cell, in order to protect it, and to see whether he could heal and save it.

CHAPTER X.

THE SECRET OF THE HANDICRAFT.

IT was upon the next day in the afternoon. Egino had lain down for a siesta, but had sought slumber in vain. He had lain so a long while, and now shut his eyes, and sighing and weary laid his head back upon the cushion of his couch. The door was softly opened; it must be his servant, and without opening his eyes, he said in a low tone:—

"Bring me some water, Götz; I wish a drink."

He heard the steps of some one passing out over the matting of his floor.

After awhile they returned, and a gentle voice said:—

"Here is water, sir."

He opened his eyes, and saw, standing before him, Irmgard — in her disguise of a boy.

"Irmgard!" cried he in surprise; "is it you?"

"It is I, sir. You desired to drink; here is a cup of fresh water."

She reached him the cup, which she bore in her right hand, and at the same time fastened her eye sharply upon his features.

"I thank you, maiden; I thought it was my servant to whom I gave the order. Why do you look at me so inquiringly? And why do you still always stick yourself in the clothing of a boy?"

"That, sir, you would have found out, if you once again should have had the goodness to inquire after your poor fellow-countrymen," she answered, with a tone of quiet reproof.

"Yes, yes; I had really forgotten you. Forgive me," said Egino, with a sigh. "Seat yourself beside me, there, and talk to me."

"As to your second question, sir: I looked at you so sharply because I believed to read in your features that it does not go much better with you here in this strange land than with us poor people. You are sick, you are so pale ——"

"Am I? Well, yes; I am a little sick. You are right. I have

brought away with me a little contagion from a corpse, it seems. But speak of yourself. Why do you say it doesn't go well with you? What has happened?"

"Nothing more than that they laugh at poor Uncle Kraps, wherever he lets himself be seen and wherever he opens his mouth. And what is worse, they laugh at him, also, even then the most, when he comes with his request to become something great and distinguished here. They likewise laugh at me with my zeal to speak for him, when I speak in the language of men here, and therein make a hundred mistakes. We have, as you know, through Donna Ottavia's kindness, found a good lodging with an honest woman, who gives us food and shelter; but a friendly hearing from the men to whom they advised us to go we have not."

"And do you go always in this costume with your uncle?"

"Can I do otherwise?" answered Irmgard, blushing. "The men,— the young men, and also the older ones, and those in priestly garb not the least, are so shameless! If I as a maiden go alone upon the streets, with my foreign appearance and blonde hair,——"

"Poor child!" said Egino, sighing, and rising to walk slowly up and down his chamber. "I fear all we innocent German bloods have come not for our happiness into this Roman world—neither you nor I, nor, perhaps, even the wonderful monk, who disturbs himself over the pictures of Master Raphael."

"Of what monk do you speak? Of the same of whom you said he could help us?"

"Of the same, — of Brother Martin, from Wittenberg."

"On his account I have just come to you, sir. I thought that if I complained to you of our need, you would show me the kindness to take me to him, that I may beg him to speak for us with his brother of the order in the papal palace."

Egino shook his head.

"To-day it would do no good, Irmgard. Brother Martin is troubled; something has, as it were, revolutionized his whole soul."

"And what has happened to him, to Brother Martin?"

"What has happened to him! Can I make it plain to you? They say whoever unveils the Truth and looks upon its countenance must die. The monk has looked upon the countenance of Beauty, and has at least become sick from it."

"That has more frequently happened, not only to poor monks, at the sight of beauty," answered Irmgard, with a fleeting smile.

"Yes, yes; still, I didn't mean it that way. The monk has looked upon a different beauty, and thereby has made the discovery that a movement, growth, and development has come into the world which is growing out over his church roof. Imagine that the mind of man is a beautiful palm, which some one has nurtured in a glass house; and in order that the glass house by which it has been cared for and protected may not burst, he has cut, capped, and deformed it. Now, however, this tree so pruned will bear no more fruit; the young shoots and sap are too powerful; the strong boughs press against the roof and glass as if they would burst through it ——"

"Then must he make the house wider and more airy," said Irmgard.

"Truly so; but can the poor monk order that, or bring it about?"

"And he is troubled about that?"

"About that — and, indeed, a little, also, that the wicked palm which threatens to break his house into atoms is so wonderfully beautiful ——"

"I don't understand you," answered Irmgard. "But what is it, then, that causes you to say your coming hither is not for your happiness?"

"With me it is another thing — and still, in the end, the same. As they have restrained the living palm tree under the dead glass house, so have they also here fettered the living to the dead, and made the dead master of the living. That is their wisdom here in Rome,— to make the grave master over the living, the letter over the spirit, and the dead over that which breathes ——"

"You speak to me in nothing but riddles, sir," said Irmgard, discouraged, supporting her head upon her hand. "In this lies poor consolation for me; and for consolation I came to you."

"If I did not speak in riddles, could it be a comfort to you? The affair is, for once, inconsolable, believe me."

She opened her eyes and observed him again.

"You appear as if you had not slept for nights, and as if you had had no rest or quiet for days. That must indeed indicate something inconsolable for you. It would be a comfort to me if you would tell me what oppresses you; for it would show me that you have confidence in me."

"And do you wish my confidence, Irmgard?"

"I mean you owe it to me."

"And why do I owe it?"

She regarded him with a peculiar glance, in which lay something questioning, almost wondering.

"Well, yes," she said then, after awhile; "it seems so to me, truly. But you are right that you find such a speech presumptuous in me, in a poor maid from the common people. I know not what is in me that makes me speak so openly! You see, at least, that I trust you, when I speak so openly what I think — even the foolish things."

"I believe that you are an honorable, faithful soul, Irmgard, and therefore do not call yourself a poor maid from the common people. For what purpose is such false humility? You are rich, because you have a pure and warm heart. For that reason also, I will gratify you by ceasing to speak in riddles. Listen to me. One evening — it was about ten or twelve days since — a friend of mine took me with him into the palace of a great nobleman here named Savelli, up on the Aventine. You have seen the castle up there near the great Dominican monastery of Santa Sabina."

"I have been in Santa Sabina — also there?"

"There I was to serve my friend as a kind of witness, and to look upon a marriage ceremony. I witnessed the ceremony. The bride was a ravishingly beautiful woman, and the bridegroom was dead!"

"Dead! the bridegroom?"

"So I said."

"So the ceremony amounted to nothing?"

"No, no! They plighted the living to the dead."

"What you say is incredible!"

"And still it is so; and in Rome not so incredible, after all. They also wed the living spirit of man with a dead institution; there the bridegroom is living and the bride dead. You gaze upon me, Irmgard; do you believe that I have become mad?"

Egino laughed bitterly.

"I must almost believe it, sir."

"Perhaps you would not be far wrong. I have become mad; my soul has been snatched from me since that moment; my mind is no longer my own; my entire thought and aim are directed to a single one — only one in all this world. I wish to free this living being from her dead. O my God! let me not be overwhelmed in the madness which flashes through my brain when I think that I must, must and yet cannot! Let me not be crushed under this iron weight which the horror, the powerlessness lays upon me!"

Egino uttered this with such a tone of despair, that Irmgard, horrified, raised her head. Silently she followed with her glance his form moving slowly back and forth.

"You are right," said Irmgard, after a long pause, "that we have come here to become inwardly distressed. But perhaps," she added after awhile with a sigh, "must the soul of man through tribulation attain to its rest. Let Brother Martin see how he will manage his palm tree, which will truly give him enough to do; for us, even it does not appear impossible to get rid of our trouble. You lead away your beautiful bride, since you are a living man; I will entice, the best I can, my unhappy Uncle from the folly which led him here, and so we will withdraw homeward over the mountains, somewhat, yes, very much wiser."

"You speak as you understand it."

"Show me that I do not understand it."

"If the Savelli have done anything so criminal, so monstrous, as they have done when they wedded that woman to a dead man, they must have had urgent grounds for acting so. There must have been for them much depending upon having this woman bear the name of Savelli,— very much. They, at least, wish her to carry what she possesses into the house. They would know how to make it quite certainly impossible for her to bear any other name."

Irmgard nodded her head.

"But if some one could be found to rescue her out of the power of the Savelli," said she, thoughtfully,— "some man courageous enough——"

"Courageous enough," said Egino, cutting short her speech; "of what use is courage here? I know that I am perfectly powerless against them."

"Don't you know anyone who could lead you as a harmless foreigner into their house, into the circle of the family?"

"Then must I play the hypocrite before them! And dare I think of that since Signor Callisto has introduced me into the palace as a young lawyer accompanying him?"

"And could you not appear again as a young lawyer?"

"Impossible — already impossible; because, if I could do it, I would not go into the presence of Corradina in a lying mask — nothing would move me to it."

"Then you have poor prospects: with open force you will not be able to accomplish it."

"Certainly not."

Irmgard rested her brow upon her hands. She bit her lips fast together; the mute play of her countenance showed an inner struggle,— some kind of difficult turning over in the mind. Then slowly lifting her face she said, with a forced jocularity: —

"For the poor Henry, a maid was found who gave to him her blood to save him; for you, Count Egino, it shall not be said hereafter that no maid was found who would give to you her innermost thoughts in order to save you; for it seems to me you need saving more than your — Corradina."

"And what are your innermost thoughts, Maid Irmgard, which you will give to me?"

"In the first place, if you will not think evil that I consider you very helpless and dispirited; and that you must also come to one's aid with good strokes; and that your passion for this woman must be very cool if a little lie, a little bit of pretence, necessary to attain the goal, is esteemed an insurmountable obstacle between it and its object."

"A lie?"

"Well, yes. Is not this Corradina of sufficient value to you, that for her sake you may so far humiliate your pride as to lie? It is as often a necessity as anything else! Could you not do it at all?"

"Now, by God! for Corradina's sake I could try it. Whether it would be a success, I know not."

"Well, try it; for without deception you will not create for yourself an approach to her."

"And with deception would it succeed? And you, Irmgard, if you know how to bring it about, how?"

"I know how to help — yes," she said, "if you promise to thank me for it, and not to despise us on account of that which I must confess to you beforehand."

"Despise — I despise you? And how should I then ——"

"Listen to me. My Uncle Kraps, you know, is a bell-founder by trade."

"I know, I know."

"And you know also that, when in a city at home the metal for pouring a bell is in the smelting oven, the old crones and the pious people come and bring all kinds of silverware, in order that it, mixed with the brass, may give a better sound; they believe this is a gift especially pleasing to God."

"I know that, too."

"But not that it is a superstition! The silver does not conduce to purity of tone; it only destroys it. Seventy-seven parts copper, twenty-one parts tin, and two parts bismuth — that gives the right ring. But whatever you will, the people will not allow themselves to believe anything but that it will not go without their silver, and that without such offering the bells would never do the right service, nor could ring away the thunder-storms and everything else they should do. And so, sir, it is one of the secrets of the handicraft. Every handicraft, you know, has its secrets and hereditary tricks, which other people not belonging to it have no need to know. One of the secrets of the bell-founder's trade is not to waste the silver brought to them by spoiling with it the tone of their bell. They take the silver and cast it through the chimney of their furnace, apparently into the mass of metal, before the eyes of the people; but, in truth, in throwing it they give it such a turn that it falls obliquely, sidewise, into the hole for the ashes under the fire."

"I understand," exclaimed Egino; "also on this account is Uncle Kraps so rich?"

Irmgard, with rather a shy glance, observed the expression of his features.

"You must not, therefore, think evil of him — of us, sir; it is just —— "

"A secret of the craft!" broke in Egino, smiling. "I find that Uncle Kraps has acted very wisely in not explaining anything openly to those old wives of Ulm which would have disturbed them with great anxiety at every thunder-storm; so now go on."

"So," said Irmgard, "we have gotten all kinds of silver things, among them some that seemed to Uncle Kraps too good for melting. He is like a child, you know; and when he anywhere received a piece that pleased him, it was like a plaything to him, which he could not make up his mind to give out of his hands."

Egino nodded his head, but, at the same time, looked at Irmgard most inquiringly, and in suspense as to whither all this might tend.

"You are wondering what I intend to do with my silver toy," she put in, smiling; "only hear me further. Among the things, now, which pleased Uncle so that he let it go unmelted, and brought it here with him, along with some engraved vases, and figures of the saints, and embossed work, is a little altar-piece with two wings made to clasp together. Upon the middle piece, not larger than a man's fist, is to be seen, in fine work artistically embossed, the holy

Dominicus, as he kneels before the Mother of God with the child; and she shows to him the white dress of the order with the black scapulary, with the little cap attached, in which the Dominicans go about. Upon the wings of the altar-piece is, upon one the dream of the saint's mother of the little dog having in his muzzle the torch which lights the world, and upon the other the saint is represented as he makes alive again the dead architect struck down under a fallen house."

"And this silver-work?"

"This silver-work you should go to offer at the altar of the holy Dominicus in his cloister Santa Sabina, in order thereby to make the monks of Santa Sabina your best friends."

"Ah! And then?"

"And when you then present to the prior of Santa Sabina the request to be received for three or four weeks into his cloister, in order to perform exercises therein, you can be sure to receive no negative answer."

"I — Count Egino von Ortenburg — shall perform exercises with these dogs of the Lord?" said Egino, with restrained laughter.

"Why not? If you will not do it in the belief that it will redound to the welfare of your soul, then do it in the faith that in the course of four weeks you can certainly find an opportunity to see and to speak to the woman who has bewitched you, and who dwells almost under the same roof with these 'dogs of the Lord,' perhaps daily walks about in the same garden with them."

"Indeed, Irmgard, your thought is excellent — it is good, very good; and so be it, therefore," exclaimed Egino, excitedly. "I will do as you say; I will, if necessary, make myself a monk among these black-white men-burners; I will let their homilies go over me without betraying in my countenance what I think of all this monkery. Give me your artistic tablet; I will pay Uncle Kraps for it as if it weighed in gold what it weighs in silver."

"Wherefore?" asked Irmgard, who regarded his excitement with a look out of which spoke something like care or depression. "Wherefore?" she asked, coolly.

"Because your advice is inestimable."

"Look upon it that way, then, and give up wishing to pay for it."

"You not, but Uncle Kraps."

Irmgard did not answer.

"Can it not be right away, to-day?" cried Egino.

"If you long so after the life of the cloister," she responded, smiling painfully, "why not? I am going to bring you the jewel," she said then, rising.

"Go, go — bring it. If we make use of the time, I can this very night sleep in a cell in Santa Sabina. While you are gone I will give Götz his instructions."

Irmgard reached him her hand quickly; he wished to say to her by a warm pressure how very much she had placed him under obligation; but she drew it hastily away again. She avoided meeting his eyes, lighted with joy and hope, and the next moment had disappeared from the chamber.

When she was outside, in the street, she went slowly, with her eyes fastened upon the ground. Before the Church of San Silvestro, at the end of the street where Egino lived, she remained standing a moment; then turned to the door of the church, lifted high the heavy leathern curtain which covered the entrance, and walked into the dark little vestibule, which was separated from the nave of the church by a high grating. Did she wish to pray in the cool twilight room? It seemed not; she seated herself upon the dark wooden bench which ran along the wall, folded idly, and as if weary, her hands upon her lap, and thus stared into the church, but as if into empty space.

The round-arched window over the altar in front of her was curtained with a green material. It must have been the reflection of this color which made Irmgard's features so frightfully pale.

CHAPTER XI.

HOW THE SOUL-PLANT GROWS.

NLY a few weeks before, even on the day on which he had in such enthusiastic terms depicted to Donna Ottavia the impression which Rome made upon him, Egino would have repelled the thought upon which he was now so rashly and eargerly about to act.

To introduce himself into a house under a false pretence; to lie; to feign a religious need which he did not feel,—he would have found it impossible!

But his nature had, in this short interval, made a whole circle of evolution. The plant of his soul had been set in this Rome as in a forcing hot-house; it had put forth the gigantic shoots of a banana, of a wild vine, in the heated, excited atmosphere wherein he had now lived for months.

The soul of man, with all its life of thought and feeling, is a plant needing a soil to which it may cleave, with which it may entwine its roots, into which it may strive to grow. There is an inner dependent being. Man is bound to something, while the animal is free. The lion roams through his desert, the eagle circles about his rocks, and the fox hunts through the forest; when the appetites upon which their life depends are appeased, they live in satisfaction. There is something absolute about the animal; it is on account of his nature. In him is the peace and rest of self-sufficiency; he has in him something of that to which the highest human wisdom or the profoundest depths of knowledge cannot attain,—which the East Indian view of the world portrays when it names the limit of man's upward development the Nirvana. This feeling of satisfied existence, which, at most, comes to us in some moments like flashes of light, which lighten upon our restless being and which we call moments of joy, remains unknown as a continuous state to the soul-plant of our nature. It has always to seek a soil for its roots, a hold for its climbing tendrils. So long as it is young it throws itself forward to meet external appearances. As the flower turns its head to the sun, so it turns itself toward the glitter of life, toward all that appears full of grandeur and triumph. It revels in the fullness of great and dazzling appearances. It shoots forth in the history of the past, of the present; the plant lays its searching tendrils about glittering, but — often hollow images.

Experiences come; the school of life gives compulsory instruction about the worth and the kernel of outward appearances, about the smallness and poverty of earthly greatness. Man turns himself from things to the idea of things; having become sharp-sighted, he seeks to unite his life to the life of thought, — to the mind-world. He stretches himself upward to the great ground-pillars of philosophic truths; in intercourse with the abstract and with the struggling after higher standpoints, he climbs to another trellis, which he entwines above, in order from its heights to obtain a view of the infinite.

But this is only for awhile; upon this struggle follows resignation: the searching glances, which would sweep into the infinite, return discouraged and weary. They turn themselves from the misty, dazzling appearances, to the only one which they have succeeded in searching out; but there the soul cannot be without clinging to something outside of itself, so it seeks something new with the spirit. Upon the mental evolution of human culture follows the spiritual. It throws all its force to this side, and at the end of the growth-period it strikes out into still, gentle, modest blossoms of the heart, which could not burst forth without another something, — a something foreign to itself, which it needs, for which they are, and through which they live.

In Egino had a similar circuit completed itself within a short time. Within a brief space impulses the most diverse had become powerful in him; it was as if within weeks he had run through that development which, at other times, might fill out a human life.

The dazzling appearances of Rome had at first taken deep hold upon him, as if unhinged him, made him dizzy. Still, on that morning in the "*parva domus*" this impulse had sounded itself fully out; but near to that which inspired and thoroughly filled him, stood too close that which repelled, aroused, and irritated him. And after the experience in the house of Savelli, the enthusiasm subsided, — turned to ashes. It had brought about a revolution of his entire being. In the hours of his solitary wanderings about he had often yielded to fits of deep melancholy; often had looked with bitterness upon the world around him here, which, so short a time before, had been so charming to him. Then, again, he would succeed in wrestling against this; in tearing himself away from the pain; in saving himself through quiet, plain consideration and composed reckoning with the facts. He had then been strong enough to find this composure. But there had lain for him no consolation in that which the reckoning enabled him to find. He was too young to console himself, as Callisto had done, with the resigned *"nil admirari;"* he brooded over the how and the wherefore of a history whose fragments lay around him, at some day to be covered with the layers of new fragments and ruins. What remained of it all? What was the eternal essence and import of these appearances? For what purposes did the centuries work upon stupendous structures which again fell into ruin and became dwarfed — upon religions, states, and universal empires, like this of Rome? Thus questioning himself, he was led to meditate upon the great cosmology which, like a gray, heathen goddess of Destiny, sat upon old Rome, or like a gloomy Christian sibyl stretched out her hand over new Rome, and in dark oracles informed her of the on-rolling, annihilating waves of the future. This absorption in the import of the world surrounding him, in the philosophy of the fixed fact, Rome, was something which filled him with endless sadness, depression, and hopelessness. There was a nihilistic nucleus in that great cosmology, which oppressed Egino's youthful soul; he dared not look into the eyes of that great goddess of Destiny, as if feeling that the lightning of her glance could make the blood in his veins stiff with cold. The thought of nonentity is as a drop of prussic acid: it stuns, it stops henceforth, in a youthful heart, every warm life-throb; and in this impulse, this agitation, this fermentation, Egino's whole being had yielded itself so much the more fully to the new current, the current of passion, into which it rushed the more inconsiderately, as bound with it was a kind of escape from a painful and unhappy condition. It was an escape from anxiety over a doctrine, a truth, which he saw rising before him, and would not see; a doctrine which is poison for the young, and not always a wholesome drink for the old.

Egino fled from his mind into his heart, in which he loved Corradina. He fled out of a cold, stormy night into a warm circle of light. Even if there was for him no hope to force himself into this circle, and therein be able to hide himself, his soul flowed out thitherward with all its emotions; his whole heart fled toward it; his eye was fixed upon that alone as his only salvation upon earth; and in his reckless impulse toward her, all his pride of virtue had been overcome. When Irmgard's advice awakened in him a hope, he felt that in his emotions lay his right. In the struggle for this right, which consecrated every weapon upon which he could seize, he did not think of refusing an armor which served his purpose, although this armor was a disguise, a mask, a lie. Love accepts laws only from itself.

CHAPTER XII.

IN THE CLOISTER.

"She walks in beauty like the night."—LORD BYRON.

 FEW hours later Egino was, with Irmgard, walking to and fro upon the quiet, open space before the church of Santa Sabina. He had sent his servant into the interior of the cloister to make known to the prior his wish, and now waited upon the return of faithful Götz.

Irmgard carried upon her arm the silver ornament of which she had spoken, wrapped in a white cloth.

"Will you visit me in the cloister, Irmgard?" asked Egino.

"It will scarcely be allowed you to receive such visits."

"Would they recognize you in your costume?"

"And if they did not, so——"

"I would not like to be whole weeks without hearing from you — from you and your poor Uncle. Let me take you with me there now into the cloister, as my trusted servant to carry this silver jewel; thus you might, indeed, receive the permission, at one time or another, to look after me here. Will you?"

"To what purpose would it serve you, sir? You have your faithful servant, whom you will need to keep with you."

"What is the servant to me? Can I talk with him as with you? And if I should fall into dangers or helplessness, where I should need counsel — I have just seen how quickly your clever brain finds out an advice."

"Well, then, if you really place much stress upon it, I will now go with you and show myself in the cloister, in order that they may admit me to you later."

"Do it, do it, Irmgard; it is to me almost as if I had found a sister in you."

"In me, the poor bell-founder's child? You, the princely lord?"

"I do not think my princeliness alters it much," said Egino. "At home it may dazzle the tenants of my brother; what is it here — here in Rome? Therefore it will not even make you proud if I say it to you, you poor bell-founder's child, as you call yourself — if I say to you, I feel it is so. It seems to me as if you belong to my life; as if you are no friend, but it lies as if in our destiny that our life-paths should cross each other, and then we should go along near to each other, rich in help one for the other in this strange land."

"And still you let yourself go a long while, sir," said Irmgard, coolly, "without being led by this feeling to see what had become of us; and only to-day, when I serve your — passion, this knowledge comes to you."

"You are right, Irmgard; but what will you have?" responded Egino, unabashed. "Is it not customary that much which lies in us first becomes known, when an emergency, an outward impulse, comes and draws it out."

Egino's servant at this moment stepped forward out of the cloister door; a monk in a white habit was with him. He had permission to conduct Egino to the prior.

Egino and Irmgard followed the monk into the interior of the cloister. Götz walked after them, a knapsack with articles for his master under his arm.

A broad, dark passage received them; when they passed farther in, it grew lighter, and opened on the left side with light, graceful arches upon a beautiful, though small, cloister court, around which a vaulted pathway ran. A fountain played within; the jet of water seemed to exert itself to spring so high that it might ascend to the region of the sunlight falling down over the roofs, which sparkled and flashed in its upper part. Some oleanders and orange trees stood motionless near by. There prevailed a wonderful quiet and stillness in the little court. At the end of the walk was a doorway closed by a curtain, which the monk lifted in order to let Egino and his companions enter. At a long table in the background of the lofty and vaulted chamber into which they came sat three monks, likewise in white habits; the black scapularies which belonged to their complete costume they had thrown aside, on account of the warm day. One could scarcely have distinguished their costume from that of Brother Martin, except the latter fastened his habit with a leathern girdle, — the only token of the rise of his order from a poor anchorite.

Between the monks lay books and manuscripts pushed together in a heap; the brothers appeared gay, and as if they had been chatting about things quite different from those contained in their books. One of them, a stately man, with a round, benevolent face, about whose shorn pate lay a wreath of blonde-gray hair, now arose and came slowly forward to meet Egino.

"Let Jesus Christ be praised!" he said. "You are a German count, and desire to be allowed to bring here an offering to the holy Dominicus for the salvation of your soul?"

"It is even so, worthy father; and, moreover, it is further my desire to be received for some weeks into your cloister, and therein be allowed to perform spiritual devotions."

"Well, well, these are praiseworthy motives which lead you to us. We hope your devotions will be as pleasing to the beloved God, as your offering to the holy Dominicus. In what does it consist?"

Egino beckoned to Irmgard; she drew back the cloth from her light burden, laid it upon the table, and opened the two wings which covered the middle piece of the little altar-ornament.

"*Ecco, ecco, è cosa bellissima, cosa rara!*" exclaimed the blonde-gray, the prior, while the other monks crowded around to examine this antique work of art.

"*San Dominico e la Madonna! è fatto molto bene!*" said one while another took up the whole thing, and balancing it in his hand exclaimed:—

"It is worth about fifty *scudi!*"

They appeared to rejoice over Egino's present as children over a plaything. The prior began to explain the figures; and when that was done, he ordered the brother who had conducted Egino, to take it to the father vicar-general of the order, that he might see it.

At all this Egino felt the anxiety with which he had presented his request disappear. He saw, indeed, how susceptible these good sons of the holy Dominicus showed themselves to have introduced in this way a contract with them, and so he brought forward with so much the less embarrassment his request to become so quartered in the cloister that he could go at all times of the day into the garden, and could keep his servant Götz with him.

"You do not need your servant," replied the prior, "for you will have one of our brethren at your service. Your additional wish, however, to be allowed to entertain yourself every hour in our garden, has nothing in its way. Our garden stands always open to the occupants of our cloister; and if you are so great a friend to walking for pleasure in the fresh air, Father Eustachius, the exercise-master (Where is Father Eustachius? Let some one call him), may show you to a cell which opens out to the garden and out of whose windows, furthermore, you can see far over San Michael's to the Janiculum."

"And will it be allowed, while I am here, that from time to time this trusted servant"—Egino pointed to Irmgard—"may come to me to bring news, if letters or messages arrive for me from home?"

"While you are here in the walls of this cloister, you must forget the world and what takes place in it," interposed the prior. "Of what use would the spiritual exercises be to you if they did not overcome the world that is in you?"

"You are right, worthy father; but I am here in Rome for the sake of important business of our house, which I have to carry on with the Rota and with influential men; and hence it might become necessary to receive and return communications."

"So, so; well, then, let it be as you wish. The porter may admit to you your page, there, when he presents himself. Your knapsack your servant may lay there on the floor; some one will take it to your cell. And there is the father exercise-master, in whose guardianship I place you so long as you tarry among us poor sons of the Saint, in order to atone for your sins, and through penitence, prayer, meditation, and the holy sacraments, to purify the garments of your soul from earthly dust."

The exercise-master, who now entered, was a meager man with a yellow face, deep-set, coal-black eyes, and a wreath of hair no less black. With his deep-cut features, his high-peaked crown, his downcast, and, from time to time, suddenly and sharply uplifted glance, he made upon Egino a disagreeable impression. For the kind of soul-washing he pretended to desire, the florid, open-faced prior, descendant of some northern land, would have been to him as a bath-master preferable to the emaciated southerner; but he guarded himself from uttering this wish, and bowed respectfully before the man, approaching him with noiseless and measured step, and above whom he towered at least a head.

The exercise-master reviewed the foreign company, his glance remaining fixed longest and most sharply upon Irmgard, and then looked speechless and inquiring at the prior.

"Our German guest is a friend of fresh air," said the latter; "let there be given to him the cell by the garden, which was formerly occupied by the Marchese del Monte. You"— he turned then to Egino's servant —"lay your master's baggage down, now; some one will take it immediately to the cell."

"Then good-bye!" said Egino, while he reached Irmgard his hand, and dismissed his servant with a nod of the head. Then he turned to the exercise-master, who still stood unmoved, and followed with keen glance Egino's retreating companions.

"Come!" said Father Eustachius, finally, after the curtain of the door had fallen behind the last one.

With a "Blessed be Jesus Christ!" the prior now dismissed his guest, and Egino followed Father Eustachius, who led him again through the same door into the corridor.

Having arrived at the archway, Father Eustachius turned to the right; soon after he remained standing before a closed door, and murmured softly the words:—

"Wait here."

He stepped away from Egino, walking slowly down the archway, then back again no less slowly, as if by walking to and fro to pass away the time of waiting.

"Father Eustachius seems to be a man of no immoderate impulse to speak," thought Egino. "That is always a good thing; he will indeed let me have quiet to think of other things besides his saints and their castigations."

A lay brother came with the keys. The cell was opened and Egino saw himself conducted into a room tolerably spacious for a cloister-cell, and already sufficiently well arranged to leave nothing else to be desired except a little more order and cleanliness.

Father Eustachius had disappeared the instant that Egino entered his cell. The latter saw himself suddenly alone with the serving brother.

"Where is the exercise-master?" he asked, a little astonished. "The man appears to be as sparing of his person as of his words."

"He will be back immediately, sir," responded the lay brother, "as soon as you shall first have settled yourself a little. What orders have you for me?"

"That you bring hither my things which my servant carried, and then bring more order into this room."

The brother went.

Egino went to the window of the cell and opened it. The prospect which it presented to him was of most captivating beauty. Above the garden lying beneath, towered, on the left, the lofty structure of the church of Santa Sabina; and above the wall surrounding the garden he saw a good bit of the Eternal City before him, and beyond the Janiculum even as far as the Vatican. Farther to the right was the Castle of St. Angelo; the Capitol, however, was hidden by the towers of the Savelli Castle. From the surroundings of this castle the cloister garden was shut off by a wall, along which, on the inside, stood a row of cypresses. Upon their dark green lay, in wonderful golden sheen, the splendor of the now fast-declining sun.

The lay brother returned, bringing with him the knapsack containing Egino's effects.

Then he began to put things in order.

"Saint Dominicus," said Egino, turning from the window toward the brother, "dwells here very close to the castle of the Savelli. Do the saint and the lords of the castle maintain good neighborly relations?"

"Why should they not?" responded the monk, looking up. "San Dominico is a great sanctifier of all that belongs to this house. You must know that more than three hundred years ago Pope Honorius III., who was a Savelli, and resided near us in the castle, erected to the saint this cloister among his own habitations, and, therefore, you see the towers and walls standing so close around. They protect San Dominico's poor sons; it is all as if one building. The Savelli have their way through our cloister when they wish to go into the church."

"Into the church of Santa Sabina?"

"Yes, sir; into our church. And they also have their own oratory in our church, and on the great feast days like Easter and ——"

"And the occupants of the castle walk through your cloister into the church?" interposed Egino, aroused.

"Yes, sir; the male occupants. The female occupants, you know, are of course not allowed to walk through the cloister!"

"But the female occupants?"

"What did you ask, sir, about them?"

"How do they get into the church?"

"They? Well, like other people; outside over the way of all — that is, such as belong to the servants; the ladies are allowed to go through the garden under this window. A little door leads from our garden into the church, but none of the domestics are allowed it——"

"So will I see the ladies of the Savelli family pass by under my window?" interrogated Egino, in a tone as indifferent as possible.

"You will not see many of them, sir; only the widow of the poor Lord Luca, who recently, so soon after he had been married, had to die. The others dwell beyond at Montanara, on Monte Savello."

Egino's heart beat so violently at the words of the monk, which opened to him the prospect of hourly seeing Corradina, that he feared to betray his emotion should he utter another syllable more. He turned again silently to the window, while the lay brother continued to move and dust the furniture, and to put in order the couch in the corner.

When the monk went out, Egino followed him. "Will you show me the way into the garden, brother? What is your name?"

"Alessio."

"Then, Brother Alessio, show me where you go out into the garden," said Egino.

"You must await here the father exercise-master, sir," said the monk.

"Must I? He has not announced to me his visit. Still, let it be so."

Egino returned to his cell, and standing at the window awaited the father exercise-master.

Father Eustachius, however, did not appear. Egino was in the act of leaving his cell, to seek for himself the way into the garden, when the bell rang, and Brother Alessio entered to call him to the supper of the monks. Egino followed him with firm, confident step through the passages which led to the refectory. He was peculiarly, but joyously and courageously, excited by the venture which gave such excellent promise of success. If he had met Irmgard in these passages, he would have embraced his clever page out of gratitude for her good counsel.

In the long dining-hall of the monks his place was assigned him near the prior. Egino had ample leisure to observe this company of fifty or sixty white-robed men, who sat down the long room in two rows to partake of their frugal evening repast of mingled wine, bread, cheese, and fruits; for they all sat silent, while upon a little platform in the centre of the refectory sat the father reader, and out of a thick Latin book read to them a long legend about a pious painter whom a miracle saved from certain death. The old monk read it with credulous fervor. The painter had all his lifetime been an especial worshiper of the spotless virgin. Hence he painted with holy zeal, as he had been commissioned to do by the brotherhood of his cloister, in a church, high up on the wall, the Madonna standing upon the globe of the earth and the crescent moon with her head encircled with stars — "the Immaculata." The evil fiend became exasperated over this, full of indignation and rage, for he had already a long time sought to destroy the pious painter; and now he seized this excellent opportunity, and cunningly sawed through the props of the scaffold upon which the painter, wholly absorbed in his work, was laboring. The scaffold tottered,— broke down; the boards suddenly gave way under the feet of the unfortunate painter. But see! the Madonna painted by him opens her arms, embraces her pious worshiper, presses him to her soft, pitying breast till some one, summoned by the noise of the broken scaffold, comes, and with ladders takes him down from where he was hanging to the wall above, out of the arms of the protecting Mother of Heaven.

The Dominican order in the beginning of the sixteenth century represented the learning of the church; it was the fountain, the guardian, of scholastic science, through which the evolution of dogmas had been carried on; it maintained the chair of literature at the academies; it occupied the courts of justice which rendered decisions over the orthodoxy or heterodoxy of opinions and of systems, and directed the consciences.

And the men of this order listened with devotion to such tales!

Could anything be more significant? Could anything be more terrible than that the consciences of men should be subjected to the verdict, to the control of men who had been brought up with such views, in such a spiritual atmosphere, and who remained therein to the end of their days?

With devotion, we said just now. But no; they did not all listen with devotion. Upon the physiognomies of the most diverse kind, young and old, with the type of the South and that of the North; upon the now broad and comfortable, now deep-cut, marked, emaciated faces, lay the expression of most diverse inner occupation of thought, or yet of utter want of thought. While to what was presented some held their ear closed, evidently only from stupid indifference, being busied only with the bites they swallowed and the contents of the mug they emptied, there were others evidently lost in meditation, and with their thoughts widely remote from this place. Some, again, looked with inquiring or hostile glances furtively and clandestinely upon their neighbors.

Egino listened carelessly to the legend of the *pater lector*. The Italian accent with which the man brought forth and Italianized his Latin, had something in it which forced him to a smile; the story itself, however, called forth in him a kind of indignant haughtiness toward this whole world. It did the last, in order to take to him the feeling of anxiety and a certain sadness with which he had crossed the threshold of the cloister.

In the monk who sat opposite him, on the other side of the table, he recognized the one whom he had seen in the house-chapel of the Savelli; who had wedded Corradina to the dead Luca Savelli.

While he was observing him, he did not perceive how sharply and searchingly the eye of Father Eustachius lay upon him, as he sat farther down on the other side of the table.

When the prior had arisen, and after the youngest of the company, at the lower end of the table, had pronounced the benediction, Father Eustachius approached Egino.

"You will see me appear before you in the morning, sir," he said, while over his gloomy face he allowed to glide a smile, which he meant to be friendly. "I think you will know how to thank me that I let you alone this evening; you are a child of the world, and when such an one enters into a circle so strange as ours is to him, there crowd upon him, indeed, many impressions. One must let him have time to overcome these, to collect himself, before requiring of him absorption in holy thoughts. Only perfectly smooth water is able to mirror the blue of heaven."

"Still, the Master passed over the Sea of Gennesaret when it was swelling with the storm," answered Egino. "But I will not contradict you, worthy sir, and thank you for your considerateness."

Father Eustachius did not reply. He seemed, after having spoken his words, to wish to lay aside all discussion of them, and silently nodding his head went out.

Egino left the refectory, and as he fell upon his lay brother outside, he repeated his request to be conducted into the cloister garden.

The cloister garden consisted of a terrace running along the side of the building in which was found Egino's cell, and another deeper-lying portion, which was inclosed by several walks hedged with evergreen plants, laurels, box and yew, and crossing each other at right angles. Behind these hedges, upon the little inclosed squares, grew nothing but a thirsty turf, which the want of sun and air had stunted. These garden-beds were there only for the sake of the garden-paths; they lay thus dry and barren, like many a human life which spun itself away in this cloister. Above, however, the terrace was planted with a row of old orange trees, upon which hung an abundance of fruit, already beginning, here and there, to become golden.

In the shadows of the cloister wall at the left, and of the row of orange trees at the right, must Corradina walk when she betook herself to the Church of Santa Sabina. On the north end of the terrace there was to be found, in a niche of the wall, a little door of iron-clasped boards with sharp, vaulted arch, which evidently led into the garden or hinder court of the Savelli Castle. At the south end of the terrace, above some steps, appeared a similar, but less-carefully guarded door, which was even only on the latch, and which led into the interior of the church.

"The life-path of Corradina runs through shadows," said Egino to himself, a little low-spirited and depressed, when he had explored the nature of the locality. "Shall I ever succeed in forcing myself to her out of all these walls, and in winning her to light and life? Will that iron-clasped door ever open itself for me, or shall I ever be able to climb over this wall running under the cypress row, and separating the region of the cloister from that of the neighboring castle?"

The wall was everywhere very steep, very high. The baron and the monk had found themselves very near together; the saints and the knights had built very close together, and shared in the same soil; and still they had found it for their good to erect a strong and lofty wall between them.

Egino went along this wall. Since the garden was entirely clear of men, — for the monks betook themselves after their evening meal immediately to rest, that they might be able in the night to apply themselves to their choral service, — he could carry on his investigations undisturbed. The wall was everywhere preserved in good condition; it presented nowhere a hole, a projection, or any assistance for a man who might have the wish to be able, in case of necessity, to scale the wall.

In a smooth right-angle it joined on to the powerful, battlement-finished and tower-defended wall which crowned the rock-wall of the Aventine, falling precipitously hence to the Marmorata, and protecting on this side as well the grounds of the castle as those of the cloister.

On this corner stood no tree upon which to ascend. One would be obliged to have wings.

Rather discouraged, Egino went from the wall back to the middle of the garden, where, in the intersection of the two chief walks, stood a great antique basin, borne upon a no less antique Corinthian capital of weather-beaten white marble. He seated himself upon the rim of this basin; folding his arms, he gazed upon the heavy, massive walls of the castle.

The latter presented to him upon this side two portions of the building,— an older one with small, unevenly disposed windows, and a higher, newer portion with symmetrical rows of windows. Both parts were flanked with quadrangular towers, and in the middle, where they were united, was placed a semi-circular, stair-cased tower. The newer part of the building, which was more distant from Egino's standpoint, had high up, running along a row of windows, a balcony lying, perhaps, above an arcade, which the wall separating the garden of the cloister from that of the castle hid from view. The shutters of one of the window-openings leading upon this balcony stood open; a gleam of light just now kindled forced itself through this opening into the darkening night, and illuminated a portion of the balcony with its feeble glow.

When Egino had stared at this awhile, there occurred what he, in palpitating suspense, had been longing for, expecting, and had already forseen as if in a dream.

A female form clad in dark robes stepped upon the sill of the window; looked a moment upon the evening dusk, which might already be called night — a moment, but long enough for Egino to recognize, or, better (for positive recognition it was much too far away, much to dark), for him through a sixth sense to feel, what he, rising and pressing his hand upon his wildly beating heart, whispered : —

"It is she!"

She stepped out upon the balcony, and began to move slowly up and down.

Egino's soul was in his eyes; as if it had been possible that his breathing could betray him, he suppressed it, while he sharpened his glance to perceive every movement of this dark form, which, as a ghost of the night, moving back and forth high above, swayed along the gloomy stronghold of the Savelli.

CHAPTER XIII.

THE EXERCISE-MASTER.

GINO may have sat thus a good while upon the old fountain-basin and stared through the darkness, when he heard a noise behind him. He turned suddenly around, and saw a white monkish form arise bright from the dark, neighboring hedge; it now came nearer him, and the voice which addressed Egino was that of Father Eustachius.

Was it not strange that the silent father was not where all the other monks were at this hour? Did he absent himself from sleep merely to watch over those placed in his spiritual care?

So it almost appeared.

"You are meditating, young sir?" he asked, in a dry, sharp voice.

Egino, with his whole soul, wished him a thousand miles away, but he could not do otherwise than turn himself away from the object which had held him enchained, and forcing himself to an unembarrassed answer, he said:—

"I take pleasure in the mild, soft night air; in the deep, dark vault of heaven, with its clear lights; and in the refreshing fragrance extracted by the falling dew from the laurel hedge."

"And that," responded Father Eustachius, turning while he spoke, and thus forcing Egino to follow him down the walk, "that disposes the soul to earnestness, and may be a good preparation for the work which you will begin here to-morrow."

"So it is," rejoined Egino, who thought so little about this work and took it so lightly, and now said to himself, with some anxiety, that this Father Eustachius might be just the man to make it very difficult for him.

"You have given yourself up to your exercises in our cloister, Count Egino," continued the monk, "with fixed grounds which caused you to prefer it to any other cloister?"

INTERIOR OF ST. PETER'S, ROME.

"Certainly, certainly; I had the most definite grounds."

"That speaks for the keenness of your judgment, and for the full earnestness with which you are striving for the salvation of your soul,— for the deep earnestness of your intentions," said Eustachius. "For you know the spirit which prevails among the sons of Dominicus is as earnest as the grave. The other orders have well comprehended that humanity wanders in darkness, and must wander painfully till the coming day. They assist the wanderers and lead them. Ours, however, has received it as their special gift to seek out in the night those wandering in their darkness, and lead them back to the right way; friendly and gentle toward those who follow, severe and inexorable toward those who obstinately call the path of error the right road — and this office is an earnest one."

"As every penal office must be!"

"As every penal office, yes, where mildness becomes sin, and kindness remissness of duty."

"And no one will reproach the sons of Guzman with such sin and remissness of duty," Egino could not refrain from saying, with a sharp tone of reproof.

"No," responded Father Eustachius, overhearing the irony of this remark; "whoever knows the history of our order will not. Every association, even the Christian, needs sacrificing men, whose self-denial goes so far that they eradicate from themselves one of the most deeply rooted feelings of unregenerated human nature, compassion for and sympathy with the contemporary creature, and put in its place in the heart a thought unyielding and inexorable,— the thought of the law that mankind should walk toward God upon the *one way*, and that sword and fire should punish them if they wander from this way."

"And the sons of Saint Dominicus are evidently now the bearers of the sword and fire!"

"So it is," said the monk; "that is our calling; therefore is our order established as the '*Militia Jesu Christi contra Hæreticos.*' To it the Inquisition is intrusted, and its judicial authority stretches out over the world — over the high and the low, over the lay brother and the bishop, over the bondman and the prince ——"

"I know," interposed Egino, fast becoming wrought up; "and the order has gloriously justified the confidence placed in it by the church, in handing over to it the office of judging the conscience. It has had chains, dungeons, woodpiles, and tortures of all kinds for the — erring; and in the great Albigensian wars, has been obliged to exterminate tenfold more of the unfortunate than there were even of the Christian martyrs slain by the followers of the heathen emperors. One might almost come upon the thought whether to the gentle, love-preaching Christ such a worship, with more human sacrifices than all the heathen themselves have slaughtered, could then be well pleasing. But the church teaches it, and the church must know it —— "

Father Eustachius nodded the head.

"So it is," said he, dryly; "we have had to bring into use various implements of punishment for the stiffnecked and obdurate; and to the fact that we did it, many peoples, the Spanish, the French, above all, also, the Italians, owe the high enjoyment of their faith. You know our order. You know it, you say. You chose it with forethought —— "

"So I did."

"And you will remain true to your decision?"

"Certainly; why shouldn't I?"

Father Eustachius did not answer; he walked in silence by Egino. Then, as if arousing himself from thought, he said:—

"Will you still remain in the garden? I advise you not; the air here on the Aventine at night, or even in the day, is not very salubrious; therefore you will do well to be careful of yourself, Count Egino. Will you still remain?"

They were at the end of the walk, and had reached the flight of steps leading up to the higher-lying terrace. The monk spoke his last words with a peculiar intonation, while he placed his foot upon the steps.

"I should like to remain awhile longer in the garden before I betake myself to rest, worthy Father," Egino answered, quietly.

"Then good-night, Count Egino. When I see you to-morrow, I will speak with you about the general confession you have to make to me. Blessed be Jesus Christ!"

Father Eustachius went up over the steps, diagonally over the terrace, and disappeared in the cloister.

Egino looked after him a little wonderingly. What had the monk wished? Had he been spying out his steps, or had he really wished to warn him, to threaten him? Was there not in his speech something like a hint not to jest with his order, as solemn as the grave? Had he upon Egino's brow read his thoughts, and discovered that very many among them were such that Father Eustachius, out of human interest in him, did not wish by the opportunity of a general confession to need to enter into an explanation with him?

Had he really penetrated his intention?

No; that was not possible!

And in regard to the other matter Egino did not trouble himself much. He hastened back to his former position, to the stone basin. The form, however, upon the balcony of the Savelli Castle had disappeared; the light was extinguished.

Early next morning Egino was awakened by Brother Alessio, who said to him that it was time to take part in the early divine service of the monks in the church of Santa Sabina. It was still so early Egino followed the brother rather unwillingly, and had himself shown to a place in the church in one corner of the choir of the monks.

After the service the early meal was partaken of in the refectory, and, still more frugal than the night meal, it consisted of milk and bread. Then, when Egino had scarcely returned to his chamber, Father Eustachius appeared.

Father Eustachius had entered silently, and silently took the chair which Egino carried forth. He gazed awhile at the floor, then suddenly, sharply fixing upon him his dark, fiery eyes, he said: —

"You know that the exercises begin with a general confession, which has to extend over your whole life, from the moment where, with the knowledge of good and evil, your moral accountability began. You can so arrange the preparation for this confession that you may divide into periods the life lying behind you, and seek to give yourself an account of your actions in each single instance; or you may fix your whole life at once in the eye, and seek to bring yourself to a knowledge of what runs through it, as the principal trait of weakness or sinfulness, and is the common cause of the single instances wherein you have sinned. If you choose the first, I will trouble myself out of the individual instances to lead you to a knowledge of the prevailing weakness of character which rules you; if you choose the other, it will be my task from the ground-failure to proceed to the separate facts, which are like the separate waves pouring themselves out of the fountain of your weakness."

"And how do most persons proceed?" said Egino, hesitating, and struggling against entering upon a theme that at this moment lay so far from him, and from which, with a Father Eustachius, at least there was no escape.

"The most persons? Most men esteem themselves gold, upon which lie only a few spots of rust, to be washed away from them by the holy water of the church. They consider themselves the victims of temptation approaching them from without. They think their fall is due to the stone upon their way, over which want of forethought causes them to stumble. And still they are not gold, but dross through and through. And still temptation does not approach them from without, but the vice in them leads them into the temptation; and still the road is not to blame that they fall, but the weakness of the feet upon which their virtue stands. So most of them complain of the separate instance, and it is the task of the spiritual father to show them that the individual sin is without significance; that the worst robbery, murder, treachery, can be pardoned by the mercy of God, but not the foulness of soul rankling in them. Men are all endowed with capacities, as plants with boughs, branches, and leaves. But only in a part of the top which such a human tree carries, living juice pours itself and life pulses; another part stands arid, dried up, leafless, juiceless. The branch of courage, of willpower, the branch of unselfishness, in one stands green and full of foliage; but the branch of chastity, the branch of fidelity, the branch of goodness of heart and of humility, stands dry and dead. With another the branches of kindness, of brotherly love, of gentleness, are green; but the branches of self-control, of faith-power, of devotion, stand dry. Now, the father confessor must be the gardener of the human plant, and he has to bring even into the dry branches life. Still, say how you will proceed."

"So let us look after my dry branches at once, worthy Father," answered Egino, smiling, for in him the deep earnestness with which the gloomy Spanish monk spoke began to inspire a certain confidence.

"Not at once," interposed Father Eustachius; "you need time in order to collect yourself, to enter within yourself, and to make clear to yourself what branches in you are dry. And when you reflect upon it, do not let one escape you; that is, on the human plant the branches mostly grow in pairs, grown upon one bough, standing together. And when you find one of these twin branches dry in you, then ask yourself whether at least the other is green. If your goodness is dry, so, at least, must your justice be green; if your faith is dry, your love, at least, must be green; and if your self-restraint and chastity are dry, your mildness and brotherly love, at least, must be green. Thoroughly bad natures are those in which both twin branches are dead; and entirely miserable are those natures which have nothing of the virtues of their faults and nothing of the faults of their virtues. The weakness which is not good, but evil; the cruelty which is not courageous and strong willed, but cowardly; the rudeness which is not honorable, but a deceiver; the haughtiness and imperiousness which are not generous, but a miser,— such are the wholly bad! Such is the dry wood with which Satan makes his hell hot. Hell is not there on their account,— that would be too much honor for them; but they are there to serve as logs for the nourishment of the eternal fire."

"And for whom is the eternal fire?"

"For the ungodly who commit great transgressions, and scorn the means of the church to receive pardon again."

Over Egino's face flitted a proud smile.

"We are all the children of God, worthy Father," said he, with a bitter, ironical tone. "And since we need continual guardianship, God has delivered us over to his church as our careful foster-mother, who takes upon herself our everlasting pupilage. Is that so, worthy Father?"

"That is so."

"Well, then, '*Sunt pueri, pueri puerilia tractant.*' How is it to be explained that God could conceive the horrible thought of making an eternal, endless punishment in hell, lasting through eternity, for something that his children, in their stupid, childish ignorance, have committed? If we were not children, it would, indeed, be otherwise. Had God treated us with the confidence that the father has in his grown-up, mature, reasonable son; had he opened our eyes to his design in this endless universe; had he communicated to us openly the mysteries of the world, and disclosed to us the secrets of his being which tormentingly surround us, instead of hiding everything from us as children and leaving us in the dark,— then would he be right to require of us so strenuously that we now behave ourselves as reflecting men, and, through our actions, not disturb the harmony of the moral order of the world. Since, however, he treats us as children under age, how can he wonder if we for our actions, as minors, refuse accountability, and find the eternal hell-punishment very unjust and quite horribly cruel?"

"How can you talk so, since God in revelation has disclosed all his mysteries?" exclaimed the monk. "Are those the thoughts with which you have prepared yourself for your confession?"

"Your speech awakened these thoughts. If it is sinful, make me see it."

The features of the monk grew dark. "I will do it," he said. "Previously, however, answer me a question — in case you are prepared to answer it at once," he added, with sharp, almost disdainfully ringing tone, at the same time rising and going to close the open window. Then he further spoke: —

"This is the question: Why have you come into this cloister, Count Egino?"

"Does it require a preparation to answer this question?"

"It seems so, since you do not know how to answer it, because you have learned it is a deadly sin to lie in confession."

"I do not lie, either in or out of confession," said Egino, proudly.

"Then answer the truth."

"That I came — you will at least maintain it — was yet no sin, and there need be nothing said about it in my confession."

"And suppose I say to you, Count Egino, that your coming was a sin."

"So I deny it ——"

"Do not deny it; you alter nothing thereby. You did not come for the sake of our exercises! They are a pretext. There is another aim which leads you here, — an aim which you pursue obstinately, for I find you here in spite of the warnings which I presented to you yesterday, and which you must have understood. Now speak — you are speaking to your father confessor."

"I have nothing to say to you in regard to it," responded Egino, "but that you err when you see something in my coming which resembles a sin, and therefore belongs to the confessional ——"

"And I tell you," interposed Father Eustachius, almost threateningly, "man is sinful through and through, and your every work, your every word, your every thought, belongs to the ear of him who can free you from sin. Therefore speak, to what end you came, and what part in it has the woman whom you led into this cloister — that disguised woman that you called your page, and who, since she passed over the consecrated threshold of this house of God, this cloister, incurred the fullness of eternal punishment?"

"You have a sharp eye, Father Eustachius," replied Egino, in surprise.

"I have; and this sharp eye has rested upon you more attentively than you were aware."

"It appears so," said Egino, feeling with angry smart that his plan was upon the point of being miserably thwarted, and that this interview must end for him in an ignominious expulsion from the cloister. And against such a disgrace, against the abandonment of the hope with which he had come, all that was in him rebelled. All his daring became aroused.

Should he fear this monk? Why should he? Had not *they* even, in the end, to fear *him*? He proudly threw back his head, and, suddenly composed, said with firm and resolute voice: —

"Well then, since I see no one can escape you, I will answer your question as to what impelled me to come to the sons of the holy Dominicus. Understand, then, there lies upon me a sin, and it is such that I, in my worldly surroundings, might repent and atone for a long time."

"And this sin, for whose repentence you need a disguised maiden — what is it?"

"The disguised maiden is more harmless than you think, Father Eustachius — but we will leave her out of the game. She shall not appear again, since you live in the remarkable belief that if a female being, let her be so innocent as St. Peter's daughter, Petronella, and so pious as St. Augustine's mother, Monica, steps over your threshold, her pure breath renders foul the atmosphere of your musty cloister passages. My sin is the following. We Counts of Ortenburg are three, — or there were three of us: my eldest brother, Bruno, the lord and heir; my second brother, Udo; and myself, the youngest, — like Udo, on account of being a younger son, shut out from the ancestral heritage. I was set apart to the service of the emperor; for Udo, provision was to be made by a marriage with a relative, whose guardian was my deceased father, and whose inheritance was adjoining our own. But my brother Udo was a wild, rough fellow. Ulrica, the relative, did not love him, and stubbornly refused to give him her hand. For this she was tormented by us, vexed and harassed in every way: we held her imprisoned; we devised every means to break what we called her obstinacy, for we were determined her rich inheritance should never escape us. Then suddenly fell a decisive blow upon this state of things — my brother Udo died. A chronic illness carried him suddenly away, before we had been able to wed him to Ulrica; and the estate of the latter, which we had long considered our own, had also in part alienated and used up —— "

"It must not be allowed to fall into other hands by the marriage of your relative, Ulrica, to another man," broke in the monk, with a scornful pucker about the corners of his mouth, "and, therefore, there remained nothing but to wed the relative by force to the dead, whose death you kept secret. After some days the death was published; the relative was now your brother Udo's widow; as his widow she remained in the power of the head of your family; and you, you Count von Ortenburg, will see who can tear her estate out of your hands!"

"By God, so it was!" exclaimed Egino, astonished at the monk's ready comprehension, but determined to throw him the guantlet completely. "Yes, we forced the woman; we found a monk, a monk of your order, Father Eustachius, who let himself be bribed, and wedded her to the dead. To atone for my part in this outrage, in this deed of violence which cries to Heaven, I come to you. I come also to receive counsel from you, whether I shall expose to the Pope the execrable monk who lent himself to this purpose, or whether I, for sake of the calling of the order, of the monstrous scandal it would give to the world, which from day to day becomes more hostile to you, and without that knows so well how to slander you, must let it alone."

Father Eustachius had looked daggers at Egino while he was speaking; upon his sallow face had momentarily flamed out a flush as of white-hot anger, which then again disappeared. Father Eustachius evidently possessed remarkable control over himself, for with the most quiet voice he now said:—

"If so unusual an action, and one so hard to comprehend in all its circumstances, disquiets and oppresses you, you indeed did well to come here. I hope you will reach your aim, and that fully quieted in your soul and in your conscience you will leave these walls. In the next place, however, I must say to you, that you need ask no advice of me whether or not you may be bound in conscience to expose that corrupted monk to his superiors; for since he is, as you assert, of my order, I cannot be impartial in this affair. Another shall advise you in this."

"Another? And who? Do you consider the matter so lightly that still another, a third, may learn of this hideous crime of the brother of your order?"

"Hideous crime! Be not so hasty with your words, Count Egino. The other person who shall advise you knows without telling that of which you speak; is fully in the secret; is, indeed, the one most concerned, — it is the wedded kinswoman herself."

"What do you say?"

"The widow of the dead — she is truly near enough to us!"

"It is she — and she ——"

"She shall advise you. You shall see her, and ask her."

"I shall see her — speak to her? You will bring that about?" exclaimed Egino, with an agitation which would not have escaped Father Eustachius, even if Egino had striven to conceal it much more than he thought he was doing.

"You will accompany me to her," replied the monk, fixing his eyes upon him sharply, quietly, and for a very long time.

"And when shall this happen?"

"That shall the signora decide. I will send to her to have her consulted, or go to her myself."

Egino, beside himself with excitement, walked up and down in his cell. Father Eustachius followed him with the little, deep-set eyes in which still something feeble, faint, indicated that he was now busy in thought with something other than the behavior of the young man.

"What can be settled quietly and peacefully," said he finally, rising, "one should not settle in anger. And this business, for whose sake I see you are here, not as a penitent, but defiantly and for the sake of a quarrel, can, I think, be settled peacefully to your satisfaction, to the justification of the poor monk whom you accuse and whom you are ready to prosecute. I wish well, not only to that poor monk, as my order-brother, but also to you, Count Egino, believe me. With this well-wishing I spoke to you yesterday, when I gave you the hint you had better leave our cloister. And with the same good will for you, I take the course of mildness in this affair, however defiantly you have conducted yourself, however imperiously you have acted. I leave you alone till I return to conduct you to the woman, who — will counsel you."

Father Eustachius departed.

VOLUME II.

THE DAUGHTER OF EMPERORS.

CHAPTER I.

CORRADINA.

Iphigenie. — Vernimm, Ich bin aus Tantalus Geschlechte.
Thoas. — Du sprichst ein großes Wort gelassen aus.
— GOETHE.

GINO awaited the return of the monk. Whether the time was long or short, he scarcely knew. The time was for him as a whirlpool,— a storm,— a wild flood, in which he was overwhelmed; they were moments of fearful agitation. Finally the door of the cell again opened, and Father Eustachius stepped upon the threshold. He remained standing, and beckoned with his hands.

"Follow me, Count Egino," he said.

Egino snatched his dagger and gloves, then his cap; he was still carrying them in his hands when he was already outside on the way in the garden. Here Father Eustachius passed over the terrace to the door in the wall which united the cloister-garden with that of the Savelli, lying on the other side. It stood only latched. On the other side presented itself the garden of the castle — not very different from that of the monks, not even in size. Pope Honorius seemed to have shared fraternally with his friend Dominicus. Only the terrace was more imposing, more elevated; it did not run along the whole garden-front of the castle; it ended at the semi-circular tower, in which a door standing open revealed a stairway leading above.

Eustachius led his companion over the terrace into this door, up the winding-stair to the first landing; from this another door led to the great balcony, upon which Egino, on the previous evening, had seen the dark form pacing back and forth. They stepped upon this balcony; there stood upon it, not far from the window-casement which led into the interior of the chambers, a little table with a footstool near it. Upon the table lay a book, with some lady's work upon it; upon the footstool lay a light cloth; the occupant of the adjoining rooms must have passed a part of the morning there. Coming near the open window, the exercise-master suddenly restrained his step; he made a bow full of monkish humility, and pointing to Egino, he said:—

"The young German lord, Madame, to whom I begged you to grant an interview."

Within the next room, scarcely a step behind the open window-casement, stood the Countess Corradina von Anticoli.

She threw upon Egino a searching, hasty glance, and without returning his bow, turned and stepped farther back into the interior of the room.

"Only follow in, and — hold your consultation!" said Father Eustachius, with a somewhat disdainful smile.

Then he turned to the little table, and seated himself upon the footstool behind it.

The slightly haughty reception and Father Eustachius' mocking smile were for Egino in this moment something almost welcome. They made it easier to him to master his emotion; he stepped over the threshold with the firm step of a man who is conscious that he comes with a definite purpose. In the middle of the moderately large room, which, with its gold-imprinted leathern tapestry, its fine mats, its artistically cut and ivory-adorned furniture, presented all the comfort and grace of a lady's chamber of the time, he bowed profoundly before the lady, who had now reached the end of the room and disposed herself upon a cushioned seat, and turned upon him clear and full her countenance.

It was the same wonderful countenance, full of beauty and dignity, which Egino had seen in the soft twilight, and which now, illuminated by the bright light of day, exercised upon him the same, and, if possible, a still higher charm. Her blue eyes under the long blonde lashes looked upon him with the fully self-conscious transparency of a proud woman, and still with an expression of uncertain curiosity, which gave to her the girlishness that would, perhaps, have otherwise been wanting. She had not put on the *bandeau*,— the cap which she should have worn as a widow; at least her gold-blonde hair, rich and wavy, parted in the middle, flowed over her shoulders just as Egino had beheld it in the marriage scene; only a narrow fillet of black velvet with some pearls set on it held it together around the temples. Her slender form was enveloped in a dress of light, black material brocaded with violet velvet.

"You call yourself Count Egino von Ortenburg?" began the Countess Corradina von Anticoli, after a pause.

Egino, who had been devouring her with his looks, almost forgot to answer "Yes," he was so surprised to hear these words addressed to him in German speech.

"And," she continued, "I recognize you. A short time ago you entered this house as a young jurist,— as the law-pupil of Minucci?"

Egino assented with a slight bow, still always asking himself whether or not merely in a dream he heard these German sounds from these lips.

"Into the cloister of our neighbors you have introduced yourself with the statement that you there wish to practice the exercises,— to apply yourself to the penal-observances."

"So it is, noble lady," responded Egino, sighing, clasping with his left hand the hilt of his dagger, while he held his right pressed upon his heart. "I came into this house by the side of a lawyer, who introduced me as his pupil. He named me so, not I; he had grounds which caused him to wish my company. I thus became a witness to the matrimonial alliance (if it is allowed so to name that which happened) which you entered into. And that which I saw, whose witness I became, left to me neither quiet nor rest in my soul; so from Signor Minucci's pupil I became a pupil of Father Eustachius, till I now stand before *you* as a pupil, not prepared beforehand to utter that which lies upon my heart; and even if I were, I am still not in condition to speak as I should like to speak in your presence — Father Eustachius has brought me here so unexpectedly, so hastily; I have been placed before you so suddenly, quite as if in a dream ——"

"Strange," she said, interrupting him, "that a German prince should appear in the role of a pupil; strange that he disquiets himself over the actions of a monk, a stranger to him, whose actions he does not understand or comprehend, yet allows so entirely to disturb him that he thinks he must prosecute the matter; and strange, also, that Father Eustachius desires that I should explain this monk's conduct to you ——"

"Do not find it strange, noble lady. Father Eustachius seems to be able to read in the souls of men, and may perceive that my soul is so filled by this affair that there is for it no tranquillity except through you. He may have discovered something in my soul with which he knows it is not good to contend, but better to yield to it."

She looked at him inquiringly,— searchingly.

"To yield? One yields to children," said Corradina, then proudly throwing back her head.

"Do I then impress you as a child?" asked Egino, no less proudly, and lifting himself up to his greatest height.

"You, indeed, believe you make the impression of a knight, who nobly takes into his care unprotected women and punishes deceit and violence," said she with a tone of jesting, which had in it something mocking, and yet, again, friendly.

"You may be so accustomed to such things that knights seem to you as children," responded Egino, who therefore took courage to answer in the same tone.

"That is a more polite answer than was to be expected from a pupil, as you call yourself," she replied with a smile. "I see you are not without shrewdness, and this will say to you that you now hear enough from my own lips in order to become satisfied about that which, as you express it, leaves neither rest nor quiet in your soul. Should this not satisfy you, however, Father Eustachius may explain the rest; I give to him the permission to do so."

"It does not lie in the power of an Italian monk to give quiet and rest to my soul,". responded Egino. "You speak German, as I do. You speak to me. Do not send me away after so few words, I beg you. You may know, I have suffered much through that which I experienced, very much in the thought of you. I have a right to a little kindness on your part."

Corradina looked upon him awhile in silence,— not kindly and benevolently, and yet not angrily, but as if with an expression of astonishment.

"Strange," she said then. "You must perceive, Count Egino von Ortenburg, that this is a strange scene. A foreigner, whom I do not know, of whom I only know he appears in different roles, stands there quite unexpectedly and suddenly before me, and speaks to me of a right to my confidence. He wishes an explanation,— an explanation of my actions, my situation, my thoughts, motives,— and all that because to him my actions, to which chance made him a witness, are mysterious. Do you not yourself feel, my German Count, that you, you to whom I only for the sake of Father Eustachius allowed entrance to this chamber——"

"That I am laughable in my presumption, you would say, Madame. It is possible I appear so to you. And still you are wrong. That I appear so unexpectedly, so suddenly before you, do not charge against me. That which comes before us most unexpectedly, and for which we are most unprepared, is often that which takes most earnest hold upon our being. What would life be if fate did not, once in awhile, as if with a holy hail-storm, seize upon us and cast us into a new road. Such a sacred hail-storm is it when a man looks upon a woman by whose appearance a hot flame and a great light falls upon his soul, — a light that shows to him he has in himself a heart, a power, a will, of whose force he was not before aware. If I were recommended to you by good friends, placed before you by your relatives; if I had met you in a gay circle of associates to pay to you my devotions, — I would not, with my interest, seem laughable. Now since I am a stranger, who presses to you in his own way, I appear so. Wherefore? Believe me, so solemn as was your situation when they wedded you to a dead man, is that which took place in me when I perceived it: that which arose in me and has mastered me since that moment, believe me, is worthy of your full sympathy!"

Egino had spoken all this with firm precision, and almost imperiously, his face crimsoning, and his head with its blonde waving locks thrown back.

The Countess had looked upon him as if more busy with the fine features of the young man than with what he said; she now answered with a tone entirely changed, softly, as if suddenly submitting to the fact that she must discuss the matter with him.

"Your name is Count Egino von Ortenburg; where lies your ancestral house?"

"In Swabia."

"Swabia!" she repeated with a peculiar tone, as if with a suppressed sigh, such as that with which a homesick person calls the name of his land.

"How long have you been in Italy?" she then asked, after a pause.

"In Italy for years. I have been in Bologna, at the High School."

"And in Rome?"

"Weeks, — months."

"Was Count Eitelfriedrich von Ortenburg your forefather?"

"He was the ancestor of the line of our house to which I belong. What do you know of him, my lady?"

"He fought," she replied, deliberately, "at the side of my grandsire, Duke Frederic von Antioch, in the battle of Benevent."

"Your grandsire Frederic von Antioch!" exclaimed Egino. "Frederic von Antioch was son of Emperor Frederic II., brother to King Manfred, to King Enzio; he was your grandsire?"

"He was. He was King Manfred's younger brother——"

"And you,—you were his granddaughter, his blood?"

"I am," she said quietly. "Duke Frederic's son was Conrad von Antioch and Alba, and first Count of Anticoli. Since his descendants were always called Conrad, or in the Italian idiom Corrado, Anticoli, their seat, is called, after them, Anticoli-Corrado, and I am also called Corradina after my father.

"And therefore you bear the coat-of-arms of the Büren! You are in a direct line an offspring of the heroic blood of the Hohenstaufen!"

"I am the last, the only remaining one of the race of the Hohenstaufen," she said.

Egino stared at her still a few seconds as if caught in a trance. Then he knelt down before her on both knees; he opened his lips, looking upward as if he would speak to her; stooped to kiss the hem of her dress; and when he again looked up at her, Corradina saw that tears were streaming over his face.

She looked with her great eyes calmly, almost absent-mindedly into his; then there came into hers a moist glance. She slowly brought her face nearer his own with an expression of infinite mildness and submissiveness, which suddenly and wonderfully illuminated her face; she lifted her hand and laid it upon Egino's head, and appeared to wish to draw his head gently to herself; then pressed it with sudden agitation from her, threw her head back, and said half-aloud, almost unintelligibly, pointing to a chair:—

"Arise! Seat yourself there."

CHAPTER II.

A PROUD LINEAGE.

EGINO had arisen and obeyed her command.

"Do you believe," she said, "when Father Eustachius presented to me his strange request that I should give to a strange man explanations, that I should have bidden him lead you to me if he had not mentioned the name of Ortenburg, and if the name had not been that of one of the truest vassal races of my house?* And now I see you have not applied this name to yourself without right; I see that you are worthy of your fathers, and a true blood is in you."

"I know from the history of my forefathers that we owe everything to your house," replied Egino. "But it is not that which takes such a hold upon me in this moment; which so convulses and rages through me; which causes me to pour forth a flood of tears, and then again rejoice over this most unexpected occurrence of my life. I see the splendor of the most illustrious race and celebrated ancestry shine forth before me in you,— in you, my lady ——"

"There, there," said Corradina, interrupting him with an impatient motion of the hand, "leave me aside, and speak of yourself; of your,— of our land, of Germany. Is the memory and the tradition still living there of that which once was when still the kingdom ——"

"When the kingdom was still the world, the civilized world, and the entire circuit of Christian humanity, and your race the shield and guardian of its greatness. Oh, certainly, the tradition of it is still living! It lets your grandsire, 'The Redbeard,' sleep in his castle; the tradition itself does not sleep; it cannot, dare not ever be lost to the German people; for therein truly lies its eternal claim to

---

* According to the usual supposition, the race of the Hohenstaufens was terminated with Conradin, 1268, and the children of King Manfred. In truth, however, King Manfred's younger brother, Frederic, had descendants, who caused the race to continue through several centuries beyond that.

imperial rank among the nations,—the eternal reminder of her duty
to stride forward in front of other peoples upon the road leading to
the goal of humanity."

Upon Corradina's features became diffused, as it were, the still
light of joy, while Egino thus spoke. She breathed quickly, and
with her great glance resting upon him she said :—

"And they still speak of the Hohenstaufen?"

"The Hohenstaufen! Oh! believe me, the name has a charmed
sound in every German castle, in every house, in every breast. It
arouses a flight of thoughts in us which are like eagles, and fly over
the land; it conjures forth pictures from the skill of powerful men
who wrestle with the chains of ecclesiastical servitude; it awakens
around us ringing tones, as if the golden strings began again to
vibrate to whose sound the singers of Barbarossa and Frederic sang
of lofty deeds of knights and of woman's love at every high feast in
golden Mainz, on the strand of the German stream, or in the castles
of Sicily, on the banks of the blue Mediterranean. Oh! the sound
of this name comes to meet us as the roaring which passes through
the tops of the German mountain forests with the old voices of the
gods. It diffuses the sunny splendor of Sicily around us; it wafts to
us the flower-fragrance of Concha d'oro, and its magic erects for us
the loftiest domes of the father-land. Forever stands the name of
Hohenstaufen hewn into the foundation above which the wonderful
structure of the human mind arises."

Corradina had arisen; with a quick movement she had seized both
of Egino's hands, and exclaimed :—

"That, that, binds me to you, Count Ortenburg, not your foolish
request to force yourself into my situation; to wish to play the
knight of an oppressed woman, for which you seem to hold me.
But these words do it; these words and this feeling out of which
they spring make me happy——"

"And how can my feeling make you happy," interposed Egino,
laying hold on both her hands, "if this feeling for you, for your
situation, should be allowed nothing, no service to her——"

"I do not need your service," said she, quickly withdrawing
her hands, and turning away as if suddenly chilled.

"Pardon, if I cannot believe it. A woman so young, so beautiful,
so lofty in thought, so warm in feeling as you, cannot be forced
to something which you still did only by compulsion, unless——"

"I did not allow myself compelled," said she, proudly interrupting him again, and throwing back her head. "The dead Luca was— my choice!"

"Impossible!" rejoined Egino.

"And still it is so. He was my free choice?"

"You surely would not, uncompelled, have given your hand to a dead man?"

"So I did—and forever. Still, what is that to you?"

"And then," exclaimed Egino, "does it not lie heavily as a transgression upon your soul,—this terrible suicide, this crime against your liberty, your life,—this legerdemain? Pardon me; passion carries me away——"

"Speak, only speak. You believe I have thereby committed a transgression? I deny it. I know what I owe to my name. You reproach me with legerdemain——"

"Yes; you have made sport of the most important, the most earnest, the most holy thing,—the vow of woman before the altar. This dark widow's garb, without having been the wife of any man, this name of Savelli which you wear,—are they anything but a lie, as a false mask?"

"I have," replied Corradina, calmly, "spoken with Father Eustachius about the matter; he is my father confessor. And," she continued, with the hint of a gentle smile, "should he not be a better judge of it than a young German count, who has, indeed, not studied theology in the school of Bologna?"

"Do you ask whether an Italian monk is a better judge than an honorable German conscience, noble lady? Oh! certainly, certainly not! And if theology seems to you a matter of so much importance, well, then, German theology will certainly feel, decide, judge as I do. If you would like to let this come to the test, I would place before you a German divine who would demonstrate it to you. Oh! if I had the mind of Brother Martin and his eloquence, to say to you what there is in me which revolts against your action, in order to tear away from you this mask of quiet satisfaction which you present to me,—in order to win you back again to the life you have renounced! I would that I possessed his tongue ——"

"In order to hold for me a penal lecture?" smilingly interposed Corradina, in a mild tone. "Who, then, is this eloquent Brother Martin?"

"A German monk, slightly my friend, and a man like an apostle."

"A monk, and at the same time an apostle?" she rejoined, with a shrug of the shoulders.

"So I say; and if you could hear him, if you could see him with his flashing eye ——"

"Why shouldn't I see him? I have no objection. Bring me the apostle; a young woman may allow an apostle to pass sentence upon her, not a young knight. Still, you may be present at the judgment, and hear him absolve me. To be candid, although I have no pleasure in defending myself before you, yet I would give a little to be pronounced free from charge in your presence, and to be justified. And now farewell. It is better that this interview end now. Come with him, your wonder of a monk, to-morrow, if you will, at this hour. Since he is an order-man; the cloister of Santa Sabina will stand open to him, and the attendance of your apostle the monks will certainly allow you — if you say I wish it! God protect you!"

She again reached him her hand, which he pressed to his heart.

"I go, happy that, as an Ortenburg, I have the right to be forever your vassal and servant!"

A cool smile and a slight nod of the head answered this exclamation of Egino.

Egino departed.

From the terrace outside, Father Eustachius had disappeared. Egino found him again, beyond, in the garden of the cloister.

"And now," asked the monk, stepping up to him out of one of the walks, "are your conscientious scruples appeased?"

"Not quite," answered Egino; "still, they shall be to-morrow. Till morning, also, you will be obliged to tolerate me here in your walls as a guest, and allow to a German monk to make to me the same road which I went to-day."

"To a German monk! Wherefore? For what purpose?"

"Because he is my friend."

The exercise-master regarded him not agreeably surprised, as it seemed. Then he said: —

"If Countess Corradina desires it, what could we have against it?"

"She wishes it."

The exercise-master merely nodded the head, and turned to pass down the nearest walk; still, after two steps, turning round, avoiding, however, Egino's glance, he said softly, and with a peculiarly earnest intonation: —

"Signore Conte, I have done for you more than I dared. I have been silent to my superiors as to the fact that I have penetrated your design; I have given you opportunity to satisfy yourself over that which you presented as burdensome to your conscience. I have also warned you not to show want of reverence toward the sons of San Dominico; now I warn you again. Leave the cloister, and forget Lady Corradina Savelli."

"She has bidden me return to her," replied Egino, obstinately. "You should not hinder me from doing so. I think want of respect to a Savelli would look as bad in San Dominico's monks, as in me the want of respect to San Dominico's monks. So I will remain, if you do not otherwise drive me out, and compel me to construct a road to her through her castle, through the open portal over there."

"That would prove a difficult thing for you," answered Eustachius, looking upon the ground. "Still, as you will! Blessed be Jesus Christ!"

The monk moved slowly away.

Egino betook himself to his cell, in order to write a letter to Brother Martin, in the cloister of the Augustines, at Santa Maria del Popolo. When he had finished it he gave it, with a bit of money, to his lay brother, that the latter might send it to his residence in the Albergo del Drago, where Götz should seek out with it Brother Martin. Alessio promised to attend to it faithfully.

CHAPTER III.

LIVIO SAVELLI.

WHEN Egino was gone, Corradina sat long upon the couch in the background of her chamber, and looked through the open casement into the far distance, with half-shut lids,— with that faint luster of the eye which indicates how far the soul is removed from the things now surrounding it. She sat thus motionless, her hands folded in her lap, when she suddenly started. Without having heard a knock the side-door opened, and Count Livio Savelli stepped upon the threshold.

He carried something in his hand, which he placed before Corradina upon the little round table at the head of her couch; then, without waiting for invitation, he took his seat upon a chair standing near, which Egino had previously occupied.

"You love these old works of art, beautiful sister-in-law," he said, showing to her, at the same time, the trifle. "See what I bring you; it is an old silver bowl, with half-raised figures upon it. The two dolphins which serve as handles are especially fine."

"Indeed, it is beautiful," replied Corradina, examining the old and but little-injured dish. "Whence did you obtain it?"

"My servant Antonio bought it from one of the Lombard peasants who come here to work in our vineyards. You know these men, while turning up the mold, find manifold treasures,— old bronzes, coins, cameos,— and they give them to one for a trifling sum. I thought the bowl would serve you for throwing into it your ornaments and rings."

"I thank you, Livio; it is valuable to me for its fine classic workmanship," replied Corradina. "How gladly would I seek for such things! Also, I think it must be an absorbing entertainment to look upon the great excavations which Master Raphael Santi has carried on in the soil of our old city."

"If you wish to see it, Corradina, I am ready to take you. As I understand, the master will in a short time have them penetrate into the earth under our feet also. He asserts that out of the substructions of the Temple of Diana, which once crowned this height of the Aventine, outlets must have led down to the river, and he intends to search them and lay them open, in order to make his way into those substructions, which he believes might also lead to the graves of the old kings Aventinus and Tatius, or even to the cavern of the fabulous giant Cacus, whom tradition has to reside just here. In any case, whether in the *area subdivalis* of Diana's temple or not, he will somewhere fall upon a grotto world; for where are they not to be found in these hills of ours? And you know how, in such protected vaults and grottos, countless remnants of antiquity, even frescoes, have been found, which they, on that account, call grotesques."

"I know; but I thank you for your offer," said Corradina. "It would not be suitable for me, in my state of widowhood, to betake myself into such a host of laboring-men."

"In your state of widowhood! You are right, *cara mia*," answered Livio Savelli, supporting his arm on the back of his chair and his chin on his hand. "You are right!" he repeated in a slow, drawling tone, at the same time observing Corradina's features with glances peculiarly lurking under his brows. "Poor sister-in-law, how long will it be possible for you to play this role?" he then added, suddenly throwing up his head in a vivacious manner.

"Certainly so long as custom bids me," replied Corradina, quietly. Livio shook his head gently.

"Do you believe it?" he said. "Do you believe you could hold out a year long in this dead, desolate castle, seasick with tediousness, ill from disgust at the monotony of your days, stupid from thinking always of the same things? They say, 'Out of a cock's egg the Devil broods a basilisk:' loneliness broods the worst and most poisonous worms out of the eggs of our imagination."

"I enjoy this solitude," answered Corradina, calmly. "I am happier here than in the excitement of hollow society, where men, under the forms of friendship, conceal how deeply they have departed from it within. I hate now for once all concealment. I have always loved solitude; what you call tediousness, I have only experienced when men around me forced me to think of things which do not appear worth the trouble that one should think of them, and yet politeness demands of me to feign an interest I do not feel. I know how to make work for myself; and I have learned so much that I know how much I have yet to learn in order to lay hold on and comprehend the least part of what I should like to comprehend. And so, then, I bless this my lonely widowhood, which is so like my maiden years at the quiet castle of Anticoli, the happiest time of my life."

"You call that the happiest part of your life, because you were then much sought for. And so it might please you. Women are pleased only with the continuance of that which helps them to please themselves. Solitude here will do that awhile. You will look upon yourself in the light of a poetic isolation. Very soon, however, will it grow tedious to you, that only you see yourself therein, and you will soon desire to learn from others how you impress them in your character of recluse."

Corradina shrugged her shoulders.

"One only would I like to have," said she, after a pause: "I would like to have Angela again as my maid."

"Have you so pardoned Rafael Riario that you no more avoid to look in the eyes of Angela?"

"I have not pardoned the Cardinal, and shall not pardon him. If I will overcome the avoiding of the eyes of Angela as a childish feeling, it is because I wish near me some one I can fully trust."

"Do you not trust me?"

"That you cannot yourself suppose!" answered Corradina, with bitterness.

"You do me wrong, deep wrong, Corradina. Your wish, however, I cannot fulfill; you must tell it to my father, who will be eager to do it."

Corradina was silent.

"Don't you believe it?" asked Livio, again lifting upon her the lurking glance.

As if to avoid an answer, Corradina took again the silver bowl which Livio had brought her, and appeared to view it attentively.

"I forgot while I was saying what I have said hitherto," pursued Livio Savelli now again, with a wicked smile distorting his lips, "that you are not entirely alone in this old castle. My father has taken up his permanent residence herein, in order to be able to fulfill the duties of his guardianship over you so much more zealously and faithfully."

"My marriage makes me of age, and this castle is large," she answered coolly.

"Very large and wide indeed," replied Livio. "On one side of it many things can happen of which one may not be aware on the other side."

"Many people can live in it without placing themselves under restraint."

"How unembarrassed you act, *cara mia*."

"What is there to make me embarrassed? The Duke of Aricia has a right to live wherever it pleases him in his houses."

Livio began to drum with his fingers upon the arm-rests of his chair, while he, apparently lost in thought, gazed through the window into the distance.

"Corradina," he then said, "let us speak candidly with each other. It only depends upon you to make an end of this jugglery of widowhood, which holds you here pent up and separated from all the joys of life; only upon you to end this danger which threatens you from my father."

"What danger? I am the wife, the widow of his son."

Livio shrugged his shoulders.

"You are that," he said; "but you see, indeed, he remains here in nearness to you in the house which you should occupy as a widow! I fear we have, with the marriage, done only half, — only what is inadequate, useless. It would have been better for you to have become mine, my wife, instead of the dead Luca's."

Corradina opened her eyes upon him; he could read in them unconcealed astonishment.

A bitter smile glided over his lips.

"For that purpose I must have been a widower, do you think?" he said. "Now, yes. Perhaps out of love to you, I might have found means to become such."

Her glance still rested upon him. Then she turned away from him, angrily knitting her brows, and with the unmistakable tone of contempt she answered half aloud: —

"I will not have heard what you say!"

"That you are not accustomed to hear what I say, I know. If you would do it you would have no man who would devote himself more entirely to you with body and soul; who, for your sake, would more obstinately challenge the whole world, not even shunning death and damnation, if it would conduce to your happiness."

"What would that help me?" responded Corradina, rejectingly; "I thank you for a happiness purchased with the danger of death and condemnation, and the friendship of a daring which challenges the whole world. And with that let us end this conversation. I do not see why you came to say this to me; you cannot possibly believe that it is agreeble to me to hear it."

"*Cara mia*," interposed Livio, "do not trouble yourself about it; for did you never say things to me which were not agreeable for me to hear? Still, I will obey you, and cut short this interview, which seems to become so burdensome to you. But I cannot relinquish the thought that it would be better for you to leave this castle, and return to the Castle Savello bei Albano. The hot summer months approach, during which the air upon the Aventine is not healthful; in the mountains beyond it is fresher — better for you."

"Do you speak in earnest?"

"Why do you doubt it? I speak so very much in earnest that I have had everything there made ready for your reception."

"You have never in your life done anything more useless, Livio!"

"I believe it not. In the first place, I beg you only reflect over my proposition; and also say to yourself a little that I have made up my mind about the matter. For since my father has now lost his head, I must, in his place, take a little authority in the guidance of the affairs of our house. I will not allow, Corradina, that you die here through the fever of malaria, through the tediousness of loneliness, or through madness from terror of my father. In the Castle Savello I will do everything to atone to you, through enjoyment and pleasure, for that which lies behind you. I will also let Angela come to you there, if you request it, although she may be pretty well grown wild with her goats in the mountains!"

Corradina had slightly changed color at the words of Livio. She was evidently troubled by them. Still she arose and answered with quiet pride: —

"You could make my stay in this house in all respects unendurable to me, if you came frequently to insult me with such proposals; yours, however, would be the last where I would seek refuge."

She stepped with erect carriage through the room, and turning her back upon Livio, entered a window-niche.

Livio's face took on a threatening, angry expression; a still fury glowed through the narrow slits of his eyes, while he stroked with his hand that part of his dark beard covering the upper lip, putting it between his teeth and biting upon it. Still, after a pause he said, with apparently perfect calmness: —

"You should not make it too hard for me, you woman of marble! Why are you so hard against me? That I should serve you, that I should assist you against all, have you willingly allowed to be pleasing to you; and yet you knew how I felt for you ——"

"Does your assistance to what your own interest constrained you, justify you in torturing me?"

"My interest because it was yours; I have never separated the two. And as to the torturing — how may you complain of trouble who swim against a stream? Cease to struggle against it! Still you will that I leave you. I will, if you promise me to reflect over my proposition."

"I promise you to forget it; that is more favorable for you."

"You will not be able to forget it; I will return in order to speak of it again. Take care of yourself in the meantime, *cara sorella*."

He departed. When Corradina turned her face from the window, to be assured that he had left the room, her features had become pale as marble.

"It is dreadful!" she whispered, after awhile. "Can I in no way purchase rest from them, — not even through the most venturesome and most difficult thing?

"And he is right in it all! I am alone, alone, — alone here! And so defenseless, so dreadfully defenseless against these men!"

She began to pace noiselessly to and fro. There came over her a sort of desperation, which, in order to escape the intolerable, might blindly enter upon that course which could snatch her away to other destinies, and these also hurl her life's boat into storm and destruction.

She strode hastily up and down. She thought of the German who, so deeply moved, so passionately, had offered to her his services. "Oh that he were only a more mature, a more discreet man, with gray hairs!" she said to herself; "I would say to him, 'Let me fly with you, — fly over your Alps, and as far as my feet can carry me!'"

CHAPTER IV.

IN THE STUDIO OF RAPHAEL.

RAPHAEL dwelt on the Tiber, on the left bank, opposite the great Hospital von San Spirito lying on the right, in a little house now destroyed; for he had not yet built his little palace on the Borgo, which is now partly destroyed, partly built up into the Palace Accorombone. Between the back of the house and the river was a little garden, which was bordered along the water by a low wall; through this wall a little grated door allowed exit to the moist, river-washed stone steps leading down into the water. One does not travel in gondolas upon the charming Tiber; still, this was a place perfectly adapted to landing with a little boat, and quietly coming ashore in the dark, silent night.

The little garden contained nothing but a starved, foot-trodden sod, and some orange trees which shaded it; some laurel bushes and oleanders, which covered from view, right and left, the walls of neighboring houses. What further filled it was not fruit or flowers, but stones; stones, however, formed by the hand of man into images as beautiful as flowers. They were exhumed relics of antiquity; reliefs, statues, busts of women, heroes, and gods,—all more or less preserved or half ruined. They stood among each other rather irregularly upon pedestals, in the grass, leaned against the trunks of orange trees. Also, now no great veneration fell to their share, for a young girl of about eighteen was even now busy winding a clothesline about the neck of a mutilated god, to whom was wanting the legs up to the thighs; and he therefore seemed sunken into the earth, as if gallantly presenting to the pretty maiden his beautifully formed neck at just the proper height.

Out of the garden a little flight of two or three steps led into the house through a door-opening, which was covered only with a blue curtain. This curtain was even now drawn back by the master of the house, and fastened at the side to a hook.

The painter stepped upon the threshold; he leaned himself with the left shoulder against the withdrawn drapery, so that one freely obtained a glance beyond him into the spacious studio, filled with a soft light, out of which he stepped.

His eyes followed the movements of the young girl.

"You throw a halter around the neck of the Apollo; has he deserved it?" he said.

"Eh, who knows?" she answered. "I only know he very patiently allows the rope to be fastened around."

"And whoever patiently allows a rope placed about his neck, also deserves it, you mean, Margarita."

"These wicked old gods have all deserved it," she replied, "and most certainly such a Bacchus as this; for it is a Bacchus, and no Apollo, as you call him."

"And will you draw the distinction between them — you?"

"Why not? Have I not yet heard you, Master Raphael, and your learned friends talk enough about such things? This quite light and tenderly rounded body," she continued, observing the marble with a precociously knowing mien, "this soft breast, these full hips, are those of a Bacchus or an Antinous, not of an Apollo, whose frame must be stronger, firmer."

"Indeed," said Raphael, laughing, "one might go to school to you."

"And still I have learned all this in your school! Otherwise what care I for these naked old gods? What you could learn from me, *carissimo*, are other things"

"And what?"

"Eh, much. Men could always learn very much from women."

"Not one thing could you teach us, Margarita."

"One? I think many, because you do not now understand many things which they try to bring to your doors."

"No; only one — how to be deprived of you!"

"And if we could, would we be willing to it?" she rejoined, smiling with her whole pretty, roguish face.

"We could not do without you — and still we have you not!" he added.

"Now I do not understand you."

"No; you do not understand that," he replied, coming out, in order to seat himself near her upon the head of an old marble bust, and to so draw the "Fornarina" to himself, that he could lay his head against her with half-shut eyes.

"You have us not?" she responded, laying her hand upon his dark hair, with a half undertone. "Did you say that to me — to me? And I mean," she continued, with louder and almost angry tone, "you would formerly have found still many of them, from your friend to whom your glowing sonnets pertain, to your betrothed Maria Bibiena, to——"

"Ah! my dear, ethereal bride — the poor, tender plant who was too sensitive for this harsh, terrestrial atmosphere — do not remind me of her!" interposed Raphael, with a sigh. "And what befell that lofty, glorious being who——"

Margarita, pettishly drawing her brows together, gave him a gentle tap on the beautiful, expressive mouth with the "well-mated lips," which seemed about to express something that could only have astonished and charmed her.

"Why do you strike me before I have spoken?" said Raphael. "Do you know what I would say? See, I meant it this way: we have in you not yourself as you cause our desires to paint you; we have not that in you which our souls yet cannot do without — there lies the pain of life for us."

"What have you not in us?" asked Margarita. "No angels, but weak women, who love you more than you faithless creatures deserve. Is it that of which you wish to complain?"

"You are right. Take it so. What shall I complain of you? What shall I reproach you for? Do you know the story of Pygmalion, the sculptor, who carved a woman out of stone, and effected that his prayers to Jove gave her a soul, and made her living? Since then it has happened to the contrary with many men; they have a living, loving wife, on whom they hew and labor so much she becomes stone to them. Therefore will I rather leave you as you are, Margarita. Is it your fault if in you that divine and eternal something in which our soul seeks its life does not burn? Not that light which your beauty seems to radiate from itself, and that is still only a reflection which our ardor throws upon you?"

"Then," answered Margarita, gayly, and little touched by this speech, "it happens to us as to the planets, to whom also their light is thrown only by the glow of the sun. What more do you want, you great proud sons of men, than to find in us living planets from your light?"

"Ah! planets are heavenly bodies — and you are vain earthly dust; painted dishes upon the table of fortune; beautiful still life — without idea! And so we end the struggle with the insatiable thirst of the soul for the infinite, which is not in you and not about you, in creating and forming as if, indeed, we reach it there! All our trouble and labor is only the restrained love-force which takes pleasure in the poem, in color, or in stone."

"So it is well that your lofty, glorious sonnet queen is not yours, as your Fornarina, this poor lantern, in whom you find no light," remarked Margarita, with pouting of the red lips; "for if she appeased your repressed love-force, you would throw away from you brush and colors, and let Pope Julius see how he would get his chamber walls painted!"

"So it is," answered Raphael, "perhaps. I would live, love, be happy and idle, throw from me the brush, all that vexed me, and — even almost forget the sermon of the rude German monk."

"Of what German monk?"

"Of a German monk who has vexed me; still, what does that concern you? Follow me; you must sit for me."

"I cannot to-day, it is so fearfully tiresome; and you always paint something quite other than myself, when I have sat there all day long with the patience of an ass, as motionless as a statue."

"I paint your hands, your shoulders, your breast, the folds of your drapery which I throw over you, but your features I cannot use. I need others if I paint an angel, my little demon; others if I represent the deepest and most sacred mother-love; for you, with your roguish eyes, your saucy lips, as red as fresh-blown pomegranate blossoms ——"

"I am no saint; I know it," replied Margarita, with a mixture of pouting and sadness, looking away from Raphael beyond the stream into the distance. "But you, — you should not throw it up to me!"

"Do I, *anima mia?*"

"Oh! you say to me to-day none but bad things; I will hear nothing more, and go to bring my washing. But let this be said to you, that I have not the least respect for your 'deepest and most sacred mother-love' as you represent it in your Madonnas, although all men praise them and outweigh them with gold."

"No? And why are you not satisfied with them? Let us hear, Margarita."

"What shall I say? That is also one of the things about which we could not teach you men anything, for you cannot understand us."

"Tell me, anyway; I will make every effort to understand your instruction, *carissima*."

"Well, then, do you believe that the Madonna was a good, honest woman, with a whole, strong, womanly heart?"

"Certainly."

"Well, then, she did not become espoused and wedded to St. Joseph without loving him. Is that true?"

"That is true."

"And do your Madonnas love their St. Joseph?"

"They love the infant more!"

"And you have never reflected over why and wherefore a mother loves her child, and when she does it with the fullness of her soul? Truly," continued she, hesitating and half-aloud, "if I had a child ——"

"You — now, you?" said Raphael, looking at her and searching her eyes.

She turned her eyes slowly to his with a half-tender, half-reproachful look, then went to the house. When she reached the steps of the door, she turned back smiling roguishly.

"Come, come," she said, "you paint the Madonna gazing in ecstasy upon the infant, and St. Joseph, delighted, in the background. That is clever, manly labor, and I will go to my stupid woman's work."

Raphael with both hands stroked the hair from his brow; then supporting his chin upon his hand, he said: —

"Margarita should take this German monk to task with such thoughts! Will that simple cowl-wearer never get out of my head?"

He sat there awhile thinking, when a servant stepped upon the threshold of the garden door.

"What do you wish, Baviera?" he asked.

"There are two gentlemen here who wish to speak with you," replied Baviera. "The one is Monsignora von Ragusa, the other a monk."

"A monk? Of what order?"

"From Santa Maria del Popolo."

"A yet young man? I am coming."

The servant stepped back. Raphael arose to go hastily and excitedly into his studio.

This was a great, cool room, lighted on the north — that is, toward the garden and the river — by a large, broad, but rather high-placed

THE HOLY FAMILY. (Raphael.)

window, in whose neighborhood stood the easel, with the adjustable stool of the painter before it. On the dark-red painted walls hung pictures in oil and sketches, mostly without frames, but symmetrically arranged. Below them extended, along the wall, a long, cushioned seat after the fashion of a divan; a smaller easel stood in one corner; a large table with papers and drawing materials upon it, all very well ordered, in the other. The whole made the impression of the utmost simplicity. All the thousand objects which fill another studio with its hereditary house-furniture, its casts, its statuettes, its draperies, its old weapons, and so forth, were wanting here. It was evident that the man who thought, felt, and created here in this one, did not have the need to become confused by a chaos of gay colors and forms, but to keep far from himself perplexing impressions.

There were also enough of those objects which pertain to the profession in the great back room opening from the studio, and into which one looked through an open door. There were a pair of young people occupied at easels, another pair sat at drawing-tables; in the background already stood Baviera, again rubbing colors, and around on the walls, on the furniture, was a full supply of those things which could serve as models or implements for any demand of the work, or of pleasure.

The young men there beyond appeared accustomed to a respectful stillness in the presence of the master. They labored in silence, or only whispering.

When Raphael had stepped into the front chamber, he found the two men announced standing in its midst.

The monk was no other than the one he had expected to see, according to Baviera's announcement; it was Brother Martin. The other was a medium-sized, strong man, whose fat, yet lively and intelligent face, with the squinting glances, the highly mobile features, was not entirely adapted to the costume of a bishop, — the violet robe, the hat with its gold-interwoven green band, in which he appeared.

"Monsignore Phädra," said Raphael, extending his hand to the latter, "you surprise and rejoice me."

"Do not say that so hastily, Master Santi," said the one addressed. "Will it rejoice you if I come for the first time to scold you that you have not come to wish me joy over the occasion of my elevation to the bishopric of Ragusa?"

"Oh! Was that not joy enough for one man like you? Should I wish you still more?" rejoined Raphael, banteringly, and inviting both men to take places on the settee.

"Does there not belong to every office understanding and happiness?" replied the bishop. "And must you not wish to a friend so much the more of these, the less of them you give him credit for? In the second place, however," continued Monsignore Phädra, seating himself, "I bring you a man here of awful learning; an incredulous, obdurate German, who places himself in opposition to your art, and, I fear, only insists upon it so warmly, that I introduce him to you because he has the intention to quarrel with you like a genuine German."

"Since you call me a German monk," here interposed Brother Martin, "I have the right to be a little rugged; and therefore I say to you candidly, my Lord Bishop, that I would like first to quarrel with you because you present so incorrectly what caused me to wish to be allowed to visit this Master Santi in his workshop."

"Well, then, present it yourself," answered the friend of Raphael, whom the latter addressed, not by his name, Tommaso Inghirami, but Monsignore Phädra. The spiritual gentleman had one time, when he was not, as to-day, librarian of the Pope, and bishop, played the Phædra in a representation of Seneca's tragedy of Hyppolytus, and therein, when a halt in the machinery suspended the progress of the piece, had with such great presence of mind entertained the spectators with improvised Latin verses, that the nickname had remained with him for all time.

"That I will," responded Brother Martin. "See, noble master, I was in the Vatican Palace, in the rooms which Pope Sixtus IV. had arranged for the celebrated collection of books, with whose oversight this worthy bishop is intrusted. He was condescending enough to lead me around therein, and show to me the learned treasures which Pope Nicholas V. has collected there, and which he brought hither from Avignon, so that our gloriously reigning Holiness has acquired them. Among them, Monsignore Inghirami showed me also a wonderful manuscript, with little miniature pictures finely delineated in gold and vermilion, and other colors such as I had never seen before; and when I fell into raptures over it, this learned gentleman laughed at me, and called all that with which these old artists presented the mysteries of faith in the living human form as a mockery compared with that created by the new school of art, and especially by yourself, Master Raphael. And so we fell into a dispute over your style of art, which ended with Monsignore Inghirami's angrily drawing me away to follow him into your place of work, where, he said, my eyes should teach me another thing. My heart now desired nothing better; for, since I have seen your pictures in the chambers of the Vatican, something has lain heavily upon my spirit, and I am revolutionized in my thoughts."

"Indeed?" asked Raphael, listening intently. "It has not gone much better with me since you recently, by your words, pressed a sting into my soul. For, to confess it to you, it has vexed me deeply that a man, who with good intellect, and fresh thought, and accurate mind, comes to me from a foreign world, consents not to that for which I strive, but falls into opposition to it. It was no consolation to say to myself: 'He is only a monk crossed in his scholasticism, and whose mother's milk was that of superstition'— pardon me the candid speech. I said to myself: 'Shall, then, all that you have reached not be great and powerful enough to overcome such a monk with his superstition and scholasticism? Are my works not eloquent enough to heal and turn back such a mind from its unsoundness? Are my forms not strong enough to compel him who, foreign to their world, steps before them for the first time to kneel down before their grandeur? Upon the brow and in the eye of this monk lay still a human challenge, whose voice I must hear!' And there seized upon me a wonderful unrest, an impulse to attain to something higher, more powerful, something irresistibly compelling, a stinging impulse of longing, and, at the same time, an apostolic inclination to manifest still more clearly, more devotedly to the world, the beauty which I sought to represent — still more illuminated by a light which can truly only stream forth from them out of a heavenly beyond. So arose before my mind the image of a Madonna, — of a woman who swayed upon the clouds, beautiful as the most beautiful woman that ever walked upon the earth, and yet from whose features, from whose eyes, flows down upon you the fullness of infinity; so that you, let you be the most obdurate monk in the world, must sink upon the knees before her, whether you will or not."

Brother Martin looked with an expression of surprise into the shining, self-glorified countenance of the painter. Then he said:—

"I had not believed that my recent words aroused in you so much reflection. What happened to me I willingly tell you,—that your works have sunk me into a real melancholy. I saw the world around me here sinfully turned away from Christianity; I saw the customs becoming savage; the church led by men who see in her a great institution of force. I saw science alienated from the faith; and I saw also, now, still the highest that man mentally creates, art, turn itself away from Christian reality! Shall, then, the Rock of Peter become a solitary, barren island in the stream, on which the waters overflow without troubling themselves further about it? Shall the faith become lost to the world? Shall worldly wisdom become our morals; pleasure, our dogma; sensual beauty, our worship? You could not wish that! Not you! Afterward I burned to ask you what would happen if art again would turn itself to the highest, to the revelation of divinity; become a theology, and Christianize morals, instead of decoying them deeper into paganism."

Raphael, meditating, supported his brow upon his hand; then he said:—

"Do I know? If art should turn itself to theology, then give us theology, so that it may be possible. Give it to us pure, great, free, in harmony with the inner life of man; give us a theology which falls like dew upon our spirits, not one which requires of our lips to babble the rosary; of our knees a gliding up holy stairs; of our stomachs to fast; of our hands gold for every kind of favor. Give to us a doctrine, not of fear and of threatening, but of love and of liberty. To it can art turn, with it go hand in hand. Fear, and hate, and horror, and devil, and hell, and torment, and death I cannot paint."

"You see," here remarked the bishop of Ragusa, "our Master is an obdurate heretic, and you will do nothing with him, Fra Martino. If I tell you candidly what I think, it is my advice to let him go as he will. Art will neither aid nor harm religion much; just as dogma, again, neither aids nor harms morals a great deal, if man looks upon it as a great whole. The heathen Nero was a very bad fellow; the Christian Ezzelin von Romano a still much worse. The Emperor Diocletian, the heathen, had very many Christians tortured to death; Pope Innocent III., of praiseworthy memory, and his great general, Simon von Montfort, these good Christians would have treated in the same way many more of the Albigensians, an upright people, if there had, indeed, been more of them!"

"And you say that,—you, a bishop?" asked Brother Martin.

"I say it," responded Monsignore Phädra calmly, "for see, I think it all depends upon man's receiving a good education, upon his being led by instruction to thought; by good breeding, to mastery over himself. As to religions, however, they and the representations of men about the future life are always very different, and yet men always have remained very much the same."

Troubled by this speech of an Italian bishop, the German monk continued:—

"I will grant to you that art has never had much influence over men,—your art, which, with all your thoughts and your knowledge, you put into paganism. Old Rome, God knows, had art enough: temples, columns, statues, baths, gold and ivory, and splendor around,—inestimable, for us, inconceivable magnificence. And all these Romans, moving about in the midst of such splendor—what were they other than miserable dogs, shabby bloodhounds all and severally? They scourged slaves; they slaughtered prisoners; they caused gladiators to tear each other's flesh for their amusement; they let poor men be torn of beasts; and they wandered at pleasure in the light of burning torches whose cores were living men. They were horrible wretches despite all their art. And so you see of what use your art is. Christianity alone has softened the manners; has tamed rudeness; has disclosed to man his inner self. A spiritual song that I sing to my lute gives to my soul more consolation, more trust in God, than all the statues of all the Grecian sculptors, than all the bath halls of all the Roman emperors. Therefore, I say, put Christianity in your art, or it is good for nothing."

"And I," responded Raphael, "answer you: Give us a Christianity that can receive into itself our art."

"You have the Christianity," exclaimed Brother Martin. "'To you it is given to understand the mysteries of heaven,' says the Master."

"No; we haven't it," replied Raphael. "Your Christianity, as you have formulated it, is not adapted to us. It has long lain upon me painfully, and often has it become a real torment to me, that I indeed felt it and still did not confess it to myself; the evidence, however, came over me as an inner revelation. Will you hear how it was? It was in Sienna, seven or eight years ago, maybe. I had come into the city in order, with Messer Pinturicchio, to paint new frescoes in the library of the cathedral. One day I was shut up alone in this great library hall. I was eager to delineate a Christian saint,—a poor suffering, female martyr. I drew,—again I erased my lines; I made them anew, and felt that I created bungling work. Vexed, I fell into an irritated humor. The saint with her moonshine body, her starved features, troubled me finally as a ghost. I could not find the form or the features; she placed upon me, as it were, an Alp which shut off my breath. Tired of wrestling with her, I mopped my brow and threw away the charcoal, and, taking a deep breath, turned away. And see! when I turned, my eye fell upon that antique group of graces in the middle of the hall; that group which, in the thirteenth century, some one in Sienna dug out of the rubbish, and which, in spite of its mutilation, shines forth as formerly in the full glory of eternal youth and sublime beauty. My eyes rested, as if bound by magic, upon these forms; it was as if invisible threads drew me to them; upon my soul there fell as if a light, and with the light there came as if an inner rejoicing over me. I seized my pencil again, moved to the profoundest depths of my being; I turned over the leaf with the misdrawn saint, and my hands, as if winged with ecstasy, drew upon the back the heathen forms of marble, — the nude women of the gods. From that on all was clear to my mind; the library hall of Sienna was my way to Damascus." *

"Paul became a Christian, you a pagan!" retorted Brother Martin, dryly.

"Not quite," rejoined Raphael. "But let us drop this contention, which would never end. Come here and see for yourself these drawings; perhaps you will sometime learn to think otherwise."

He arose and went into the room where his pupils were busied.

Here he opened a portfolio, and drew out of it a great leaf, which was covered with drawings. With it he returned, and placed it upon his easel.

"See," said he, when the two men stepped up, "that is the sketch of a picture which I have designed for Messer Agostino Chigi. He is to build a villa over there on the banks of the Tiber, and I have undertaken to adorn it for him with frescoes. He wishes one of them to be the story of Galatea. If you are less versed in heathen mythology, our learned bishop here will be able to give us reliable information who Galatea was."

"The information stands at your service," said the learned bishop and librarian. "You must know, in the first place, that there are three Galateas. Theocritus speaks of one; she is a young, sensuous Sicilian, who throws apples at the sheep of Polyphemus, in order to attract the attention of the giant to herself, and to excite his desires.

* The leaf is still in the Academy of Fine Arts in Venice.

The second, the Galatea of Lucian, is not so bold and wanton, but a haughty village beauty, the beloved of Polyphemus, and very proud of the conquest of the giant. Quite different is the third, a Nereid, described in the Metamorphoses of Ovid. She is a charming woman inflamed with passion, who loves the beautiful Acis, and one day, resting by his side, she is surprised by the uncouth giant, who, burning with jealousy, hurls a piece of rock at the poor Acis, which crushes him in pieces. Galatea, however, in deadly anguish, escapes the giant; she throws herself into the sea, in order upon its bottom to save herself in the house of her father Nereus."

"Now, see," said Raphael, as Tommaso Inghirami finished, "this drawing. If I were a heathen, as you say, I would have preferred the sensual, inordinate Galatea of Theocritus, or the self-conscious one of Lucian, haughty and glad of her beauty; I would have chosen one of them for my representation. I chose the one of Ovid, because she alone allows herself to be represented as pure and chaste, and, so to say, with a soul within,— with a soul full of beautiful, ennobling, human grief over her slain lover. This grief gives to her something sacred, glorious, chaste — so, at least, I have thought and willed. I have wished to represent an ideal beauty and an existence of soul which, finally, I do not believe you will find with the heathen!"

"And that," put in Tommaso Inghirami, contemplating Raphael's drawing, "have you accomplished in a masterly manner, friend Raphael. This nude beauty, this unveiled, blooming young body, with the noble head looking upward as if complaining, has gone beyond every conceivable desire, because you knew how to place in her a soul; and where a soul is, there is no more what our German brother chides as paganism. Your works, Master Raphael Santi, are like children's faces, which bear in their features, strangely mingled and no more distinguishable, the physiognomies of the father and mother.

"There look out of your works both paganism and Christianity; the form-beauty of the one, the soul-beauty of the other, — the depths of soul which could not yet be given to the world without Christianity. Fervor and dissolving in God's love, enthusiastic living beyond into the other life, Giotto and Fra Angelico have already known how to represent. You, however, have understood that after which our art, for a century perhaps, has already struggled, what our minds in our free culture require,— to find the free, beautiful form for the soul-life, and put to it, while you bring it into this form, that which made tattered and distorted the true nature. And so you have, it seems to me, through the blending of the heathen form and the Christian ideal of our time, impressed upon it its highest seal."

"You praise me too much, Monsignore," said Raphael; "if it were as you say, our German monk here would also be satisfied. And still he quarrels with me!"

Brother Martin stood silently absorbed in the contemplation of the drawing of Galatea.

"I quarrel with you because," he now said, "in spite of all this worthy bishop says about Christianity, you do not serve God. There is nothing of doctrine in your works. Doctrine, however, is our spirit-sun. What help is it to me that from this sun you let fall, perhaps, a little light upon your works, a little warmth, perhaps, upon your forms. Paint the sun itself as it rises upon the world and gives it light!"

"The monks," answered Raphael, smiling, "have made too much dust and ugly clouds before the sun; one sees it no more."

"And if we poor, much-chided monks again removed this dust and clouds, would you then paint it?" asked Brother Martin, as if low-spirited.

"Yes; give to your doctrine, which is now nothing but the dressing of thoughtless men, again its soul; make of it the doctrine of love, which reconciles and blends the human with the Divine, from the oneness of the human with the Divine through love, and I will paint for you pictures for this new doctrine. I will no more paint for you merely the beautiful thought-world, but pictures wherein earth and the other world shall meet: the Madonna who is the woman and still also Heaven's queen; the Transfiguration, which, through the mortal body of Christ, lets his heavenly nature shine through; God the Father, himself a man like Jove, and yet the eternal spirit of the world, the All-Merciful. Zeal and inclination for such figures shall not be wanting in me; you only take care that your sun, over which you have hung so many 'holy Passion week napkins, and Swiss kerchiefs of Veronica' and other patchwork become clean and bright, so that I can see it through your doctrine."

"Then," said Brother Martin, smiling ironically, and still yet with a sigh, "we must truly already take heart and see, let what will be,

SISTINE MADONNA. (Raphael.)

the patchwork torn away and clouds driven off which obscure the sun from you."

"And so," interposed the Bishop of Ragusa, jestingly laying his hand upon the shoulder of the monk, "will this our learned speech have still the effect that you, my zealous brother, return into your wrong-headed and strife-loving Germany, and there begin a great cloud-chasing, a great dusting-off and cleaning-up in the church, only therewith that Master Santi can paint here more pious and mystical pictures; and when you from the sun have torn away the patchwork, and have again brought forth the Word of God pure, and the world has taken a revolution to Christian and purified doctrine, Master Santi will paint for you pictures such as the world has never seen, — this world illuminated by the world beyond; the world beyond plastically become this! That will indeed be very beautiful and edifying; still, I advise you in your church-cleansing not to whirl off too much dust. You might get much to swallow — much, even to suffocation."

"You jest," responded Brother Martin, throwing his hands over his breast, and directing his fiery eye upon Raphael. "To me, however, comes in earnest the feeling that a pair of righteous men could lend great service to the world of to-day. The world of to-day needs men; in truth it needs them!"

Tommaso Inghirami listened no more to these excitedly uttered words, even so little was he aware what feeling would be produced by his jestingly outspoken words. For how the simple Brother Martin, who stood before him there, would go home over the Alps in order indeed to lend the world a "great service," he could not foresee. He could not foresee how this service, the leading back of the world to a deeper and more sincere laying hold upon the doctrine of Christianity, the whole revolution in feeling and thought so soon following even in Italy upon that "service," would work upon the great Master von Urbino, whose turning to the visionary, to the transfigurations, to works such as the Sistine Madonna, the Vision of Ezekiel, the Saint Cecilia, the Spasimo di Sicilia, and the like, yet indeed stand in inner connection with the new world-current into which Luther led the souls of men; with those analogies of Protestantism which, at the same time, led Sannazar to write a poem "*de partu virginis*," and the most celebrated humanists, as Bembo, Sadolet, Contarini, a brotherhood, to compose an "*Oratorio del divono amore*," to which, perhaps, Raphael himself also belonged; so that one could say Raphael had been a pagan, and had become a Protestant Christian.

Tommaso Inghirami, as has been said, had heard nothing more of Brother Martin's answer; he had just turned around and taken his gold-adorned hat to depart, when Margarita stepped into the studio, accompanied by a young maiden of foreign appearance, who carried a paper in her hand.

"The maiden will not allow herself restrained from intruding upon you, signori," said the 'Fornarina;' "she asserts she has something important to communicate to one of the gentlemen, and to deliver to him a letter which admits of no delay."

"Pardon that I intrude," said, in her German-accented Italian, the apparently heated and excited young maiden, who was no other than Irmgard; "I have a letter for Brother Martin. You must be he," she added, approaching nearer the latter. "Here is the letter; it comes from Count Egino von Ortenburg; it was brought by his order to his lodgings, and was to be quickly forwarded. That appears alarming to me; the letter certainly contains nothing good; I pray you read it,— read it!"

Brother Martin looked at the young maiden a little surprised that she held out to him the writing in such urgent haste; then he took the letter, opened and read it hastily, while Irmgard anxiously studied his features.

"There is strange information in the letter," said Brother Martin. "Count Egino has encountered a wonderful adventure; he has withdrawn himself into a cloister, and in its neighborhood has found— well, we will say, he has unexpectedly found a great treasure, a royal jewel of the olden time, of which men have ceased to think. I shall come at once to see him, to pay my respects to this treasure, and to him with it."

"And that—that is all?" said Irmgard, gasping between the words.

"All? Is it not enough?"

"I only thought there might some accident have befallen him,— he might have fallen among wicked men."

"Nothing of that, my child, is in the letter, and you may calm yourself," answered Brother Martin. "How was it possible to you to find me out here?"

"In your cloister they told me you had gone to the library of the Pope; and when I searched this out, and knocked at the door, a servant opened it for me who told me that a German brother such as I was seeking had gone out with the Bishop von Ragusa, and that the latter had left word he was going to Master Raphael Santi. So I inquired my way here."

"You have also made your way through difficulties in your care for this young Count von Ortenburg," replied Brother Martin, looking fixedly upon her.

While she blushed more deeply at this glance, Raphael laid his hand gently upon her shoulder.

"And since you have now become calm, young lady, let me look once into your eyes!"

"What do you wish of me?" answered Irmgard, almost harshly, turning toward the painter, who was viewing her sharply, and, as it seemed to her, impertinently.

"You must know," replied Raphael, smiling, "you have here fallen into something like a lion's den, out of which a creature formed by nature as you are, and who has such a countenance as yours, will not escape again so quickly. I will send away these two worthy gentlemen and keep you with me."

Irmgard stepped back alarmed, and exclaimed angrily:—

"That is a wicked jest which you allow yourself."

"No jest, for I wish to draw your portrait! Where could I find again, indeed, such a graceful copy of blonde German maidenhood? Are you now appeased?"

"I have not come to have my portrait drawn!" answered Irmgard proudly, and with irritation.

Raphael and Tommaso Inghirami laughed.

"And why not?" exclaimed the latter. "You must know, proud and coy maiden, that princesses and cardinals are vain of becoming drawn by this master, and of being immortalized upon his tablets."

"And I," said Irmgard, "am much too little vain to wish to take a place among such distinguished persons, even upon the tablets of this master."

"You will not do it in truth," exclaimed Raphael, "even if I tell you that I wish it? that I will be thankful for it? that I will reward you for it with whatever you ask?"

Irmgard shook her head very energetically, and turning to Brother Martin, said:—

"I know the way to the Count von Ortenburg. If you wish to be led by me, worthy brother, I am ready; I would like to go."

"You will go," asked Tommaso Inghirami, "before you have even looked around in this room,— have even thrown one glance upon these drawings, upon these works? Do you know in what man's house you are?"

"In a painter's house,— and it is not the first time," answered Irmgard, coolly. "At home, in Ulm, such a painter was our neighbor. I saw very often his productions with the colors and the brushes, when he painted saints for the stations in the church, or white horses and golden lions for the signs for inns."

The three men laughed heartily.

"You see how inexorable she is, and you must let her go now with me," said Brother Martin.

Then he took leave of the bishop, and with a warm pressure of the the hand also of the master, and departed with the young maiden, who undertook his guidance.

"Now you see the artist's reward, Monsignore Phädra," exclaimed Raphael, when they had gone out, sighing audibly. "To this monk all my work is a vexation, because I do not paint in an orthodox style; and this maid throws me in with her neighbor, who paints sign-boards for inns! Is it not discouraging? Truly I will beg of you to go to our Holy Father and ask him whether there is anywhere in the neighborhood of Ragusa a bishopric with which he could provide for me!"

"Why not?" answered Monsignore Phädra; "a man such as you deserves not only a bishopric, but even a cardinal's hat."

"I am satisfied with less," responded the painter, smiling; "and if you obtain it for me, I will turn over to you as a reward the first beautiful work of art which I discover in our excavations."

"That would be a transaction!" interposed Inghirami, laughing; "some beautiful Venus, Diana, or Leda for a cardinal's hat."

"I am in earnest," continued Raphael, likewise smiling. "I shall in a few days have excavations begun in a yet unsearched place, and hope to find there wonderful things."

"Ah! remain in your place of work, Master," said the bishop, preparing to leave; "and even if it were only sign-boards which you painted, you would be happier there than if you should go about in a violet or red coat and do nothing. There is no more bitter labor than enjoyment which becomes labor. Besides, you must hold your brush in readiness to redeem your word to this German monk; for perhaps, like a wonder-worker, will he redeem his. The man has in his eye something which reminds me of the great Girolamo, only it is brighter; one does not feel afraid in its presence. And now farewell, dear Master. Have you heard the latest court news — that Fabricio Colonna, the brave commander-in-chief, who was once Alfonso von Ferrara's prisoner of war, and in this imprisonment became his friend, has effected a peace between Alfonso and Our Holiness, and Alfonso will appear at our court?"

"I heard it, and rejoice to be able to greet the art-loving duke here and do homage to him! Perhaps, also, is Messer Ludovico Ariosto in his retinue."

"Hardly," interposed the bishop, smiling. "Messer Ludovico has once succeeded in beholding the countenance of our Holy Father and does not desire it the second time!"

"Indeed; I forgot that," replied Raphael, lightly, laughing aloud.

"Now good-bye, beloved friend," said Monsignore Phädra, and he reached Raphael his hand as leave-taking.

CHAPTER V.

BROTHER MARTIN'S RESOLUTION.

 A HALF-HOUR later, Irmgard and Brother Martin had reached the heights of the Aventine. When they had arrived in front of the Cloister von Santa Sabina, Irmgard, who was to-day in her maiden-garb, had to remain behind, and Brother Martin reached to her the hand while he said: —

"And now I thank you, my friendly guide. There is the door of the cloister, and I need you no more."

Irmgard, however, remained where she stood.

"I will first see whether or not they let you in," she replied.

Brother Martin rang at the cloister door; a slide opened on the inside, and the countenance of the porter became visible. When the latter espied a monk, without questioning he opened one shutter of the door. Irmgard was just ready to turn and go, since she saw Brother Martin step over the threshold, when she heard him utter a few loud words, and immediately perceived, as she stepped back, how the shutter of the door just now opened for him was again so quickly shut upon him that he was plainly pushed out.

She hastened to him.

Brother Martin exclaimed, coming to meet her: —

"But Count Egino is no longer in this cloister."

"He is no longer there?"

"No; the brother porter says he has already departed this morning."

"That cannot be."

"The brother says so, and pushed me out rather crossly."

"Count Egino himself sent this letter to his residence, wherein he has invited you, as you say, to come to him at this hour — here, in this cloister; so it stands in the letter?"

"In the letter it stands so."

"And now should he be gone? Impossible."

"Who knows what has caused him to do it!" responded Brother Martin.

"It is certainly, certainly not so," remarked Irmgard, disquieted. "Oh! I beg you ask this porter again, once more. Say to him——"

"My child," replied the German monk, "I have not the least desire to do that; this brother porter is brutal as Cerberus, and gave his information with an irritated definiteness."

"Then there is nothing left us but that we hasten to the dwelling of the count, to seek him there. I beg of you to go down there with me; it is on your way."

"I will go down with you," answered Brother Martin, "just for the purpose of seeing you quieted, for it is evident that you have a needless anxiety about him."

"I have an anxiety about him, and I have grounds for this anxiety; for, to confess to you — but come, let us hasten."

Irmgard stepped quickly forward, and in going she confessed to the young monk with her, who had on the way hither already completely won Irmgard's confidence, exactly what had led Egino into the cloister, and what dangers might threaten him there in case he should fall into the hands of the Savelli.

Brother Martin had listened to her highly perplexed. Excited, he exclaimed: —

"That is a very wonderful story which you relate to me. In the letter of the young count, all that is only indicated with some mysterious words, which I now understand; but you yourself, — how is it you know all that so exactly?"

Blushing, Irmgard also gave answer to that: how Egino had found them and received them here in this strange land as fellow-countrymen; how he finally let her entirely into his secret; indeed, less, she added, blushing again, out of confidence in her and in the supposition that she could be useful to him and help him, than because he had the need to utter what was passing in him and so oppressed him.

Brother Martin nodded.

"It may be so. It is also good, my child, that you so comprehend it; you may also yet be able to help and be useful to him in his condition if he should really be fallen into danger and embarrassment, which does not now seem to me improbable. He has even played with danger; the Italian cunning is capable of much of which one of us would not think; and that Brother Cerberus appeared exactly as if he gave his information about Count Egino with a bad, though quiet conscience, as Saint Thomas Aquinas says. God shows his power most willingly through a weak vessel, and so we will hope that we can do something to rescue this poor youth out of the danger into which he may have fallen, if he has acted without foresight as a right unreflecting young blood. Yet let care go, so long as we have hope to find him again. Perhaps he will come forward, well preserved, to meet us on the threshold of his dwelling, in a few minutes."

They finally reached the lodgings; but Brother Martin's hope was not to be realized. They heard some one ascending the stairway to Egino's chambers, a sound of voices in conversation above, and soon saw upon the landing the faithful Götz standing with a stranger, to whom with great effort he sought to make himself intelligible in his broken Italian. Irmgard knew the stranger; she had seen him out in the villa with the "*parva domus.*" It was Signor Callisto Minucci.

"The gentleman asked for the count," exclaimed the servant in German, when he caught sight of Irmgard. "I cannot understand him; see if you will get on better with him. He appears to be in distress about my master."

Irmgard addressed Minucci in Italian. The latter answered:—

"I see that you can serve as interpreter, and that happens fortunately. I would like to speak with the Count Ortenburg, whose servant, however, says to me his master is not at home, and that he is in the cloister Santa Sabina; but I cannot understand what in all the world can have led him thither."

"So the young man is, in truth, not here?" said Brother Martin.

"You see," said Irmgard, "I had only too much right to be alarmed. Let us walk into the gentleman's room, Götz," she then turned to the servant, "that we may be able to talk at leisure about what to do now."

Götz opened the sitting-room of his master before them, and all four entered.

Signor Callisto dropped upon a chair, and turning to Irmgard, he said:—

"You are the young German maiden whom the count brought to my wife. And you?" he added, looking at Brother Martin.

"A German monk, who has come with me on account of anxiety

about the count, whose friend he is," replied Irmgard, quickly interposing. "I pray you tell us what brought you here, for you see we are troubled about the fate of the count."

"So am I," replied Signor Callisto; "uneasiness about him has brought me here. You must know that Count Egino, a short time since, accompanied me to serve as witness at a marriage ——"

"Oh! we know that, signor, we know that; I pray you go on," said Irmgard, interrupting him.

"Well, then, you will comprehend my uneasiness," continued Signor Callisto, "when I tell you that this morning I saw suddenly appear at my villa, out yonder, no less a personage than the Duke of Aricia. He stopped on horseback at the steps which lead up to my residence out of the garden."

"'Signor Minucci,' he said, when I appeared at his call above him, on the terrace, 'only stay up there, and do not invite me to dismount and walk into your dwelling, for I have not the time for that, because I am on my way to the Prima Porta. In passing by your villa a thought struck me, which caused me thus to startle you from your work. Tell me, then, who was the young man recently accompanying you—at the marriage of my Luca, you know—whom you introduced as your pupil?'

"I communicated to him," continued Signor Callisto in his narration, "the desired information. He inquired then about his native place, about the relations of the young man, about the standing of his house in Germany, about their possessions and influence. When I had given to all this such an answer as I was able, I asked him: 'And what interest does Your Excellency take in all this?'

"'Only an accidental and quite superficial one, my dearest Signor Legista,' responded the duke. 'The young man is in the cloister of the Dominicans, with my pious neighbors of the Aventine, and has requested to practice exercises there. The good monks, however, have not discovered much piety in him, and do not know exactly what to do with him; whether it is more advisable to attack his heretical tendencies with their moral thumb-screws, or his body with their iron ones—or to let him run. The prior has accidentally communicated that to me this morning in a conversation; and since I, without that, was passing by your residence here, I promised him to obtain from you information concerning the German youth. I thank you for this, Signor Minucci, and commend you to the protection of the Madonna. Good-bye! You see if I do not now give rein to my horse, turning like a top here, he will tramp up the sod and Donna Ottavia's flower-beds; besides, my people await me out there on the street.'

"With a wave of the hand the duke rode away, as if he were desirous to avoid a further conversation.

"He left me so much the more uneasy," continued Signor Callisto, "because I could not deceive myself into believing that he would have come into my villa without quite a different interest in our young friend, and that the secretiveness with which he denied it, and represented himself as merely the messenger of the monks, could betoken nothing good."

The narration of the lawyer could only increase the anxiety of Egino's assembled friends to the most painful height. They conversed and deliberated a long time about what would be best to do, and each took upon himself to follow up most zealously the means and ways by which he would be in a situation to find out what had become of Egino. Signor Callisto, who knew the body-servants of both Savelli, of the father as well as of the son, and besides these Sor Antonio and Sor Giovanni Battista, still other dependents of the house, would seek to get something out of them. Irmgard should take Götz with her as a protection, and try to find out in the neighborhood of Santa Sabina whether any one had seen Egino leaving the cloister. Brother Martin should, if possible, through his orderbrethren of Santa Maria del Popolo, obtain information concerning the monks of St. Dominicus. Also, so soon as they should have news of Egino, they would turn to Father Anselmo and beg his intercession with the Pope: for that, however, they of course needed beforehand more definite points of information about Egino's fate. If they should wish to present a request to this exalted personage, they must be able to carry something definite and reliably positive. They determined on the next day, at the same hour, to come here again to Egino's dwelling, in order to report what they had accomplished.

Irmgard was so entirely unnerved and thrown out of balance that she had taken very little part in this whole conversation. She had only looked with her great frightened eyes from one speaker to the other.

The men left. Götz accompanied them out, and then hastened to his room, to make ready to go out as a companion of Irmgard. The latter had remained sitting still and unmoved in her place; she stared with ashen face upon the mats which covered the floor at her feet.

The door opened again, and Brother Martin came forward, having turned back once more. He came quickly to her, and laying his hand upon her shoulder, he said:—

"Irmgard, poor child, I saw how troubled you are ——"

"Have I not every cause to be?" she exclaimed, suddenly bursting into tears; "was it not I who gave him the advice?"

"Console yourself; what depends upon your advice,— upon the advice of a girl, of a child? The count must have known what he did: console yourself; commit it to God, who watches over us all, and trust that we shall find him again. Signor Callisto said just now, as we were stepping out on the street, that he is invited to a feast at which the Duke of Aricia will take part. He can introduce me there; and I, although it will be little appropriate for one of my cloth to be seen there, will, nevertheless, go. It is, indeed, not contrary to the custom here, that a monk, a priest, appear at the luxurious feasts of the reveling children of the world. I will go for the sake of the missing friend, and a little, also, for your sake, because I desire to see you quieted, Irmgard."

"Oh! how good you are, Brother Martin," broke in Irmgard. "Count Egino has not celebrated in vain your noble spirit."

"Has he?" replied Brother Martin, smiling. "I shall, alas! not be able to reward him to-day; but, on the contrary, I shall be obliged to say of him a good deal that is bad ——"

"Bad? You? Wherefore?"

"Don't you understand? Upon that rests my plan. Did I not say to you the Duke of Aricia will come to the feast?"

"Certainly; and will you say to him something bad of Count Egino? Oh! I understand, — you are here as his opponent; you carry on against him a contest at the court of justice ——"

"So it is," interposed Brother Martin, "just that. I will seek to approach this duke; I will say to him that I have learned how he was asking information about my antagonist; I will make it count that I am his countryman and his opponent. Do you not believe the duke will then see in me a man toward whom he need not be on his guard? that I will, at least, entrap him into indicating what has become of Egino? Besides, in the excitement of such a feast, when wine opens the heart and makes the lips voluble, it must be very unskillfully managed by me, or I must have great ill luck, if I do not succeed."

"Oh! certainly, certainly," exclaimed Irmgard, the color coming again to her cheeks with hope and joy. "You have found out the best way, and that you will go in it is so much the more noble in you, because it will be hard for you to go in a way costing you cunning and dissimulation."

"You are right," responded Brother Martin; "but we cannot do otherwise. I console myself, when I commit such a sin of necessity, through the likeness of the Master, which allows me even to work on Sunday if I do it to save the poor animal fallen into the ditch; and through that other which permits me to take the ears of corn of my neighbor if I am hungered. And so God protect you, my dear countrywoman. I hope to be able soon to bring you consolation."

He gave her his hand, and departed; immediately afterward Götz came to accompany Irmgard.

CHAPTER VI.

CINQUE—CENTO.

*— dando non deficit; unum
Hoc sat habet, si se scit retinere sibi.*
—J. C. SCALIGER, about Augustin Chigi.

HE feast to which Callisto promised to conduct Brother Martin took place in a house which lay on the other side of the Tiber, and not far from the Cloister von Sant Onuphrio, about where, at present, along the Strasse Longara, the Botanical Gardens spread out at the foot of Monte Janiculo, shaded by the precipitous, wooded bluff of the latter.

The house was not large, and although it had a portal adorned with an old coat-of-arms, was scarcely to be called by the name of a palace, to which the coat-of-arms and portal formerly gave a house the right. It stood alone; high walls separated its surroundings right and left from the street, and green treetops extending above these walls showed that it lay upon an extensive garden; and, indeed, this garden was its chief distinction.

One passed through the portal into a stair-cased hall, and from the first landing of the broad stairway leading upward in the background of this hall, into a dimly lighted vestibule. From this, one entered into a great festal parlor, with paneled, artistic ceiling of wood and walls which showed mythological designs painted *a tempera*. Out of this, one stepped into a garden; next upon a broad, marble-paved terrace, upon which benches and tables along the wall of the house invited to sit down; while upon a balustade inclosing the garden, and sustained by a pillared elevation, were displayed beautifully chiseled busts of celebrated men of antiquity and of Roman emperors, with whose names, such as those of Marcus Aurelius, of Trajan, of Antoninus Pius, and of Titus, are connected thoughts of human culture.

From the terrace led very broad, low steps, scarcely perceptible to those going down into the carefully tended garden with its dark evergreen hedge, upon whose background gleamed forth the white statues of Mercury. A marble statue arose here at the end of every sidewalk, — an image of still and chaste beauty in the umbrageous, luxurious world of plants.

Opposite to the terrace steps leading down into the garden, at the end of the broad middle-walk, was presented a decorated wall higher than a man's head, constructed in a semi-circle with a vase-crowned balustrade above it. A round basin was half encircled by this wall, and in it a fountain with distinct murmur threw a strong column of water high up into the air. Right and left from the round basin of the fountain led gently winding flights of steps up to a terrace lying much higher than the first, of the same height as the ornamental wall. Its breadth lost itself in the forest, which here arose on the side of the mountain with a close undergrowth and magnificent cork trees.

Right and left at the end of this terrace were two ornamental structures, — little halls or pavilions, open in front and supported by pillars, with draperies of colored material, which when let down formed the most secret hiding-places out of these little graceful buildings.

The house belonged to the rich Messer Agostino Chigi, from Sienna, as they said ; the richest merchant of Italy, who had removed to Rome to carry on his extensive traffic. He was a friend of Raphael and Michael Angelo and of many distinguished men. He was the same Agostino Chigi for whom Baldassare Peruzzi built, farther down on the bank of the Tiber, the beautiful villa which the Master von Urbino had mentioned in the conversation with Brother Martin. Until its completion, Messer Agostino gave here his luxurious and celebrated feasts, at which he knew how to bring together what Rome possessed of the great names of prominent men and women. These were feasts which united with their customs many which, justified by the standards of the time, would to-day no more be called the elegance of the gay enjoyment of life, but often licentious indulgence and riotous wantonness. Rome did not possess that which Florence and Naples possessed in their academies, — those central points for the nurture of the scientific and spiritual interests of the time, and also of its thought-power ; but Agostino Chigi's house presented something similar, only more unrestrained, — more according to the chance of who might be at home there when he brought his guests together.

He gave his feast to-day as a kind of farewell for many of his acquaintances whom the approach of the hot season drove away from Rome to their seats in the mountains or on the seashore.

When Brother Martin, at the side of Callisto, entered the house, and they had reached the already darkening anti-chamber filled with servants, they found torches stuck upon high, bronze candelabra, of which three were burning. This was a sign, as Callisto explained to his companion, that three cardinals, or Roman princes, would honor the feast with their presence.

A garland of flowers festooned the entrance-door of the festal-hall, on whose posts sonnets were nailed, welcoming poetic greetings for the guests; other poems, brought by friends of the house, they found fastened to the walls of the banquet-hall itself. In this latter appeared a richly covered table, set with artistically wrought sets of plate, flowers, and polished vases, rich silver mugs, and glittering things of every kind — in the condition it is wont to be when just left by the guests. The host had invited the nearest of his acquaintances and friends to the meal; the wider circle of them, however, to which Callisto belonged, to the *Conversazione*. Therefore the hall was already well-nigh deserted by all the guests; the whole gay crowd enlivened the terrace before it, the garden, and the higher terrace in the rear of the garden.

A gay crowd it was indeed; gay through the rich, luxuriously colored garb of the time, whose costume now began to supplant the strongly defined mode of the past by a tendency to the fantastic, which created the most various and the most picturesque garments. It is often incomprehensible to us how those who wore these garments found the patience and the time to put on, fasten together, and to carry, this constraining style,— these slit and puffed waistcoats, these ruffled linens, all these over-garments with flounces of lace and ornaments of precious stones and pearls. Already were the bluntly cut off shoes not left unslit, and without the lining of colored leather or silk pushing through. The folded coat, with its broad, thrown-back collar, was not without the addition of double sleeves hanging free from the shoulder or the elbow. The great heavy hats were not without feathers, clasps, and golden chains, which bore medallions.

The women, whom Brother Martin perceived assembled in groups upon the terrace, wore the hair simply parted on top of the head and bound behind under gold-adorned caps, or under hats ornamented with feathers and pearls, after the style of the men's hats; or else hanging down free between the shoulders in wavy curls drawn together in a knot below. Over broad-folded, long garments, was thrown the *camora*, a broad, loose-fitting garment, or the *vesta*, a close-fitting jacket of light silken stuff, bordered with golden fringe or broad guipure. For going out and traveling, the *sbernia* was thrown over these, made out of darker and heaver silk, edged with fur, and provided with very long, wide-open sleeves. Besides all this, there was a great predilection for ornament, consisting of rich jewelry, which often hung down in the form of strings of precious stones or pearls; with some ladies present, there was also displayed a taste for the most wonderful gold embroidery, in the form of flowers, animals, and the signs of heaven.

When Brother Martin beheld the glittering appointments of this house, the table furnished with such splendor in the elegant festal-hall with its adornment of pictures, and then cast his eyes through the open window-casements out upon the terrace, with the richly and luxuriously clad women and men upon the background of a garden laid out so charmingly and with so much noble and pure conception of the beautiful, the whole made upon him the impression of an enchanting dream-world. It needed not the soft and melting tones of music sounding above, and the sound of fine male voices, which let itself be heard from one side of the terrace, in order to make this impression more perfect. Such a world of ideal life in a surrounding composed of purely artistic forms, upon which the splendor of an evening sun poured in golden light from the dark-blue heaven, over which vibrated the tones of a powerful and penetrating voice, now swelling out, now softly dying away,— all this was to the German pilgrim, who at home had seen nothing much worthy of mention outside of the narrow cloister-cells and the not much larger bedrooms and other chambers of the German dwellings or of the small castles, a sight which filled him with astonishment. It also increased the anxious timidity with which he now walked by Callisto's side among all these strange men, who bore so much wealth, honor, or proud name — he the poor, nameless miner's son, in the white gown of the hermit monk.

Callisto led him to the master of the house,— a small, very mercurial man, who was now standing talking vivaciously to a still younger and handsomer man in the red robes of a cardinal. The latter leaned indolently back upon the balustrade of the terrace. The cardinal looked down haughtily and with wandering attention upon the monk, while Callisto presented him to the master of the house.

"Messer Agostino," he said, "allow me to introduce to you a guest who causes me with more assurance than if alone to enter your noble house, the meeting-place of so many learned and distinguished men. For while I otherwise feel that I appear indeed poor and ungifted here among so many rich and honorable guests, I know that I bring you to-day something in the person of this friend, a learned German, just so much versed in the writings of the Old World as he is unversed, indeed, in the ways of the Roman world. I would not, moreover, let him return home without having learned to know you and your house, for then he would have failed to become acquainted with the finest bit of the Roman world."

Messer Agostino Chigi, coming forward, reached Callisto and then Brother Martin the hand, and, smiling, said to the latter : —

"You are welcome, heartily welcome. What you, in any case, have already learned to know of Rome, is the most eloquent of all the procurators of the Rota ; only, Signor Callisto, you should not go so far with your eloquence as to shame me, and to awaken expectations in your friend which my house can fulfill only when honored with guests such as I am rejoiced to see with me to-day."

Messer Agostino at this made a slight bow to the cardinal, who smilingly turning to Brother Martin, said : —

"You see that in a good turn of speech, Messer Agostino comes short of no procurator of the Rota."

"I see," replied Brother Martin, "that he is very kind to receive the uninvited guest with so much good will."

Messer Agostino smiled at the foreign accent with which Brother Martin spoke his Italian ; and while the cardinal again regarded the monk with cold, haughty glance, Agostino said to Callisto : —

"You must now, however, take it upon yourself to care for your friend's comfort and refreshment, also his entertainment, and to make him acquainted with men with whom he can wish to come in contact."

Callisto bowed silently, and stepped back with his companion.

They went to take their places upon an unoccupied seat behind a little table which was laden with wine, fruits, and loaves of bread. The friendly reception of the host, and the noticing that many men in church garments and in the garb of the orders were in the company, had relieved Brother Martin's timidity; which had, indeed, been quite uncalled for, as he saw from the unrestrained manner in which everything was carried on, and in which every one moved about.

Callisto filled for him and for himself a pair of high beakers with wine, and said:—

"You will not be entirely without acquaintance in this company, Brother Martin; I see there now Raphael Santi and Monsignore Phädra; they are going up the steps yonder on one side of the fountain."

"You are right," interposed Brother Martin; "but who is the tall man near them, who ascends the steps with such heavy strides?"

"Don't you know him? Every child in Rome knows him, and would know him even if he did not have this powerful frame, and the ugly, broad nose which Torrigiani mashed for him when a boy. It is the Florentine Buonarroti."

"If he did not have that dark hair, I would have accosted him as a German," said Brother Martin.

"Of the German he has only the hard, stubborn head," Callisto smilingly answered. "I wonder that he has come; for although Messer Agostino's friend, he is the most unsociable and most retired nature of which you can conceive. That he goes about silent and alone as a hangman, Raphael Santi indeed retorted upon him, when he one day reproved the latter for always going about with a swarm of followers, like the *bargello*, the chief of the bailiffs. But cast your eyes upon the two men there, who are now passing diagonally over the terrace entering into the garden."

"Who are they?" asked Brother Martin.

"The one in the robes of a prelate is Messer Pietro Bembo, a man distinguished by fullness and amiability of spirit, and the most elegant writer of our time; he belongs to the splendid Court von Urbino, celebrated for so many great men. He has been led here, they say, through the wish to win our Holy Father to the establishment of a school of short-hand, since he is striving to revive anew the art of short-hand writing, as Cicero already made use of it in taking down his orations: in fact, though he may be here as much for the sake of his lady-love, the charming Marosina, to see her and induce her to follow him to Urbino. Have you not heard of the book "*Gli Ascolani*," wherein he no less analytically than elegantly discusses the nature of love, into which Madame

Marosina has so thoroughly initiated him — perhaps, as the wicked world says, also Madame Lucretia a little?"

"I read," replied Brother Martin, shaking his head, "not the dialogues in which men of the church, as he evidently is from his dress, speak of their love!"

"Then you dare not read the wanton comedies which make the other of the two men celebrated; for he is also a man of the church, as his dress indicates, and Bembo's friend; an eloquent and very witty man, — Bernardo Dovizio, called Bibiena ——"

"You have not yet told me," interposed Brother Martin, "who is the cardinal with whom Messer Agostino was conversing, and who looked down upon us so proudly when we came up to them."

"That is Cardinal Rafael Riario; a man of illustrious mental gifts, as his stately and fine exterior evinces. He is from a distinguished house, clever, cultivated, ambitious. There is nothing lacking to him that should hinder his obtaining at some future time the triple crown, — unless, alas! the reputation for better morals. They say he has too much favor with the women, and too much zeal in seeking their favor."

"He has a fine countenance," replied Brother Martin, "and yet something which repels me. He brings over me a feeling like that at the first sight of men with whom one shall meet later in life, and then in close dispute ——"

Their conversation was interrupted by the loud laughing and chatter of a group of women, young without exception, who were approaching them with an offensive and peculiar freedom of manner. They were surrounding one of their number, who, for the amusement of the rest, was making very graceful movements with a strange bit of clothing which she wore. It was a head-ornament of silk gauze, fastened at one end to the girdle; the beauty, however, was throwing it around her head as if at different aims, — now as a cap, now as a veil, now as a covering for other parts of her person, — and appeared to be giving the others instructions in it amid laughter and noise. Such were the conclusions drawn in regard to this dangerous weapon of coquetry, which they called the *caudale*, and which, as Callisto understood from their talk, was of Venetian origin. Men stepped up to the circle; it was soon surrounded by spectators. Cardinal Rafael Riario had also come forward to it; but soon, as if wearied with the play, he laid his hand upon the bare shoulder of one of these women, the most beautiful and stately of them, and drawing her gently to himself, he stepped with her down the terrace. He let his arm and hand rest upon her neck and shoulders, while he walked along by her side.

"See how confidentially Cardinal Riario talks with that lady!" whispered Brother Martin, looking upon them in astonishment. "Is she his sister?"

"Sister?" responded Callisto, smiling. "Good brother, what are you thinking about! It is Imperia, the most beautiful of the Roman courtesans. See, they turn this way, and approach us again. You can now see for yourself how noble and beautiful is this proud woman's countenance."

"By all the saints, I see only that this is the most dreadful scandal which has yet aroused me to revolt — this behavior of a cardinal! And a courtesan, you say that beautiful woman is?"

"Certainly — as are the whole group of these ladies playing here with the Venetian head-dress. Over the door of more than one of them, you may read, *'Honesta meretrix.'* This Imperia is for a part of the Roman world what Aspasia was for a part of the Athenian. Those others are as much like Lais, or Phryne, or other celebrated courtesans of the Grecian world. They belong to our customs; they make, in part, our morals. They form a central point of a part of our social life, and there are among them women of good birth; women who have every quality of mind and heart except virtue. The beautiful Julia Farnese, the lady-love of our former Pope, Alexander VI., who made her brother a cardinal in spite of his wild life, was not much else. And still, that greatest of all sinners had her painted as a Madonna, and himself kneeling at her feet. You are horrified at this? You are right, Brother Martin; but observe life as it is here, and then confess that such phenomena as this condition of honorable courtesanship have their good and use. We have thousands of men in different positions who, because they belong to the church, are allowed to take no wife. We have thousands of other men, scholars, artists, soldiers, whose occupations do not allow them to establish a household with a wife of equal rank. Shall they, on this account, be consigned to sink with their need of love into the lowest and most common spheres, which are, alas! not wanting to us, and to which a countless mass of our population belongs? No, no; the Grecian and the Roman courtesan is an institution which represents a great advance out of crude immorality. A broader and more wholesome advance would be for us to return to something like the Roman legislation about marriage, when we would have, besides the solemnly celebrated '*justæ nuptiæ*,' a second form of contract recognized by state and church, which, concluded under easier conditions, might also be allowed to those in the service of the church. Then there would cease much of this which shocks you and gives offense to every one, and there would not be so many illegitimate and unfortunate men, who often descend from a good relationship justified by fidelity and self-sacrifice for each other ; but they have no right, because our legislation has a deficiency, or our customs do not recognize this necessary institution. You Germans have in your law the *Matrimonium ad legem Salicam*, but only for princes. Let that be made a universal institution, and the morality of the people would only win thereby.

"You comprehend all that very well as a jurist!" answered Brother Martin, shaking his head.

"Would it not be well if we jurists, and not the church, should control the state?" remarked Callisto with a smile.

Brother Martin arose.

"Let us not contend over that," he said ; "only come away out of the neighborhood of these laughing women, and the vicinity of this cardinal, strolling at pleasure with his honorable courtesan, as you call her. I cannot look upon them, or breathe the same air with them."

"And yet there is no better place than this for viewing the company ; but as you will. It may also be time for us to call to mind the aim of our being here, and look about us for the Duke of Aricia."

"Certainly; if he is not on the terrace, let us go down into the garden."

They passed by the cardinal and Donna Imperia, in going to the garden-steps, and Callisto said in passing : —

"You are, however, still wrong, Brother Martin, not to look at this maiden, or woman, as you please to call her. Look at her features. You do not easily see a finer and more soulful face, or a nobler form. She has also often been sung by our poets. One, inspired, celebrates the tasteful magnificence with which her dwelling is adorned, and the splendor of the feasts she gives therein to her friends. Still more, they magnify her knowledge, the abundance of learned books which occupy a place near the fragrant ointment and essences of her dressing-table, and the poems which she writes in Italian, or Latin speech."

Brother Martin had for all this only a displeased shrug of the shoulders, while he quickened his pace. Thus they reached the garden below. The walks of the garden were also filled with guests, who walked up and down, or sat under the statues of Mercury, upon marble seats in the shade of the evergreen hedge-walls and the old cypresses, and gayly entertained each other; while the sun, sinking by degrees behind the mountain ridges, threw here still bright beams and golden glow upon the whole dazzling picture of this world, though over other places a dim half-light already was spread.

Callisto asked one of those he met about the Duke of Aricia, and received for answer that he had been seen at the end of a walk. When Callisto and Brother Martin passed farther down the walk, the former saw the Duke in animated conversation with a handsome, dignified lady: she was one of those ladies whom Egino had seen at the marriage of Corradina.

"The man with the nose of a hawk and the heavy, shaggy brows is the Duke," said Callisto; "the lady who sits before him on the bench is his daughter-in-law, Madame Cornelia Savelli, of the house of Colonna Palliano."

"Will you present me to him?" asked Brother Martin.

"Let us sit here and wait till this heated conversation now occupying him is interrupted," responded Callisto, slowly walking nearer him and taking his place upon a seat near the two talking together.

Detached words of the interview forced their way to them, — unintelligible to Brother Martin, with his feeble knowledge of the speech. Callisto understood a single word; still, if he had wished to listen, he would soon have been disturbed, for a lively, restless little man stepped up to them, reached Callisto his hand, and began with great volubility a conversation with him. He appeared to be one of that rabble in the great exchange of society who knows everybody, takes an interest in everything, and who expressly fumes with sympathy for persons and objects, — a sympathy which then truly is only smoke.

"You come late, late, Signor Legista," he said; "and where is Donna Ottavia, your wife? Have you not brought her along? She doesn't like large companies, I know, but to-day she should have come; for our noble host, Messer Agostino, this king of all merchants, has prepared for us the most beautiful surprises. I was just now over there in the forest, and threw a glance into the mysterious tents, out of which some kind of a secret will come forth to meet us. You see the curtained pavilions at the end of the terrace up there—but I will betray nothing of that which will surprise you; you will see it indeed, and then will you admire these magnificent little kingdoms, which certainly rather go through the eye of the needle than for a camel to come into heaven. Even the man most afraid of his kind of any man in Rome has been decoyed here."

"You mean Buonarroti?"

"Even him; and what is still more, he has read aloud for us, at the breaking up of the table, a sonnet, so well composed and fine, that I maintain one must admire him far more as a poet than as a sculptor and painter; for in both arts, you know, he is not quite according to my taste."

"Not according to your taste, Master Sylvestro? And what fault do you find with his style?"

"What do I find fault with? You see, Master Raphael Santi also paints much incomprehensible and unsubstantial stuff. For example, now, up there for our Father Julius, on the walls, he paints upon one and the same surface all the apostles and fathers of the church together, part in heaven, part on the earth, without one's knowing wherefore one part of them are in heaven and the others still on the earth. Opposite these, upon the other side, he paints all the philosophers and thinkers meeting in one and the same hall; and now I pray you, Signor Minucci, is not that madness? Are there men stupid enough to believe these people have all existed so in one heap together? How childish that is! But the Master von Urbino paints them at least pleasing, graceful; every individual form is beautiful. Does Buonarroti do that? He only wishes to show that he is a wizard in drawing. He laughed aloud at me grimly when I told him that; but am I not right? Is it not mere foolishness with which he fills out the Sistine Chapel,—nothing but occurrences, and forms, and stories, which never were and never will be, and, besides, so wild and desolate that the looker on becomes afraid before this world of giants? 'Messer Michael Angelo Buonarroti,' I say to him, 'you are a man of so much insight, and throw away your time on the representation of things in which no one believes any more, and which, as you represent them, could also please no one. Why do you do that? Why do our artists always still represent pictures and scenes out of the Christian mythology? or why have they in more modern times gone over to that, since this Christian mythology finds no more believers? or why also represent scenes of heathen mythology, of which one believes still less? If you paint for me how Socrates or Phocion, these noble men, were compelled to drink the poisoned cup, would that not be to me a more moving picture than the wild, naked, mortal coils of your Last Judgment, over which I laugh, because it belongs to the realm of fables?"

* * * * * * * *

Brother Martin, who had listened with ever-increasing astonishment to the talkative man, interrupted him here, while he deliberately arose before him with threatening, flaming eyes; but restraining himself, and suddenly turning to Callisto, he said:—

"Is this babbler all in earnest? or does he wish to ridicule my calling?"

Callisto laid his hand upon Brother Martin's arm, and drew him again to his place.

"Do you not see, then, that such a design never entered Signor Sylvestro's head?" said Callisto, smiling.

"And you really think as you speak," continued Brother Martin to the gentleman, who turned in surprise, now upon Callisto, now upon the monk, "you have really thus relinquished all faith, all fear ——"

"Faith!" Signor Sylvestro exclaimed, laughing aloud. "Good brother, you are comical. I go to the confession and the Lord's Supper, and take indulgences and order masses, as does every good citizen and Christian. But if I pay for all that my good money, what more do you then desire? The church sells to me her wares; I pay for them in good coin — now, do you also wish faith? Has the merchant who gives to me his wares and receives for them my gold, to ask after my thoughts?"

Brother Martin was dumbfounded. He looked with gloomy eyes upon the man; it was a relief to him when the latter, laughing, turned away to accost some one going by.

"You are as if crushed, Brother Martin," said Callisto.

"That I am," he responded. "Do many men think as this one?"

"Many," said Callisto.

"Your Master Santi, I observed, had only coolly turned away from the church; but this man has become her enemy!"

"Oh no!" rejoined Callisto; "don't believe that. He submits to her, as we all, indeed, must; and since he submits to her, she lets him go his way! But let us think about our purpose. The duke arises now; let us step up to him."

The duke did get up, sure enough, but for Callisto to speak to him remained impracticable; for the lady, his daughter-in-law, who had been sitting near him, arose at the same time, and seizing hold of his arm, as if to hold him back, said in a louder tone than she had hitherto employed, and eagerly: —

"Your Excellency must tell me still more about this. You do not escape so!"

"I know nothing more, as I told you," replied the duke, — "nothing further than that Livio has had a violent and hostile encounter with a strange man, a German, whom he discovered with her; and that I think Livio will now learn, when he must, that Corradina does not love him, alone, but also carries in her heart another, who, without our being aware of it, kept himself in her presence. Livio will now let go his foolish plans upon Corradina and become reasonable. You know that I, uneasy and concerned lest Livio have the design of some deed of violence against Corradina, am staying in the castle on the Aventine, in nearness to her ——"

"I know that you remain in her vicinity, and certainly only to protect her, truly!" interposed Cornelia Savelli, the words a little mockingly intonated. "For," she added, "since you out of fear of Livio were prevailed upon to consent to the marriage, which was yet planned by them only to play you a cross-stroke, it seems to me you could no longer have other interest in the matter."

Without expressing himself in regard to it, the duke continued: —

"I can only give the advice to you, Cornelia, now, since Livio must be, at least, a little cooled from his misplaced passion, to do your best to cure him entirely."

"I should have much to do indeed to heal all the misplaced passions produced by Corradina," responded Cornelia, sarcastically, in a tone of opposition. "So that is all you will confess to me?"

"What shall I say more, Cornelia?" replied the duke, now also with a wicked smile. "Corradina's German lover and his fate will not interest you; and since, as you say, it interests you so little whether or not Livio, your husband, after this experience, can be again won by you, we may as well let this conversation end. Give me your arm; the sun is set, and the coming night-air warns us to withdraw ourselves to the terrace or into the house."

He reached her his arm. Since, however, the peculiar carefulness of the Romans against the influence of the evening air after the setting of the sun had already led many of the guests the same way, the Duke of Aricia could not pass Callisto without observing him. He returned his salutation with a curt —

"Ah! Signor Legista — *bona sera* — it appears you are now also giving instructions in theology, since I see you with a young monk, as you not long since were with a student of law!"

"I give instruction in everything, Your Excellency," responded Callisto, unabashed; "still, not yet in theology, but in Roman personages, occupations, and customs. My companion, this young Augustine brother, you must know, is a novice in all things, since he has only a short time since come out of Germany. But since you have reminded me of my former pupil, the jurist, now let me add that this is even his opponent, in a most especial sense — opponent in a lawsuit. He could also give you information about him which you asked of me, and which I was in a condition to communicate only so imperfectly: he could give it so much more reliably, as he who contends with him here at the Rota, knows well his descent and relationships."

The duke measured Brother Martin with a distrustful glance, and then having turned very scornfully, he said to Callisto: —

"So, so — it is likely this is the German brother for whom the young gentleman of whom I asked you had sent, — probably to conclude with him a compromise in his suit! Say to your new pupil, then, Signor Minucci, that he has done well not to come and accept a compromise. That German gentleman will, I fear, be hindered a long time from prosecuting his suit energetically, and his opponent will now have doubly favorable play. *Felicissima notte*, Signor Minucci!"

The duke passed on with a haughty nod of the head; Madame Cornelia swept past at his side. Callisto, a little put out, looked after him, and then at Brother Martin.

"There is nothing to be done," he whispered; "the duke is suspicious."

"Indeed, he is a cunning fellow; my unfortunate countryman must also have spoken of the fact that he expected me in his cloister. One could hate him on account of his endless improvidence. The poor Irmgard. She awaits comforting news from me — and I shall have none to bring her."

"And what evil fate may we not fear for poor Count Egino,

from the scoffingly intonated words of the duke?" said Callisto.

"It is an unhappy story!" said Brother Martin. "Instead of going to her with consolation and a good hope for him, we go with doubled care. Can we go?"

"Not well," replied Callisto; "you see they are all crowded together upon the terrace and in the festal-hall, where new refreshments are being served; they would scarcely let us through there if we should wish to go now. Messer Agostino has still somewhere in reserve a surprise for his guests,— a spectacular display. It would attract too much attention if we were to go; and if this cunning duke should see it he would certainly entertain the suspicion that we came only for the purpose of approaching him. Therefore you must still hold out awhile longer."

"Which will be hard enough for me!"

"Why? Is not this society splendid, enlivened with the forms of beautiful women and distinguished men? Gayly and pleasingly the company moves about in the forms of the finest pictures, and the music, the surroundings, this festal-hall, this garden, does it not form the most beautiful setting for a talented company? Does it not teach you to know the world, a world foreign to you?"

"The lesson which it gives to me," answered Brother Martin, "presses a sting to my heart, as if a red-hot steel; and if it were unknown to me it would be better for me. Will it ever be possible to call back to the right path men who think as these do, and to save their souls? If they were only, as Master Raphael Santi, seeking spirits! But they are that no longer. The 'Christian mythology' or the heathen, it is all the same to them. They are no more like the lukewarm, which are spit out of the mouth: their heart is cold, cold as nothingness. They thus stand over the abyss, and the voice of one who would snatch them back from the steep brink of eternal destiny, would be as the voice of one crying in the wilderness!"

"With many of them, perhaps. Many others of them the voice would call back, if it should be the right voice!"

"You yourself?" here interposed Brother Martin, with a quick, sharp look at Callisto's features. "Say now for yourself, what is your creed?"

"My creed? That is a question of conscience, good brother," gave Callisto for answer. "I have no creed; but I have a view, a philosophy, if you will; and if it is not exactly a dogmatic creed, it is yet for me sufficiently a conviction to furnish me a good moral law reaching out to all the relations of life. It is the philosophy of all the enlightened minds of our time, — the philosophy of Plato."

"Is it not sufficient for you, as for so many 'enlightened minds,' to have the illusion that the philosophy of Plato is in you, without your being able to give an account of what the philosophy of Plato then is?"

"No," replied Callisto; "do not consider me so superficial. I know well what of Plato, what of the notions of the Stoics, what also of the Christian refining and deepening of pagan views, is in my thought. Believe me, in spite of all the stagnation of the church, of all the wantonness of morals, of all the crudeness of the passions, and of the insolence of egotism, which we perceive in our time, there still lies over its nobler spirits a very earnest, consecrated temper; a longing after the Beautiful and a desire for the True, as, indeed, over no earlier time. It is as if the eve of an event in the spiritual world as of a coming dawn, as a still presentiment in the souls which are listening whether or not through the tops of the cypresses under which the quiet thinker rests, the meditating artist dreams the Master will pass with a gentle murmuring. If you wish to find that out, read the hymns like the meditative poem of Lorenzo de Medici, the Magnificent, wherein he has his teacher in the Platonic philosophy, Marsilius Ficinus, to represent the blending of this philosophy with Christianity."

Brother Martin did not answer. He walked along by Callisto looking upon the ground. They mounted the steps to the terrace, where Callisto was accosted by one of his acquaintances, and became engaged in a conversation that did not seem inclined to come quickly to an end, since the acquaintance began to speak to Callisto about legal affairs.

With gloomy eyes Brother Martin turned from them, and again descended the steps into the garden. There he walked down the broad, middle path to the fountain. It was well for him to be alone for a time. It had become very oppressive to him; he breathed with difficulty. Indeed, the evening was very close, as if a storm might be at hand; clouds had collected in the sky, which continually grew darker. On this account the twilight which had followed the sunset had, with unusual suddenness, spread itself over the garden with deep darkness.

Brother Martin came as far as the fountain; he ascended the steps to the right of it, up to the higher terrace lying in the background of the garden. He saw that some men were busy here setting out and preparing some iron vessels, which looked like coal-pans, also spreading carpets, and moving here and there low seats; while another brought a bundle of short spears, and then played with a pair of fine wolf dogs, which followed him.

The German turned and threw back a glance upon the garden and house; the festal-hall began to glitter with lighting up, and to pour out the glow of countless lights upon the terrace in front of the house, upon the costumed forms enveloped in the manifold light-effects from the brilliant illumination.

Brother Martin stared awhile on the spectacle below; then came to him the thought whether, if he would go straight on and pass into the forest covering the steeply rising mountain-side behind him, he might not soon reach the inclosing wall above, and somewhere in it find a way of exit. He would give much to be able to slip away to be alone with his thoughts.

He therefore left the terrace which he had mounted, and clambered through the thicket behind it quickly upward, through the underwood and under lofty trees high up. It was remarkably lively in the woods; forms, which as if fleeing from him, glided through the bushes, dazzling white, and — in fact naked forms, two half-nude maidens they were, who now slipped before him around a thicket, and laughed and whispered.

Astonished, he remained standing; he rubbed his hand over his face. He was certainly only in a dream!

He then went farther, and again remained standing; he breathed quickly; his pulses began to beat wildly; his breathing stopped, and it was as if a swoon must come upon him the next minute. What was that? What did it mean? What meant these forms which now, a short distance below him, on the cliff, assembled from the bushes on all sides, descending to the terrace—a whole host, all scarcely half-clothed, or naked in spite of a light, fluttering drapery? What would they do down there? Why did they let themselves down on the carpets, reclining one upon another, the one in this, the other in that place, here singly, there in groups of five or six? And now, in truth, fires became kindled, which flamed forth from the arranged fire-basins; a sudden dazzling glow coming forth as if by enchantment, in order to throw a light upon these nude women, while a crashing hunter's fanfare sounded out, and then passed off into a soft music.

So it was; it was really so. A great commotion arose over there in the festal-hall, as Brother Martin could perceive through the lighted windows. All rushed out upon the terrace lying in front, laughed, clapped their hands, let a hundred bravos peal forth.

"*Brava, bravissima*, Diana and her nymphs!"

"*Montium custos, nemorumque, Virgo!*"

"*Diva triformis!*"

Brother Martin heard it. It was as if Signor Sylvestro cried it out; countless other cries followed.

The words gave him something like a key to what was transpiring under his eyes. It was a representation of the hunting-camp of Diana and her huntresses; a living picture, as we would say, which Messer Agostino Chigi had arranged, and which upon the height of his terrace, with the background of the green bushy woods, with the cleverly planned illumination from beyond, might be from below picturesque and enchanting enough to behold. At any rate it was received with loud rejoicing, and the enthusiasm increased as the flames in the coal-pans began to beam forth in variously colored fires,—to flash up now purple, now violet, now green.

Seen from above, from Brother Martin's standpoint, the picture of the goddess of the chase, with her nymphs, with her spears, her dogs, this confusion of naked bodies and limbs, with every colored drapery of light material between, was quite wanting in the enchantment which it had for those standing below. There was wanting the conception, as a whole, which only the right arrangement, the right light could give. If it had not been for the notes of the music, which for Brother Martin were something softening the shock of the scene,—something which, as it were, took away the common reality, and lifted it out of the real life into the land of dreams,—he would not once have felt the gentlest excitement of the senses; he would simply have felt outraged and horrified.

And still, as it was, he felt outraged and horrified; he stood and looked staringly upon the whole picture before him there below: this camp of Diana illuminated by every kind of dazzling and colored lights, then the dark garden out of which the music resounded; the host of guests, who noisily crowded out from the house through the garden, to observe the picture more closely in its individuality; the brilliantly lighted house, out of whose interior, as from a feast of Sardanapalus, gleamed the splendor and wealth of the ornamental furniture and the golden tableware of the richly dressed and luxurious persons within.

He stood there and gazed down; how long it continued, this spectacle, he would not have known how to say. He observed, all at once, a very suddenly occurring excitement in the camp of the nymphs: they drew themselves together; low cries became heard; some sprang up and drew what clothing they wore close around them; the others followed their example. There were drops of rain falling, which, striking on the naked shoulders and backs, had so suddenly thrown a panic over this camp. The drops rustled now already over Brother Martin's head in the leaves of the trees. Diana and her nymphs fled before them, to the right and left, seeking shelter in the two pavilions at the end of the terrace, and after a few minutes had disappeared behind the curtain.

The thunder-storm, which the dark clouds rolling themselves together had announced, seemed inclined to break out; the thick, down-showering drops were its first greeting. A whirlwind hurried down from above over the mountain-side, twisting the tops of the trees. Brother Martin slowly descended, to seek shelter in the house. He came to the terrace below him, and passing diagonally over the carpets lying there spread out, he suddenly stopped in its midst, in order to look upon a contorted streak of lightning. He felt, at the same time, the falling of the drops had ceased; only a second wind-gust came, and moved violently, right and left, the flashing, colored flames in the coal-pans.

So he remained standing, his arms thrown over his breast, looking up to heaven as if expecting a second flash of lightning would come to inscribe its indentations upon the inky wall of the skies.

The lightning came; it rent asunder suddenly and crashingly the cloud-masses to the very earth, and a sullen thunder growled after it. Brother Martin involuntarily stretched out his hand, as if in an ebullition of angry joy over this crash that he might have liked to hurl down at his feet upon this world, as a terrifying call of God.

"Only see the monk up yonder," said one of the guests among those upon the lower terrace at the house, turning back to another.

"Ah!" the latter exclaimed, "how pale the wind throws over him the blue flame of the coal-pans!"

"And now, where the lightning flashes quickly over him, he stands there like a threatening vision."

"How threateningly he stretches out his hand against us!"

"Girolamo Savonarola, who comes back again in the fire!" exclaimed a third, smiling.

"To send his lightnings crashing into our feast."

"Not yet," remarked a voice in their vicinity—it was that of Signor Callisto; "this threatening form up there on the height, which seems to you as a vision, is only a German monk, Brother Martin Luther, from Wittenberg."

TRANSFIGURATION. (RAPHAEL.)

CHAPTER VII.

DOMESTIC LIFE IN THE HOUSE OF THE SAVELLI.

ET us turn now to Egino von Ortenburg, and look after the fate that had befallen him, over which the Duke of Aricia showed himself so silent even in the presence of his daughter-in-law, and still more toward Callisto.

On the evening of the day on which Egino had spoken with Corradina and had written that letter, which, as we have seen, did not reach the hands of Brother Martin till the next day — on the evening of this day, Egino was in the garden of his cloister.

It was after the supper-time of the monks, who had already betaken themselves to rest; only out of a few cells still shimmered a weak, reddish light. Perhaps it was the learned men of the order, who were there remaining awake with their books, and who preferred to the early time of rest the waking thought-life in which they carried on their theological investigations.

Fra Eustachio had compared man to a tree. One could then compare the thoughts in which they live to the leaves with which the tree clothes itself. There lies in this picture a consolation. If there should seize upon us a despair over the prodigious heap of humanity whose whole mental life is wasted upon the untrue and upon false systems, upon the suppositions of scholasticism, let us remind ourselves that men are trees which must put out leaves, common forest trees, which bear nothing but leaves, or needles like the pine. Why do we struggle against it, if only the forest is green? if these leaves and needles are worth nothing? if it is their lot in the autumn to fall away and moulder? And have they not, also, a value as fertilizers of the ground for the coming race of trees, among which are also even glorious fruit trees?

The greatest quiet prevailed in the garden. Out of the broad plain into which the Tiber threw itself southward after it had mirrored the rock-wall of the Aventine, came the evening breeze rustling in the tops of the laurel trees of the cloister garden, and whistling a low, mournful tone of complaint through the old cypresses which stood along the wall. Crickets chirped; now and then a bell tolled or a clock struck in one of the many hundreds of towers of the slumbering Eternal City. Otherwise, however, all was silent, and the air so clear and still that one could perceive the plash of the fountain which murmured in the quadrangle of the intersecting walks. One might believe when he raised his head aloft to the innumerable stars which glittered in the dark but unclouded vault of the heavens, that he could hear the crackling of these eternally twinkling and sparkling little beams of fire.

As upon the previous evening, the window-casement was open upon the balcony of the Savelli Castle; a light forced its way out from the interior.

But Corradina did not, as upon yesterday evening, appear upon the balcony. Egino gazed from his former place upon the basin of the fountain across to the balcony, and did not grow weary of gazing. The time went by; Corradina did not appear. Instead of this, he observed a few times a shadow gliding past the door, which momentarily obstructed the light falling out upon the balcony; only a moment, yet some one must be walking very rapidly through the chamber.

Once he thought he heard thence the buzz of voices through the night. Certainly he had deceived himself. All sank again into the former stillness. Then he perceived it again more distinctly; and then — was not that something like an angry outcry, or, indeed, a cry for help?

No; all died out again. It was very foolish in him to disquiet himself about it. The shadow no longer glided as before past the casement. Still, it drew Egino nearer. He passed along the cloister and came to the wall door, which led into the garden lying beyond. It was again locked as on yesterday. Again he looked scrutinizingly at the wall, at the cypresses which stood beside it.

Why should these cypresses so stubbornly lay their boughs against their trunks! If they would only have stretched them out as other trees stretch out their boughs from them, it might thus have been easily possible on a strong branch to help one's self upon the top of the wall. Egino racked his brain over the possibility of such a thing; for in spite of all the stillness now fallen upon the castle over there, his uneasiness had not ceased.

Suddenly he struck himself upon the brow, while he murmured : —
"How stupid I am! If no bough willingly extends itself over the wall, one must compel one of them to bend over it."

He swung himself nimbly to the trunk which appeared to him most suitable, and clambered up higher than the dividing wall; which was very easily done, on account of the innumerable boughs rising from the trunk. Then he climbed up on one of those boughs till it bent under the burden ; now he let himself sink down with it Thus Egino succeeded in stretching one leg over the rim of the wall ; and a slight swing now enabled him to sit astride upon the wall.

Egino looked down into the garden of the castle, which lay there deserted as that of the cloister. When he let himself down, clutching with his hands to the rim of the wall, the height was no more so considerable that one might not be able to spring upon the ground without danger. To succeed in again returning over the wall was truly more difficult ; there stood no helpful cypresses on the side of the castle garden.

Although his standpoint now was much nearer the lighted chamber with the open window-casement, yet every tone of the interchanging voices escaped him ; he only saw anew, from time to time, the swiftly moving shadow gliding before the light in the interior of the chamber.

He had so sat awhile when this shadow, again emerging, again darkening the light falling upon the balcony, suddenly thickened into a form, and stepped into the frame of the window-casing.

It was a masculine form, whether young or old, Egino could not determine on account of the distance and the darkness, and it also moved so quickly ; it stepped, evidently excited, to the balustrade of the balcony, and exclaimed, turning back the head to the open window : —

"Your will! a woman's will! Have you seen the riders in the arena hold out the paper-covered rings? And how they shy before this hindrance? As these jugglers go through such a paper ring, I go through your will! You will spend to-morrow night in Castle Savello!"

An oath thrown out upon the night followed these words, during which the man reclined with his arms upon the balustrade of the balcony. These words made Egino tremble in his very soul ; they went through him like a sword. He knew the voice. He had already once heard it. But had he now the leisure to think about to whom it belonged? Enough, the voice was angrily threatening, threatening violence — that was enough; that tore him away up there to the side of the woman exposed to violence. In the next moment he had as noiselessly as possible slipped down from the comb of the wall, and sped below along the wall in its shadow to the terrace, to the open entrance to the stair-cased tower; then he climbed the steps softly, ascending them two at a time, and stood above upon the balcony.

The figure which was just now leaning upon the balustrade had already disappeared. It had again stepped inside. This was fortunate for Egino, since it otherwise must have perceived his movements in the garden below.

It was also fortunate for him that the conversation within now became so loudly heard that he, without any care, could step close to the open door.

Here he must stop. The beating of his heart threatened to suffocate him. He must take breath. He heard the following words spoken by the voice of Corradina : —

"Fool that you are! Scorn, if you please, my will. You have seen enough of it, I think, to fear it."

"What have I seen of it?" exclaimed the voice of the man, mockingly.

It was the voice of Livio Savelli.

"What have you seen of it? Have not you, all of you, wrestled with me for years — sought to enslave me — mistreated me as if I were a bond-woman, in order that I, this wretched one, might become the wife of your brother Luca? Has my will triumphed, or yours?"

"Praise yourself for that! If it had not been for my father, with his idiotic passion for you——"

"Well, then, has the idiotic passion of your father triumphed over me, in spite of all its efforts to break me? or has my resistance, my will?"

"Not your will has done it, but mine, which assisted you."

"Your assistance! Would I have been obliged, then, to take hold of the resolution to wed myself to the dead Luca, in order thereby, once for all, to escape the wooings of your father?"

"My father would not have let you marry the dead Luca, of that be sure, if I had not willed it, — if you had not have had my determined help in this resolution."

"It may be; it was foolish in me to accept this assistance, and, at the same time, suppose you were acting merely from pure unselfishness; merely from the consideration that your father must be hindered from again taking a wife, and perhaps giving to you brothers, with whom you would in the future have to share. I see now you acted with secret cunning from a double selfishness———"

"To be sure," laughed Livio, a little constrained. "I also acted in the hope that an hour would come when I could make my service count with you, Madame Corradina; what do you wish? We men are all selfish, singly, doubly, or a hundred-fold. But never, I think, has a woman reproached a man for being inflamed with love for her; for suing for her; and because he wishes to possess her. Such selfishness lies now in human nature, as in the flame lies the nature that what it has laid hold of it consumes; or in the wave the nature to flow downward, not upward."

"And as a flame will you consume me?" she interposed disdainfully. "I thank you!"

"I will save you."

"Save! And from whom?"

"Can you not tell yourself that?"

"I do not know what threatened me,— what forced me to fly to you for assistance."

"You may pronounce that as haughtily as you will, it cannot, at the same time, be well and peaceful for you around the heart."

"I assure you my heart will beat very quietly as soon as I see you depart," replied Corradina.

"I receive the confession gladly that my presence makes it beat uneasily," answered Livio, smiling. "It would also be strange if the beating of mine did not affect you. But can you be sincere when you say you fear nothing when you are alone in these broad, desolate, as if depopulated chambers of the old castle, where no one is near you for your company, for your help, for your defense?"

"I am not alone; I have my servants."

"Whom my father, who wished also that you should pass the year of your widowhood in this old, desolate castle, sought out for you! They would be a great assistance to you!"

"Because your father sought them out for me?"

"Corradina," now exclaimed Livio, with elevated voice, "you cannot be so foolishly simple as you represent yourself. You know my father well enough to know what you have to fear from his passion for you."

"And what should I have to fear from him?" said Corradina, with a voice wherein were mingled ridicule and contempt.

"Everything, fool, just everything! And strange that you assume the appearance of not fearing him! If you did not fear him, why did you seize upon the expedient, the cruel expedient, which would erect an insurmountable barrier between you and his desire to make you his wife? Speak. Why did you declare, when Luca lay at the point of death: 'You have wished to couple me with him for the sake of my inheritance. I have resisted, because I despised him. Now, since he will die, let me wed him. I am then yours, and my inheritance is yours!' Yes, why did you remain by that resolution, when during the preparation for the wedding, which my father would have opposed, but dare not from fear of me, Luca died under our hands?"

"You know; you have said why I did it. Because I would put an end to your father's importunities. And also because I, above all, would become the wife of no man — no man on earth. I know, now that I am Luca's widow, you will be careful that no other, no stranger approach me with proposals and attentions, and thus draw away from you what you have devoted to yourself for the future."

"It may be, it may be; but upon one thing you have misreckoned?"

"What is that?"

"When you believe a step which cuts off from my father the possibility to make you his wife, will make an end to his passion. Do you really cherish this illusion? The love of a young man is a glow which becomes extinguished when it finds no nourishment: the love of an old man is a bit of the flame of hell, which consumes and yet does not die; which is never extinguished; which no means of force extirpates; which fears no means of force; which impels to deeds of madness!"

Corradina was silent.

The mute shrugging of the shoulders, the proud throwing back of the head, with which she answered Livio's speech, Egino could not perceive.

"You are alone," he added, "here in these desolate chambers, in which one could kill you without your cry for help reaching any mortal ear, or at most that of the servant, the old waiting-woman, who would run away at the first danger. Can it be your desire to remain at this place?"

"It is," she answered quietly.

"Your desire," he continued vehemently, "to doze away here your days in dreadful solitude? to pine away in tediousness, friendlessness, melancholy? Impossible! You make no visits, you receive very few of them; the women who are related or otherwise bound to our house you do not love, and they do not love you. You are too beautiful and too proud not to be hated by them in secret. My wife, who should be a sister to you — well, we know her, truly! The condition of widowhood binds you to the house. There are for you no feasts, no gay society, no rides in the free air here,— nothing, truly nothing! Can your books, your embroidery, compensate you for all this? It is impossible! And it is your duty to tear yourself away from this destiny. You will at the Castle Savello find everything which can pleasantly shorten the time for you; I will sacrifice my whole life for you; all my hours shall be devoted to you, to the effort to make the time pass gently by as a happy dream to you. We will invite our friends there; we will give feasts; we will chase the stag in the Albanian Mountains; hold regattas upon the Lake of Nemi ——"

"Cherish good neighborship with the Colonna at Palliano," threw in Corradina, tauntingly.

"Also that, if you will," replied Livio, coolly. "My wife knows she has lost the right to lift a protest against my inclinations. My wife!" he added, with a peculiar tone of most bitter contempt.

"Your wife, Livio, was once good and noble! She was a proud nature, — too proud for the impure. You have broken her pride, and what she is now, that is, in short, your work — then truly also that of your customs, of the ways and dealings of you all. And do you know I have taken her for an example for myself?"

"You? An example from her?"

"Yes, from her, — from her fate. I said to myself that I would not let take place in me what has taken place in her. I will not. I will not become the wife of one of these men of whom none of them all is better than Livio. I will not let myself be mastered, be broken, by any one of them, — be led into the mire of their sins. I cannot live with them; I will not let the white garment of my soul be drawn away, to be pulled into the naked orgies of their immoral thoughts, the filth of their revelings. I have not your faith that I, when I have spotted my soul with a sin, have only to call to a priest of the piazza to read me a mass, or to hang somewhere a jewel before the Madonna in Sant Agostino, or buy me an indulgence, and all is good! Your God may thereby become reconciled to me, but I will not thereby become reconciled to myself. And as I have not your faith, I cannot have love for you. So my course was determined. It was not merely the helplessness of the moment which impelled me; not merely to make it impossible for your father to force me to his will. Let me once be the wife of the dead Luca, and his widow, then I would be free from every wooing for all time. You will, from now on, find means to keep at a distance from me the wooing of every other man."

"That last you have now already thrown up to me the second time, and so bitterly that it sounds as if it were not much after your mind," remarked Livio, jeeringly.

"I throw up nothing to you except your avarice, — the avarice with which your father has taken possession of my inheritance; with which you became my ally against your father, in order thereby to make impossible to him something which could at some time lessen your estate."

"I became your ally, Corradina, because I saw it was your wish; and your wish goes beyond everything for me."

"My wish is that you leave me; that you never again speak to me as to-day; that you leave me here to spin out, quietly and peacefully, the days of my year of widowhood. Do you hear, Livio? That is my wish. Let it be said to you, compel me not to withdraw myself somewhere into a cloister; cloisters are hateful to me. And now go!"

"Not yet. A peace is concluded only when each surrenders something of his will. Submit your will to mine in that you follow me to the Castle Savello; then I will there submit mine to yours, and not trouble you with my importunity."

"I would be very foolish if I believed you."

"I will swear it to you."

"I do not believe in your oaths."

"And also not in the danger which threatens you here?"

"I believe in the danger, and also in my power to defy it."

"Will, power, defiance, — truly you show best that you are nothing but a weak woman, even by the haughtiness with which you throw about you these words! Suppose I now laugh at your defiance, and break your will?"

He stepped up to her and stretched out his arm toward her.

"Do not touch me, or I shall call for help!"

"Call; you will see whether any one hears you!"

He grasped her by the upper arm, but quick as lightning she tore from him and fled out on the balcony.

"You can hasten down," exclaimed Livio, following her quickly, "but the garden is locked."

"I can throw myself over the balustrade and kill myself," replied Corradina, stepping to it; "perhaps I can also hurl you over."

"To that," he exclaimed angrily, stretching out his arm to enclasp her and snatch her back, "to that your strength does not suffice!"

"But mine does, I think!" here said Egino, emerging from the shadow, and suddenly standing near Livio, whom he had as suddenly seized by the neck with a powerful grasp, and snatched to himself.

"Count Ortenburg — you!" exclaimed Corradina, frightened, struggling for breath. "Is it you? Oh! stop, stop!"

She uttered this exclamation because Egino now also, with his other hand, seized Livio in the side, and lifted him up as a light burden,— as if he would, in truth, hurl him over the balustrade of the balcony into the depth below.

"Stop, stop!" she exclaimed, laying hold of Egino's arm with both hands, as if to tear him loose from his victim. "I command you to do it!"

"If you com——"

Egino did not finish; he suddenly drew himself together. Livio, who kept his hands free, had won time after the first shock to grasp after his dagger, and with it make a thrust. The blade now for the first time became visible, gleaming in the light, when Livio drew it out and again lifted it to inflict upon Egino a second stroke.

Egino evaded it, at the same time clutching after the balustrade with his left hand, in order to support himself. In the same instant Corradina was between him and Livio.

"Demon!" gnashed Livio with his teeth. "Away from there, or it strikes you with him."

Corradina held in her grasp the wrist of his uplifted hand; they struggled together.

The young woman seemed, in this moment, to possess more strength than the man; the latter let the dagger fall, and with a sudden turn ran from them.

"Save yourself, save yourself, Egino!" exclaimed Corradina, now.

"He will bring people, and they will kill you, as certainly as those stars twinkle above us."

"If they kill me, I shall die with the thought that I lose my life for your sake."

"What help would that be to me? Oh! away, only away! Flee! Are you wounded?"

"Here in the side," whispered Egino, in return. "I feel no pain, but the warm blood."

"And still you must flee instantly! O my God, how dreadful! If you could flee, flee to the ends of the earth, I should like to flee with you out of this horror! Still, away, away; if this wretch had not himself removed the servants to a distance, they would already be here to murder you."

She seized his arm and drew him away with her; he moved with feeble steps. Now that he moved, he felt a violent pain in his side.

They had reached the entrance of the stair-cased tower, when he said:—

"Shall I there below climb over the wall? I will not be in a condition for that."

"No, no!" she exclaimed. "Did you come over the wall—not through the gate?"

"The gate is shut; I came over the wall."

"O my God, how bad that is! Stay,—wait here!"

To keep from falling over, he leaned against the wall near the entrance to the stair-tower; she flew back. After a few minutes she was near him again.

"I have the key," she said; "now away!"

Supported by her, he reached the steps below, then passed through the garden. When they had fortunately arrived at the little gate, heavy, hastening steps already rang out on the stone plates of the balcony above. With trembling hand Corradina unlocked the gate in the wall and pushed Egino through, pressed the key into his hands, and hastily ejaculated:—

"Take it,—take the key with you, or they will wrest it from me."

She then banged the heavy little door to, behind Egino.

Livio and the servants who followed him came too late. Livio pushed Corradina back from the door.

"The key, or I will throttle you!" Livio, in unutterable fury, gnashed from between his teeth, pressing the wrist of her hand as in a cramping-iron.

She tore her hand away, and turning to go, she said: —
"Look for it! I threw it far from me into the garden!"
She stepped away.

The servants rushed to about the place in the garden that she had indicated. Two persons with flaming torches now came hastening over the balcony. The servants below called to them to aid in the search. Livio stood with angrily heaving breast, breathing audibly. A moment he watched the servants in the search, then he hurled out an oath.

"Blockheads!" he said. "She would not have told us the truth!"
And then following Corradina, he whispered to himself: —
"This is, then, the cause of her resistance! This is why she would stay so defiantly in this house! A man concealed in this garden! *Corpo della Madonna!* A man whom she loves! The wretch! To the monks, now!"

Livio called to the torch-bearers; they must pass up the tower stairs back into the castle, through the chambers and corridors there above, finally into the little passage connecting the castle with the cloister. In the cloister everything was buried in profound repose. Livio sounded an alarm. He aroused some of the monks. Drowzily the lay brethren heard it, and came in response. They began to search; Egino's cell was empty, so they hastened into the garden. Here they found the wounded man lying helpless upon the terrace. Livio desired to remove him into the castle. The monks, in spite of Livio's rage and wild threatenings of death, took him into their protection. During the contention which took place about it the lay brethren bore him into his cell, and brought to him the Padre Infirmario. Livio's commands, threats, ranting, prevailed not over these monks. He must go back frothing with rage. He had only, by the noise which he made, rescued Egino from the fate of remaining prostrate on the terrace all night to bleed to death from his wound. Now the Padre Infirmario stood by his couch intent upon rendering him aid; washed his deeply gaping wound, which extended in his right side diagonally over several ribs; and had brought to him probes and bandages by Brother Alessio.

CHAPTER VIII.

THE INQUISITOR OF HERETICAL DEPRAVITY.

THE order of the Dominicans had two cloisters in Rome; that of Santa Sabina, and that of Sopra Minerva, lying down in the city, in the neighborhood of the Pantheon.

In the latter dwelt the general of the order, the worthy Fra Thomas de Vio; the man who became so celebrated in Germany; to whom Pope Leo X. lent the cardinal's robe and the see of Gæta; who also, as cardinal legate Cajetan, showed himself, at the diet of Augsburg, so unyielding and implacable; and who yet, from contact with the great German reformer, returned home with thoughts which drew upon himself later the condemnation of his writings by the Sarbonne.

In the cloister of Santa Sabina was the highest dignitary, the Inquisitor Padre Geronimo.

Padre Geronimo was a perfect contrast to the slender Padre Eustachio, the latter bearing in every feature the type of the southerner. He towered half a head above the latter; he was built with a large frame, had a full, red-brown face with hanging cheeks.

Padre Geronimo was a Swiss, according to descent, from the Rhætian part of Helvetia.

On the following morning he stood in the cloister passage leading into the Church of Santa Sabina, on the point of repairing, in company with Father Eustachius, to the early divine service in the choir of the monks.

On the way hither he was detained, laid hold of, by the Duke of Aricia and his eldest son Livio.

They had talked to him very vehemently; the Inquisitor had then let Padre Eustachio give information minutely, and thereupon had said:—

"You hear it. Father Eustachius tells you, as he has already yesterday made known to me, that this German has brought over the threshold of this convent a disguised maiden, into this sacred cloister. Not to consider his heretical speeches, his design to deceive us as a wolf in sheep's clothing, his lies, that sacrilege alone makes him answerable to our court of inquisition. There is no other jurisdiction which takes precedence of ours, not even yours; and had he transgressed tenfold worse your domestic authority, Your Excellency, I would yet not be able to consent to have him delivered over to you."

"We must submit ourselves to that," said Livio, thereupon, with a face evincing displeasure, "if you promise us that the manner with which you deal with him grants to us full satisfaction."

"We will deal with him according to justice and according to the law. The law has strong measures against the hard-hearted and the impenitent; mild, however, toward the penitent," replied the Inquisitor, with coolness and dignity.

"And those who act merely in youthful passion and thoughtlessness," added Father Eustachius, looking at the ground.

"Correct — toward fools," said Father Geronimo.

The Duke of Aricia, with his agitated face, whose muscles were convulsed with inner excitement, looked, with his keen, piercing eyes, at the head of the order. He did not understand this man, and the latter's cold indifference stimulated in him the aroused fury, the jealous hatred, with which he wished to see Egino instantly subjected to a thousand deaths. He did not comprehend how these saints could be so cool, where he, the knight, stood so much in flames. What cunning was hid in these monks that they would not, with willing submission to him, deliver up this criminal to the house of Savelli? And if they wished to reserve him to their judgment as a criminal against the church, as a heretic, what could they then have against incarcerating or burning him to-day to please the duke?

The Duke of Aricia did not consider the fact that he, although a duke, was yet only one of the laity, and that the church likes to manage its affairs without the protest or advice of the laity. He also did not say to himself that Egino must possess in Father Eustachius a natural protector, whose humble utterances, thrown out in subdued tones, had much more weight with Father Geronimo than all the heated speeches of the two Savelli. Father Eustachius had already on the evening before broken, in presence of the prior and the inquisitor, his previous silence about Egino: he had received a rebuke that he had not earlier made these communications. He had through his forbearance with the young man burdened himself with a sin; but this sin of human sympathy with Egino, this indulgence and mildness became so much the less and so much the more pardonable, the less Egino's guilt was; and it was also only natural that Father Eustachius represent this last in a mild light. He had told all that could be charged against Egino, but he had also not kept silent that he considered it the consequence of the idiotic passion of the young man for Corradina; and therefore was the great Inquisitor of heretical depravity, the saint, so cool toward the strong pressure of the knight.

"Do you consider him a fool?" exclaimed the latter, after the last words of the monk, — " he who came to you with the intention of thanks for the hospitality you granted him, to accuse one of your number, and thus to bring upon your whole order ignominy and shame?"

"So it is," said the Inquisitor; "that is, alas! this young man's offense; but since it appears not a depraved spirit has impelled him to it, but the transient weakness of the flesh, the mind-dethroning passion for a woman, upon whose power, indeed, more than half of the sinfulness of the world rests, so we must judge with mildness the misdeeds of this German."

"I am astonished at this mildness of yours, Padre Geronimo," here put in Livio. "Let his sinfulness rest upon what ground it will, do not forget that the audacity of the evil-doer went so far as to order for himself a German monk whom he would introduce into our house secretly, without our knowledge. What was this monk for?— for what purpose was he ordered? Was he probably to wed this bold man to Corradina? Would he then take her away? Would he flee with her over the Alps? Against elopement is Corradina assured at this hour; yet your mildness with such plans and audacious strokes seems to me out of place!"

"What is in place, Count Livio," responded Padre Geronimo, "we must consider, and decide accordingly, as we are the lawful judges of the man."

"And we who are, as well as you, trespassed upon and insulted by him — are we, I mean, to have a voice in it!" exclaimed the duke.

"Certainly," responded the Inquisitor, with an affirmative nod of the head and a fatherly tone. "You have a voice in it, and, as you see, we hear it now. When has our order not listened in all things to the voice of the Savelli? I think there was a proof of this recently, when we yielded to you in spite of serious scruples in that affair, and were accommodating wherein you so urgently desired of us a service; you know — in that wedding consummated by means of one of our brethren, which now exposes us to danger, as this case with the young German proves."

"You must also reflect, Your Excellency," remarked Father Eustachius, half-aloud, "that the young man concerned appears to belong to a princely house in Germany; and that our order has beyond the Alps houses and numerous brethren, for whom it would not be well done to expose them to the vengence of powerful lords."

"Ah! does the wind blow that way!" murmured Livio, displeased, to himself.

The duke said: —

"I hope to be able to satisfy you in regard to that. The young man is not without acquaintances here; and as to what pertains to his transalpine princeliness and its importance, I can draw out information from them."

With this the interview of the men was broken off. The Savelli betook themselves again to their castle, and on their way home the duke said: —

"These priests! They have no higher interest than their lust for power! Therefore they draw away from us the man who yet, according to all right, should have fallen in our jurisdiction; and they will not act against him, because it might appear they obey us therein."

"So it is," responded Livio. "It would be best if we should take the German from them by stratagem or force, and make him harmless in our way."

"The best — but it would be difficult," replied the duke. "Through force? Their vaults are fast, and to break in openly we dare not. And through cunning? Do you contend in artifice with such a band of priests?"

"Priestly cunning is woman's cunning grown up."

"That means ——"

"I think Corradina would not refuse to free the man who, on her account, has fallen into this situation."

"What a thought!" exclaimed the duke. "I do not wish her again to hear a syllable from this man."

"It will be meditated upon," replied Livio, thoughtfully, and as if not hearing the words of his father.

"Do you hear? I will not have it!" repeated the latter, loudly.

"What can it help that she nevermore hears from him, since she will still think of him enough? Leave the business to me, father. It is best this man be dealt with quickly aside; and since we cannot get possession of him by force, we must see if we cannot, in some way, get him out of the hands of the monks into our own through stratagem. It is certain, however, that he would most willingly and most without suspicion surrender himself to the guidance of Corradina."

"And can you send her into his prison, that she may lead him out and deliver him into our hands?"

"Let me think about it."

Father and son separated. The former strode through the castle, and reached its court. He had brought before him a saddled horse, in order to ride upon it to Callisto Minucci, and with him have that short conversation whose import we know, and which had caused Callisto, as we saw, to repair to the residence of Egino, the next morning, still anxious.

CHAPTER IX.

THOUGHTS OF A GERMAN MONK.

GINO'S three friends, two days after the feast of Messer Agostino Chigi, found themselves together at the dwelling of Egino, each without having discovered a trace of the missing. They talked much about whether it was to be supposed he had fallen into the hands of the Savelli, or was held a prisoner by the monks. In the former case it was easier to obtain information about his destiny than in the latter, where it had fallen into darkness and secrecy. Callisto was of the opinion that the latter was the case.

"The duke," he said, "would not have drawn out information from me, if Egino had been in his power. What would he care about the young man's kin? The monks, however, have grounds to be careful. Their cloisters are scattered all over the world. If Egino's nearest relatives are powerful landlords, in whose territories are cloisters of the order, these last might have to feel severely whatever evil the brethren in Rome might do to Egino. Only this consideration could lie at the bottom of the inquiries of the duke."

Callisto then informed them how he, true to the task taken upon himself, had not restricted his quiet investigations to the cloister, but through many kinds of means and in ways standing open to him as the legal friend of the Savelli, he had sought to obtain information about all that had taken place, or was still going on in their different houses. The threads which he had knit together extended over the castle upon the Aventine, over the palace of the Montanara, over the Castle bei Albano, over the Corte Savella in the Via Giulia. The only definite result that he could acquaint them with was, that Egino had been led neither into the dungeon of this Corte Savella nor to the Castle bei Albano.

Brother Martin had drawn into his confidence a few of the brethren of the order, who had promised him to approach the brethren of the order of Saint Dominicus, and to elicit information. He had heard from them that everything belonging to the Sant Uffizio remained covered in darkness and silence; still it appeared so much the more certain that Egino's affair had not, up to this time, been pending before it.

Irmgard had in vain by day, and almost still more in the hours of late evening and of breaking day, watched, circled around, and guarded the Aventine. Often had she allowed herself to be accompanied by Götz; often, also, had she gone alone, impelled thither by her uneasiness. She appeared pale and exhausted. The boy's clothing, which she then wore for the sake of safety, had become large for her and in folds. Her eyes had something peculiarly unsteady; the sun, the air, the inner unrest, which had laid hold of her countenance and given to it an expression of suspense, had marred her pretty features: she was much disfigured.

She spoke little in the assembly of Egino's friends; the fearful idea had taken fast hold of her that Egino had been killed. She let the men hold counsel over the further steps they would take; she had the horrible presentment that all was too late, all in vain.

"There is only one way," she said at last, "to obtain certain information,—which is to force one's way to the woman for whose sake Egino has risked all. She cannot be indifferent to his destiny; she must, as we, wish to see him saved; at least, she owes to us the truth."

"You are right," replied Callisto; "but I would not advise you to make the attempt to reach her. I have already requested my wife, Donna Ottavia, to go to the castle on the Aventine, and there ask that they lead her to the Donna Corradina Savelli. But they have rudely turned her away. They have said to her that the Countess Corradina is not in the castle, not in Rome; that she has withdrawn to the Castle bei Albano. Since I know now that this is not the case, it is clearly to be inferred from this that they hold Corradina in a kind of seclusion or imprisonment; and from this it follows, furthermore, that they suspect her,—that they charge to her a participation in Egino's venture,—and that you will hope in vain to have a better chance than my wife."

Irmgard did not answer; she folded her hands in her lap and looked down reflectively.

"The worst is," continued Callisto, "that we have not the least prospect to win in any way the intercession of a powerful and high-standing man. We cannot go to Padre Anselmo, because we have nothing definite to ask of him. We can also not represent Egino to any one as innocent; and if he were, or if one were able to represent the thoughtlessness with which he believed himself able to deceive the monks as a pardonable, youthful want of consideration, there is yet no one who, for his sake or ours, would like by an intercession to make the monks of Santa Sabina trouble, and mix themselves with the affairs of Sant Uffizio. The Holy Father himself does not meddle there."

"And I—and I!" said Irmgard, in deep despair, in a low tone to herself, "who brought him, by my advice, by my assistance, into all this misfortune!"

"What did you say?" asked Brother Martin.

"That we ourselves must save him,—we, we, his only friends, if it is not too late!"

"No, no; that it is not, believe me," remarked Callisto. "Egino is held in durance by the monks; and if the monks torture, they torture long. They hasten over nothing."

The conversation ended with the vow of the three not to be willing to leave off their search, and to wish, after some days, to find themselves again together at Egino's dwelling, for further conference. Then they separated, Irmgard going alone to the little house on the Quirinal, in which she had found a residence with her uncle; Callisto and Brother Martin going together, since Callisto, in order to go home, must pass Brother Martin's stopping-place in Santo Maria del Popolo.

They walked along together awhile in silence.

"If they do yet mar for me here this pure, noble blood, this offshoot of German princes," exclaimed Brother Martin after awhile, "so, so——"

"You do not finish," said Callisto.

"What is the use, Signore Callisto," replied Brother Martin. "You even do not understand what there is here to turn a German spirit round and round. Since you recently took me into the sinpool of your feast, it seems to me that I must also hate *you.*"

Signor Callisto smiled quietly, and with an expression of superiority, as he answered:—

"Do I bear the blame, good brother, if you, in this Eternal City, which still remains always eternal, find so much that is different from what you honorable Germans there at home imagined it?"

"Yes, so it is," said Brother Martin, bitterly. "They should forbid us to make pilgrimages to Rome. There is much here different from what we believe it in Germany. There goes as if a deep rent through my soul, now I perceive so clearly how men live in Rome; how they who have the power act as the heathen, and they who think, think as the heathen. Even you yourself, also. It is as if a band of robbers had entered and taken possession of a beautiful and dazzling palace built for the mildly ruling father of the land, and from thence were exercising sway over the land. And as 'like prince, like people,' there is no more any restraint, and almost no hope. That confuses my thoughts; and when I sit in my cell reviewing the things I experience here, it oppresses me sorely, and I cry out, 'Lord, Lord, what must be done in order to drive out the robbers who have broken down thy sanctuary, have drunken out of thy cups, and have intoxicated themselves with wine out of the vessels of thy altar?' And because I am deprived of breath, I hasten out into the open air and throw myself down upon the barren heights, and look down upon this great gravestone of history — this Rome! Is it destined, also, to become the gravestone of all that constitutes the religious connection of humanity with their God? Shall the faith be buried here where the Apostles are buried? Shall the basilicas, at some future time, stand there exposed to the winds and weather, robbed of their roofs by the storms, clothed with wild vines, the marble of their pavements overgrown with luxuriant nettles, just as now stand the temples of Pæstum and of Agrigentum, — monuments of a dead thought-world, supulchers of ideas, which we no longer grasp? Shall the world sometime smile over the saint, as we now ridicule the misconceptions of our childhood? Will the world give up its adoption by God as a childish dream?"

Callisto looked at him, surprised at the warmth of this outburst.

"And if it should come to that?" he then said earnestly, and as if meditating. "The church has become a worldly institution, and everything worldly, earthly falls to pieces,— everything!"

"You say that so calmly! Oh! imagine it, even — the world unchristianized! Think of it! The churches only ruins! The bells silent; no more those which ring out for you the evening blessing; no more those which call you to a love-feast with all the brethren; no more the Easter bells, which ring into your life its consecration and comfort; no more a choral song, which speaks over your grave of the promise of resurrection; no more a tone sounding out into your burdened life from the eternal kingdom of faith; no more a priesthood, to bless your entrance into life, none to bless the bond of your love; no one into whose silent breast you can pour out a sin! No more talk of God, of the world beyond, of the Father's hand which leads us! What a world! Humanity would become as an instrument from which the vibrating strings had been torn away. A world without tune——"

"Not merely strings of faith have been stretched over the instrument of humanity," answered Callisto. "There are still other strings which vibrate in the human soul."

"And what would they be?" asked Brother Martin, quickly interrupting. "Strings? Yes; but only religion gives to them a tune."

"It may be! Religion, indeed! But you yourself have a presentiment that the existence now calling itself religion, the official, scholastic, dogmatic religion of Rome, leads the world in such a direction that, as you say, one day the basilicas will stand as do now the temples of Pæstum. And this presentiment of yours is exactly the same as that existing in me. Look around you here. The people are still well trained. They pray off their rosaries, they walk in their processions, they kneel and sprinkle themselves with holy water. They hear masses and go to confess; they reach into their purses and bring forth offerings, and pay for indulgences. All that is training, all of it. The means of training — with the dog it is the whip; with people, the punishment in hell. The whip is something real; the hell is only an idea. The idea will one day fail. People will laugh over hell. And then? The means of training is forever gone."

Brother Martin did not answer; he walked on in silence, looking before him.

"The thought steals over me once in awhile," continued Callisto, after a pause, "that Christ, with his loving anxiety to bring the truth to mankind, has come into the world too soon. Mankind should have been required to struggle longer to come by its own power to a finer human development. A race refined by culture would have understood him. Now, the world has not comprehended him, and he is dead for it. The priests have done their best to make dead the proper, living, true Christ. The church takes the field with a dead commander, as the Spaniards with the dead Cid."

"And who,— who is able to awaken again for the world the dead Christ?" said Brother Martin. "There must,— there must be a power found for it, for the world has need of Christ! Only through him can it become justified; only through him can it become moral!"

"Perhaps," said Callisto, "mankind will, in the future, find another law upon which to build its morality. Who knows? Are you, however, so firmly convinced that they need Christ for their morality, then you may also take on the consolation that God will not leave them much longer without that power which may wake him up. Perhaps this power will give itself utterance only in the pronouncing of a single great word. Perhaps it will know how to make as a law, instead of fear which trains men, love, which draws men to the bosom of Christ through the impulse of the heart, and not into the church through fear. Such a word would make resound in the ear of mankind again all the Easter bells which would rejoice over the newly risen Christ, and a great and powerful feeling of the divine, like a full chime of bells, would pass over humanity; they would again have their music, their voice out of the eternal!"

"Christ could awake the dead," said Brother Martin, half-aloud, and, as it seemed, affected, for his voice trembled noticeably. "Should a man be able to awake the dead Christ?"

"A man? Not a man, but a divinely inspired thought, which a man may utter. The world has seen such miracles, and they are the only ones which it has seen."

They went along together in silence, and thus they came to the cloister of the Augustines.

"Here we separate," said Brother Martin; "still, I have a request to make of you."

"What is it?"

"For the maiden, — for Irmgard. She loves Egino, and grief has made her sick. If your wife would take an interest in her."

"Certainly," said Callisto. "Donna Ottavia thinks with motherly care about your poor countrywoman. She has, as you know, recommended to her a suitable dwelling with an excellent woman up on the Quirinal, near the Baths of Constantine, and has already been there herself to look after her. The woman Giulietta is just as honest as she is intelligent, and takes the best care of her tenants, Donna Ottavia says."

"I thank you, Signor Callisto," replied Brother Martin, "and only request that, for the sake of comforting her, your wife speedily make a fresh call upon the young girl. My calling hinders me from bringing her consolation as often as I should like — and she needs it, you see yourself."

"That is so, as you say; still, you may be sure that my wife will not neglect it."

They shook hands, and Callisto turned, in order to pass through the Porta del Popolo to his domestic hearth. Brother Martin pulled the bell at the cloister-door, and immediately disappeared into the interior of the building. He sought out his cell, and seated himself upon an old, hard wooden chair, — except a pair of stools, the only seat which the poor little room contained. It stood before the window. Through this window he looked out upon the height rising close before it, steep and barren, only set here and there with scanty bushes, among which a flock of goats sought out a meager sustenance. The brow of the hill was crowned with an artistically constructed wall-work; the last remnant of some magnificent building which once arose here in the luxurious gardens of Sallust, formerly covering these heights.

Half-way up stood a picture of the Madonna, above some crumbling stone steps; upon the lowest lay, sleeping, a ragged youth, the shepherd of the goats.

Martin lifted his eyes to the picture of the Madonna.

"Poor woman," he thought, "why hast thou the countenance of a sufferer? Because the world and the time have killed your Son? Because they have done violence to his mind and his soul, that both may be stifled, and die? Is it then true what this Roman says, that the world will turn its back upon all this strange miracle-work, with which as an armor they have clothed the dead heroes? Will the world reduce to ruins their pictures and your own? The youth there sleeping at your feet — will he, when he has become a man, lift up a stone and hurl it at your head as thanks for the shade you have expended upon him to-day? Is mankind on the point of awaking as if out of a sleep, and ridiculing the dreams it had, and destroying the pictures? Will one, at some future time, pass through our forests and find no more the pious shrine of the saints at the crossroads, around which, as to-day, some poor maid with a care-heavy heart places a wreath of oak-leaves, or entwines the golden broom?

"Will no cross longer mark the still, cool graves of our dead? When one passes through a peaceful village in a green meadow-vale, will he there ask, 'What ugly, dark heap of ruins is that in the midst of your village?' And will one receive the answer: 'Those are the ruins of a church, as our fathers called it. They assembled there to honor their God, but they had a priest as servant of the altar in this house of God who told them so many unreasonable and incredible things about their God, who so long threatened them with his wrath, and so long drove bargains with his favors, that they began to laugh at him, and resolved to bother themselves no more about God, but only about their daily labor'! Will it come to that? Will the lean kine thus consume the fat, the curate beat the vicar, and the common people the curate? Will the last Pope with his cardinals, a little heap of feeble diminutive old men, sit upon one of these seven hills, like Pope Benedict upon Peniscola, hurling upon the world, which has forgotten them, excommunication which no more excites them? Cruel thought! The world without Christ! A world which casts its glance only upon the ground, upon the earth at their feet upon which they labor, no more forward into the infinity of their future; no more upward into heaven! Men nothing but leaves upon great trees appointed to fall off to make fresh place for the new, which come only to fall away and to molder; the world a great heap of refuse! A thus wider, buzzing child's play, eternal, eternal in cruel monotony!"

Brother Martin had supported his head upon his arm resting before him on the widow-seat. He now let his eye sweep above to the overhanging mountain-cliff, which suddenly took on a wonderfully rosy glow, and looked up to the sky glowing in most magnificent purple from the reflection of the evening light.

"*Ecce signum omnipotentis Dei!*" he continued, in his silent monologue. "Dost thou come to say to me that I am a fool? That thou canst not have kindled this immeasurably wonderful sunlight in order to lighten up the childishness of an aimless perpetual motion? and that thy Word, thy Spirit will flame further through the ages than this beautiful, indestructible globe of the sun? That I am a fool, with my oppressed, downcast heart, if I suppose the dark funeral company which buried the Master could take from mankind their eternal need, the faith, if I see the crosses destroyed, the churches of our German villages lying in ruins, the former voices silent in the towers of our cathedrals, the last monk speedily starving in some rocky desert? Is it a crime in you, a sinful despair? Lord, forgive me; I see indeed thousands, hundreds of thousands of honorable men in whose inner being the crosses are already broken, the churches already lie in ruins, no tone of a bell calls any more to faithful meditation ——

"And still, it cannot,— cannot be! This Roman is right. Only the word must be found,— a word of new life! Whence is it to be taken? Where is it to be found? What did that wonderful Master Raffaelle Santi say — he has made himself free and found beauty — I should, through freedom, find truth? Freedom? Shall the living word preach liberty — liberty from that funeral company? Shall it say, 'We shall each go his own way to Christ, and walk without you to God?'

"Is that enough? No. The black company has stirred up the intellect and the reason, and thus raised men in revolt against God. What quiets the disturbance must come from the soul. From the soul, the word that saves us! From the soul ——"

Poor Brother Martin! if you should come to these Romans with your German soul would they understand you?

He thought awhile; then, rising, he said: —

"And if not, what difference would that make? The German understands the word of the soul; and if the Romans do not, so may every people become saved in their own way. It is better that they go different ways, each guided by his own indwelling nature, than that one lead another astray, and draw him into the abyss."

He sprang up as if revived. With both hands he stroked his thin face, his luminous eyes, and concluded his soliloquy with these words: —

"And now let us go down to these monks below."

CHAPTER X.

GOSSIP OF AN "ARTISTA."

WHILE the German monk and Callisto walked along the street in such an earnest interchange of thought, Irmgard had gone back alone to the little house in which she, with her uncle, upon the recommendation of Donna Ottavia, had taken up her abode with the widow of a worker in marble and her son. As said before, the house lay upon the then still desolate Quirinal, at whose western foot arose the palace of the Colonna, the oldest of the still-standing palaces of Rome; while upon the height above, stretching to the ruins of the Baths of Constantine, extended the garden of the palace. The whole square above was still, and deserted by men. On an old wall of the baths reclined the little house of the widow; it was surrounded by a garden, in which the woman raised cabbage and artichokes, and a hedge of a prickly shrub fenced it around. In the corner of the garden, in a thicket of shrubbery, stood a plane tree and a mulberry tree in a group together; under them, a stone table; a piece of a marble frieze out of those old baths served as a seat behind it. Irmgard, when she came home and had looked after her uncle, seated herself there, and looked with her careworn glance over the city, which now, flooded with the bright glow of the sun, she could look down upon from this height. It was the sunny splendor of the Hesperides, which lay lighting up in her presence the Eternal City. She saw the cupolas and the monuments of Rome before her. A gentle breeze blew a coolness through the shady nook under the trees in which she sat hidden. This breeze, which drew so gently through the leaves of the laurel bush near her, bore to her the fragrance of blooming oranges from the gardens of the Colonna. Irmgard was young; she was strong and healthy; every breath in this pure air should have streamed through her with a feeling of a full, joy-creating life-force.

STATUE OF RAPHAEL.

And still — she sat drawn together as if bound around with the weight of pain. She bore the blame of Egino's misfortune. She knew not how to live longer without the hope to save him, with the consciousness that she had led him into destruction.

She felt herself lacerated, consumed, dying under this thought.

She was where she found herself surrounded with everything to live for, everything for a happy, physical being, and a thought killed her.

Nevermore except through pain does man perceive that he is entirely soul, — entirely mental life, — entirely a world of thought and feeling; that his physical being is nothing but the fragile glass vessel which contains his real self. Pain is the great revelation of immortality.

Pain is the great revelation which speaks to us out of the glowing thorn bush of our own inner self, and for which we need no testimony, no miracles.

While Brother Martin and Callisto talked of faith and of a new foundation for the ethics of the future, Irmgard received through pain the lesson which develops man into moral perfection here, and forms him for its reception in eternity.

Irmgard sat thus a long, long time. Through the open window of his room she observed Uncle Kraps; he had no more the pleasure of looking out upon the world through panes of glass, for the widow's little house did not have any: if one would look out, he must have the wooden shutter opened just as at home in Germany. Uncle Kraps had become reconciled to this, as to many other things. He had become reconciled to seeing his dreams of titles, and robes of state, and extraordinary distinction disappear; he had become reconciled to having men laugh at him here, just as they did at home in Ulm, whenever he let himself be seen; he had even become reconciled to the goat's flesh and the bitter, roasted bird of the Campagna set before him by his landlady; for all these things he had a solace, and it was the sweet, golden drink of Orvieto.

Uncle Kraps was on his way to that philosophy which forgoes to master things mentally by the use of dialectics, and confines itself to becoming their master through the frame of mind; a philosophy so much the wiser when it allows itself to have and to create more easily this temper than the mind or the thoughts. Uncle Kraps had brought to himself one, two, three, four flasks of Orvieto wine, and also of others, — of Rocca di Papa, of Marino, of every different sort, "*Dei piu megliori castelli*,"— and the frame of mind was there.

Irmgard had in the last days forgotten to guard her uncle, and his progress in the art of getting the better of life by tonic incitation of this frame of mind had escaped her; she did not see with what beautiful results his practice of this art of overcoming the world had been crowned, for Uncle Kraps was a silent nature. His voice at home had had something bleating about it; and if in the evening hour she perceived something of stammering, it was hard to recognize this alteration, because it had been brought about by a peculiarly gentle transition. So about Uncle Kraps there was no anxiety to be entertained; he was, on the contrary, an element of gayety in the house of the widow. Beppo, her son, the marble-workman, broke out into a laugh every time the remarkable man opened his mouth to utter one of those Italian words which belonged to his rather scanty vocabulary, and which he brought forth so comically and accented so falsely.

But what could cause the grief of the young German maiden, who was evidently under the pressure of some suffering of the soul, who no more ate or drank, who seemed to ramble restlessly around?

Thus questioned the kindly widow, Signora Giulietta, and Beppo, her laughter-loving son; in whose countenance the laughter always died out, and who always threw back his dark head to shake from his brow the raven locks when he espied Irmgard.

They had no answer for this question, and still it appeared to occupy them more and more every day — at least Beppo, who for some time came home more regularly of an evening, and much earlier from his work at the studio of his master, a sculptor, or from the excavations under the guidance of Raphael, with whom he also worked.

Beppo was a stonecutter, and therefore called himself an "artista," and was, in his way, a cultivated young man. They are all the product of the ancient life-culture, these happy sons of Ausonia; to each one of them has been handed down a greater or less share of the ancestral heritage.

Beppo had a pair of deep black eyes, and these always glowed more than usual when they lay upon Irmgard. Irmgard, truly, had observed it; she had, therefore, always been monosyllabic and quiet when the young man was there, and Beppo was therefore shy, going about her as about a mystery.

"She has a love-sorrow, the Giovinetta; she has left her heart behind her in her land," said the widow, when she was alone with her son, and he began about the strangers.

"No, no; I'll wager it isn't so," then asserted Beppo. "When they came to rent these two rooms, these remarkable people, the maiden was well and gay, and now she is no longer so. Her trouble lies in Rome. Ask her about it, mother."

"As if I hadn't done it!" answered Frau Giulietta, shrugging her shoulders.

"And what has she replied?"

"That she is not well."

"Not well! And yet she is on her feet the whole day; still she is up on the Aventine more than in her room."

"On the Aventine?" said Frau Giulietta. "And how do you know that? Have you slyly followed her?"

"I know it," replied Beppo, coloring slightly; "we have been working there under Santa Sabina, in the old vaults. I know that if her grief lies in Rome, it lies on the Aventine."

"*Ecco, ecco!*" exclaimed Frau Giulietta; "only do not give yourself anxiety about it."

Beppo turned and went out into the little garden, and saw Irmgard sitting under the trees in the shady corner.

He stood and looked over at her, which he could do without restraint; for she sat motionless, her glance fixed upon the ground, so lost in thought that if she had looked up, she would not have perceived that she was observed by him.

Beppo finally took courage and went to her.

He stationed himself near her; with hands behind him he reclined with his back against a plane tree, and said: —

"It is fine up here in the fresh air, Signorina. Do you not find it so? When the evening breeze comes hither from the sea, it is always so mild and refreshing; one breathes with redoubled joy when he has crept around all day in the dark under-world, like a blind mole."

"And in what under-world have you crept around, Beppo?" asked Irmgard, raising her glance, but inattentive, and not looking at the young man.

"I have assisted at the excavations," continued Beppo; "there are twenty artists and workmen of us — besides, Master Raffaelle Santi comes from time to time; the Holy Father has intrusted to him the entire oversight. We rummage around in old, obstructed vaults, dark chambers, and lofty passages. You would not believe what a frightful under-world it often is; sometimes it is broader, grander, higher than in the largest palaces here above; baths, they call them then. We shovel and dig by torchlight, like a troup of demons. You should see it, Signorina; it is indeed a strange sight in the damp, moldy vaults, where the water often drops from the walls, and toads or salamanders glide or hop over the floor, when the unaccustomed beam of light falls upon them——"

"And why do you do it?" said Irmgard, interrupting him. "Do you seek for treasures?"

"Now, we do certainly seek for treasures," exclaimed Beppo, smiling, — "for treasures of every kind; of course, those of the best kind, such as gold and jewels, we do not find."

"What, then, do you find?"

"Busts, coins, vases, statues, sarcophagi—ah! what all do we not find! Under the rubbish of Rome, you must know, lies a world of precious relics; the entire possessions of ancient times, as much as has not been destroyed. It is like a house that has been overthrown by an earthquake. We find works of art in marble and bronze, tablets with inscriptions, stones with reliefs; in the Baths of Titus we have found remnants of wall paintings. I tell you no disagreeable and trying labor is better rewarded than ours!"

"And have you carried on such work to-day, Beppo?" asked Irmgard.

"Of course, even to-day."

"And have you found much?"

"Ah! no, about nothing," replied Beppo; "and so we have come away tired and disappointed, and must hope to have better luck to-morrow. It is the fate we often have, to see that others have already been there long before us, and have hunted and rummaged through everything; not, indeed, for the sake of the art things, but for treasures. For in olden times people cared very little for art; they were in this respect great barbarians, our forefathers, Signorina. Scarcely twenty years have flown by since they began to carry on excavations and searching for artistic things. In the Catacombs, indeed — have you ever heard of the Catacombs, Signorina?"

Irmgard, who for a long time had no longer followed Beppo's chat, only shook her head gently.

"You have never heard of them? Oh! you must see them; you must let me take you there," exclaimed Beppo, eagerly. "You can have no idea of this world of death and of horror. Long, long labyrinthian passages, narrow and high, hewn out of the tufa and clay in the dark earth; also little halls, chapels; and, right and left in the walls, one above another, the *loculi*, or grave-niches, wherein the bodies of the dead have been placed,—the dead and slain Christians and martyrs. I tell you, it is a world full of the horror and dread of death, and therein have the poor Christians hidden themselves, and have celebrated the holy sacraments in secret stillness and dread of the persecutors, who have often broken in upon them even there; and then they have poured out in streams the blood of the poor flock of God, and have then shoved the bodies right and left immediately into the wall-niches and put before them a stone to close them. Ah! you must see it, Signorina. You cannot otherwise understand how yet since then the beloved God has been so gracious to his church, and how great and powerful it now is. I went for the first time into the Catacombs—it was exactly ten years ago; and my father, who was a very pious man, Signorina, very God-fearing, and only too good to the poor and to the monks, who did not then neglect our house—now, of course, since the mother is poor and feeble, you see them give us a call less frequently—but what was I going to say? My father had taken me with him just ten years ago, and on that day it was that Madame Lucretia went in procession to Ferrara as a bride. When I came out of the dark depths, where once the poor persecuted martyrs, the poor Christian lambs fleeing before heathen wolves, hid themselves in their distress, and now slept in this world of the dead extending for miles, I was quite wretched and sick at heart from all this. My limbs trembled with cold, and my teeth chattered. But in the bright sun shining without, on that bright, warm winter day, and in the midst of the people that we saw streaming to the Corso, and that bore us with them thither, and when my eyes soon fell upon the finest festal procession which the world has ever seen, then I was quickly healed! I was an urchin, Signorina, hardly fourteen years old, and one that forgot nothing soon! But the procession, which I have never forgotten and shall never forget, such a magnificent and glorious thing it was! Just over the Catacombs, in which we had been with the dead martyrs, it was passing along; the Holy Father, and his daughter, and his son, Don Cesare, and the sons of the Duke of Ferrara, and the cardinals; the hollow ground must have echoed with the tread of their proud steeds, and the joyful shouts of the people must have penetrated even to the quiet *loculi* of the poor saints. Oh! you should have seen it! Such a sight one beholds but once in a lifetime, and only in Rome. The Holy Father gave them his attendance as far as the Porta del Popolo, Don Cesare to the Ponte Molle, and the nineteen cardinals to the Prima Porta and farther. Not to be overlooked was the number of pages, of body-guards, of nobility, of high officials; and inestimable was the magnificence of the costumes of scarlet and gold, and of silk entirely hidden by embroidery of gold and adornments of precious stones. Don Cesare wore a splendid coat-of-mail held together by a golden girdle; the saddle cover of his powerful war-charger alone was valued at ten thousand ducats. Madame Lucretia, however, wore a close-fitting dress of crimson silk with a *shernia* over it of golden tissue, with broad, flowing sleeves, and bordered with ermine. Covering her head, with its flowing golden hair, was a hat also of crimson silk with a proudly dangling plume, and upon the left side hung a string of pearls down to her ear; she was so beautiful, Madame Lucretia! A band of musicians in costly robes marched before her, but the cries of the people sounded above their tune. And how great the procession was you will be able to form an idea, Signorina, if I tell you that the number of horses and mules which the Holy Father gave away with his daughter might carry no less than a thousand; there were two hundred wagons; and of the cardinals who gave her escort, each had two hundred nobles, halberdiers, pages and servants in his retinue. Oh! you should have seen it. My young heart rejoiced in me over all the glittering magnificence, and my pious father, who stood behind me, laid his hand upon my shoulder and said: 'You see now to-day, my son, how God is with his holy church; out of the darkness of the Catacombs and the misery of martyrdom, he has led it to the highest worldly glory, as it is said in the book of Judges, "I have saved you from the hand of the Egyptians, and from every hand which oppresses you, and have given to you your land."'"

Beppo was obliged to take breath, he had fallen into such eagerness in his narration, accompanied by the most animated pantomime.

"You are right, Beppo," answered Irmgard, with a painful twitching of the mouth. "He has lifted it very high. Still, there are always martyrs who languish in the Catacombs, as you call them."

"Martyrs?"

"Well, yes. Has not the Inquisition dungeons?"

"Ah!" exclaimed Beppo, "but those who languish therein are not martyrs, but heretics!"

"Of course; but, in any case, their lot is to be pitied."

"Holy Mother!" exclaimed Beppo, "the lot of heretics to be pitied? But if men did not judge them what would our lot be? Would not God seek us out with all the plagues of the land of Egypt, with famine, and pestilence, and earthquakes, if we were remiss in defending his honor, and did not take vengeance with the edge of the sword upon those who sin against him? I pray you, Signorina, what would become of us?"

"You are right, good Beppo; your God has need of vengeance. And that he may obtain it, he has here upon earth the judgment of heretics, and there beyond the eternally flaming woodpile of hell."

Beppo looked at her in astonishment, his eyes dilated. Did the maiden speak so impiously in earnest? He was going to answer her, when she continued: —

"And so is the whole life such a world: down in the depths of dark labyrinths for the poor, the bondsmen, the outcasts; and up yonder above, the immense festal procession of the great and powerful!"

CHAPTER XI.

WHO KNOWS?

HILE Irmgard thus listened to the chatter of Beppo, and in her grief looked upon the world as divided by fate into two halves, one dark, subterranean, for the poor care-burdened ones, and one bright, sunny upper world for those born to privileges, she was not aware that among this privileged class, in the proud occupant of a princely castle, she had a sister in pain. Upon the high-towering balcony of the Savelli house, which presented a view of the Eternal City, and seemed lording over it, sat Corradina, as isolated, as full of care, as Irmgard in her poor little garden.

And if Irmgard, from pain at Egino's fate, from anxiety about him yet, felt upon her heart the pressure of bitter reproof made by her conscience — Corradina, besides her anxiety for the missing one, felt the pressure of uneasiness about herself, her own fate!

The pain of the child of princes was no less than that of the poor maiden from the people.

She sat upon the balcony near the little worktable; upon it lay a little book with parchment leaves closely filled with writing, bound in a gracefully wrought cover of shining metal. She had just been reading in it; the finger-tips of her right hand still lay upon the lower edge, to hold it open. But she was looking beyond the leaves, away; what she had read must have occupied her mind profoundly and intensely.

As if arousing herself from thought, she then closed the book and pushed it from her.

"If there could a man be found," she whispered, sighing deeply, — "a man for this book! They seek the 'philosopher's stone,' and here, here it is, the stone for a philosopher; but where is the philosopher for it? Where is the slinger powerful enough to hurl this stone at the head of the Goliath? Where is the hand strong enough to bear this formidable weapon forged by my ancestor? Shall it never be of further service than to pour anger into the soul of a young maiden, and through wrath give her strength?

"Strength, strength! Ah, how I need it! And how long will that which is in me suffice, hold out, to keep me upright?"

These words, which came gently and as if complainingly over the lips of Corradina, were to-day uttered by her for the first time; and the feeling which they expressed had a few days since come over her soul for the first time.

Something like a defiant pride, a lofty self-consciousness, as well as the union of her fancy with forms of the past, had up to this time kept this thought far from her. She could not have grown faint-hearted, if she had said to herself that the men and women whose blood coursed in her had stood in such infinitely greater and more difficult struggles.

To-day such considerations had no more for her the tempering effect that they formerly had.

The wrestling with personal cares, the anxiety seizing immediately upon her heart, lay upon her too heavily to be removed from her by forms of the remote past, let her fancy occupy itself ever so much with them, let them draw ever so near her. What were all the lofty, deceased ancestors to the living, breathing form so near her of a young man who, for her sake, with such foolhardy fearlessness, had rushed into a danger before he had even taken a moment of time to reflect upon the greatness of this danger.

She thought of the host of men who, enticed by her wealth or her beauty, had sued for her favor. While over all these she curled her lips with an expression of contempt, she felt a kind of pride in this German, whom she looked upon as a countryman; a kind of pride in his preference, which had manifested itself so chivalrously.

Egino von Ortenburg stood no nearer her heart than any other man. Such a sudden surrender would have been impossible to this heart. If she had seen him for the first time in an assembly among other men, her glance would have glided indifferently over him. But his warmth, his ardor for thoughts which lay now in her own soul, had influenced in her a feeling of sisterhood for him,—a feeling of stronger, more sacrificing friendship; and now, when his actions had wrought upon her fancy, when his condition had awakened all her anxiously concerned womanly sympathy, she thought more of him than of any other man on earth.

With an infinite relief she had found out from Livio that the monks over there had not delivered Egino to her relatives. She had had Father Eustachius brought over to her, and sought to obtain from him information about Egino's further fate. Eustachius had been silent about it; he had been unwilling or unable to tell her anything more than that, in the first place, nothing could be undertaken against Egino, because he was too severely wounded. He had also tried in his severe, but at the bottom of his heart not hard and loveless way, to console and quiet Corradina. She placed her hopes in Eustachius; had he not from the first shown himself remarkably mild and indulgent towards Egino? If he had not had his monkish notions, there would have been something free and humane in him.

Still, Eustachio's words did not reach so far in appeasing Corradina as to induce in her a passive inactivity. She tortured her brains with plans and thoughts of helping the prisoner, of rescuing him. Of all her servants she could trust no one — she knew that. She thought of drawing into her confidence Livio's wife, Cornelia Savelli. Was it not possible the latter would find a satisfaction in getting away the German knight from the hatred of her husband, to play upon him a stroke of revenge? Corradina knew Cornelia too well not to find this probable; but if she spoke to this Cornelia of the German, she knew that Cornelia would believe in her love for the German, and in her mind she saw already the eyes of this frivolous woman resting mockingly upon her. Corradina's pride revolted at this idea most violently, and thus there was wanting to her the courage for such a resolution.

With gold and with promises of greater gain to herself she had sought to bribe her body-servant, whom she knew the duke and Livio had already bribed. She had thereupon received the most beautiful promises in return. And, indeed, the woman had at least been able to bring her news, which Corradina was obliged to receive as true.

Teresa was even now stepping through the window-casement out on the balcony, with a face as if she had something important to communicate.

"What news do you bring, Teresa? what have you found out?" asked Corradina, in excitement, "good or bad?"

"Eh," replied the maid, "who knows! I have found out that Count Livio, with his servant Sor Antonio, has gone down into the vaults and cellar-rooms under us, and that they have stayed there a long time."

"Ah!" said Corradina, "that clearly enough betokens to me the worst; for what can Count Livio wish except to look around in the vaults and deserted places for a dungeon for the unhappy German? Perhaps he has recovered, and the monks show themselves ready to deliver him up?"

Teresa shook her head.

"Possibly, possibly," she said; "but I do not believe that the monks will give him up. He is said to be a heretic, Fra Alessio has told me in confidence, and then they dare not give him up; the heretics belong to their order, Madame."

"But what do you think, Teresa, could otherwise have impelled Livio to go down there?"

Teresa lowered her voice to a whisper.

"The vaults below are adjacent to the vaults under the cloister, where the prisons are."

"They are adjacent? But they are still separated by thick walls?"

Teresa shrugged her shoulders.

"*Chi lo sa?* Who knows?" she replied, "whether Count Livio will find the walls separating them so thick as to hinder his going through, in case he wills to do it!"

Corradina, whose countenance had gradually grown paler, was silent awhile. Then she said:—

"But how could it help him to force his way through, Teresa? You have assured me of having found out from Fra Alessio that Count Egino does not lie imprisoned in the lowest dungeons, but in a cell higher up, and that the Padre Infirmario is taking good care of him?"

"So it is,—so it is; Fra Alessio said so," put in Teresa; "but can I know whether or not Fra Alessio is telling the truth? And whether, when perhaps the German is cured, they will not bring him into the worse dungeons, perhaps even into the Chapel of the Immured? Do they tell us the truth in such things?"

"You are right," responded Corradina, with trembling lips, and feeling her anxiety inexpressibly increased.

"And then," added Teresa, "I must confess to you that yesterday, also, I saw this Fra Alessio in a private conversation with Sor Antonio over there in the cloister-garden. I can overlook the cloister-garden from the window of my room up there. So I saw them; they sat under the olive tree of the Holy Dominicus and conversed quite heatedly together. Do we know now whether Alessio tells what comes from himself, or what has been put in his mouth by Sor Antonio?"

"Do you believe that, Teresa?"

Teresa shrugged her shoulders.

"That we know as good as nothing?"

"If it were not that what Alessio said is also the most probable, I would think so."

"And Eustachius has also led me to suppose the same," said Corradina.

Teresa nodded; and since she knew nothing further to communicate, she left to find out as much as possible in secrecy what Livio was doing in the lower regions of the castle. She left Corradina in greater pain and uneasiness. The young woman tortured her brain with thoughts and plans of saving Egino, and among them all was no one which held even the remotest hope of success.

After awhile she put both hands before her face, and then made a movement with these hands as if to motion something away, as if to ward off a picture of fancy, and at the same time as if a light shudder passed through her frame.

"Away with it, away!" she whispered. "Why does this horrible form thrust itself before me? In truth, through him, through him it would be possible — through this Cardinal Riario! He would render aid; but could I sink so low? Would Egino himself wish me to humiliate myself so deeply for his sake?"

"And still — still, why am I not educated to such humility, such dovelike softness? Upon this road might lie rescue for myself and the German. If I could open my lips before Riario and reveal my heart to Egino, I would be happy. With the rescued one I could flee into a better, nobler, a peaceful world; before me would lie a future, — a life with hopes, with pictures of future happiness in it! And now, — now lies before me darkness and dread of the coming day and what it may bring!

"But I cannot do otherwise! I cannot degrade myself, and if I could, I could not do it to such an extent as to forget I had degraded myself, and then I must hate myself an account of it.

"So the fate must be borne until it pleases God to avert it, and to have mercy upon a soul which is, as yet, the way he created it — and on this account very, very unhappy!"

CHAPTER XII.

A WAY AND A HOPE.

IT was on the next day. Irmgard, as if tired out, as if despairing in her search, had spent the morning at home, and had assisted Frau Giulietta in her little garden, tearing out dry pease, and placing them upon the wall of the house to finish drying them. While doing this she had perceived much noise and disturbance, which must prevail over in the gardens and courts of Colonna Palace. There came to them only a muffled sound; the walls were high; the palace lay still rather far down below them, on the square of the Church of the Holy Apostles. But still they perceived that something unusual must be going on there, and Frau Giulietta did not delay in telling Irmgard the cause of it. She was even initiated into all that happened over there; she and her son Beppo, indeed, belonged to the clients of this powerful house, and the chief servant over there was Frau Giulietta's special friend and patron, who, when he was passing her house and saw her, never failed to stop awhile and have a little chat, now over this, now over that.

"That they are somewhat in excitement over there is no wonder," said Frau Giulietta; "for in the night, you must know, cara Irmgarda, they have received a guest, a very eminent and noble guest, who has ridden in with many lords and servants. It is the Duke of Ferrara, Lord Alfonso von Este, the husband of the beautiful Madame Lucretia, if you have ever heard of her."

"Oh, yes! Beppo, your son, has told me about her. And has the duke brought with him this Madame Lucretia?"

"Oh! not that," answered Frau Giulietta; "the duke has not made the journey hither for feasting and pleasures, but only that our Holy Father may absolve him from excommunication. The Holy Father has put him under ban, and that was right; for the duke made an alliance with the French king, and has thus carried on war with the Holy Father and his ally, the republic of Venice; then, however, the King of France made peace with the Holy Father. You can have Beppo tell you about it, as he knows everything as it took place; he understands everything that happens of the nature of war. In this respect he is at home like a Swiss race-runner, or a German summoner; and if he did not have his poor mother, who is alone in the world, and but for him without help, he would certainly have run away long ago in full armor to become a soldier. As it is, however, he must indeed remain at home, and be an honorable laborer, which supports one, — in a kind of a way, you know, — for the marble-work doesn't pay much, in truth. But the wages in the excavations are good, and they must be; for if they were not good, you understand, Irmgarda, it would be a bad thing, with all the beautiful, costly things they find. Who would otherwise answer for it that the people would not then make themselves even for what they believe themselves to have earned by their sour toil? Human nature is weak, and one could not look after the fingers of each one; and so they must seek out honorable and reliable people for the purpose, and reward the labor respectably, or else respectable people will not come to them. But to come back to the Duke of Ferrara, I was telling you that he, deserted by his king, could not alone offer resistance to the Holy Father,—for the Holy Father is a mighty master of war, before whom stronger ones have already humbled themselves; and that, in fact, the duke wished also to do, but the Holy Father would know nothing about it, and treated his embassadors in such a manner that they sprang out of the window through fright. Now, you must know, however, that the Holy Father has a very illustrious and celebrated commander, and that is Lord Fabricio Colonna, who once, some years since, in a battle, or in a conquered city,—I believe it was Ravenna; Beppo would know,—fell into Duke Alfonso's hands, and was conducted to Ferrara, and there was treated so lovingly by the duke that they become quite intimate friends. To Lord Fabricio, then, Duke Alfonso finally turned, and the former has secured for him now peace and the deliverance from excommunication by the Holy Father; and so the duke has come, and there will be great splendor over there. There are such powerful and rich lords together that there are no more like them in Rome,—and, indeed, not in the world."

Frau Giulietta began now to chatter about their patrons, the Colonna, the Lord Marc Antony, the son-in-law of the Holy Father, and Prospero, and the wild Pompeo, who would so gladly have been a soldier, and whom they had brought by force under the priestly tonsure, and finally of Fabricio, again, the commander of Pope Julius II.

Irmgard had long been listening with only half an ear, when she, looking up, saw Brother Martin coming, walking slowly through the garden. He nodded to Frau Giulietta; he gave Irmgard his hand, and said that he only came to exchange greetings and to look after her. He was carrying a heavy book under his arm, which Irmgard took from him, to lay it upon the table under the shady cluster of trees, whither she led him, in order that he might rest himself and wipe away the sweat standing in bright beads upon his brow.

Brother Martin was silent and absent-minded; he was just from an hour of instruction which he was accustomed to take in the forenoon from a learned rabbi named Elias Levita, in order to learn the Hebrew language. Alas! the hours did not continue to be devoted merely to the suffixes and prefixes; it came also to disputations between the learned young monk and the wise old rabbi, and in these the rabbi was not always to be beaten, and proved fallacious; and today, especially, had he vexed Brother Martin with the assertion that there could exist a thoroughly religious people living within the narrow limits of moral law, entirely without dogmas, and that such a people the Jews were. They had, he said, no creed except that of the one God and of the coming of the Messiah.

This contention still echoed in him to such an extent that he let fall a few words of it in presence of Irmgard. Irmgard became silent thereupon; then, after a pause, lifting her eyes to him, she said:—

"Give me one piece of information, Brother Martin — will you?"

"And what?"

"Tell me, in what do people believe who believe nothing?"

Brother Martin smiled.

"That seems a childish question, and yet there lies in it profound wisdom; the feeling that to human nature faith is an inextinguishable need! What do they believe? You would not understand me, Irmgard, if I were to speak to you of their ideas; it is, indeed, finely and enchantingly thought out, and for subtle minds like a pleasure garden, in which to rove about and lose themselves to their hearts' delight. But for a man who thinks and cares for his sinful nature, how he is to become justified before God, it does not quicken the soul."

Irmgard looked meditatively before her. Then she asked: —

"And what do you think we should believe of justification when we feel that we are unworthy of pardon, and still do not believe that we can atone for what has happened through rosaries and fasts?"

"Does that also torment you?" asked Brother Martin, looking at her in astonishment.

"It also torments me, for I bear a sin upon me. And you see it has become clear to me that I cannot through works, through a whole sea of good works, wash it away from me. Good works do not make good. This Rome is built of them, and they rise in churches and cupolas in all magnificence even to the heavens. Men, however, are not good therein! Therefore must sin be atoned for through something else, and I am of the opinion it is only through penitence, through sorrow. Dare I say it? I am of the opinion Christ did not come to arm God's wrath against unhappy mankind by a bit of death, which could not fall heavily upon him, for it was still only in appearance and blinding the people, who found him again, after three days, alive and well. I am of the opinion that Christ came as an embodiment of pain, as pain clothed with form, to show us that the saviour, the redeemer, the mediator, is pain."

Brother Martin looked at her with an earnest countenance, and almost becoming angry.

"Is all the world, even you also, running out of the school of faith? Does it lie in the air? Is it a contagious fever? A pestilence and an illness? Pain? Well, yes; the pain of penitence is the saving bath of the soul. But above the pain is something higher, to which the soul must force itself as to the high-hanging jewel with which to purchase its pardon; otherwise the pain avails nothing. That is the action."

"Action?"

"Yes; the action of inner surrender to Christ in fructifying love, out of which then, as out of a freely gushing fountain, follows the impulse to works of love for our fellow-men; yes, even for the unknowing animal, that is also a creature of God."

"You are right, truly," replied Irmgard, thoughtfully. "What I said was the feeling of a woman who feels herself weak and helpless for the deed of love for the brother on whom alone she can think, whom she would most willingly help."

"I understand it, Irmgard," responded Brother Martin, seizing her hand with emotion. "I will also only scold you because you lose so easily faith in the protection of God, and the help of the Providence watching over us all."

"Your God is so hard," she said. "He is not good, your God; if he had been good, he would never have created men. What a God who makes for himself men, and then such a thing as hell for them! A good man cannot be the inventor of a horrible rack of torture. A good God would not do that which leads him to invent something still horribly worse! Tell me now yourself, would you procure for yourself three little dogs, if you knew two of them must be thrown into the water and pitifully drowned? Would a good God create for himself men, when he knows that two thirds of them must be thrown in the fire and consumed?"

Brother Martin was silent. He felt himself in presence of the young maiden still more helpless than in the presence of the wise rabbi; he felt profoundly such simple reproaches against the weakness of the theological armor with which he had gone forth equipped into the world.

He thereupon confined himself to reviving her hope with mild exhortation. The best consolation he left her was something definite about Egino's fate, which he was able to communicate to her before he left. He had heard through an order-brother that Egino was still in Santa Sabina, and that he would probably be guarded in a prison cell in the broad vaults and rock-hewn chambers under the cloister. The order-brother had not been willing to name to Brother Martin the source of this information, but assured him it was reliable.

There lay at least the satisfaction for Irmgard of knowing that the worst of her fears had not yet been realized,—that Egino had not yet been put to death by the wicked men in whose power he had fallen.

When Martin was gone, Irmgard turned to the house to spread the table for Uncle Kraps in the great cool chamber which they both occupied, and in which Irmgard also slept, while her uncle found lodging for the night in a little adjacent room.

After eating, Uncle Kraps rested, as was his custom of old, and Irmgard betook herself, with some work, again into the garden to the seat in the shady thicket whither she had previously led Brother Martin. There she reflected over Brother Martin's words, over his words about the action standing above the pain; and as it was with her now about the heart, she could not come to any clearer or stronger feeling about the inner act of surrender to God and to his love. She must be with all her thoughts occupied with the deed to which all her being urged her,— the deed of help, of rescue. And ah! it was so impossible to her, so past finding out — how well may that be said, the higher is the deed; but how inconsolable was it for him who had no hands, no arms, to do anything?

Then came Beppo, stepping into the little garden through the opening in the hedge. Irmgard heard him talking with his mother; he wished something more to eat. While Giulietta went to warm him some food he came to Irmgard.

"You, Sor Beppo?" she said. "You come home to-day at an unusual hour — in the afternoon instead of in the evening!"

"That's so," replied Beppo; "but I come as tired on such a hot day as if I came in the evening; besides, I am as hungry as the wolf that suckled Romulus and Remus, and must have had much to do to still a pair of such wild youngsters. We have worked hard yesterday and this morning; but we have been obliged to give up the work; it didn't pay."

"And where were you then?"

"On the Aventine."

"On the Aventine?"

"Yes, Signorina Irmgarda, right there. Master Raffaelle Santi was intent upon uncovering there the passages to the old burial-places of the Latin kings. But we have found nothing of them, and the work has been left off; we will be to-morrow on Monte Celio."

"And where were you on the Aventine?" questioned Irmgard.

"We have been at the foot of the rock-wall which goes down against Via Salara and the Marmorata. There is an old arch forming a gate into the rock. In the room behind it a merchant of the Campagna has had his wine-cellars, which are now empty; but at the end of the room a passage leads farther into the rock, which is obstructed, and we have cleaned out the rubbish, and have thus reached a higher-lying vault. The vault had been broken through above, and a mound of rubbish lay under it; when one climbed up on this he could reach with his hands the rim of the opening high above him. I forced myself up into the room above, and what did I find? That everything had been known and searched through long ago! In one corner of the upper room, into which I had forced my way, was even an old, rusty, iron-grated door, which must lead into the vaults and dungeons under Santa Sabina, and under the cloister in which the heretics are confined."

"Into the dungeons under the Dominican cloister?" said Irmgard, growing pale, and speaking half-aloud with a trembling voice.

"Just so," added Beppo.

Irmgard looked at him awhile, as if lost in thought. Then, while a slight flush mantled her cheek, and gasping deeply, she said:—

"Listen, Sor Beppo; I am for one time a curious woman, and the desire torments me to see once —— "

"What do you wish to see, Signorina?"

"These prisons,— the heretics, who languish in the cloisters under Santa Sabina."

"And are you not afraid of the sight?"

"Not in the least."

Beppo clapped his hands together in astonishment. "Demonio!" he said, "you, a girl, have more courage than I."

"Possibly! Would you also not have the courage to conduct me thither to where you were to-day — to that grated door of which you speak?"

"Holy Mother of God! you would not, in fact —— "

"In fact, Beppo, I should like once to reach it."

"Impossible, impossible! And if the monks should find you there, the watchmen —— "

"It must be in the night, when the guards and monks sleep the sleep of the righteous."

"But the door is locked," exclaimed Beppo; "to force one's way in would be quite impossible."

"Perhaps so. That would then be my business. You would only have to guide me to the door, no farther. Still, if you will not risk it, we will talk no more about it."

"Nevermore, nevermore!" said Beppo, scratching his head, and still all the time very much frightened.

"You would have thereby rendered me a great service," added Irmgard, with a deep sigh.

"Yes; see, Signorina," answered Beppo, "I should like to render you a service, willingly for my lifetime. But only think, if they should discover us there; if —— "

"If they should discover us, we must have some pretext in readiness."

"And what pretext could we have to explain that we wished to force our way into the dungeons of Sant Uffizio?"

"You, Beppo should not force your way in there," said Irmgard. "You should only lead me to that rusty iron door. Could you not answer now, if one should see us there and require us to tell whither we thought of going, that you had lost some object of value to you while working there, and came back with us, as your friends, to hunt for it?"

"*Ecco, ecco;* what clever notions you have, Signorina!" exclaimed Beppo. "Such a thing anyone must find credible; and that so much the more as it would occur to no one that anybody would think of forcing his way into the dungeons of Sant Uffizio."

"Well, then," added Irmgard, "what could you have lost?"

"What could it be? If I should possess jewels, I would not wear them at my work."

"That's so; then, if it should be the case that we should be observed and questioned, say it is a silver *Agnus Dei*, that you are accustomed to wear as a memento of your pious father."

Beppo nodded his head.

"That is good," he said; "but," he added, as if in suddenly recurring anxiety, looking upon Irmgard with a beseeching glance, "but must it really be, Signorina?"

Irmgard forced herself to a smile.

"Have you not heard that what a woman sets her head on must always be done?"

Beppo nodded again.

"Yes, yes;" he said, sighing; "then I shall not be able to escape you. But understand clearly, I lead you only so far as the way is without danger—to that highest vault."

"Only so far," assented Irmgard. "Where the danger begins you turn back, and let me go on alone."

"No, no," exclaimed Beppo, reddening; "it is not on account of the danger, but such curiosity as yours is a sin, which I cannot assist without a sin of my own."

"Quite right; you shrink only from the sin," said Irmgard smiling. "As far, however, as you are able without sin, you will guide us, myself and my uncle, whom I will take with me, and who will protect me; and, for the purpose, dear Beppo, provide a pair of lanterns or torches, which we shall need,—will you?"

Beppo stood staring at her and scratching his head, in great disturbance of spirit.

Irmgard suddenly arose to go ; she gave him her hand.

"I have your word, Beppo," she said — "I have your word, and you must redeem it. I let you off no more. I go now to my uncle, to speak to him about it."

She went hastily to the house.

"Holy Mother of God!" said Beppo, with a deep sigh, looking after her. "If I gave you my word, I must truly redeem it! But whither is this maiden leading me astray! If my mother were aware of it! May all the saints help us!"

CHAPTER XIII.

NELLA PERDUTA GENTE.

N a thoroughly idealistic nature such as Egino's, it may be a benefit to be for once surprised and cast down by a stroke which reveals to it the entire misery of humanity in its perfect wretchedness, without a veil, without any kind of mitigation, without any possibility of diminishing through the beautifying art of speech the dread which chases the serpent-covered head of this human wretchedness through the soul, through the joints and marrow.

Without an experience of this kind, such idealistic-winged souls never learn what the world is, and what men are. Without it they never become startled out of their stubborn confidence.

Egino was to have such an experience. He lay imprisoned in a narrow, musty chamber, within four gray-black walls of stone, under a cloister of the Dominican order—in a kind of intermediate story between the deep dungeons below and the cloister-rooms above him. This chamber or cell was yet one of the best of these horrible, un-ventilated places. It had a bed with a coverlet, a table, and a couple of chairs. There were no chains and no rings fastened to the walls; no preparations of this kind were there to awake in the prisoner that most horrible feeling, the anticipation of that which was ahead of him. There only hung from the vaulted ceiling a chain about two feet long with an iron ring attached. What did this betoken? What purpose was this ring to serve? Egino did not know, did not comprehend, but his feeble glance was often riveted upon it. Often when he lay upon his bed in a half-slumber, loathsome, horrifying pictures twined themselves about the rusty black ring; goblin eyes coming forth out of the twilight peered through the narrow circle; the ugly phantoms of a diseased imagination hung to this horrible and terrifying mystery over his head.

And then the cell had light. A weak and insufficient light forced itself through a narrow, high-placed, unglazed opening in the wall. It was not grated; that was unnecessary, for it was too small to allow a man to slip through it. The sunlight of the south, however, is strong and powerful. After accustoming himself to it a few days, it sufficed for Egino to see all objects with more perfect distinctness.

He saw that the four stone walls surrounding him were like four leaves of a book, — of a book of wonderful contents. It was like a book which the naked human soul, in its purity and beauty, in its delirium, and, again, in cynical shamelessness, had written, as if it said, "You have torn away from me the last garment; now see what I am!" All that could be extracted from human nature under the pressure of despair, had written itself here upon these walls in confused outcries, in blasphemies, in curses, in abominable pictures, and in noble rhymes, in prayers, in verses of moving beauty. There were verses from Dante and Petrarch scribbled upon these walls of stone; passages from Plato, Boethius, Horace, near passages from the Bible; forms of saints and heads of angels were drawn there near the most obscene and most filthy things; then again an Agnus Dei, rosaries, amulets, scapularies, — all the childish puppet-play of superstition.

Egino had been nursed the space of a few days in the infirmary of the cloister; when it was evident that his wound was not dangerous, that his enfeebled condition was only the consequence of a great loss of blood, and when the fever from his wound quickly subsided, Padre Geronimo had ordered him to be brought into this cell. The Padre Infirmario visited him here once a day to look after his wound, to renew the bandages; at the same hour Brother Alessio brought him his food and water. They had also brought to him his clothing from the cell above; nothing indicated that they wished to treat him with hardness. But they did not speak with him; the Padre Infirmario talked only of his wounds, Brother Alessio was perfectly mute — and nothing, absolutely nothing, not once the thought of rescue, of flight, which seemed impossible, of which Egino in his feeble prostration did not possess the energy to think, broke in upon the dreams, the meditations, the inquiries of the prisoner, upon the feverishly throbbing pulses of life-thought in him; upon which heated ground, however, the soul-plant within waxed so much the stronger and more powerful.

His inner life, as we saw, had become a life of the soul. His idealistic nature, in the hands of his passion, had fled into the saving shelter of soul-life from the shock with which the cosmology of Rome threatened him. He had clung to his love, and in its presence what there was in him of original, innate piety, as if recollecting itself, was newly inflamed; the beautiful resignation to the Divine which characterized his childhood, this sweet poesy of the young human soul, had returned to his heart like a warm flood of sunbeams. Love, poesy, religion, they are one and the same feeling; the trinity of that which fills the human soul; the longing, the longing for the beautiful, let it be the beauty of the earth or the beauty of heaven. The poet, who gives himself up to his dreams; Dante, who follows Beatrice through the endless spaces of creation; the stigmatized saint; the enraptured anchorite, who pursues the Madonna to the cot of eternal peace under the palms under which resound the harps of the angels,— they all equally obey the one impulse of the human breast, the impulse toward the beautiful.

Egino must, with this thought, find himself in the dirty, dark cell of the church prison in order to feel with an overwhelming force the horribleness of a theology which used such means of compulsion — of compulsion to faith! To think of forcing into the human breast by dungeons, racks, iron rings and piles of fagots, the freest things in the innermost being,— poesy, love, religion!

It was fearful. It was madness seated upon the throne, with the sword of the highest judgment in the one hand, with a book of law written by a demon in the other.

Egino felt that if ever again he should leave this cell, the last bond would be rent asunder between him and this ecclesiasticism; that he would hate it to the death; that he would seek his God with the free impulse of his soul. With this impulse must he find him truly. The stream would not rush in unrestrained course through the land, if the ocean for which it strives were not really there. The thirst would not exist if there were no water at hand to still it; the eye of man, with its desire of sight, would not be created if there were no light; and so the eternal thirst for God would not burn in the human soul, if there were no God into whose bosom outpours this stream of longing which, for thousands of years, runs through humanity with equal strength.

Out of such thoughts flowed over him a peculiar quiet, a peace. He had, with a profound German fidelity, held too long to the faith of his fathers; with hundreds of threads it had been wound about his innermost heart. There had been deeply written upon his soul what this faith had once been for the moral order of the world; what the church had effected as the great mother of culture; what it had won for mankind, and to what manhood it had led; how it had restrained savageness, subjugated and enchained the passions, inspired and ennobled rude existence. The inner falling away from this faith could not take place without a painful hesitation and struggle. In this cell, however, with his eyes directed to these walls, to the leaves of this horrible book, which he had to see daily and to read, it became no less clearly inscribed upon his mind that the ecclesiasticism which imposed itself upon his age had forfeited its right to existence.

Meanwhile, as with dreadful monotony and tediousness one day vanished after another, his strength gradually returned. He was still very weak, but the feeling of life stirred more and more powerfully in him. This had about it something alarming. Some one tells of a prisoner who saw the four walls of his prison being gently shoved together, and could foresee the day and the hour when they would touch each other, suffocate him, crush him to death. For Egino this growing strength of the feeling of life brought something similarly grievous. In the proportion that his bodily weakness departed from him, arose in him the need of light, of air, of liberty, grew in him the feeling of the intolerableness of his condition; the imprisonment became to him a gentle pressure of the heart becoming continually harder and harder. The effort to hold out in this dungeon preyed more and more sharply upon his strength. He could look forward to the moment when this power would disappear and be consumed; when it could no longer be endured; when he would become deranged or must kill himself,— let himself starve.

VOLUME III.

THE DAUGHTER OF EMPERORS (Conclusion).

ST. CECILIA. (RAPHAEL.)

CHAPTER I.

LIVIO'S STRATAGEM.

IVIO SAVELLI would not have been Livio Savelli if he had not entertained the firm conviction that an avowed, and perhaps guilty, relation existed between Egino and Corradina. Neither the customs of that time, nor the hot blood of the South in him, nor his inferences from the circumstances, could allow him to think otherwise. Would Egino have exposed himself to so great a danger without being sure of a reward for his venture? Would it have been possible for him, without the joint knowledge and assistance of Corradina, to force his way into the garden of the castle? And would Corradina have saved him if she did not love him?

There was still continuously boiling in Livio Savelli a venomous rage over it. All his meditations and thoughts were involved with it. He must annihilate the German and subjugate Corradina to himself; the passion in him which desired possession of her, had, through the thought that she preferred another, become something which racked him continually; it had become an unceasing torment.

Should he leave Egino to the monks, to their Inquisition?

The Inquisition was, on the whole, a mild, negligent, drowsy creature just at that time. It was like a fully sated tiger digesting its repast. It had burned, racked, allowed to pine away, incarcerated mangled; it had exterminated entire populations and drunk streams of blood. This last, however, had taken place years before. Now it had become indolent and a little childish; it had gone out of style. Once in awhile the tiger still stretched itself, as if to test the strength of its limbs; it administered a stroke with its paw, and then a funeral-pile flamed forth, like that of Savonarola. But what could it do then other than again fall into slumber, in a time when the people of culture read the writings of Plato instead of the Gospels; when Bembo, the cardinal, wrote to Sadolet, that he did not like to read the Epistles of Paul, lest he should injure his style; when even the Popes, such as Alexander VI., Julius II., and Leo X., troubled themselves very little about theology; when it could be told of Leo X. that he had said to Pietro Bembo, "All ages have been witnesses of how useful to us these fables concerning Christ have become." This was a slander, but it was significant that such a thing could have originated and have been repeated innumerable times. The Inquisition had become something which no longer made itself at all felt in certain lands of Italy; as, for example, during the entire long reign of the formerly strong believer, Hercole I. von Este, not a single trial for heresy was held at Ferrara. In other lands it was something that moved only by starts, in especially provincial opportunities, where cunning and wickedness united in the transgression of dogmas and ecclesiastical law. And even in Rome it was no longer that which could have given Livio satisfaction, if Egino only knew any way to defend himself skillfully.

And as concerning Corradina — should he carry out against her that which he had threatened? Should he carry her away by force to his Castle bei Albano?

He dared no more to use violence towards her. He had his father to fear. Since the day when the latter had learned of the scene with Egino, he had no more left the castle on the Aventine; he occupied there the chambers always standing prepared for the head of the house, and was now always at home.

It was evident that he had resolved in jealous passion to stand guard over Corradina.

Livio could reach his aim only through artifice, also that of taking vengeance upon Egino. He combined both aims into one plan, and hit upon his preparations.

"Corradina," he said then, walking into her chamber on the same day in which Beppo was urged by Irmgard, and induced to risk with her the dangerous undertaking, — "Corradina, I beg you not to be alarmed at my coming to you to-day. I come to conclude a peace with you."

Corradina looked up and inquiringly directed her great eyes upon Livio.

"I do not fear you," she answered; "but the peace which you come to offer — from your evil, angry countenance, you appear to wish to unite with it severe conditions."

"I come not to make conditions with you, although, perhaps, to utter some reproaches."

"Reproaches? And wherefore?"

"Why did you not tell me candidly that my passion for you was hopeless?"

"That is the last reproach I could expect from you! I mean that candor has never been wanting to me, and you cannot have forgotten that I have very often, and very, very definitely, declared it to you!"

"What were these declarations! With a woman whose heart does not belong to another, a man always has hopes. Only when it beats for another, does a reasonable man relinquish the hope. Why did you not say to me that your heart was given away to that German?"

Corradina shrugged her shoulders.

"I do not love the German," she replied; "and if I did, you would be the last one to whom I would intrust the fact."

"You would answer me more amicably if you knew with what an honorable effort I have conquered my passion for you, and have torn it forever from my heart!"

"You — know how to conquer your passions?"

"It is as you say, Corradina. If you, however, will not accept it that it has been by a good emotion of my soul or by a moral power that I have conquered this passion, then take it that it has been by the pride in me."

"The pride?"

"So I said."

"Do you feel yourself degraded by that which you call your love for me? That would be a more righteous emotion than I supposed you capable of."

"I feel myself degraded by it, but in another way than you think. I feel myself degraded by the thought that another man has been preferred before me. In the first hours, days, after the discovery, I would willingly have killed this man; I could with pleasure have seen him die under unutterable torments; I have cursed myself that my dagger did not penetrate more deeply, strike more truly. Since then, calm reflection and cool understanding have become my master; I feel compassion for this poor devil of a German and for you, Corradina."

"I do not need your compassion; but speak further."

"You do not need my compassion, but my help."

"Your help? For what?"

"To save this German."

"Do I wish to do that?"

"Most certainly. He has, for your sake, fallen into danger and into prison; what is more natural than that you would even go to any length to free him from it?"

"Granted that should be the case, your help is the last upon which I would count."

"Corradina," said Livio, after a pause, while he strode through the room, reclined with his shoulders against the wall near the window-casement, and folded his arms over his breast. She, meanwhile, was looking through this window straight before her, beyond the garden beneath, into the glowing evening-sky beyond the Janiculus, which poured over her head in a peculiarly rosy golden sheen. "Corradina," he said, "through all this bitterness and sharpness you only show to me best what you wish to conceal from me,—that you love this German; you forgive me the most natural act, the simple deed of defense which I committed, not because it was directed against him."

"I have never loved a mortal man," replied Corradina, "not even him!"

"We will not contend about it. In any case you wish to save him. And I—I wish to take you away from the neighborhood, the reach of my father's power; but you will not go."

"Not to your castle."

"You could seek refuge in some other standing open to us, if every other did not belong to my father, and also stand open to him. Only that of Albano belongs to me, as my own assigned portion. I am the master there; and the drawbridges there rise and fall at my signal, and at that of no one else in the world."

"Speak further."

"You save the German, and, since he is still sick from his wound, conduct him to my castle and nurse him there."

Corradina slowly lifted her head to Livio, and looked at him questioningly with her great eyes.

"Are you in earnest?"

"I swear it to you."

"You save him if it is possible to save him. Why need I to do it?"

"I would finally, also, do that, if I were certain he would consent to become saved by me. But if I should force my way to him, he would certainly not follow me. And can I think of carrying out my plan by force, — with people to force my way into the dungeons of the Inquisition? Would my people risk open violence, even if I were willing to risk it? You alone can carry it out — you alone, and in stillness."

Corradina did not answer, and Livio continued: —

"Listen to me. The affair is not difficult. Count Egino can easily be saved, if he only will trust himself to follow the one who forces the way to him. The rooms over there under the cloister are separated from those under the castle by a not very strong dividing-wall. I am at this hour having that wall secretly broken through. Beyond it a narrow passage leads to a round chapel; around this lie the cells of the dead; at the side of the chapel a stairway leads above into an upper passage, to which other more airy and more roomy cells are adjacent. In one of the last have they confined Egino von Ortenburg. It is the third. The key is in my hand; I have had it prepared from a wax impression which I have obtained. You go, now, at the fourth hour after Ave Maria, when the monks lie asleep, to the prisoner, and he will follow you, as Paul the angel who stepped into his prison. If I should come he would surely resist, and create a disturbance, which would bring the monks on our necks; and, although my name is Livio Savelli, I should not like to fall into a close contest with the Inquisition. I can also send no one; there are no people who, with me or alone, would press into the dungeons of Sant Uffizio. If it is to take place, you must do it yourself, Madame Corradina."

Corradina had remained silent all this time.

"In all that you are right," she said at last. "And so I will do it, then. It is not possible that cunning and treachery lingers behind the whole thing. You are not bad enough for that, Livio. You could have no interest in letting me fall into the hands of the monks of Sant Uffizio."

"No," responded Livio, dryly, and entirely avoiding her glance. "You will do it entirely without danger. A part of the way will I accompany you myself, and be your guide. You will free the German, and lead him back through this castle; in the court below two mules will be awaiting you, and two armed servants, in order to bring you to Albano. There no one shall harm a hair of your head or his.

So we both will have accomplished what we wish. He will be saved, and that is what you wish; you will be removed from the power of my father,—that is what I wish!"

"And I will be given into your power!" remarked Corradina.

"How inextinguishable and cruel your mistrust is! You do me wrong, Corradina."

"I have reasons to be on my guard," said Corradina, curling her lips with an expression full of bitterness, "toward you no less than toward your father, and all that surround you."

"But you hear now that my mind is changed since I know that you love this German!"

Corradina shrugged her shoulders.

"So much so that you give yourself all the trouble," she replied, "to find out where Egino lies imprisoned, how these dungeons are arranged, how one can force a way into them, that you will defy the danger of penetrating into them—all of that out of zeal to rescue a man whom, as you believe, I love? What magnanimity! Messer Ludovico Ariosto should devote to it a dozen stanzas in the heroic poem on which he is laboring!"

Livio smiled.

"Messer Ludovico Ariosto!" he exclaimed.

"Why do you repeat the name?"

"Because he stands in nearer connection with the matter than you are aware."

"Who—Ariosto?"

"If not he, exactly, still his court, his master, the illustrious Alfonso von Este, and his consort, the golden-haired Madame Lucretia."

"Will you have the goodness to explain that to me?" asked Corradina.

"I will tell you everything, to dissipate entirely your mistrust. You know, years ago, when the Borgia were still our masters, and your Luca, Don Cesare's friend, I was, to some extent, the friend of Donna Lucretia. We all, all the young nobility of Rome, and I, most of all, then lay in her bonds, the beautiful, charming woman."

"I know; so much as a child can find out of such things. I heard of it."

"Well, then, Lucretia has since become the wife of Alfonso von Este; and Alfonso von Este is here."

"He is here, the Duke of Ferrara? He is carrying on war with the Pope, and is here?"

"Just so. He was the Pope's truest ally and gonfalonier of the church; then, when our Lord Giulio with his help had conquered his enemies and made a conquest of Romagna, the Holy Father concluded peace with the former enemies, and carried on war with his ally. Ferrara may have seemed to him very suitable to round out the conquests in Romagna. In this contest the fortune of war went against the duke; he wished for peace, and has several times sued for it in vain. Once he sent Ariosto with such a message, but in vain; finally he has found a friend in Fabricio Colonna, who has rendered the Holy Father favorably disposed toward him, and he is here to perform the act of submission and homage required of him. I saw him yesterday in the house of the Colonna. He brought to me greetings from Madame Lucretia, and invited me to Ferrara — heartily and pressingly. I burn to see Madame Lucretia again as the faithful, modest housewife and beautiful princess of Ferrara, in the midst of a splendid court, surrounded by talented and noble men."

"You will indeed go to Ferrara?"

"Even so; you know that 'old love never dies.' I will accompany Alfonso on his return home; and thus, I think, you have a key to that which you so bitterly name my magnanimity. I cannot go away and be quiet in soul, if I leave you behind here in this house. You, however, I say to myself, will not leave it if the German does not leave it with you; so save the German for yourself, then leave it."

Corradina looked upon Livio's countenance awhile in silence.

"Who can look into the heart of man?" she said then.

"I have let you look into mine," rejoined Livio, quietly. "Make up your mind!"

"Is the German, then, so recovered from his wound that he is in a condition to flee?" she asked, after a pause.

"He was prostrated by fever from the wound. That is past; he is still feeble, but sufficiently recovered to hold out for a short journey. So they have informed me."

"Well, then, I am ready to do what you wish."

"And you relinquish your mistrust toward me?"

"Do you make that a condition of your assistance?"

"No; I only wish it. I require no conditions of you — not a

single one. If I say to you to conduct the German to my castle and have him cared for there till he is recovered, that is also no condition which I require of you, but only the pressure of circumstances which demands it."

"Well, then, Livio, I will believe and trust you," said Corradina. "You will not deceive my confidence, will you?"

"Nevermore. Do you wish oaths?"

"No. I am even ready to do without that what you advise."

"Good; so we are agreed. I rejoice over that, and hope we shall evermore do so. Give me your hand. I leave you now. I am going to see how far my trusty laborer has advanced with his still work deep under our feet. You may now take for yourself the key to the German's cell.

"Also till the fourth hour after Ave Maria," replied Corradina, taking with emotion the heavy key which Livio drew forth.

"Till the fourth hour. Be ready then, and clothed for a ride in the cool night air. I will have a mantle for the German thrown on the mule."

Livio departed.

Corradina listened to the receding steps. When they died away she sprang up and went hastily out on the balcony, and there walked to and fro.

"What trickery lurks behind this?" she asked herself. "Does Livio believe I am really so easy to deceive as to see in all his speech nothing but a sincere goodness, a returning to virtue, or the wish to be able to travel quietly to Ferrara? O my God! have you men for this purpose surrounded me for years with the wild scenes of your passions to let me believe in your honesty?"

Her step became more slow; folding her hands, looking at the ground, she moved slowly up and down.

"If I were to refuse," she said then in a low tone, "Egino would then remain in the dungeons of the Dominicans perhaps long years, perhaps forever! He has acted too insolently not to call forth their vengeance: he has the secret of my marriage, and they must fear him. There is no hope for him if I do not save him as Livio has planned."

"Well, then, I will do it! I will do it even at the risk that even there lies the snare into which Livio wishes to entice me. Yet no, it does not lie there; it cannot. He cannot wish that his sister-in-law, a woman bearing the name of Savelli, fall into the hands of the Inquisition, and that the world find out that the house which gave to the church three popes, saw a heretic among its members. The snare into which I would fall lies beyond these walls. The passion of his father is a danger, but also a protection for me. I am to be enticed out of his father's neighborhood to Castle Savello, into his house. Against that alone am I to guard myself. And I will do it! Let me be out there in the night, on the back of a strong mule, under the protection of Egino, and I will ride, not to Castle Savello, but to Palliano. To her, to his wife, will I flee; and she will receive me with rejoicing, and protect me, in order to put him in a rage. Oh! these men. And what a humiliating situation when my safety depends upon having the evil passion of one to protect me from that of the other! I am horrified at all these men and their wild career. And how long will it be, if I save Egino, till I shall also be filled with dread from his passion? Also he, also he will begin to utter these speeches which stir me up, — which say to me I was born to be a man's true helpmeet; while I scorn entirely to become the companion of a life which is worthless in the world, like a wave more or less in the sea, — but false and cunning as they. In short, that they will make me a wife dishonored, treated with disrespect, as they all are. Will he also talk in that way? God stand by him, then; the others I scorn, but him — yes, him I could hate. I believe I could kill him if he should open his lips to talk to me as the duke, as Livio presumes to do!"

After uttering this in most violent emotion, she sank into silent reflection; then, as if rising out of thought, she smoothed with the palms of her hands the hair from her brow.

"Let us think now only of saving him," she whispered.

She went into her chamber, in order to prepare herself for the journey which stood before her in the night.

Would that she had been able to look down from her lofty balcony into the little house far below, by the gardens of the Colonna, where even now a poor German maiden was preparing for the same dangerous passage which she also wished to go over this night!

CHAPTER II.

IN THE NIGHT.

IT was, according to our reckoning, the eleventh hour of the night.

Livio stepped into Corradina's chamber; he found her prepared for departure. She wore over the bodice a *camora* of warm cloth, the shapeless, loose-fitting jacket, and over that the long *sbernia*, a broad over-garment of black velvet with trimming of dark fur. Covering her head was a hat of the same material as the *camora* with a pearl buckle, otherwise unadorned, without a feather.

At her girdle hung down under her *sbernia* a budget, a graceful leathern pocket swelled out round and hard. Corradina must have put in it what it would take in of ready cash and little necessities.

"You are ready, I see," said Livio; "it is just the right moment. In the castle everything is still, and over in the cloister the monks in their first deep sleep."

"I am ready. What servants will you furnish me on the way to Castle Savello?"

"Niccolo and Giuseppe," answered Livio; "they wait with the mules in the shadow of the archway down in the court."

"Only they?"

"Certainly, only they. Do you think I would have intrusted our secret to more than necessary? You may yourself suppose that it is convenient for me that the monks never find out, in regard to the stroke which we play them, that I have had a hand in the game. Upon Niccolo and Giuseppe I can depend; also upon the mason waiting below, in order, when we have accomplished the deed, to close again the opening in the wall, so that no one may notice what has happened, and the monks will believe in a miracle."

"And who will light us?"

"I, myself. My body-servant, Antonio, is waiting out there with torches."

"Call him in here."

"What for?"

"That he may carry down out of my bedroom for me the valise which I have packed with my most necessary articles, and buckle it to the saddle of my mule."

Livio nodded, and went out to send Antonio upon this errand. Corradina then took her gloves, felt about her girdle to be assured that the dagger stuck in it was there, then stepped out. Outside came Livio with the burning torch of the servant, who went now to attend to Corradina's charge. Livio walked in advance. Through an angular passage they came, treading softly, to a landing of the great stairway, which discharged itself below into the court under the same inclosing archway. Corradina heard the stamping of mules and whispering voices in one of the angles. She went on, following Livio, into the rooms of the basement; then down into a region which she did not know, into which she had never been before. They passed through a half-open door, behind which a steep stairway descended, at first built out of stones, then hewn out of the rock; there was at the foot of the stair a vault, the walls of rock, the ceiling arched with dressed stone; several of these rooms succeeded, separated by immense pillars which supported the vault; here and there the way was narrowed by partitions of wooden planks blackened by time; the floor was dirty, so that they now slipped, now trod upon some kind of broken pottery, now sank in as if stepping upon modern remnants of refuse. The last room was inclosed by a wall in the background. When the light of Livio's torch, which lighted this under-world glaringly and with ghastliness with its red flame, fell upon this wall, Corradina saw that it had been unartistically constructed out of the most unlike materials,— out of layers of brick, of bits of old marble, of old building-stones. In the middle of it an opening had been broken large enough to let a man through. The stones that had been broken out lay in orderly heaps near by; the light of the torch also fell upon a vessel with mortar and upon the tools of a mason. It was as Livio had said,— everything ready to close the opening again, only the man who should do this was not visible.

"I have sent him away," whispered Livio; "it is not necessary that he should see you!"

Corradina did not answer; she followed courageously through the opening, when Livio had forced himself through in advance of her. Beyond, a room surrounded her similar to the last, only it was smaller, and opposite to the broken wall-opening a passage led out of it farther into the substructions of the cloister. Livio also here still walked in advance, a distance of about twenty steps, to a great expansion of the passage. This expansion formed a circular room, which had the appearance of something like a subterranean chapel. A strong pillar stood in the middle supporting the vault, and to this pillar a little altar was attached; it stood elevated above a few steps; a lofty crucifix arose over the gray altar-plate, which no altar-cloth covered.

Livio extended his torch before him into the room, and pointing to a place which lay next to him of the encircling wall, he said in a low tone: —

"This is the Chapel of the Immured. There are their niches."

The flame of the torch dwindled and burned less brightly. In the room prevailed a peculiar, inexpressibly disgusting smell, — a pestilential atmosphere, under whose influence the light of the torch diminished.

"There are the niches," whispered Livio, while he pointed to the wall.

Around the chapel deep recesses had been built of masonry or hewn out; walls either inclosed these entirely in front, and in them was then formed a little quadrangular opening, which allowed one to look out, and through which food could be shoved, — or the walls were broken down to about three feet from the floor.

Corradina was seized with shuddering; she shrunk back.

"O God!" she said, "and do the unfortunate ones languish here?"

"No," whispered Livio, in return; "there would then be a light burning on the altar: they kindle a light for them, that they may recognize there the Christ who does not help them."

"To whom they are brought as human sacrifices! It is horrible!" whispered Corradina, staring around at the walls, and as if fixed to the floor by fright.

Livio held the torch higher. Its light fell upon the ugly caricature over the altar, that appeared dark, blackened by time and dust, unspeakably frightful with its disfigured features.

"O my God, what have they made of him?" whispered Corradina, taking a deep breath.

"That which they need,— an idol," answered Livio. "But let us not make observations about that. Here, behind the pillar, you see, a narrow stairway leads up into a passage in the upper story; it is the third door, you know. Have you the key?"

"I have it," she replied almost inaudibly. "Give me the torch."

"Wait — we will light the altar-lamp; I think there will still be oil enough in it. It would make me gray to be obliged to stay behind, here, in the dark."

He pushed nearer to him the earthen vessel half filled with a thick, dirty oil, which, serving as a lamp, stood upon the altar, and he succeeded in lighting the half-burned wick therein with the torch. It crackled awhile, and threw out little sparks; then the slender wick began to burn brighter, and sparingly lighted up the round chapel room, the altar, the picture of Christ over it, and the stone surface of the pillar behind it. When Corradina withdrew in order to enter courageously upon the course she was to make alone, and when she disappeared with the torch behind the pillar, the lamp threw only a feeble twilight around; it sufficed only to make visible the circular wall and the niches in it.

Livio seated himself upon the steps of the altar. He listened to the steps of Corradina gently and carefully mounting a stair. They died away after a few moments. Then all was still; only the lamp sputtered; it struggled with the air in this room. Livio's breast also began to struggle with it. He breathed with difficulty. And — what was that? Livio thought he heard a suppressed breathing; he turned his head and looked behind him. It was nothing.

Livio waited long.

Also outside, up in the castle court, the men tarrying there waited long.

The mules, placed in the shadow of the archway, began to stamp with waxing impatience the broad stone slabs with their hoofs. To Niccolo and Giuseppe, who held them by the reins, to Livio's trusted servant, Antonio, who clasped to one of the beasts Corradina's valise, had stepped up the mason, who awaited the appearance of Livio, and the order to repair below and take up again his work on the penetrated wall. He came to them to shorten the time of waiting through chat. At length, also, out of some lurking-place in the broad, adjacent court, slipped three wild-looking figures with goatskins on their legs and firearms on the back; genuine bandits, than which the Sabine or Volsci Mountains never produced any more picturesque and more forbidding in appearance.

"Holy body of the Madonna!" exclaimed one; "if nothing is to come of the affair to-night, Sor Antonio, His Excellency should tell us, that we may go and sleep."

"You can sleep the whole day to-morrow," glumly answered Antonio, an elderly, meager man, with a slow, peculiarly muffled nature. "Go back, so that the Lady Countess may not see you when she comes with the German whom she believes herself to have rescued. You know, indeed, she must not be aware ——"

"We know that, we know that," said another; "but we should also like to know ——"

"*Benedetto!* A man who would like to know!" said Antonio, interrupting him. "The less you know, you blockhead, so much the better for you. Do you comprehend that, just so you know enough for your job!"

"If His Excellency wishes us to wait still longer, let him send out to us a brazier," remarked the third of the bandits, wrapping himself closer in his mantle.

"Or a brazier with liquid fire in it, which warms the stomach and keeps one awake," said the first.

"The devil!" here said Giuseppe in a low tone; "that would not be bad, Sor Antonio, for the night is cold, and waiting makes the stomach empty."

"If these dogs, whom the Countess Corradina must not see, will creep back into their kennel, I will go and fetch what you wish," whispered Sor Antonio. "Go, Lanfranco," he turned then to the first of the three bandits, "go, and press yourself into the shadow. I will bring you then hither a warm jug, as you wish, but be still. Niccolo, give your mule a kick in the belly, so that the beast will leave off his stamping."

Niccolo snatched the head of his mule high up by the bit.

"Accursed beast!" he exclaimed, "I will stick a knife into your body if you do not stand."

Giuseppe stroked the neck of his beast to keep it patient.

"My dear, my sister," he said, while doing it, "patience, patience; then you shall carry the most beautiful countess into the mountains, far, far away; my sister, you shall carry her, only you!"

Antonio had, in the meantime, turned and passed diagonally

through the archway to the stair leading upward into the interior, when, from up in the inner part of the building, from far off, and perceptible only on account of the stillness of night, one perceived the shrill note of a whistle.

"*Ecco!* They come," said the men standing around the mules; and the three bandits slipped away, in order not to be caught by Livio, who had commanded them to show themselves for the first time when they were outside of the city.

On the first stair-landing which Antonio reached he remained standing. He heard the shrill whistle again.

"*Corpo di bacco*," he whispered to himself; "that sounds out of the rooms of the old man! We shall fail if he mixes himself in the affair!"

Antonio took one of the two burning torches which were stuck into the wall-rings on the stair-landing, then he mounted higher, and having arrived above he passed into the passage, in order to bring out of some room the wine which should appease the impatience of the people; yet before he had reached the door of this room he saw, at the end of the passage, a form emerge, which was likewise carrying a torch in the hand and coming quickly to him.

"Eh, Antonio, what is the matter there?" exclaimed the figure, with a loud voice.

"Giovan-Battista, you?" answered Antonio, with displeasure. "What do you want? Why are you awake and up?"

"The old lord has wakened me," said Giovan-Battista. "He says he has perceived in the court the hoofstrokes of horses or mules, and other noises. What has happened? What is going on?"

"It seems to me the old lord has ears like a mole," replied Antonio. "Why doesn't he stick his gray head into his pillow and sleep?"

"Ask him yourself. In the first place, speak and give me information."

"Information? About what?"

"About what is taking place. Why you are here, Sor Antonio?"

"Does that concern you?"

"Not me, but His Excellency wishes to learn."

"Then tell him Lanfranco and his two nephews have come from Albano, and have brought four barrels of oil. I go now to bring the fellows a drink of wine."

"You lie, in fact, Sor Antonio; but I will go to tell him what you say —— the devil! There he is himself."

The Duke of Aricia came striding down the passage. He was just placing a leathern girdle around the long robe into which he had thrown himself; it was provided with a cowl, and he looked like a monk as he came quickly striding forward,— only it was evident when he reached the light of the torch that the robe was of dark-red velvet, and too costly for a monk.

"Antonio," he said, with his hawk eyes blinking, and on that account holding his hand as a shield against the dazzling flame, "whither are you going? What means that noise in the court?"

"Your Excellency," put in Giovan-Battista, "it is Lanfranco with his two nephews, who bring four barrels of oil on their beasts of burden from Albano ——"

"Go forward with the torch," broke in the duke, without listening to his words.

"Excellency, do not go, but let me give you information," said Antonio, who in an instant had calculated that if he could detain the duke with a narration, he would thus create for his master just that much space of time in order there below to carry away Corradina and the German in the saddles, if, perhaps, Livio was just now returning with them.

"Well, then, speak," answered the duke.

"Giovan-Battista should not hear it, Your Excellency."

"Then step back, Giovan-Battista," ordered the duke to his body-servant.

Giovan-Battista drew himself farther back into the corridor.

"My Lord," now began Antonio, "has forced his way into the prisons over there under the cloister ——"

"Ah! Livio has forced his way in there, and without telling it to me?"

"Just so, Your Excellency. I have been compelled some days ago to speak with one of the lay brethren over there,— Fra Alessio, he is called; and he is a good-natured old boy, who comes from my neighborhood, from Marino at home, and a kind of a cousin he is; a man, Your Excellency, like a child, who ——"

"To the devil with your Alessio! Go on, go on!" exclaimed the duke, angrily.

"From Alessio I have found out where they have confined the young German count, and then I have had him take a wax impression of the lock of his cell. It is the third when one goes up out of the Chapel of the Immured, and comes into the passage above; also where the Chapel of the Immured lies, has Fra Alessio described to me——"

"All out of good nature?" asked the duke, interrupting.

"As you please to call it, Your Excellency," responded Antonio. "Out of good nature, perhaps, also, a little out of excitement over fifty *scudi* which I had brought him from Count Livio, and had stuck into the sleeve-opening of his gown."

"Go on."

"Thereupon Count Livio has had a key made from the wax impression, and as he was ready; to-day, in secrecy, in the twilight, he has conducted a mason into the vaults under the castle. What the man has done there and what he is still to do, he can tell you himself, for he is down in the court, awaiting Count Livio's return."

"And Livio is even now down in the vaults? He will bring the German out? And is he alone?"

"No; the Countess Corradina accompanied him."

"Corradina is with him? Holy Mother! And all that behind my back! But what are the mules for? If he wishes to get the German away from the monks, what need has he of the mules? Have we not here in the castle dungeons in order to confine a malefactor, and firm stones to lock him therein?"

"I do not know, Your Excellency. Countess Corradina appears to wish to ride away with the German, accompanied by Niccolo and Giuseppe. Besides, Count Livio has also had Lanfranco and his nephews to come; they shall follow unobserved. And what more they are to do I know not; Count Livio has not given his orders; I do not know them."

"*Accidente!*" muttered the duke between his teeth, stepping quickly forward down the passage. "This tricky Livio, who wishes to steal the German from the monks and Corradina from me. Giovan-Battista," he called, turning; "where are you, blockhead? Listen to me —Antonio, forward; I will see for myself what your master is doing down there."

"To tell you the truth candidly," whispered Antonio, now already near his hastening excellency, who was descending the stairway leading down into the court, "it is preferable to me that you have come to see about it; Count Livio tarries so immeasurably long, there has fallen upon my heart a heavy anxiety about what can have happened to him."

"Anxiety? What is there to happen to him?" said the duke. "Granted, even, that he should be surprised by the monks — he is not the man to let them cut off from him the way of retreat; and I do not think the idea will occur to them of trying to cut off Livio Savelli's retreat. How long is it since Livio went?"

"Almost a half-hour, Your Excellency."

"A half-hour! Most blessed! that is truly a long time. And why have you not followed him, then, Antonio?"

"Because he has expressly forbidden it, and because I had not the desire to fall under ban, which Count Livio risks more easily than his body-servant, Antonio Tarmucci."

"In spite of that you will now let it come under ban, Antonio Tarmucci," said the duke, redoubling his steps. "You will call the mason hither, and you two will then lead me the way which Livio has gone with the Countess Corradina."

They had arrived down in the archway. Antonio walked quickly over to where the men stood near the mules, beckoned to the mason, then turned, followed by the latter; after a few moments they had been received by the rooms into which Livio and Corradina had disappeared. Antonio went in front with his torch, the duke followed, the mason and Giovan-Battista, with the second torch, closed up the rear, on the way down the stairs and through the dark cellar rooms.

They moved in silence; they reached the penetrated wall; the Duke of Aricia stepped close to the opening, listened, stretched his head forward, then passed with courageous step into the dark room beyond, while he, turning back, whispered to his son's body-servant: —

"Everything is still. I see only a shimmer of light; it must be in the chapel of which you spoke, Antonio."

CHAPTER III.

IN THE CHAPEL OF THE IMMURED.

HE light was glimmering out of this chapel. We have there left Livio sitting upon the steps of the altar, awaiting Corradina's return. The minutes had gone by slowly to him. It had begun to chill him in the musty, damp-chilled room; a shudder passed over his limbs. Staring upon the niches before him, he felt his glances gradually becoming dazed, as if fettered by them through something unspeakably dismal. There, in the twilight depths of these niches, behind the half-broken-down walls by which these were inclosed, did there not move shadows,— shadows of something living, slowly rising, and, again, sinking down,— as if these niches still had their occupants, their victims,— as if there were still in the dark recesses of the walls, beings convulsed by the death-struggle?

It was stupid and foolish to look at it, since it was only the effect of the gentle movements of the oil-lamp upon the altar, which was still sputtering there from time to time, and carrying on the struggle for its existence in the heavy atmosphere; it was stupid thus to stare upon something which was not there at all; and still Livio was filled with dread thereby.

He heard again also a breath. Foolishness! As if forms that were not there could breathe! And then a slight crash, as if a sole had been gently pressed upon the floor. Was there something living in these vaults? No, nothing! Nothing but the silent shadows were there which attracted Livio's glance, and from which he turned himself away by an effort of will.

He felt for his girdle, and drew forth the dagger hanging down from the girdle by two silver chains. The handle was round and engraved, the blade three-edged. Livio tested the point upon the nail of his left thumb. Still it was too dusky in the room to be able to see how deep the point cut in. Livio placed the weapon between his knees upon the altar-steps under him, drew his knees up and hid his face in his hands, in order not to be obliged to look any more over into the recesses.

"She stays a long time," he whispered. "Perhaps he is dead, perhaps Alessio has let me be deceived; perhaps my first stroke was enough, and there is no need of the second. Then, however, how to get her to Castle Savello?"

Awhile he sat there in this way; more minutes long in which he might have busied himself with plotting how he should allure Corradina to his castle at Albano, if Egino was dead from his wound. Then he heard the breathing again.

A strong, no more to be mistaken, almost snorting expiration — close before him.

Livio raised his head, and his wide-open eyes perceived something which filled him with a perfectly unutterable dread.

His heart ceased to beat; his eyes seemed bursting from their sockets while they stared upon this object, which had grown up out of the floor before him.

There — immediately before him — dazzlingly lighted by all the light which the lamp behind Livio could emit, stood a figure of a man, if it was not some hideous offspring of the night, — a devil — an inexpressibly ugly, grinning head, with wild, gray hair grown low down upon the narrow brow; with a nose like that of a mask; under this a hump; and hanging down right and left of this two long arms, — long enough to be able almost to touch the floor.

It was frightful. Standing before Livio in these surroundings with this suddenness, in the red glow of the struggling oil-light, it was a surprise which could deprive a man of weaker nerves than Livio's of his senses.

The man, or the ghost, or the devil, whatever it was, grinned; under the thick, protruding lips gleamed forth huge, long teeth. Still he appeared not to have stepped to Livio so stealthily with any hostile intent; and when he lifted his arm, it was perhaps because he believed Livio to be asleep, and wished to waken him.

But Livio's fright did not permit him to make such observations. In the same instant when the heart, standing still in the first moments, began again with powerful throbs to propel the blood, which suddenly returned to him, he followed the instinct of fear, of self-preservation; he seized the dagger between his knees, and the blade flashed in the light of the lamp. It cut already the cheek of the frightful form there before him; when just as quickly a powerful fist laid upon his throat a grasp like that of a cramping-iron, and a long arm stretched itself out so far that Livio could only thrust about in the air with his dagger, but no more reach his antagonist.

"Now stab!" was growled forth in hollow tones from the breast of the monster, while Livio's struggling to free himself only had the effect of causing the throttling fist to grasp his throat with redoubled force.

And in this instant another, a second form, was there near the first, throwing itself between the latter and Livio. Livio perceived it, and his hand flourishing his dagger thrust toward it, and struck it; that he felt, but then it became dim before his eyes. He could no longer distinguish who or what this second supposed antagonist was; he could no longer hear how a voice whispered entreatingly:—

"Let loose, let him loose, for God's sake! You are choking him, Uncle."

"If I let him loose, he will call for help and call the monks hither, who will burn us up," exclaimed Uncle Kraps between his teeth. "I will make him cold, the dog, for stabbing me!"

Irmgard wished to make an effort to tear away the dreadful hand of her uncle from Livio's neck, but in this instant she felt herself suddenly become powerless; besides, she felt a violent pain between her breast and shoulder. She sank back, gliding down at the side of her uncle. Thus she sank upon the uppermost altar-step.

"Now you will not stab again!" said Uncle Kraps, without observing her, with a grin of triumph over his fearful strength distorting his visage. "You will not stab again; now lie there in company with your knife!"

He threw Livio, who no longer moved, full length upon the floor.

"O my God!" whispered Irmgard, speaking with difficulty — "Uncle, Uncle, what have you done! You have strangled him, and I could not help it — I became so weak. We must get away, away! Help me get up, and then away!"

"Are you struck?" said Uncle Kraps, stooping to Irmgard, to take hold of her and lift her up.

"Struck — here!"

Irmgard pointed with her left hand toward her right breast, and lifted herself up.

"Come, only come," she added; "if only the lantern is not gone out! I let it fall to the floor in fright when I saw what you were doing."

Uncle Kraps took Irmgard up, in order to carry her forth, when a bright light suddenly fell upon the chapel; softly hastening steps, at the same time, with the loud crackling of a resinous torch, became audible,—double steps, as if of two, who were approaching.

"Some one is coming; away, away!" gasped Irmgard, hastening a step forward.

Then, however, she fell all doubled up.

Uncle Kraps was just on the point of taking her into his arms like a child, when a hand was placed upon his shoulder.

Turning his head, he looked into the pale face of a man glancing at him with fever-lighted eyes,—a face that he knew. Near it was another,—that of a woman strange to him.

"Count Egino!" gasped Irmgard in this moment. "O Count Egino—you—you rescued?"

Over the Uncle's countenance spread a peculiar grin as of defiance, and at the same time of shame. As if Egino's sudden appearance were the most simple and explicable thing in the world, he pointed to the corpse of Livio, and gasped forth, rather than spoke the words, breathing hard:—

"I have made him cold! He has stabbed me!"

Uncle Kraps had evidently at this moment only sense and thought for the one deed that he had strangled a man; only the one impulse to justify his deed, like a surprised child. Egino, however, stared with horrified glance upon him, upon Irmgard, who was drawn up in the arms of her uncle now supporting her, upon the corpse of Livio, around upon the room, and with weak voice he stammered:—

"What a dream this is,—what a dream!"

"It is no dream that you see," whispered a voice,—the voice of the female form which stood near him, carrying a torch in one hand, with the other encircling Egino's upper arm. "The corpse is Livio's! Who are these people?" she added, hastily.

"My best friends," said Egino, still continuously staring upon the group as if he did not trust his senses.

"Count Egino, come,—come and follow us!" exclaimed Irmgard, with difficulty, while she closed her eyes, and let her head fall motionless upon the shoulder of her uncle.

Uncle Kraps walked away in a direction exactly opposite to that from which Corradina had previously come with Livio. He carried

Irmgard like a child upon his left arm, with the right he picked up, in going, a lantern lying upon the floor; it still was burning, and let one descry the dark passage opening in the chapel wall, to which Uncle Kraps approached with his burden, lifting the lantern high up.

"Let us follow; let us follow; let us flee with them!" exclaimed Egino, making a few steps forward with tottering foot.

"With them?" said Corradina. "Yes, yes, let us flee with them; what else remains for us! Come, come; support yourself more upon me; lay your arm upon my shoulder,—come!"

She led, almost carried him. Her right arm had enclasped him, his left hand rested upon her left shoulder; with the left hand she bore the torch.

"We must go with them," she said, "and see if there is an exit into liberty. I dare not go back whence I came. We would pass for Livio's murderers. I would rather, since you are too weak to kill a man, they would kill us both on the spot!"

"And to those others," replied Egino, quickly, "you may with impunity intrust your fate."

"I am compelled to do so. Then on! God will protect us!"

They disappeared in the narrow passage, through which the yellow, dazzling light of their torch flickered before them.

Into the chapel the former stillness and twilight again entered, with which the little lamp on the altar struggled.

Thus a considerable time fled by, till from the side of the castle steps and voices were heard; it was the duke and his companions.

Antonio came first.

Antonio was the only one who, through Fra Alessio, had any definite knowledge of the arrangement of the rooms, and according to Alessio's description, he had also been able to initiate his master therein.

The rest followed the duke; all four had soon reached the chapel, where the little oil lamp burned on the altar. Now the bright torchlight poured itself into the twilight room of the Chapel of the Immured.

"Most holy Madonna!" exclaimed Antonio, espying the lifeless body of his master.

The next moment the duke stood near him.

"The master, the master,—he has been killed!" exclaimed Antonio.

Already the duke had stooped over and taken him by the shoulder, as if to lift him up; then he hastened to rise again. With a cry which trembled with peculiar dismalness, echoing in the dreadful chapel, he exclaimed: —

"*Iddio!* Livio! He is dead,— he is dead!"

Antonio threw the light of his torch on the pale, disfigured face with the protruding tongue, the outbursting, wide-open eyes.

"He has been strangled,— choked!" exclaimed Antonio.

The duke smote his hands together; rubbed his temples with them, as if to hold them around his head, that it might not burst, with all the horrible thoughts which rushed through his brain; wrung his hands again, and said in faltering accents : —

"O God! who has killed him ? Who has killed my child?"

"Poor Master?" said Antonio, kneeling down near the body of his master and breaking into a flood of tears.

"Where is the murderer, that I may tear him in pieces,— that I may make him die a thousand deaths!" exclaimed the duke suddenly, in an outburst of rage, raising his folded fists high above his head.

"The murderer?" exclaimed Giovan-Battista, struggling for breath ; "where will he be? Up there!"

"Whereabouts up there?" asked the duke.

"Eh, do I know? But yet a child sees into that! The monks have surprised the poor Lord Livio in his sacrilege in forcing his way into the dungeons of the Inquisition, and have choked him for it. The Countess Corradina, as less guilty, they may have dragged up stairs there, and secluded her somewhere."

"Impossible!" cried the duke. "How would they have dared to do it? And still, how can it otherwise have been? How can it otherwise have happened? O Antonio, Giovan-Battista, run, bring me weapons here; wake my people; we will strike them dead, all of them, to the last one. We will burn the cloister down; we will put powder into the vaults, and send everything that stands over it to the devil, in revenge."

While the duke, with frothing mouth, continued to vent himself in threats against the supposed murderers of his son, the mason plucked by the sleeve Antonio, who was kneeling over the corpse.

"Sor Antonio," he said, "look here once."

Antonio arose and followed him.

The mason, who, during the foregoing, had been looking around the chapel, led him to the opening in the circular wall through which Egino and the rest had saved themselves.

He pointed to a drop of resinous matter lying upon the floor, which was still smoking, and which had evidently dripped from a torch.

"Body of the Madonna!" said Antonio, "here is another way which does not lead up into the cloister, but probably into the open air."

He went with the mason farther into the passage. Holding the torch to the floor, he found, from time to time, more of such drops of resin.

The duke and Giovan-Battista followed them as they were disappearing.

"Whither will you go? Whither does this passage lead?" cried the duke to Antonio.

"We are examining it," answered the latter; "we find drops of resin and footprints. More persons have, a short time since, come through the passage, Your Excellency."

What Antonio said was not to be doubted. The floor of the passage was of rock, but here and there it presented a soft, muddy earth, as if formed out of layers of dust centuries old, and here were also fresh but confused footprints.

The men pressed forward; they came, after they had gone a distance of perhaps sixty steps, to the end of the passage. An old, rusty, iron-grated door formed of strong bars stood open; it stood in a large, dark room, had evidently been forced open, — for the iron slot in which the bolt had been held had indeed been bent to one side by some kind of strong instrument, — and lifted half out of the old wall.

Antonio lifted his torch higher, in order to light up the dismal room into which they were now looking.

The wall-work showed that they had to do with a very ancient structure, quadrangular, with the corners cut off and arched,— some kind of an old temple substruction; still, there must be somewhere a connection with the outer world, for a gentle draft began to blow back the flames of the torches; Antonio, also, after making some steps forward, cried out, while violently bounding back : —

"Back, back; the floor is broken through here!"

All yielded back, in order not to precipitate themselves with the broken vault upon which they stood, as was shown by the rim of an opening a few steps before their feet. Only the duke tore the torch out of the hand of Antonio, and stepped forward, close to the edge, in order to throw the light down.

"There lies a heap of rubbish under there; one can easily spring down," he said.

"For what purpose, Your Excellency?" replied Antonio, taking the torch back out of his hand. The fresh air streaming in to meet us shows that those who have broken through the grated door have found an exit down there. And so all is explained. The German has indeed been freed from his prison-cell, but, in the Chapel of the Immured, he has refused to follow Count Livio. Your son, Your Excellency, has wished to force him; the German has struggled with him, and choked him, and has then fled this way with the Countess Corradina."

"Then this German, who was still sick and enfeebled by his wound," said the duke, shaking his head, "must possess the strength of a lion, — or the Countess Corradina must have aided him with all her powers. Perhaps it was she who knew this way and told him of it."

"Perhaps," responded Antonio. "But come back, my lord. My advice is that we carry Count Livio away into the castle; that the mason, as he was ordered, build up again the forced opening in the wall, and the monks will never learn that Count Livio, that we, ourselves, have broken into their domains. They may ascribe to a miracle the manner in which the German has escaped them. It is better so, that upon the house of Savelli no suspicion fall of having seized upon their right, and of having committed a sacrilege."

"And who, who obtains revenge for me? Would not these monks be just the best bloodhounds to find out for me the fugitives?"

A low, lingering note trembled feebly through the dark halls.

"Come, come, Your Excellency; the matin-bell is being rung. They will be wakened in the cloister; let us hasten, or else they will hear us, and take us by surprise."

Antonio then seized by the arm the duke, still standing at the edge of the vault-opening with folded arms, staring into the black depths, and drew him away.

They hastened back, and after a short time Livio's body had disappeared from the Chapel of the Immured. In the last cellar-room under the castle of the Savelli, however, was the mason, with Antonio's help, busily engaged in replacing stone upon stone in the breach of the wall, so that only a thorough investigation could enable one to discover what had happened here.

Up in the castle, in the room in which we have already once looked upon the corpse of a Savelli, feigning life, however, and arrayed for a wedding, lay, upon Luca's bed, the rigid body of his brother; and near the bed, looking down upon him with staring glance, stood the Duke of Aricia, pale, quaking, murmuring incoherent words.

Giovan-Battista, who glided with noiseless step over the carpet, in order to light countless waxen candles upon the silver candelabra, did not understand them.

Niccolo and Giuseppe, however, sprung long since upon the mules, which had waited so long in the court, now through the night hastened to the castles in the mountains, to Aricia, to Albano; other servants to dependents and clients in the city, to let it be known that the last heir of the house of Savelli had been murdered.

CHAPTER IV.

BROTHER MARTIN.

T was the hour of noon of the following day. Brother Martin had, in the morning, quietly taken his language lesson with the old Hebrew. Now, he was much excited by that which his order-brethren were telling at the noonday meal of what had taken place. The rumor of the death, of the murder of Count Savelli had penetrated even into the cloister walls, as it had now already been heard in every house in the city. They also knew of the disappearance of the Countess Corradina; and the hasty conclusion that she had killed her kinsman, was too closely bordering upon it not to be immediately formed by each one who manifested any interest in the occurrence.

Of the flight of Egino the brethren had not spoken. The sons of St. Dominicus must not have found it for their good to let that become known. One knew nothing but the two facts that the Countess Corradina, in the past night, had wished to ride to a castle in the mountains (wherefore, in the darkness of the night, was a mystery); and that to the people of her retinue, waiting ready in the court, the news had come that Count Livio, the heir of the house, had been found strangled or poisoned, and that the Countess Corradina had fled, no one could say upon what road.

Brother Martin was, of course, surprised and excited over all this; he was also wonderfully moved by the way and manner in which the news had been received at the table of the monks. It was about as one to-day, in a great city, in the morning receives the news that there has been a fire in one quarter of the town. It was then a customary thing in Rome for one to find in the morning hours three or four murdered men upon the streets.

They would not have spoken of the accident at all, perhaps, if it had not occurred in so great a house as that of the Savelli, and if it had not possessed the charm of mystery.

LUTHER'S MEMORIAL AT WORMS.

Brother Martin had returned to his cell, and was on the point of going out to Signor Callisto Minucci's, to talk with him about this event, when he heard out in the passage, called very loudly and by several voices at once: —

"Fra Martino! Fra Martino!"

At the same time, just as he shoved back the bolt, the door of his cell was hastily torn open; two monks, behind whom stood a man clad in a waistcoat of dark-red damask, with a short, black mantel over it, rushed in, and cried at the same time, in excitement: —

"Fra Martino, you shall come to His Holiness; the Holy Father wishes to talk with you."

"With me?" asked Brother Martin, in alarm.

"So it is; here is a courier who is to bring you in haste to the Vatican."

The courier made with the uplifted hand that gesture which appears as a waving off, and yet which, to an Italian, signifies, "Come here!"

At the same time he said: —

If you are the German monk who recently accompanied Monsignore di Ragusa to the house of Raphael Santi, you must, without delay, just as you are, follow me to the Holy Father."

"I am the German monk," answered Brother Martin, "and I will follow you; I am ready to go out."

The courier turned about.

Brother Martin followed him, and the monks, in astonishment, looked after them both.

"What does the Holy Father intend to do with the poor Fra Martino?" they asked themselves, and then went to spread the news in the whole cloister.

In order to answer this question, let us go in advance of Brother Martin to the high-towering castle into which the German brother has been ordered to the presence of Christ's vicegerent.

CHAPTER V.

THE INCARNATION OF CHRIST IN THE VATICAN.

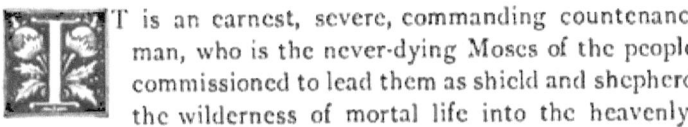T is an earnest, severe, commanding countenance! This man, who is the never-dying Moses of the people of God, commissioned to lead them as shield and shepherd through the wilderness of mortal life into the heavenly Canaan, not according to a pillar of fire, but truly according to the divine illumination, which blows upon him from the gentle vibrations of the dove of the Holy Spirit fluttering around his head — this man had something of the form and features of Moses, as Michael Angelo has carved out the powerful statue of the latter in marble. Giuliano della Rovere, as Pope Julius II., was sixty-seven years of age, but his powerful and firmly built frame stood erect, as is fitting in a commander. His rather blunt than sharply chiseled features evinced that he had lived,— lived in labor, in exhausting excitement, and in enjoyment; but the marks of growing feebleness and relaxation were not in them: the man was full of elastic strength in his step and in his gestures, which became something violent, angular, when excitement broke through the assumed dignity. He spoke abruptly, loudly, and with sharp accent; his voice easily took on a tone which sounded like anger.

The characteristics of his appearance were ennobled by the gray beard, which, in spite of the long-disused style, he had allowed to grow to its natural length.

In one of the chambers of the Palazzo Vecchio, that part of the Vatican building which, as we said before, was at that time covered along its front by the scaffolds of the loggia structure, he was walking to and fro, in a large and beautiful room with heavily carved wooden ceiling adorned with paint and gilding. Costly stuff wrought into tapestry covered the walls, and a great carpet extended itself through the chamber, at whose upper end a table and a high-backed easy-chair stood upon a platform. Upon the table were a high crucifix, writing materials, some paper and parchments with seals attached; near the chair a footstool. By the wall of the room were some divans, and in one of the deep window-niches a little table with mosaic top, upon which stood a decanter, a Venetian glass, and two gilded bowls, one containing fruits, the other confections. Julius II. was not intemperate, but he loved wine. His enemies accused him of liking it too well. In his long, white house-robe he walked slowly to and fro; but he interrupted his course, from time to time, to step up to the window-niche and drink the dark-red juice of the grape contained by the decanter.

There were, besides him, four or five other men present in the room. Three of them we have seen before. One was Padre Anselmo, the sacristan and father-confessor of the Pope; the second, the fat man with the florid face and the strongly squinting eyes, was Monsignore Tommaso Inghirami, his savant, the man who gave information where any question arose for the settling of which we to-day have recourse to an encyclopedia; finally, the third was Padre Geronimo, the Dominican, the Inquisitor of heretical depravity. The first two sat upon the long divan by the wall, where a nod from the Pope had permitted them to take their places; Padre Geronimo stood in the middle of the room, while Julius II. was speaking with him and walking past him up and down.

"It is, indeed, a very mysterious story, Your Holiness," said Padre Geronimo. "Count Livio Savelli is dead, — is choked to death; Countess Corradina has fled; but can she have choked him, — she, a weak woman, choke a strong man? No; certainly not. For choking there is needed the fist of a man, and a strong and sinewy one at that!"

"And where did they find him strangled?" asked the Pope.

"That I cannot tell you, Holy Father, for the Duke of Aricia gave only evasive answers. But in the same preceding night in which Livio Savelli was put to death, the German count, Corradina's lover, as we have said, has also fled from our keeping. We know not who has led him out of the cloister; we know, however, that he has escaped, and we have been able to pursue the course which other persons, whose tracks we found, had taken with him. Have these men, not satisfied with slipping secretly into our cloister and freeing the German, afterward forced their way into the castle of the Savelli in order to steal away Corradina, and at this opportunity throttle Livio Savelli? It is not credible; one may say that would be an altogether impossible temerity! And yet the murder, the flight of Corradina, the flight of the German, must have a connection."

"You capture these people," said the Pope. "Have you not bloodhounds enough? Capture them, and you will ascertain the connection. Bring, then, Livio Savelli a worthy death-offering. I grant it to this poor Duke of Aricia. The man is to be pitied. His Livio was a pliable fellow. But these men all go to the ground because they are not what they ought to be; that is the part of the affair which is not obscure! These barons! God has placed them as watchmen and servants around this our Holy Chair, as he in heaven has placed around his throne the archangels and legions. They, however, have believed that, instead of its protectors, they could make themselves its tyrants, and have beaten it in pieces in order to take its fragments for their own! God punishes them. He has punished them through us, as we have broken their power, and their children choke each other or suffocate together in the mire of their sins. What more do you wish, Padre Geronimo? Go and let spies be sent after the fugitives; since, as you say, this German count is still weak and sick from his wound, before inflicted upon him by Livio Savelli, he cannot have fled beyond the city."

"We have sent out detectives, Holy Father," answered Padre Geronimo. "We have first sent to his lodgings; the keepers of the hotel and his servant appear not to have learned anything of him."

"And his friends? Watch them; keep their houses under guard."

"Has he friends? We know of none. The Duke of Aricia mentions the procurator at the Rota, Signor Callisto Minucci, as his friend. If he is his friend he will betray nothing; and ought we to seize upon and subject to the rack such a respectable and esteemed person without any definite suspicions being advanced against him?"

"I might be able to mention to you a friend of the young German, Padre Inquisitore," here put in Monsignore Inghirami, arising and coming forward.

"See, see," the Pope turned to the latter in a jesting and bantering tone. "Monsignore Phädra! Why, Fra Geronimo, did you not ask him sooner? Such a learned man as he knows everything. He knows from his books what is taking place on the moon and on the earth."

"And Your Holiness knows what is taking place in heaven," said Monsignore Phädra, smiling, "so the world has need to turn to only us two. But this time you would do me too much honor if you understand that I have obtained this out of the books intrusted to my care. The best things we learn are not in the books of Your Holiness."

"Do I so often express a desire for your books that you must force this wisdom upon me? Say what you know!"

"I was with a young German monk of Padre Anselmo's order at Master Raphael Santi's; there the German monk received a message from the escaped Count Egino, who ordered the monk to come to himself on the Aventine. Also, this German monk is a friend, a confidant, of the escaped German Count."

"In truth," remarked Padre Geronimo, "you remind me of it; Livio Savelli also recently spoke of this German monk, saying the escaped man wished to conduct him to the Countess Corradina. And did the message of Count Egino fall upon him at the house of Master Raphael Santi? Did it reach him there?"

"I myself showed him the way to the house of Santi, with whom he had before become acquainted," responded Tommaso Inghirami. "Why are you surprised at that?"

"Strange," replied Padre Geronimo, "very strange; for at Master Raphael Santi's bidding in the days just past, they have been working in the rock-vaults under our cloister-buildings; and only thus was it made possible to escape from the dungeon-cells under our convent. If there had not been an opening just the day before through the excavations to pass through the old vaults and hitherto obstructed passages into the open air——"

"What would you say, Padre Geronimo?" cried the Pope, standing before him, and evidently likewise surprised. "Would you insinuate that my incomparable Master Santi is in a complot to release a guilty person from the hands of Sant Uffizio, and to strangle Livio Savelli! Take care! Do not touch the man!"

The Pope had exclaimed this loudly and angrily. Turning from the Inquisitor, he murmured to himself:—

"Accursed monk! Is he right? Certainly; it is so! This audacious man! To steal from the Dominicans their prisoner! *Accidente!*"

Julius II. stepped meditatively to the mosaic table in the window-niche, emptied the half-filled glass, and muttered further to himself:

"And a German monk should know about it! They will seize him, rack, and torment him, till he confesses everything. Poor Master Santi! We will protect you! By Bacchus! we will. They shall not lay hold upon you!

"Let the monk be brought to me. Procure for me the German monk on the spot; I wish to speak with him instantly!" then suddenly exclaimed the Pope aloud, turning around. "You know of him, Phädra; give the order that some one fetch him!"

POPE JULIUS II. (Raphael.)

CHAPTER VI.

ALFONSO VON FERRARA.

ONSIGNORE went out in haste to have Brother Martin produced.

When the Bishop of Ragusa came back, there stepped near him through the lifted door-curtain at the same time a servant, who said: —

"Your Holiness has arranged for this hour the audience of the Duke of Ferrara. His Excellency waits in the ante-chamber."

"Ferrara, Ferrara!" murmured the Pope, and stroked himself several times upon his beard, as if losing himself in thought. Then throwing up his head, he nodded, and with the words, "Then lead him in to us," he went to seat himself upon his chair, while those present, who were sitting on the divan, arose to their feet.

The servant went back; immediately thereupon the door-curtains were pulled back by two guards. One saw beyond these, still in the ante-chamber, a man richly clad in white-spotted gold brocade, handing over to the servant his dagger and his gloves; a prelate, the major-domo of the papal residence, then stepped forward and walked in with the Duke of Ferrara. In the centre of the chamber, near Padre Geronimo, the major-domo remained standing; the Duke Alfonso von Este, a man of medium size, with a mobile, bright face, dark-hued skin, and a sharp glance from the black eyes, stepped with firm and measured tread to the front of the Pope's platform, let himself down on both knees and kissed the foot, then the ring upon the hand of the Holy Father.

"I bid you welcome, Duke," said the Pope, "since you humble yourself before us, and come to sue for peace. To grant peace is our office."

"I thank you, Holy Father," replied the duke, with a soft and pleasing voice, "for these words, which it makes me happy to hear from your lips. Your commander, Fabricio Colonna, who through his intercession won your pardon for me, has informed me how graciously you require nothing of me except here in your court to express my penitence for having carried on war against you,— against you, the Holy Father of Christendom, and lord paramount of the Dukedom of Ferrara, as which I am here now to acknowledge you,— loudly and openly acknowledge you. I repent not alone having fought on the side of the King of France against you, but I also recognize the ban of the church hanging over me, as I deserve from my conduct, and beg you humbly that you now, moreover, remove that from me."

"Arise, arise, my son!" replied the Pope, taking the duke by the shoulder to lift him up.

Duke Alfonso stood up, and the manner in which he threw back his bearded head with the short, curling hair, showed that he, perhaps the most powerful, and, at any rate, the best Italian prince of his time, had lost nothing of his self-respect by an act of submission, which, in the eyes of his contemporaries, was considered as little disgraceful as kneeling before an altar. Had not, before this, Count Raimund von Toulouse allowed himself to be bloodily scourged to become released from ban? At a later time did not Henry IV. of France make peace with the Pope under much more ignominious conditions than those required of the duke? Did not the representatives of the king throw themselves down before the throne of the Pope erected on the square in front of St. Peters? and were they not obliged to receive absolution with a stroke of the rod?

Alfonso arose, and the Pope added:—

"We shall, I hope, be good friends from now on, Duke Alfonso; so good that I shall have the great pleasure of keeping you here in this noble city of Rome, in which I have collected the greatest masters in every art. For you will not dispute that my fine Raphael Santi is the first of painters; my rude Buonarroti the first of sculptors; and my ardent Bramante the first of architects. You, however, I am told, Duke, would be the first master who fell upon the art of moulding artillery; and such a man this our Holy Chair may well use in such wicked times, when it must defend with cannon its own right and that of Italy."

"Holy Father, you have already, without my artillery, done such brave wonders in this defense; you have contested so victoriously every foreign mastery of our beautiful peninsula, and founded for yourself a kingdom so powerful——"

"For myself?" said the Pope, vehemently interrupting him. "Do not say for myself; do not say it, Duke! My predecessors have fought for themselves,—that is, for their house, for their nephews. I have no house, I have no nephews. My glory is that I have struggled for the sake of the church. Let it be said to you that you may thereby comprehend what you have done when you directed your accursed artillery against my cities and my people in arms; they were battering-rams brought out against the walls of the church, against the house of Christ. And will you make it good by consecrating to the church your art? You are so great a master in every smith's-craft; you understand how to harden steel, also to build fortresses, and, besides, to arrange gay feasts of every kind, to erect stages and theatres,—the world tells of the wonders of Ferrara. Would not Rome be a better place for such arts? And then you would bring to me, also, with your suite that merry knight, Messer Ludovico Ariosto, and our court would possess in him, also, the man whom they extol as the first of Italian poets."

While the Pope thus spoke, sharply bringing forward the words in his way, the duke fixed upon him a questioning glance; he evidently perceived something in these words which caused him surprise. Would Julius II. only provoke him? Was it a merry jest, which, from the severe countenance and the harsh tone of the Pope, only sounded a little pungent? Or had the latter the intention to indicate that he, the duke, had been reduced to so dependent a vassalage of the Holy Chair, that such proposals were allowed to be made to him?

However that was, Duke Alfonso had not come, had not been ordered to the presence of, the Pope to contend with him over that matter, and so he restricted himself to answering quietly:—

"Holy Father, Messer Ludovico is, in truth, a faithful servant of my house; but to follow me to Rome, I would find it quite difficult to induce him. Your Holiness remembers I at first sent just him to effect for me a peace with you. Your Holiness, also, full of graciousness, granted to him an audience, and, as was fit, he had himself conducted to your palace and to your presence; yet, scarcely had my ambassador, Messer Ludovico, stepped over your apostolic threshold, when Your Holiness wrathfully cried out to him that he should instantly get out, if he did not wish to be thrown from the window. He fell into a great fright over this; he mounted his mule in hastening flight, and rode without stopping till he felt himself safe in Ferrara.

Now he would not again trust himself in the neighborhood of your power, even if you were to promise him to crown him upon the Capitol as poet!"

"These poets!" laughed Julius II. "Since Horace left his shield in the lurch, they have always remained the same hares!"

The laughter of the Pope had about it something forced; also an expression came over his countenance which showed to the duke that he, if he had intended to humble himself before the Pope, had, indeed, drawn himself out of the affair. He had insinuated that the power of the Pope did not extend over Ferrara, and at the same time reminded the latter of an outburst of brutal temper, which mention could not have been pleasant to him.

The countenance of the Holy Father had, indeed, darkened a little, when he now continued:—

"You see I have received you better! What concerns the conditions of peace, we shall, no doubt, quickly and easily agree upon. To establish these conditions with you, we have commissioned six of our worthy brethren out of the number of cardinals. You may go, now, Duke Alfonso; settle with them. As a sign of reconciliation and of your absolution, we will give you our apostolic blessing."

While Duke Alfonso threw himself down upon his knees, and again kissed the ring upon the left hand of the Pope, the latter made with the right hand a sign over his head. Then the duke arose, and, with quick, firm step, inwardly rejoiced and relieved, at the side of the major-domo he left the chamber.

Julius II. arose from his chair, stepped down from the platform, and began again to walk up and down, as before.

"Padre Geronimo," he said, after a pause, "you are, in truth, a saint, as we know; but you are still, on that account, no statue of a saint! How can you stand so long? Do as Phädra there, who is no saint at all, and seat yourself. What do you say to this Duke of Ferrara and his bearing? A proud man that! If I were a theologian, as you are, I would quote against him a verse from the Old Testament — alas! I no longer know how it sounds or where it is. Monsignore Phädra, do you know it?"

"Perhaps Your Holiness is thinking of the verse in the first book of Kings: 'You are high in your defiance, but before the Lord will his adversaries become frightened, and over them will he thunder in heaven!'"

"You see this Phädra knows everything. Perhaps you also know,

Phädra, how long this monk whom we have ordered to us will still let us wait."

"In any case longer, Holy Father, than is good for the poor monk, if he should find you in other than a gracious temper. Think graciously that he is one of those slow Germans, and that the road to his cloister and back here is long!"

The Pope turned back to his seat, and dropping down, he said:—

"Pity he cannot make the distance with your tongue, Monsignore di Ragusa, which is quicker; in the meantime we will abbreviate the moments by corroborating these briefs."

Julius II. took a great reed pen, and unrolled the first of the parchments lying before him on the table. After reading it he muttered some unintelligible words, and signed it deliberately with great characters. Then he took a second; in the midst of reading it, he interrupted himself, and said, looking up:—

"Monsignore Phädra, through whom do you have your bishopric of Ragusa managed?"

"Through a Franciscan, Holy Father."

"And you, there, Monsignore di Sienna,"—he turned to one of the other gentlemen in the robes of a prelate, near whom Padre Geronimo had now taken place,—"who manages your church while you draw up at the court these writs which you compel me to sign?"

"Holy Father," anwered the Bishop of Sienna, "it is a brother of the Holy Mount Carmel to whom I have intrusted it."

"And here," continued the Pope, signing the parchment, "I assign now the power of managing the archbishopric of Sevilla to a Capuchin. What true shepherds of your flocks you are; everywhere you give them over to the mendicant monks! Truly, they do it for the lowest wages; and they are better guards of the faith at their posts than you would be, Phädra, for you are a pagan, but they will yet become the whole church—the whole church a mendicant order!"

CHAPTER VII.

FAITH AND WORKS.

Motto: Gieb du mir Antwort auf die Lebensfrage,
Ob die vor Gott geringre Gnade finden,
Die demuthsvoll sich nahn mit ihren Sünden,
Als die mit Stolz auf das, was sie gethan,
Im Ueberfluß der guten Werke nahn?

— M. ANGELO to V. COLONNA.

JULIUS II. was interrupted by the valet's entering.

"The Augustine brother after whom you asked, Holy Father," he announced.

The Pope nodded his head; the servant went back, and immediately thereupon the door-curtain again arose to admit Brother Martin.

Brother Martin's face bore all the marks of heat and of excitement. He had been compelled to make the whole distance at a headlong pace; to mount thus the steep entrance to the Vatican, the innumerable steps of the stair — that even would have taken away his breath if there had not been added to it the excitement of the moment wherein he, the poor German monk, was led before the vicegerent of Christ upon the earth. He grew dizzy; everything whirled before his eyes, so that the objects around him were confused and swimming. The exalted, white-clad old man, who was throned upon an elevation at the end of the great room, swayed before him almost like a vision of dreams. If the usher had not, at the entrance, repeated to him that, so soon as he had crossed the threshold, he must kneel down, he would have remained standing at the door like a pillar of salt.

However, he humbly observed the custom.

Julius II. threw upon him a hasty glance; then he said to the Bishop of Ragusa:—

"You know him; conduct him hither!"

Tommaso Inghirami approached Brother Martin, and touching him on the shoulder, he said:—

"Come; the Holy Father graciously grants to you that you may kiss his foot."

Martin arose; he went through the chamber at Inghirami's side; he knelt again on the platform to touch with his lips the gold-embroidered cross on the white shoe of the Pope; and then he stepped back, in order, breathing deeply several times and composing himself, to direct his glance freely upon the countenance of the Pope.

The Pope looked searchingly upon these features now directing themselves so openly and freely toward him; they appeared to strike him. Passing the hand over the middle of his face, he said:—

"To the mouth, you appear like a jolly brother and a clever fellow; and below that like an exorcist, before whom the devils tremble. Have you ever cast them out?"

The Pope had said this to him in the Italian speech. Brother Martin had, by degrees, become so versed in it that he could answer in the same tongue:—

"No, Most Holy Father,— at least not out of other men's souls; at the most, only out of myself!"

"Out of yourself? And what devils have hidden themselves in you, that you must drive them out?" asked the Pope, with a tone of ridicule.

"The greatest one that has taken possession of me is the devil of despondency, of hopelessness."

"How can one who has faith despair?"

"The faith itself made me despair."

"The faith?" threw in the Pope, distractedly, and evidently more occupied with the personality of the monk than with his words. "That sounds strange. How did the faith make you despair? It must be, then, that you have despaired of the faith."

"And that is even so, most Holy Father; and if you wish to hear my confession of sins, I have fully despaired of the faith, and on that account have suffered much pain! How can I, I asked myself, do enough to deserve pardon and to be justified? How can I, weak one, find the strength to do the works which procure for me salvation? How can I save myself before the angry justice of God? And the anxiety of heart overpowered me; the fear of God came over me with a force which destroyed my consciousness and deprived me of breath."

Pope Julius II. listened to him attentively; what the German there indicated to him in such few words, moved him, perhaps, as something wonderful, strange.

"And this fear of God," he said, shaking his head, "was a devil — a devil which you had to drive out? 'The fear of God is the beginning of wisdom;' now, shall the beginning of wisdom be the Devil?"

"Why not, Holy Father? The Devil can have the beginning of wisdom, but not the middle and the end. The middle of wisdom is love, and the end is peace."

Julius II. again shook his head.

"Fra Anselmo," he cried to his Father Confessor, "listen only to your order-brother. Have you more of such metaphysicians among you?"

"Not so many, Most Holy Father," answered Fra Anselmo, rising, "that it will not repay the trouble to listen to him."

The Pope nodded.

"He may speak further. He may tell wherewith he exorcised his devil, and thereby succeeded in getting rid of the fear of God, like a heretic."

"I have not rid myself of the fear of God," replied Brother Martin, "but out of the fear of God the Devil twisted for me a rope which he placed around my neck, so that I was even at the point of death, and I have torn this Devil's halter away from me. Believe me, Holy Father, it was a hard, hard struggle! I had the book of the Holy Scriptures in my cell, and out of it I drank full draughts of the water of life and of eternal salvation. But immeasurable anxiety and inexpressible pain of soul streamed in upon me with this living water, as a flood in which I believed myself swallowed up. For many weeks no sleep settled down upon my eyelids; the fever threw me upon a sick-bed; the thought of my sinfulness preyed upon my physical strength,—the thought that, as I could not fill the broad, boundless ocean, I, through my works, could not win the boundless eternity of salvation — nevermore; that I could not turn upon me the favor of God, even though my weak human strength should be increased a thousand-fold for doing what the church prescribes for obtaining justification. Out of this situation I have forced myself to a knowledge that all this doing is a subordinate, an incidental thing; that we have only to immerse our whole soul into the faith, in order to feel streaming out of it into us the blessed, peace-giving rest of the soul. For faith awakens love; and because our love sues for the love of God, we are allowed to throw ourselves with a quiet spirit into the arms of God, who will, no doubt, grant to us salvation. The heart filled with fear and anxiety cannot love; only the calm heart can do that. And because I found this out, and thereby became of a joyous spirit, I said, Most Holy Father, I have cast out the Devil from me."

Luther's eyes flashed while he spoke. His countenance was agitated more like that of a man who declares his passion to a woman : more like that of a child who pours out to his mother the outgushings of his enthusiastic heart. He was carried away with the thought that he was speaking to God's deputy upon earth, to the father of all the faithful ; he could not do otherwise before him than to throw the door of his heart wide, wide open. While he was speaking it came into his thoughts that now, directly from the lips of this apostolic veteran, who was, indeed, a living bit of revelation, the Holy Spirit must breathe upon him and pour itself into his open heart ; for, in spite of all the sores and wounds of the church, there was, for him and for millions of others, the Head of the Church, standing high above its degeneracy, still the true and infallible expression of its original principle ; it had remained so, in spite of all that happened.

Pope Julius II., however, shook his head, murmuring some unintelligible words.

In fact, he would have answered, had not Padre Geronimo, Anselmo, Phädra, and the others been present; they were such sharp theologians! Julius II. feared theologians, because he felt himself weak in their science ; and he preferred, in their presence, not to venture upon the smooth ice, — to express no further opinion than to throw in, dryly, the questions : —

"And how have you arrived at this beautiful knowledge that works are of no use, whereby you should hang your gown upon a nail? whereby the sacraments would cease to be sacraments with fasts and castigations? whereby you should throw into the fire your pilgrim-staff, by which you made your pilgrimage to this holy city, Rome? and whereby, in the end, you can become a heathen, — for even the heathen can believe in their gods and love them?"

Over Brother Martin's features glided an expression as of severe disappointment.

With surprise, and a little less loudly, he answered : —

"Holy Father, become a heathen ? I have, indeed, spoken of the

Christian faith, because I recognize how gloriously Christianity outshines all other religions. With faith and love, the man baptized into Christ finds the only mediator; for, of all religions, Christianity alone has a mediator. In all of them there is no one who lifts up man again when he is fallen; to whose breast, to whose love, the sinner can flee when he will atone for an offense; at whose feet he can lay down all his human misery. For the Mediator was a man, as we are; he knows human nature in all its depths, also the impulse of the polluted soul to the new birth. How could a man thirsting for religion, be untrue to the faith which satisfies the heart and the thoughts before all others, to become a heathen?"

"It may be, may be," interjected the Pope, impatiently; "still, you are a fanatic. You think too much, you Germans! What need has a mendicant monk of thinking? Read your masses, sing your Psalter off, and then lay yourselves upon the ear on your straw sacks. Through your thinking you come to heresy. Isn't that true, Padre Geronimo? Let the church think for you, as the church lets us, her only Supreme Head, think for her. And even we do not think; for if we were to rack our brains with thinking, we would at last know no more whether what we have thought out is our finite wisdom, or the infallible suggestion of the Holy Spirit."

"But the brain of man cannot stand still, Holy Father."

"Why not? Is not the Holy Spirit brains enough for mankind? Do your hard German noddles need more? Will you speak against it? Will you raise yourselves against the works laid upon you by the church? Only look at this brother! Throw the stupid monk out for me, Phädra!"

Pope Julius II. began to speak in anger, which was so easily enkindled in him. Fortunately he was appeased by Phädra's remarking:—

"Your Holiness wished to examine him on account of his connection with the German Count ——"

"Did I? Well, he will not know much about it. Had the German had need of a monk for his flight and for the abduction of Luca Savelli's widow, he would not have taken this simple fanatic. You question him, Padre Geronimo."

Padre Geronimo turned to Brother Martin, and said:—

"You know the Count Egino von Ortenburg?"

"Yes," replied Brother Martin, looking absent-mindedly at the

Dominican, and wiping away the cold perspiration which his inner excitement now drove out upon his brow.

"He wrote to you that you should come to him in our cloister at Santa Sabina. What for?"

"Because he had become acquainted with a noble lady, to whom he would lead me."

"For what purpose?"

"I know not."

"Do you know that he has fled, after having killed Count Livio Savelli?"

"I heard that Count Livio Savelli had been killed. I do not believe that Count Egino has killed him, unless it has been in righteous self-defense, and from compulsion. If he has escaped I wish him good luck in it; for I wish to him, as an honorable young German prince, every good."

"How did you become acquainted with Raphael Santi?"

"The Bishop of Ragusa, there, had the good will to me to take me to the celebrated master."

"Have you seen him since then?"

"No."

"Whither do you suppose Count Egino has fled?"

"I do not know, and suppose nothing about it."

"You stand in the presence of our Most Holy Father; in his name I require of you to speak the truth; I require it of you by your vow and your obedience to the church. What do you know of the occurrences of the past night in the Savelli Castle?"

"Nothing," replied Brother Martin, calmly.

"Do you believe that Master Raphael Santi knows of them?"

"*I cannot believe without grounds of belief. The foundation of faith is testimony, unassailable testimony, which, subjected to investigation by my reason ——*"

"Isn't this monk beginning his homily again?" here angrily put in Pope Julius II. "Throw him out, I tell you; he is a blockhead, you see, and knows nothing. Let him run, Padre Geronimo; let him run. I will that they let him run, and that they no more mention Raphael Santi in this affair, nor disturb him; do you hear? I will it!"

Brother Martin, who was gazing upon the reddening countenance of the Pope, felt himself seized by the shoulder. It was Monsignore Phädra and Padre Anselmo, who had hastened forward to take him away, as they knew how dangerous it was if such an order of the Holy Father did not receive immediate execution.

And so, before he was aware, before he had come to his senses, he stood outside in the great ante-chamber. He walked slowly, seeking his way alone through the valets, and porters, and Swiss guards; through great rooms; down many, many steps; over St. Peter's Square, with its chaos of building materials; through the Borgo; finally homeward, to his cloister.

How much poorer a man he was than when he had come this way in such haste, with heart beating so high!

He was affected as is a child that sees his highest upon earth, his father and mother, committing a sin, for whom, then, the illuminating star of his trust sinks into the dirt.

He had in Italy and Rome seen the church in its most unrestrained worldliness. He had been stirred up by the moral degeneracy of those who called themselves priests, by the entire shipwreck of religious feeling in most of them, by their blasphemies and their vice. But as the poor wanderer who has fallen into cold and night, doubts not in his heart of the existence of the sun, so the poor German cloister-brother entertained in his deepest heart his trust in the indestructible power of the principle; and in the sunlit splendor of this principle, the Head of the Church, although imprisoned in bonds of mortality, had yet always stood for him as the highest guardian of the truth, as the last sustainer of his silent hopes.

And now these hopes had taken their flight.

This Pope was a phenomenon as worldly, as earthly, as without love, as unconcerned about the truth, as the hundreds of others that he saw.

To this man, who must be the gentle shepherd of his flock, the father of the faithful, also his own father, Brother Martin, in the full, warm impulse of his heart, had at once, unreservedly as a child, spoken out, as well as possible in the few words granted to him, that which filled his innermost soul.

What had moved, and tormented, and agitated him in many sad hours for months and years; what had been the object there at home of so many profound discussions with pious and learned friends, with his noble and mildly paternal Johann von Stanpitz; the whole inner life of his mind, the sickening of his spirit and its recovery; the darkness of his soul and the light; and the thought out of which, as from the moving star of the Wise Men, this light had fallen upon him, — all this he had told in quickly winged words to his spiritual father.

The Pope had not understood him. The spiritual father had had no ear for the speech of his child.

And, still, he *had* understood him. The Pope was, like all the rest — a shrewd man.

He had perceived on the spot that Luther's thought, like an atlas, took upon itself the centre of gravity of Christianity, removed it from the place assigned it by the church, and cast it into a region whither only German minds could follow it — into the region of the inner being; into a region where good works could no more be offered for gold, as if they were wares representing economic values!

Brother Martin slowly wended his way home. He was not shaken in his conviction, but he was sad, just as he had been there at home in the quiet cloister-cell in Wittenberg. Never did he feel more deeply the sentence he has uttered, "The human heart is a defiant and despairing thing." His heart was so dauntless for the truth it had found, clinging to it so inflexibly, yet so despondent in the feeling of his weakness in presence of the world which will not have the truth!

The consciousness of having a truth which the world has not and will not have, is for noble minds a greater martyrdom than is consequent upon struggling for truth.

That saying of Hamlet,

> "A rent goes through the time; accursed the hour
> Which gave me birth to heal its wounds,"

contains for deeply feeling natures, fanatically ardent for their truth, like Hamlet, the outcry of a fearful anguish of spirit.

Each one is conscious of his mission, but the still dumb prophet feels that the great word which he bears in him yet unspoken, more mighty than himself, will force its way over his lips to make of him a Laocöon; that, so soon as the word is spoken, the great, deep, and filthy pool called life will spew out against him its serpents to encircle and suffocate him. Luther felt, with shuddering and stagnating heart, the soft creeping of these serpents.

When he should succeed in finding the world-moving Word, which should wake again for humanity the lost and dead Christ, and which should overthrow the idols that had usurped his place, then there was no power upon earth to protect him in the conflict which must rage against him. This hour had taught him that the infallible, supreme head of Christendom was his enemy, as all others. He who would be victor there must be stronger than Laocöon.

CHAPTER VIII.

IN THE HOUSE OF GIULIETTA.

BROTHER MARTIN, lost in thought, moved slowly through the streets of Rome.

What he had learned up there in the chamber of the Pope, caused him now to take a different road from that he had intended before the courier from the Vatican had ordered him to the Holy Father. He did not go to the house of Callisto, but turned himself toward the height of the Quirinal, in order to talk with Irmgard.

He would bring to her at once the information which he had obtained of Egino's flight. He knew what a message of joy it would be for the young maiden, and he felt that for himself, in his deep despondency, the only comfort, the only balsam for his wounded spirit would be found in pouring balm into another bruised human heart. His unselfish disposition changed the sentence, " I suffer so others may suffer also," into, " I will bear my sorrow if I can only remove that of others."

As he was passing the entrance to the Colonna Palace, at the foot of the hill, he saw a crowd of people just dispersing. Some gentlemen in rich clothing stood before the door; horses in gay trappings were being led up and down in the court: it was still a part of the retinue with which the Duke of Ferrara had ridden to the audience with Julius II., and they had just now reached home. Inside, in the Colonna Gardens,— Brother Martin perceived this when he was mounting by the side of the lofty wall surrounding these gardens along the Quirinal,— the duke must already be celebrating with his friends and entertainers the good result of the audience, for they were talking very loudly and joyously over there on the other side of the wall.

As he was passing by a great iron door in the wall leading out of doors, he also, with a cursory glance, saw the company. Just then they were tipping their glasses and drinking the health of the Pope and the Duke.

Martin walked on; he reached the widow's house. There, where the hedge left open the entrance to the garden, stood a man clad in black, talking briskly with Beppo; Beppo appeared extraordinarily surprised, and very pale. As Martin walked past him in the garden he was just uttering some exclamations: "Eh!" and "Oh!" and "*Accidente!*" and Brother Martin then heard him cry out:—

"Sor Antonio, you can rely upon me as if I were a client of the noble house of Savelli, and as if my father and all my ancestors since the days of Romulus had been. You may rely upon me!"

"I rely upon you; and since my poor murdered Lord Livio's wife, his poor widow now, is a Colonna, the clients of the Colonna must, of course, stand by us."

"Certainly, certainly they must; but let me see now whither this brother will go."

"See to it, Beppo, and do not forget what I said to you."

"No, Sor Antonio; and I will bring you news so soon as anything the least suspicious occurs."

Beppo had a peculiarly quick and excitable nature, and on that account he left Sor Antonio standing and ran after Brother Martin.

"Whither will you go?" he said, when he overtook the latter at the house-door, which was locked to-day, and laid his hand upon his sleeve.

"To the Germans who dwell with you."

"For God's sake," whispered Beppo, anxiously, "speak low! To the Germans? What Germans? Do you know them? You yourself must be, according to your speech, a———"

"I am a German, and a friend of your tenants."

"Well, well, I will believe it of you."

Beppo knocked at the door.

"I will lead you to them," he said, while knocking. "But if you are their friend, good Brother, do not speak to any human soul———"

Beppo was interrupted, for the door opened, and Frau Giulietta stuck her head through.

"He is a friend, a German, mother," whispered Beppo to her.

Frau Giulietta opened the door entirely, and admitted Brother Martin, whom she recognized.

Beppo remained outside.

The widow led Brother Martin through her sitting-room, which the hearth pointed out as, at the same time, the kitchen, past an open door, through which one could look into a room full of tools, — implements of Beppo's craft,— and opened the door to the part occupied by their tenants. Stepping into the room, Brother Martin was startled when his first glance fell upon an old canopied bed in the background, and saw that Irmgard rested upon it, and with a motion indicating the utmost feebleness turned her head to him.

"Irmgard," he exclaimed, "what has happened to you? Are you sick?"

Uncle Kraps, who, like a picture of grief, sunken into himself, was seated at the foot of the bed, had moved away at the entrance of the monk. When he heard the German words, a wonderful distortion convulsed his face. He stammered out sobbingly:—

"Some one has stabbed her; some one has stabbed her to death, and I have made him cold! He has not moved a limb any more; but now I have the sin upon me, the mortal sin upon me, the mortal sin!"

Brother Martin fixed, with astonishment, his glance upon the remarkable form talking as if in ravings; then he turned to Irmgard, and repeated:—

"What has happened? Speak, poor child!"

"I have been wounded last night," said Irmgard, with a weak voice.

"Wounded — badly wounded?"

"The physician says so, and I feel that it is really severe!"

"Just God! you poor, poor girl! You have also a physician?"

"He has been here twice, already; the son of our landlady has brought him. He bound up my wounds this morning."

"But tell me how it has occurred."

"We had found an entrance into the cloister — into the dungeons. At the same time the Countess Corradina with Lord Livio Savelli, had come into the same rooms to get Egino out. We met, and — speaking is difficult for me; I have lost too much blood before I was bandaged, the doctor says; let my uncle tell you. My uncle has killed Livio Savelli. Now, the murder lies heavy upon his soul, and he is grieving for some one to whom he can confess it. Let him confess it to you!"

"Yes; I have no rest, no rest more, till I can confess it. Let me confess it to you, Brother!" sobbed Uncle Kraps.

"Well, well, that he may," assented Brother Martin. "But first tell me, where are they — where are Egino and this Corradina?"

"Both in the house — of Signor Callisto," answered Irmgard, uttering the words with difficulty.

Brother Martin looked around in the spacious chamber. His glance flew over the few pieces of old furniture; over the picture of Christ that hung in a dust-blackened frame on the wall; over a great white marble bust, the image of a beautiful, but severe-looking, heathen goddess, which stood by the wall opposite Irmgard's bed. He took a chair and placed it in the most remote corner; Uncle Kraps followed him, and knelt down before him and wept and whispered his confession. Brother Martin questioned him now and then, and thus he obtained information of the events of the past night so far as Uncle Kraps could give it. When he had communicated the absolution, he arose and took the place left by Uncle Kraps at Irmgard's feet. His eyes rested a long time with a moist glance upon the poor young girl.

"Irmgard," he said then, softly, and with a voice through which emotion trembled, while he seized the hand resting upon the coverlet, "you have also endangered your life for the sake of this young man, who yet loves another."

"If he loved me," she replied, with a feeble smile, "it would be no great service. Then my death would be his misfortune. Now, I die for his happiness. Is it not better so, Brother Martin?"

"You are an angel in spirit!"

She shook her head.

"An angel? I repent only one sin. It was all, indeed, only the consequence of my unfortunate advice!"

"Such consequences you could not foresee."

"Yes; but the impulse to help him made me so sinfully inconsiderate, that I gave him such an advice. And, perhaps," she added, sighing, "perhaps there was still another sin besides."

"And what, Irmgard?"

"Can I tell it to you? When I advised him to go into the cloister, in order thus to come into the vicinity of the Countess Corradina, there I fought against my own heart. I chided my heart for what existed in it, sinful, — sinful jealousy! Perhaps that was wrong, — that I exercised violence against my own heart."

"That was not a wrong," put in Brother Martin.

"Do you know that so positively? Is one allowed thus to repress her heart and her whole soul? Is one allowed to act thus against her strongest, best emotions?"

Brother Martin did not answer. He only looked at her questioningly and in surprise.

"You do not need to quiet me over this consciousness of sin," she continued, smiling. "I have meant it for good. I have yet also done the most if he is saved, and now becomes happy. Corradina said — when we were in the flight she said it — that on the way in which she would have led him into liberty, through the Castle of the Savelli, there certainly would snares, or murder, even, have been lying in wait! Now he is free — by me! I am not sorry that I have death from it. I do not cling to life. If only some friend would care for Uncle Kraps! I wish that it should go so well with him. He can become so wild,— as wild as a beast. But still he is good. Even when he grieves that he has committed a murder, I still love him. He would only defend himself; and, besides, his wildness came upon him. I still love him, but love life no more. See, there,— I will gladly go to Him with the bleeding crown; he is my brother; I will go to him. Is it not true that he is my brother in pain and good will?"

Martin followed the direction of her eyes, which lay upon the head of Christ on the wall.

"So He is," he said, also casting his eyes, large and luminous, upon the picture. "He is your brother, and is near you. For you they have not been able to slay him; your spirit keeps him alive for you. And even without the pain he would be your brother, as he is that of every human soul that seeks and loves him!"

CHAPTER IX.

THE PICTURE OF CHRIST AND THE HEAD OF THE GODDESS.

AFTER Frau Giulietta had conducted Brother Martin to the room of the sick, she had gone back,—back to Beppo. She found him standing in the middle of the garden path. He had torn off a leaf of a bush and was chewing it, and looking at the ground, lost in thought. When his mother laid her hand on his shoulder, he started violently.

"O mother!" he exclaimed, taking a deep breath.

"Will you now tell me what all this means?" said Frau Giulietta, in great warmth, and still with a subdued voice. "May I now learn how it comes to pass that you bring that poor girl to the house, wounded to death, in the middle of the night? And why does this Pasquino, this wine-bibber of a dwarf, mutter to himself as if he had become deranged? And why did that great, black-clad man come to you, who just now left? And why should I keep the house so carefully locked? And why do you put off my questions about this with nothing but evasions and confused exclamations, as if I were a child, and without right to know?"

"My dear mother," exclaimed Beppo, laying his clasped hands upon her shoulder, and looking upon her with tears in his eyes, "I will confess everything to you, everything, everything — what a blockhead, what a dunce, what a brainless fool I was! Oh my God! if now, now, where this Sor Antonio was and chased a mortal fright over my members, I did not have you, in order to acknowledge and confess it to you, it would break my heart."

"So, now, speak,—speak what has happened! Tell where you were with these foreigners last night."

"Where we were, mother? You have heard that Livio Savelli was killed last night, and that his sister-in-law, Countess Corradina, has eloped."

"Holy body! You surely would not have killed him?"

"Who knows, mother, who knows? By Heaven! it is not impossible!"

"Not impossible that you,— that you —" cried Frau Giulietta, in horror, and seizing with trembling hand the arm of her son, as if to hold herself upright in her fright.

Beppo led her to the seat under the plane tree and the mulberry tree. There he dropped down near her, and laying his hand upon her shoulder, and staring upon the ground as if annihilated, he whispered : —

"See, this is all that I can tell you. The young girl heard from me that we had made excavations, and had found an entrance to the subterranean rooms under the cloister of Santa Sabina, where they, the Dominican monks, as they say, have their cloisters, and where the immured languish. Now, she wished to go in there."

"In there!" cried Giulietta, in the utmost astonishment. "Impossible!"

"It is so, mother. She wished to go in there."

"But, Holy Mother! why — for what purpose?"

"She wished to see the ones immured there."

"To see the immured — she, the German girl?"

"She wished it — she wished it, at all events."

"See the immured of Sant Uffizio!" repeated Frau Giulietta, unable to recover from her astonishment.

"She had set her head upon it."

"But didn't you say to her that the Sant Uffizio is a sacred thing; that ——"

"I told her everything; but she begged and begged, and I, — I was such a fool, such a wretched fool, that I promised to show her the way."

"And you did that, — really did that?"

"I did it. I procured one of the great lanterns which we use in the excavations. At the third hour after Ave Maria we went, — an hour before midnight. You were fast asleep, and did not notice how we stole away."

Frau Giulietta struck her hands together with an "O God!"

"We went to the Aventine; there, where, left of the Marmorata, lies the débris at the foot of the rocks, you know, there is an old, now unused wine-cellar; through this one succeeds to the vaults under the cloister. A passage, which had been obstructed, leads upward, and this passage we had opened the day before; Master Raphael Santi had ordered it. Through this passage I led her, and then through an opening in a vault up into a great room, — great, desolate, and dark. At the end of this room, in one corner, is an old, iron-grated door, through which one comes farther, and perhaps into the dungeons, perhaps into the cloister itself. There I remained behind, mother — believe me, I remained behind, I had such dread of sacrilege —— "

"Go on! Tell me further!" interjected Giulietta.

"I saw how the German dwarf shook at the iron door; how he drew out a piece of iron, and broke from the old wall-work the slot in which the bolt stuck. I believe he could have done it with his mere fingers, for this hunchbacked, wrinkled man has the strength of an ox. I believe he could take a buffalo on his crooked back. He broke the slot out as if it had been set in rotten wood, and then they both went, he and the young girl, through the door, and took the lantern with them, leaving me behind them in the dark. I saw how they stole along the passage farther and farther. Like dark shadows they glided on; the light of the lantern traveled over the dark passage-walls near them, growing ever smaller and weaker. Finally it disappeared altogether. Everything was now still,— was night around me. I heard my heart beat; I heard the dust gently falling down; I heard my anxious breathing — that was all. And then suddenly voices,— voices, but quite from a distance. I was dreadfully frightened, you may yourself think; I wished to follow them, but groping forward, I struck my forehead against the iron door standing open in the room in which I was waiting. That made me more considerate. I also soon saw the light of the lantern again shimmering, and then a bright light as of a torch glowing. It came nearer and nearer; the shadows were there again, two, three, shadows; one shadow so broad and large, what could it be? They hastened and came quickly to me. God, mother! how I was frightened when I saw that the great shadow was nothing but the crooked dwarf, who was carrying the young maiden in his arms; and as if dead, as if dead forever she was, her head falling back like that of a corpse!"

"Most Holy Virgin!" exclaimed Frau Giulietta. "And the other shadows?"

"Did I know them?" said Beppo. "A tall, beautiful, proud lady, and a handsome, but pale, young man, who came weak and tottering, and whom the lady led, who supported himself upon her so."

Beppo laid his left arm around the neck and upon the left shoulder of his mother.

"So they walked, and when they saw me they beckoned with the hand, and murmured, 'Away, away, Beppo.' The dwarf said that, and held the lantern to me, that I should carry it; but the lady gave me also the torch, and so I took both; and so we hastened farther, springing through the opening in the floor down upon the heap of rubbish lying under it, and through the passage, and, finally, into the open air. Out in the fresh night-air the German girl recovered from her unconsciousness, and whispered with the others, and wished to go upon her own feet; but the dwarf would not permit it, but held her in his arms. They talked together in their German speech, and then the dwarf walked forward with his burden, and carried her here. I walked in advance, showing the way. I had then only the lantern; the torch I had hurled away into the Tiber; and so we came back, the dwarf carrying the girl, and I breathlessly hastening on in advance."

"And the gentleman and the lady?"

"They had disappeared as we came on,— vanished into the night. The gentleman and the lady must have fallen upon another way, on a spot where they could remain behind without my perceiving them. They had already disappeared when we were passing over the Campo Vaccino; there I looked around after them, and saw them no more."

"And who, I pray you, were they? Whither did they come? Who has thus mortally wounded the young girl? and what has Livio Savelli to do with it? and who has murdered him? and ——"

"Mother, I have told you all,— all that I know; but the man who just went away from me said ——"

"Who was he?"

"His name is Antonio, the body-servant of the murdered Livio Savelli. He said the sister-in-law of his master has fled, and at the same time a German count, Countess Corradina's lover, out of the Dominican cloister; and they must be the murderers, and all that belong to the house of Savelli search and spy after them, and guard every road and bridge; and we, we who are clients of the house of Colonna, must assist them. Sor Marcello, the master of affairs over in the Colonna Palace, had told him he should, in passing by, let me know, and commission me, in Marcello's name, to help discover the fugitives. How that man has perplexed me, I cannot at all tell you!"

"Oh! we poor, poor creatures!" exclaimed Frau Giulietta; "into what misfortune we have fallen through these Germans and through your folly, Beppo!"

"Yes, through my folly!" said Beppo, the tears coming into his eyes.

"Will they not track up, investigate, search, till everything in this dreadful, dark story lies as clear before the eyes as daylight; till they know that you were the guide of these people; till they seize upon you, and — O, my God, my God!" groaned Frau Giulietta, who from dread and horror could speak no further, but broke out in a flood of tears.

Beppo folded his hands, held them between his knees, and staring upon the ground, he said: —

"All that I say to myself, mother. Oh! if I could only do something to make it good again; only something with which to punish myself right severely for my brainless stupidity!"

"Think of nothing further than saving yourself," sobbed Frau Giulietta. "You must flee, Beppo,— you must flee instantly. You must be far, far from here when they find out the connection of this affair, and then the bailiffs and their chief come to take you prisoner!"

"And if they then take you,— if they drag you before the court, as sharing the knowledge of the affair, as an accomplice? No, mother, I will not flee; I will leave you in no case, mother."

"You must, Beppo ——"

"Say nothing more about it. I can do only one thing to atone for my follies — only one; to stay with you, in spite of my anxiety; to remain to protect you; to be able to say that I will make known all that I know, but leave my mother untouched, for she,— she knows nothing about it. I will take upon myself the anxiety for your sake, mother. It is the only thing I can do to atone for my sin,— the only thing! Say nothing further about it; I remain with you, mother."

Frau Giulietta found Beppo immovable in this; also when she pleaded with him, if he would not leave Rome, to stay, but to flee into one of the numerous asylums to which transgressors took their flight, — into a church or a cloister, or into the court of a cardinal.

"That would be foolish," he said; "for thereby I would betray myself even before they have a suspicion against me, and betray with myself that poor German girl."

"The poor German girl! Do you speak thus of these abominable

Germans who have led you astray, and think more of them than of your mother's anxiety of soul?" sobbed Frau Giulietta.

Loud talking and gay laughter at this moment penetrated from without, into the quiet corner of the garden in which Frau Giulietta and her son sat in such deep trouble. Beppo sprang up and stepped out of the thicket to the lower hedge, to see who was coming: he espied a whole crowd of young people, about twenty, who were passing by. In advance went a handsome and finely built young man with a long neck, a little bowed forward, and pale, evenly olive-tinted skin. He was clad in black velvet, with a dark-green over-garment, over which a golden chain adorned the breast, while from his black cap fluttered back a long, white plume. Another young man similarly clothed, only without the chain, bore in his hand after him the sword of the first, fastened to him by a fine golden pendant.

Beppo made a profound bow when the crowd, which appeared as if some prince had come hither with his suite, was opposite to him. The young man at the head saw him, and recognizing him, turned and stepped to the hedge behind which Beppo stood, while the newcomer gayly cried out : —

"Ay, isn't that Beppo, my industrious workman? Do you live here, Beppo?"

Beppo bowed again, slightly reddening, and answered : —

"Just so, Master Raphael Santi."

"And this is your little house, and your garden? Look, look, how cleverly this Beppo has housed himself! Can there be fresher air and a finer prospect in all Rome? Let me into your garden; and I wish to see your house, too, Beppo. Come here, you Giovanni ; we will make our call upon Beppo instead of upon the great Alfonso von Ferrara and the mighty Fabricio Colonna, over there. They can forego our company, the proud lords ; but Beppo is a brave youth, and will rejoice if we visit him. Will you not, Beppo?"

"Ay, long live Beppo and his little house!" exclaimed the others, the pupils and art comrades, in overflowing humor, and always ready to act upon the suggestions of their young master.

"Long live the fresh air in Beppo's garden!" was further cried out, in good-natured sport.

Raphael had stepped into the garden, to whose entrance, on the inside of the hedge, Beppo had approached, with his cap torn off. Now, for the first time, Raphael perceived the poor fellow's deeply downcast mien.

"Eh, brave Beppo, what is the matter with you? Have we so frightened you with our noisy breaking in? Do you fear that we will voluntarily tread down your cabbages and your artichokes here?"

"It is not that, noble master," stammered Beppo,—"only that I cannot at this hour lead you into my house, because,— because——"

"Has he just hidden his sweetheart in there, whom he will not let us see, this rascal of a Beppo?" exclaimed laughingly the one with the sword.

"Because a sick girl is in the house," exclaimed Beppo, with a suppressed tone, whispering.

"That is something different," said Raphael; and showing the pupils back, he added:—

"Who is she? A sister? your mother? poor Beppo!"

"It is not one belonging to us; it is a foreigner, who lives with us for rent."

"A foreigner? And still you seem so troubled and pained? Is she so dear to you? or is her condition so bad? Or is it want and need? Can I do something, Beppo? Is any assistance needed? You can speak openly to me, you know; I gladly help——"

Beppo looked with emotion into the features of the master, who, with such a noble expression, gave utterance to so warm a desire to help. He was tempted to trust to him at once his whole grief, when the house-door was opened, and Brother Martin, coming out, stepped upon the threshold.

"Ah! is it so bad you have already sent for a priest?" said Raphael, with a glance at him; and then recognizing Brother Martin, he went to him with a "How, is it you? you here?"

Brother Martin, seeing the company of young men, had remained standing on the threshold. His eyes lighted up when he recognized Raphael, and without saying a word he beckoned to him quickly with the hand and stepped back into the house, out of which he had come, and whose door still remained open.

Raphael followed him. He followed him through the room which was at once sitting-room and kitchen. Through the door which Brother Martin gently opened to the right, Raphael entered Irmgard's chamber,—the bright, pleasant room with old, but well-waxed and polished furniture, and the white, fine mats over the red bricks forming the floor. What Raphael next observed upon entering was the white marble image which was placed to the left by the wall on a pedestal rudely formed of wood. He recognized a very good copy

of the fine head of Juno, which to-day is called the Juno Ludovisi.
A talented young man, Beppo's friend, had intrusted it to his care,
since the former had gone to his native place, Ceprano. Opposite to
this, on the opposite wall of the great room, upon the bed with plain
curtains of green serge, which were drawn back, he discovered Irmgard, her face flushed with a strong glow of fever, her eyes large,
with a weak, indifferent look directed toward those entering. At
the foot of the bed sat Uncle Kraps, again drooping over, staring at
the floor, moving his lips, still without uttering an intelligible word.

Raphael approached the bed.

"Is it you lying here in so bad a condition?" said he, full of sympathy, seizing her hand. "Poor child, so far from your land! Have
you good nursing and everything you need? Shall I send my
physician to you? Shall I send you my Margarita, that she may
look after what is to be done? You seem to be here with none but
men."

"My mother nurses her," here whispered Beppo, who had followed
the two men into the chamber. "We do everything possible, master,
to alleviate her bad condition. We have also had here Messer Arran-
ghi, who is a skillful surgeon and a reliable friend."

Irmgard nodded her head to Beppo as if in gratitude, and while so
doing smiled painfully, as if she would say, "From a physician is no
help for me." Then her glance wandered from the men who had
approached her bed, and was directed upon the wall before her, where,
over the head of her uncle, hung the painting in the old, black
frame,— the pale head of Christ with the crown of thorns; an old
and unartistic picture of the time of Masaccio.

Her eyes took on something indescribably mild, spiritual, soulful,
as she directed them from those present toward the picture.

Raphael observed her awhile still with aroused sympathy; yet,
since she did not again turn to him her glance, did not speak, and
seemed to forget those present, he turned away to the window,
through which one could overlook the little garden, at whose entrance one perceived the troop of the master's companions waiting.

"Why have you led me hither, Brother Martin?" he here whispered to the German monk. "If I can be of use here, tell me."

"See what she is looking at!" responded Brother Martin, just as
softly.

"At the *Ecce Homo!*" replied Raphael. "What of it?"

Brother Martin did not answer. He took him by the hand and led him out of the chamber and out of the little house.

Not till they were again in the garden did he say:—

"I have brought my head back out of this chamber full of thoughts; and when I saw you, I beckoned you hither to show you something which may also give you something to think about. That young creature in there has a great heart and a deeply feeling soul; there is a full and pure human spirit in her! She has, in the past night, fallen into a remarkable adventure, and in it has been wounded, so that she will hardly come out of it with life. She, at least, thinks that she will die. And now, Master Raphael, have you followed the glance of her brightening eye? Did she look upon the masterpiece of heathen art in her chamber, the head of a goddess gloriously hewn out of marble, or the picture of Christ, of which you will best know that it is indeed only right feebly and unskillfully painted? To whom did her soul fly? To what did her heart, thirsting for consolation, cling? And where did she find comfort?"

Raphael was silent awhile before he answered:—

"You are thinking about our last discussion, and believe you have vanquished me now by a tangible proof that to the human soul in pain, only the art which serves faith is of benefit."

"And am I not right?"

"No; a Grecian maid in dying would certainly not have looked upon the bleeding head of a tortured mortal, but the beautiful head of the mother of the gods!"

"Would it have given to her the comfort which the poor maiden imbibes from the countenance of the Redeemer, and which is reflected by Irmgard's looks?"

"It all depends," said Raphael, without answering the question, "upon the ideas and thoughts which we have learned to associate with the pictures. Let us throw all that aside; still the truth remains that the head of Juno is beautiful, the suffering head of the primitive Christ is deeply moving. Out of both looks forth something pure, great, human, in its noblest form. The one looks down upon us from the height of beauty; the other, out of the depths of soul. The one compels us through the form; the other, through the spirit which stands beyond earthly beauty."

"Does not the spirit stand high above the form?"

"Let us not contend about it! Let us strive to unite the form of one and the spirit of the other; let us represent the perfect, but pure, beauty of earthly form unabridged and undraped, but in the light of most heavenly thoughts, in the midst of the clouds of heaven!"

Brother Martin nodded.

"Well, well," he replied, "with this word of yours I will then be satisfied; and let us also bring our discordant opinions to an agreement, for I see I can yet reach no more with you!"

"And now tell me," continued Raphael, "by what adventure has this maiden —— "

"I cannot!" Brother Martin put in. "It is a secret of the Confessional. The girl's uncle has confessed it to me. This deranged and half-beastly man has no greater desire than to be able to confess what has happened —— "

"Then pardon my question," broke in Raphael, "and farewell, Brother Martin. My time presses. You know my house and the way to me, in case you need any assistance for your German friends. Good-night, then; and also to you, Beppo, good-night!"

Beppo had kept himself at a respectful distance upon the threshold. He came now to accompany the master through the garden. Brother Martin also took his departure; he went overwhelmed with his thoughts, excited as he had scarcely ever been in his life,—a feeling in head and breast as if they would burst.

CHAPTER X.

THE WATCH-DOG.

T was a desolate road through a but scantily built-up, ruin-filled neighborhood of Rome upon which Brother Martin entered, over heights upon which arose the old Sabine city of Quirium and Rome's most ancient capitol. Over the ridge of the Quirinal Hill he wandered northward to Monte Pincio, which was no less desolate; for then Sixtus V. had not yet built here, nor formed the streets which still to-day are called Via Felice and Via Sistina, after this sarcastic and cunning, but brave ruler.

There stood on this road poor, solitary houses covered in part with reeds; churches lying isolated with cloister buildings attached; ruins of old baronial towers; darkly massive, broken-down archways of antiquity; mountains of rubbish and fragments of fallen structures towering aloft; between them cultivated fields, upon which, according to the customs and rules of their forefathers, as already complained of by Virgil, three or four kinds of products were being coaxed at the same time from the same piece of ground.

The neighborhood was unfrequented, and so Brother Martin, without becoming disturbed by meeting persons, could allow himself to sink into the seething thoughts which, without his perceiving it himself, now stormed forth in the hastening step; now made him stand still as if rooted to the ground, directing his eye feebly upon some point to his left in the panorama of the Eternal City below him,— a point which he still did not perceive.

What he had experienced on this day!

The Pope had thrust him back with his soul-life filling his whole heart. He had seen how from up there the church was ruled by the "Holy Spirit!"

He had, through that which Irmgard's uncle confessed to him, thrown a glance into the dark, wherein lay the weapons with which the "Holy Spirit" defended and maintained its government. The picture of the "Chapel of the Immured" stood before him, and caused the blood to congeal in his veins.

And while he was now walking along, agitated in his innermost being, as if incited and scourged by the storm in him to some strong, violent action, to some deed which could save him from distress, it seemed to him as if something ran near him,—an evil spirit, a cunning, jeering animal, which looked at him as that watchful dog of the poet,—

> "Within the heart-depths most profound
> Of e'en the most avowed believer,
> Sits Doubt, the ever-watchful hound,
> To bay at Christ as a deceiver."

It was heart-gnawing doubt which ran near the form of the unhappy German monk walking along over the heights of Rome.

He fixed his eyes upon it as the shadow lengthened which the sun, setting behind the Vatican, threw near him upon the dry, hard grassplot, drawing upon the ground a giant image of the dark man in the gown, with the ends of his garment fluttering behind him in the wind.

Had he been able to exorcise the Devil, as the Pope gave him credit for, he would have hurled his most powerful exorcisms against this Devil. He could not do it.

The dog barked on and on.

"There is no original sin!" said his barking. "It is not true, that proposition about original sin. And upon this rests everything. With this everything falls. What impelled this confounded half-witted old man to confess to me, with such anxiety of soul, that he had killed a man—that he was the murderer of Savelli? What else but because the most enveloped human nature is something originally good, which impels it to remove from itself the evil, to hurl it away, and to become healed from it, as from a cancer?"

If he had heard Beppo's confession to Frau Giulietta, Luther would have added: "What impels this young man to atone for a sin with which he reproaches himself through a pain, through anxiety and distress, which he takes upon himself? What is this pain in him other than the bitter medicine which he will sip against the evil that has come into his good nature? The evil, sin, is only the foreign, diseased stuff, the matter which shall suppurate in pain and smarting. Man is good, is originally good, not originally bad. The conscience is the umbilical cord by which he is connected with the original maternal good. The feeling that he is descended from an original good, that he is a piece of it, gives to him faith. Faith is the perception of the good ruling the world. The illusion of hereditary sin creates the illusion of the Devil. Evil is only a sickening of the good, — an illness, as a fever is an illness. What is a fever? Is it a being? No. It is nothing lasting, nothing having an existence. No, no; the strings of the human soul have a beautiful and pure tone, although they may get out of tune. Getting out of tune, not the tune, is the evil. Cold is only want of heat. Evil is only want of good. Therefore do not ask, 'How came evil into the world? Through a serpent?' Foolishness! Did not Moses hang your loathsome serpent around the cross? The serpent which you have wound around the cross, that is your lie and fraud. The cross! That calls to mind the voluntary death of Him who was willing to take upon himself the suffering of mankind; and from those features, even now, the sick Irmgard derives consolation. Upon himself, the blessed one, for he is stronger than we all. If we think of all the grief of the poor human race, the impulse seizes us to take upon ourselves a bit of all this sorrow around us. We would like to bow the neck to fate, and call to it: 'Place upon me a part of the burden; I will help the unhappy one to bear it; give my brother's care to me for one day. Let him for this one day rejoice!'

"That lies in human nature. Is human nature bad?

"Is there a hereditary sin in this Irmgard, who does not complain, and is consoled because she has sacrificed her life for him whose life and happiness she believes herself to have purchased through the sacrifice?

"Is it a depraved nature which looks out of her eyes upon the picture of Christ as upon that of a man who is her God, but also her brother in pain?"

So barked the dog which ran near the monk over the precipice of the Pincian Hill,—a heretical dog; an animal like the "poodle" of Faust, but, truly, the "poodle's" inner nature was different. Still, his bark tormented the poor monk inexpressibly. Since he felt himself as if broken, and since to his breast the act of breathing became difficult, he dropped down upon a ridge covered with short grass, which lay vacant between two built-up pieces of ground. He mopped his brow with his handkerchief, and then supported his broad chin upon the arm propped up by his knees.

With gloomy brows drawn together he looked over to the "Eternal City" and to the Vatican, which, with its proud and firm mass, was darkly delineated upon the horizon, because the sun stood already behind it.

Over there in the Vatican this Master Raphael Santi painted on the walls his pictures for the Pope, beautiful, sinless human forms such as Plato considered the embodied thoughts of God.

Was not this Raphael right? Brother Martin began to understand him. But then, then, if he was right, then everything, all theology and all scholasticism, tumbled into a heap. Mankind had been for so many centuries a wanderer in the night!

After awhile there came this way an old man driving a donkey before him. He stopped before the monk, and asked:—

"Eh, brother, do you wish to get the perniciosa?"

Brother Martin looked up.

"What shall I get?"

"Do you not know that whoever sits upon the ground here contracts the fever,—the perniciosa?"

"The perniciosa," replied Brother Martin, smiling bitterly; "certainly, certainly. I know it seizes upon the human frame here, and I believe it shakes mine already."

He arose and walked on to his cloister.

CHAPTER XI.

SAN DOMINICO'S TORCH AND SERPENT.

WHEN Padre Geronimo, the Inquisitor, had returned from the Vatican to his cloister at Santa Sabina, he had the prior and Father Eustachius called to him into the cloister-garden, into which he had gone down. He had asked to have himself informed of what had happened during his absence, and the prior had imparted to him that the order-brethren down in the city, at Santa Minerva, had undertaken the careful oversight of the German servant of the escaped Count Egino, of whom it was to be supposed that he would seek out his master, in case he had not been informed of the latter's stopping-place; also, that some one had discovered the trace of the German maiden who had accompanied Egino at his first entrance into the cloister; that she had some weeks before arrived from Germany with a kinsman, had resided at the German inn, and after some days had withdrawn from there — no one knew whither, but some one from Santa Minerva would use all diligence to find her again. "And, finally," said the prior, concluding his information by bringing the most important last, "some one has again undertaken an examination of the vaults, and has discovered that the wall separating the subterranean rooms of the cloister from those of the Savelli Castle have been broken through, and walled up again with careless haste."

"One thing yet you have forgotten to mention, worthy father," added Father Eustachius; "that is, that Brother Alessio has become sick of a fever, which seems to have its foundation more in an excitement or anxiety of mind or a suffering dread than in any other cause."

"The lay brother Alessio?" asked the Inquisitor.

"He was intrusted with the service of the German count," added Father Eustachius.

"That is remarkable; you may investigate what is the matter

with him, Eustachius," replied Padre Geronimo, while he seated himself upon a stone bench under the old olive tree which tradition asserted Saint Dominicus himself had planted. "But," he continued, "it is not strange, what you inform me of the penetrated wall. How could it all have been possible without that? It was just a long prearranged plan, in which two strong and clever men have labored to each other's hand. From one side they have caused that dividing wall to be broken through; from the other, under the pretext of searching for the treasures of antiquity, they have built for themselves a way into our vaults ——"

"What are you saying, Padre Geronimo?" exclaimed the prior, in astonishment.

The exercise-master only smiled; it was only what he had long suspected.

"So," continued the Inquisitor, "they have forced their way in, and set the German count free. In the same hour of the night, the Countess Corradina has come hither from the side of the castle, prepared for flight; Livio Savelli has surprised them, has opposed her flight with the German, and the accomplices of the two fugiitves have choked him. Thus it has happened; it can only have happened thus. I see through it all!"

The prior nodded.

"Yes; it must have been so!" he exclaimed. "If we could only succeed in getting hold of this malefactor, this German count!"

"This malefactor, this German count, has done something that is only natural; he has sought his liberty," responded Padre Geronimo; "perhaps only allowed himself led into liberty by those who acted for him. The wicked ones are those who, insolently and sacrilegiously, have forced their way into our sacred precincts, not those who have fled from them."

"Well, yes," said the prior; "and they ——"

"And over them we have no power," said Padre Geronimo, interrupting him; "they stand, at present, too high for us to do well in stretching out our hand against them."

"Too high? Who in Rome or in the world can stand so high that you, worthy brother, are not allowed to call him before your judgment-seat, even though he were an anointed king?"

"Of course," answered the Inquisitor, "we are invested with all rights and all power; there are wanting to us neither laws according to which to pass sentence, nor arms with which to execute it.

But there is also no lack of wisdom which says to us when it is time to let those laws rest, to let those arms lie unused, and to keep ourselves silent until the hour for action has come."

The Inquisitor might possess this wisdom; but to the prior, that of understanding his reasons was wanting.

"But I pray you, Padre Geronimo," he said, "if we may not punish that which happened last night, or let it go unnoticed of our own accord, it is all over with our authority and all the hitherto wholesome dread which the Sant Uffizio ——"

Padre Geronimo made with his hand a motion of warding off.

"Don't be concerned about that," he said. "'*Raro antecedentem scelestum deseruit pede pœna claudo*,' writes even Horace, the heathen poet."

"But these offenders who stand so high," remarked the prior; "who should they be?"

"Of these offenders, one is Master Raphael Santi," said the Inquisitor.

"Raphael Santi, the great master from Urbino?" exclaimed the prior.

"He," replied Padre Geronimo,—"no other than he. That German monk of whom the talk was, who is named Fra Martino, and who is of a heretical spirit through and through, has had some intercourse with Master Raphael; for what other purpose, pray, but to induce him to make the excavations through which all that has happened has first become possible. For certainly the gate of the castle over there was too well locked and guarded for an entrance from that side to have seemed possible to them. So just as the Countess Corradina has stood on one side, Master Santi has stood on the other, to dig under our feet this mine of wickedness. I see through that only too well; and you, worthy brother, will now see through my motives when I say, Do not, in the first place, let this German monk escape your eye, and follow the road which he traverses; but against the others, let us not act to-day, nor to-morrow, but when the time shall come."

The prior nodded understandingly, and Father Eustachius said:—

"You are right, Padre Geronimo. Perhaps over this Raphael, who is a noisy fool and heathen, as are all these art folk, this San Gallo, and Buonarroti, and Bramante, this whole sect of Plato, will also yet come the turning about and enlightening."

Padre Geronimo shook his head.

"Let us hope," he said, "that soon something else will come over them,—the wrath of our Holy Father. And it *will* come upon them. The Holy Father does not understand that one may jest with him, and they, these masters, are haughty and overbearing, and will risk everything. Just see how they stride about here, Santi like a prince with the retinue of his court. They say he also intends to have a princely palace built in the Borgo. And Michael Angelo Buonarroti, indeed! When he comes stalking past, with his broad ox-head and the shoulders of a wood-carrier, alone and with clownish bearing, one might think he looks upon the world as if it is a bad block of marble, without value till his chisel may hew it right! And has he not already once defied the Holy Father, and been obliged to save himself by a hasty flight to Florence and Venice? Such an hour of anger and of disfavor will sooner or later come over that other one, him of Urbino. Then will the time have come for us to talk with him and his whole crowd about Plato. The church forgets nothing. If from the protection of those who have become intoxicated from the sinful cup of their 'beauty,' they are too powerful for us to-day, San Dominico's holy torch burns yet farther in stillness, and at some future time it will throw its enlightening rays down into the writing-room of the Platonic thinkers, and the workshop of these artists,—into all these armories of the Devil! Go, my brethren,—go now; they are ringing for the vigils. Go and pray that the hour may come."

The prior and the exercise-master departed. Padre Geronimo, however, remained yet longer, sitting meditatively upon the stone bench under the olive tree of the great saint. Desponding thoughts came over him. Had it really come so far that the penal power of the church was not free,— that it could no longer seize upon one who seemed to it guilty? Had the sons of San Dominico to make themselves reproaches that they exercised their office too idly and negligently, and therefore the blossoms of sin stood so flourishing in the world? Was it on that account that everything that called itself cultivated had fallen away from the faith, despised the sacraments, and danced about the golden calf of classic heathenism? Did they, on this account, ridicule the doctrine of the church concerning hell and purgatory, and swear, according to Pliny, that there is no difference between souls of men and those of beasts?"

Padre Geronimo became absorbed in meditation. It was clear to him something must happen contrary to this condition of things.

The church had let her two punishing arms fall asleep, and she must lift them up. Every force calling itself infallible needs these arms to maintain itself. It needs censorship for the minds and the sword for the bodies. *The Inquisition is no mere outgrowth of an infallible church; it is a consequence, a necessary consequence of the principle, and will always be there again so soon as the circumstances of the time make it possible.* Behind the infallible and absolute power of princes stands the traitor's gallows; behind the infallible church, the funeral-pyre.

"But," Padre Geronimo asked himself, "was it enough, as things stood to-day, if San Dominico's sons protect themselves, and swing their torches over the great orgies, the 'Platonic feast of souls'? Must there not be created near the power which judged and punished, a new one, which also essentially subjugated souls? Should it not be just as it was when, against the great apostasy of souls in the Albigensian times, there were drawn into the field two powers, Arnold, the legate, and Simon von Montfort, the general? Could an order, one of the oldest orders at that, be looked out to take charge of this mission? Was there one in a condition to march out against culture with equal armor, against the science of the learned with knowledge? No, no; there was none. If the lion of St. Dominicus drew out to the contest, a serpent must be near him to give him aid; and this serpent was not there in the ark of the hierarchy. A greater charmer must throw his staff upon the ground, like the magician of Pharaoh, out of which must proceed an entirely new serpent, one never before seen.

Padre Geronimo clung to this thought, which, after thirty years, was to find its fulfillment, not through the initiation of a great wizard, but through that of a Spanish knight-errant,* who, with the comprehensive and tragic fanaticism of Don Quixote for Donna von Toboso, devoted himself to the service of Donna Infallibility; and to him the world is indebted if since then, in the mental crop of mankind, in the fruitful valleys of science, an injurious insect, a black grain-bug, has been committing ravage.

Padre Geronimo at length arose. The twilight had settled down, and out of some windows of the neighboring Savelli castle one saw the bright glimmer of light force its way; also a low, swelling choral song of monks became perceptible: it came out of the chamber in which the body of Livio Savelli lay in state.

---

* Ignatius Loyola, founder of the Jesuits.

CHAPTER XII.

CORRADINA.

ON the evening of the next day, Brother Martin passed through the Porta del Popolo, down the Flaminian Way, to the villa of Signor Callisto.

When he knocked at the gate in the wall shutting off the villa from the road, there appeared an old gardener, who shoved him back. "No one is at home," he said; "Signor Callisto has gone on a journey." Only upon his urgent request to speak with the mistress, did the old man conclude to announce him.

Now soon, thereupon, Signor Callisto himself appeared in the reopening door.

"I guessed that it was you, Fra Martino!" he said. "Step in quickly; it is not necessary that any one should see us."

After Brother Martin had entered, the door was again secured by a heavy bolt.

Brother Martin's eye, as he was walking through the garden at Callisto's side, rested upon a picture of great beauty. Behind him, behind Monte Mario, the sun was going down. From the reflection of the evening glow, the eastern sky before him was overspread with indescribably beautiful tints of rose and violet, and of the finest blending of green and gold. Upon the background of this ravishing play of colors arose the "*parva domus*"; and upon the *pergola* of this charming, green-entwined building sat, with arm resting upon the parapet, a female form, whose contour, full of grace, was delineated upon the roseate surface.

It was Corradina, who, her chin supported upon her hand, was gazing upon the sinking sunlight and the purple glow of the golden, flaming evening sky.

When Callisto had led the monk up to her she cordially reached him her hand.

"You are the man," she said, "of whom Count Egino would

have me receive a castigatory sermon. I hope, though, the courage to blame us will fail you when you see in what trouble we are. Have you learned anything of the poor German girl who showed us the way to rescue?"

"I have spent part of to-day with her, and I come from her, countess," replied Brother Martin.

"And in what condition is she?"

"Not good, I fear, for she is very weak."

"How you alarm me! Has she a physician? Has she a nurse?"

"Both."

"God be with the poor girl! If I could go to her — if I dared to go! But I dare not, truly! Upon her no suspicion will fall; no one will think of her,—of her or the dreadful man with the strength of an ox who accompanied her. After me they will put out spies at every corner. I dare not take a step out of this villa."

"No; you dare not do it," remarked Callisto,—"not at the risk of your life! Believe me, the Germans are well provided for by their worthy Frau Giulietta, and no one suspects them there. The only thing you can do for them is to endanger them by no approach, or even message."

"I understand that, Signor Callisto; but you,"—she turned to Brother Martin,—"do not tell Count Egino that she is in such a bad condition. He also lies prostrated with fever, which has returned violently in consequence of the excitement of night before last; he needs indulgence!"

"I will obey you, countess."

She arose, and beckoned to Brother Martin. He followed her with the lawyer into the sitting-room adjoining the *pergola*. There she showed him through an open door into a second bright and beautiful room, into which the purple evening light of the western heavens threw its full splendor. Egino lay upon a couch, half enveloped with a coverlet. Joyously he extended his right hand to Brother Martin.

"Brother Martin, how fine that you have come!" he exclaimed. "Is it not true that you are rejoiced to find me alive and at liberty,— rejoiced as a true friend? Of course you find me a little sick and weak, but not bad; to-morrow, day after to-morrow, the old strength will return. Bring me good news from Irmgard, and I will throw from me all care, in order to become well. Do you look at me questioningly and in wonder, Brother Martin? You believe just anxiety must kill me,—anxiety about my noble lady, the Countess Corradina, and her destiny, and the fearful situation in which even I, no one but myself, have brought her through my passionate action; that penitence, torturing of conscience on her account must not let me breathe? Ah! you do not know her, Brother Martin; you do not know with what kindly words she has comforted and quieted me! You do not know with what graciousness she condescends to me, most needy one that I am, and tells me that she is not angry with me; that she receives what has happened quietly and calmly as a dispensation of Heaven to lead her out of a far more dreadful condition into liberty and independence. You do not know ——"

Corradina now stepped up, and placing her hand upon Egino's arm, she said:—

"Count Egino, you dare not talk so much; do you hear?"

"You are right, Countess, and I obey. But Fra Martino will be eager to hear our story."

"Then I will tell it to him, if you wish him to know it; but in the meantime you must listen in silence, without interrupting me with a word. Do you promise that?"

"I promise to obey every word of yours to the end of my life, Corradina, my noble lady!" replied Egino, drawing her hand to his lips.

"Well, then, seat yourself, Fra Martino," said Corradina, while she seated herself upon the foot of Egino's couch.

Martin took his place upon one of the high-backed chairs standing around.

Signor Callisto brought a bowl with some cooling potion, and placed it upon a little table close to Egino's couch. Then he went out, as Corradina had, on yesterday, given him an account of the whole story of her flight. Had he been aware that the countess was upon the point of relating to them, not only the experience through which she had been led into his house, but her whole life-history, so that Egino might now hear it, he would certainly not have shut himself out from the circle of those remaining behind. But Corradina did not detain him. She sat erect with her hands folded in her lap, turning her wonderfully beautiful countenance to the glowing skylight; while Brother Martin, tired, and still in suspense, had sunk back against the cushioned back of his chair, and the sick man had supported upon his arm his blond head, with his glowing eyes directed upon Corradina.

"If your German friend," began Corradina, with a look as of inquiry resting upon the young monk, "is to judge of my actions, he must know everything that has led me where he now sees me, in this retreat, hidden, fleeing, poor and outcast. He must know how I grew up; how I came to years of maturity; what I experienced; what I have had to struggle through up to this hour. I grew up, without a mother, in the old, large, and ruined castle of Anticoli, at the side of my father; a severe and hard man, who, through his narrations of the power and elevation of our great and once world-ruling race, of the deeds of those who were the most illustrious bearers of its great and incomparable renown, did everything to make me proud and self-conscious. He could not do this without, at the same time, bringing into my young soul a great bitterness, through the contrast of these reminiscences, with the needy and ruined condition around me, — with the restricted circumstances of our house. Fortunately there lay an antidote in the peculiar bitterness of his heart over these circumstances. The soul-weaknesses of parents are seldom the inheritance of the children; they only early take an example from their parents. My father was not poor. Our possessions were large, but they were encumbered with debt. Since the great invasion of Rome, instituted a hundred years ago by the Colonnas, with whom we have almost always been allied, our house had suffered a great deal. Paolo Orsini, the Pope's commander-in-chief, had taken my forefather, Corradino di Antiochia, prisoner, and had him executed, and much of our possessions had then been taken from our people. My father had a Savelli for a wife. Her estate had served to liquidate the debts, to lift again mortgages and alienations, to bring the estate into better condition. The utmost economy sustained my father in this struggle, in which all his thoughts and all his activity were engaged; for our house did not become more habitable, our number of servants greater, our table better furnished, our gate more frequently opened to guests, as we became richer. When I was eight years old my mother had died, and my entire companionship consisted, from that on, of an old nurse and a very young goat-shepherdess, whom my father had given to me as a chambermaid. His daily company was Fra Niccolo, the house chaplain, who instructed me in reading and writing, and then in Latin, while my father taught me German. He almost always spoke German with me: speaking German was a tradition in our house. So I grew up. Of the world I saw and heard nothing, only what was related to me by rare, individual guests who came out of it and took lodging with us;

they were mostly those belonging to the house of Savelli. As I said before, my mother was a Savelli of Aricia. She, however, who had brought to our house new prosperity, desired that this wealth should at some time flow back to her house, and that I should be wedded to one of the sons of her cousin, the duke. I was, indeed, the only child, the only heiress; she had never presented to my father a son. So it was decided that I should marry Luca; my mother was still resolved upon it. If Luca Savelli came to us, he called me his 'spouse,' even at an age when this 'spouse' was not much larger than the largest of her dolls. We played together, and quarreled, and fought: although he was much older than I, he occasionally got the worst of these encounters. I believe he hated me on that account, just as I found him intolerable. I had a playmate who pleased me much better; he was of my own age, and instead of calling me 'spouse,' as Luca did, and wishing to rule me, he was intent upon doing everything I wished, and granting to me everything that I suggested. He was the brother of my chambermaid, and as poor as she, and guarded the goats upon the cliffs and in the bushes around our castle. His name was Mario, and he had eyes of wonderful beauty, large, and dark, and soft, like those of a young girl. Angela and Mario and I, we formed as peaceful a company for play as only brothers and sisters could. I know not which I loved better, Angela or Mario. My father troubled himself little about me. In fine weather he let me tumble around out of doors; in bad weather he let me take refuge in the parlor, where stood a great old chest, in which were preserved manuscripts, parchments, and books, old as well as new. I read first in the new ones — secretly, for Fra Niccolo must not see it. He called all new books homilies of the Devil and poison for the soul; and he was right. These new books were novels and stories of wanton import: as that poison which dilates the pupil of the eye and sharpens the vision, it sharpened my eye for things I should not have perceived at that age. I grew upon it. Guests now appeared more frequently at the Castle of Anticoli, and among them young men, relatives, friends of the Savelli, whom they brought with them. There was a cardinal among them, a relative of the Colonna of Palliano, with whom Livio Savelli was to become connected by marriage. Livio brought him to our house. Cardinal Rafael was archbishop in one city, bishop in two, had abbeys and benefices, and was not yet thirty years of age; but he was clever, eloquent, even learned, and they said he would yet become Pope. With all this he sued earnestly for my favor; but only too soon I understood his passionate nature, and the fire in his eyes when he spoke to me, and I shrank from his approaches. I could not refuse a costly present which he brought to me from Rome, one day; my father did not permit it. I could not speak to my father, I would not speak to Luca, openly, about the cardinal's advances. But I avoided him; I fled from him now. Fra Niccolo reproached me for it. He praised for me Rafael's high rank and merit; he brought to me secretly a letter from the cardinal. I was horrified at this behavior on the part of the pious brother whom I had respected. While I tore this letter in pieces, I had a feeling as if the earth were giving away under me, — as if a flood of hatred came over me against these priests, against these men. In the presence of Fra Niccolo I stamped the pieces of the letter with my feet. The cardinal did not allow himself frightened off. He pursued me as before. I stole away from the castle as often as I could when he was there. I complained of my trouble to Angela, and Angela related it to her brother; and when I next saw Mario, he swore that, as soon as the cardinal should hunt again with Livio in the forest of Anticoli, as he was wont to do, he would crack his head with a stone out of his pouch with his shepherd's sling. Fra Niccolo surprised us, Mario and myself, in innocent, confidential chat. He may have long been suspicious of my intercourse with Mario, the foul man. He threatened me with the wrath of my father. I answered him defiantly, and turned my back upon him. Still, he did not carry out his threat; but he must have presented the matter to Rafael, for the cardinal took it upon himself next day to make me the bitterest and most passionate reproaches for throwing myself away, — for rambling about like something wild, and having intercourse with a barefooted boy, as if he were my equal. He dared to inveigh against me as if he had a right. Aroused, I cut him short. 'And what does it concern you,' I cried, 'if I converse with my playmates, and who my playmates are? If you were even Luca, who calls himself my spouse — I hate him not much less than I hate you — but from him it would be less mad! But you — you are nothing to me, nothing but an object of abhorrence! I hate you, — I despise you! To me, Mario's honest eyes are dearer than all the cardinals in the world, with Luca included, who is none, but deserves to be."

"Rafael, mute with astonishment and pale with anger, left me alone. On the very next day he took his departure. But he

had taken care to revenge himself. It fills me with horror to
tell you how. For that which I had said to his face, he made
poor Mario suffer. He was fallen upon by bandits, and they thrust
his eyes out.*

"That is dreadful!" here put in Egino.

Corradina, as if to appease him, laid her hand upon his uplifted
arm, while her glance maintained the same direction,—straight
out into the glowing evening sky. Brother Martin had raised
himself erect, and then bowed forward; propping his hands upon his
knees, he stared at the narrator.

"Mario is dead," she said; and then added, with a painful sigh:
"I had not loved Mario; never, except in dreams, had the thought
come to me that I could be his wife. But my grief for him was as
great as if I had loved him, and all the power of rebellion in me
became aroused, and mingled itself in this grief with a bitterness
I cannot describe. From this day on, I was as if transformed.
I became fond of solitude, shy of people; I secluded myself all
day long with the books of my father, among which I now began to
prefer the ancient ones, the chronicles containing accounts of my
forefathers, to those which had before kept me occupied. I sent
Angela from me, because I could not endure that her eyes
should look upon me, for they were the eyes of Mario. I began
to live in a world quite for myself alone, which was peopled
with gentle, motherly women and noble, strong, knightly men,—
creatures of the imagination; to whom I gave the names of my
ancestors found in the old history books and annals,—the names
of Manfred, Enzio, Constanze, Beatrix, Isabella, Elizabeth, Sibylla.
I dreamed myself in the midst of these; I saw myself standing
near them and talking with them; my young wisdom gave them
advice, which being followed would most certainly have guarded
them against their tragic fates, if they would only have listened
to me in my youthfulness. Oh! certainly then would Corradina
have crushed to the earth the bloodhound of Anjou, and Manfred
would not have been beaten by Benevent! And in an old
manuscript proceeding from my grandfather, from him who was the
dearest and most beloved of all, from Frederic II., I buried myself,
and read it again and again, and brooded over it, and inquired
about separate places and sentences, whether the thought I
placed there was really that which stood there; I racked my brains

---

*Compare this with a similar deed in Roscoe's "Life of Leo X.," Vol I. p. 431 of the German
translation, and Gilbert's "Lucretia Borgia," p. 279, of the German edition. (Leipzig, 1870.)

over it, uncertain, anxious, fearing that it was so, and still again exulting that it was so; for these passages and sentences were alarming to my childish faith, but they gave me revenge upon the cardinal, upon Fra Niccolo, upon the men around me. There lay therein the thoughts, the most secret thoughts, of a man who surveyed the illusions surrounding his contemporaries, as a mountain-peak the mist and vapor of the valley; thoughts and truths, like the mountain-brook coming down from the heights clear and crystal pure, in order, ever roaring more loudly, to become by degrees the mighty waters, — the broad, flowing stream which has become irresistible in his course, and widely masters the land."

"And what manuscript was that?" here asked Brother Martin.

"I will yet tell you about that; let me go on now," answered Corradina. "When I became torn away from my solitude, and forced into intercourse with men, I showed a disposition entirely changed. I was no more talkative, loving harmless chat, still timid and bashful, and my composure easily disturbed by a word, as I was before. I had become monosyllabic, but more certain; I spoke little, but that was what I thought and held for true. I learned to dispute, to have courage with my opinions. He who put himself into a war of words with me did not always end it as victor; and since I spoke out of the bitter feeling which filled me for the men around me, I must very often have been wounding, bold, and imperative in my speech. And still this appeared to offend no one; on the contrary, it was as if one now, for the first time, was rightly intent upon showing me favor.

"When I became nineteen years of age I lost my father, after a short illness; he spoke to me still upon his death-bed of Luca Savelli as my future husband. I would not trouble him, dying, by my opposition; I was silent, and submitted, also, when the Duke of Aricia, chosen my guardian after my father's death, ordered that I live from now on with his daughter-in-law, Livio Savelli's wife, and in the world should there become schooled and cultivated. I must leave our castle. It was to my spirit as if I were taking leave, not only of my father's house, of all associations, of my liberty, it was more: it was to me as if I were taking leave of myself; as if I would be treated like some kind of stuff, a pleasing metal, which one changes and pours into a new shape; and that I would be turned into a new being and a new appearance in Rome, in the castles of the Savelli and Colonna, in their company, in their restless doing and living, that was for me like the life of an entirely different kind of people. And yet — how did I remain so entirely the same; how did I, in this world which repelled me, remain true to feeling and thinking entirely my way; how came a stubborn power of resistance over me in the midst of the immoral extravagance surrounding me! Livio's wife was unfaithful to her husband, and put herself to no trouble to conceal this from my eyes. Livio, on the contrary, conceived a passion for me, but he had not the courage, or he considered it not prudent, to confess it openly to me — he let me guess it; he played the part of restraining, mastering himself, and became his brother Luca's apologist to me. He played a finely weighed game! He calculated how, when I had become Luca's wife, my husband would make me miserable; and how then, in my distress, I should be obliged to fall into his wide-open, protecting arms! The more plainly I gave Luca to understand my abhorrence of him, so much the more he treated me as his own property,— his slave. We often had struggles; and then his father, my guardian, stepped between us, and took me into his protection so excitedly and passionately, that I soon lost my candor toward him also. Even he, even the man of fifty, began to woo me, and to increase the despair with which I became filled in this circle, which should have formed for me the protecting family circle! Fortunately the duke was shy of his sons; he feared Livio, and Livio was aroused when he made the discovery that his father had conceived the thought that he would himself make me his wife, since I would not have Luca.

"Those were dreadful days for me, a poor young creature who had no friend, no help upon earth. My servants had been sought out by the duke; Livio's wife believed her duty toward me fulfilled when she had imparted to me the refined customs of society, and the art of clothing and adorning myself with taste. She jested over her husband's devotion to me; she called me the marble princess, and took delight in the way in which I rudely and sharply defended myself against the men, whose passions I only thereby aroused and stimulated.

"How often in those days have I envied Angela; how often have I wished myself in the place of this girl, who was again guarding her goats, barefooted, upon the forest heights of Anticoli!

"Two years thus fled by; we were mostly in Aricia, also in Palliano, or in Livio's castle at Albano, which the duke had cut off for him at his marriage; occasionally we were here in Rome.

Finally, Luca's increasing illness compelled us to a longer stay in Rome; and here it was that I declared my resolution to become the dying Luca's wife. It seemed to me the only way to become free,— free from the wooings of the duke, whom I most feared, and independent as a widow, to whom one must give back part of her possessions; free for the future from the addresses of other men, for I hated them all. Luca died the morning of the day set for the marriage. I still remained ready for this marriage. Livio insisted now, likewise, upon the ceremony, with the concurrence of his wife, who thought as did he about the intention of the duke. I agreed; the duke dared no opposition — and so that occurred of which you were a witness, Count Egino."

"You allowed yourself wedded to the dead?" exclaimed Brother Martin, horrified.

"I allowed myself wedded to the dead!"

Brother Martin gazed upon her. A pause followed. Egino reached out his hand to clasp that of Corradina; as if absent mindedly she indulged him, and placed her right hand in his. Her glance remained fixed, directed into the distance.

The monk supported his brow upon his hand, and said, looking at the floor:—

"And then? Tell me all."

"Count Egino may relate to you further how he forced his way to me; how he then fell into the prison of the Dominicans; how I then found him sicker and weaker than I had supposed. Livio made it possible for me to get into his dungeon. I was aware that some kind of a trick, a something kept back, was lurking behind his goodness — and still I consented. If I should refuse, upon Livio's suggestion, to go in and lead Egino out of the cloister, there was no other rescue to be hoped for him who, for my sake, had fallen into this distress. When I had led him out, it was always to be hoped that, through prudence and courage, we would succeed in making vain the artifice, in escaping the snare, in attaining to liberty. So I undertook it. I found my way, as it had been described to me, into Egino's cell."

"Like an angel of light, you came in the night of despair," exclaimed Egino; "and if I should die for you ten times, I should not have repaid you the happiness of the moment in which my confused senses became composed,— began to believe that it was you,— you."

She withdrew from him her hand, and placing it upon his arm, as if again quieting him, she continued:—

"I led him out. We came into the Chapel of the Immured. What happened there the German maiden has already related to you."

Brother Martin nodded gently with his head.

"I know what happened there," he said.

"So I may end here. When we, following the man who was carrying the wounded girl, found ourselves outside in the dark, narrow streets, we said to ourselves that no one would pursue them, of whom no one knew, but would only pursue, spy out, and seek us; that we should therefore owe it to them to separate our lot from theirs, so that they might not, at least, become endangered; that we must, at any cost, seek to get outside of the gates, now while they were not yet guarded. So we separated ourselves from them, and, fortunately, without being detained, passed through the gate to Signor Callisto's house, who has continuously shown to me good will and kindness, and for whose true friendship Count Egino stood security. We have not been disappointed in the noble man. And so you find us here."

"And now," Corradina said, concluding her narrative, "now, Brother Martin, ponder in your heart whether what you have heard is a story of sin and transgression, or a human destiny, appointed by God's paternal hand, and guided upon the road to the goal whither he willed to lead me. Tell us to-morrow, for it has grown late; the sun has set, and the night must find you in your cloister."

Brother Martin arose.

"You are right, countess," he said gently. "I would also not be in a condition to say to you a word about it. My soul is filled with all that these days have brought to me, as if a mountain load lay upon me. Let me go. I feel as if I had been snatched into a roaring whirlpool. I must get my breath before I can speak."

He reached his hand to both of them, and passed, with difficult pace, through the room and ante-chamber to leave the villa.

CHAPTER XIII.

A MONOLOGUE OF THE MONK.

HEN Brother Martin had again reached the portal of his cloister, and had found admittance, he slipped quietly and noiselessly into his cell. He wished to be heard by no one, to be seen by no one; he wished to meet no idle questions to which he must give answer. He locked the door of his cell and threw himself into the chair at his window.

The full, round face of the moon was looking in.

Folding his hands, Luther breathed deeply several times; then he rested his temple upon his hand, and looking up at the moon he murmured:—

"Upon what a world does this round disc, there, pour its soft, peaceful light! O my God, upon what a world! As the pious mother, earnestly and with astonishment, looks into the mildly heated countenance of her child, so this face looks in upon this world!

"What men! They have the high, mild light of heaven, the glittering stars there which flicker in eternally twinkling motion, as if they would speak to men in anxious excitement, telling them to be good; and they have the soul-light beaming forth from the pure doctrine of the gospel! And still they live in darkness, and act like robbers and murderers.

"Into the pure, gushing fountain of the teaching of the Saviour, they have thrown the dead carcass of their institutions, and no pure mouth may any more drink from this water. For the sake of the faith, they imprison one another, kill, and burn. The Devil has passed by a tiger's den and has hurled to them their faith, that the beasts may have something about which to fight and tear each other's flesh. In this wild struggle they have beaten to death the living Christ, and dark birds flutter about his corpse; the raven-nature loves the odor of a corpse!

"O Lord, O Almighty God, who art able to bring forth thy lightnings! No, no; thy thunders have rolled enough, and they have taken no alarm! O thou who couldst tear thy sun from the vault of heaven and hurl this flaming, primitive doctrine under them, and couldst cry to them, There, you have light, and now see, you blind!"

Exhausted, Martin sank down. Never had come out before his eyes with such affecting force the gaping contrast between the world of that time as it was, and the world as, according to the "doctrine," it should be; between the ruthless contempt for the inner purport of the doctrine, the insolent unconcern about its moral precepts, and the violent cruelty with which they defended its outer authority, its forms, the scaffolding of its hierarchy.

He saw standing before him the form of this Pope who had shown him out of the door, and forbidden to him and to mankind the right of thinking. And near the Pope stood Padre Geronimo, the executioner for thoughts; and far behind them was as if a broad plain, upon which the sins and passions of mankind, who were not allowed to think, were flying about in a wild chaos.

The evil, bitter doubt, which had already once barked at him so poisonously, came back more painfully, more goadingly. It was a real misery that it brought over the poor monk so disturbed within. He had doubted the principle of the whole system,— the fact of the original sinfulness of human nature. Now there seized upon him a doubt of the power of the entire theology,— of its ability to lead men in general to goodness and purity. In his agitation and mutiny he could have thrust this theology, this scholasticism, from him with a stroke of the foot; he could have seized it, shaken it, and would have liked to thunder at it these words:—

"Now give me an account of your foster-child, humanity; to what have you brought it? Are not you, you yourself the serpent of which you are eternally talking, which made humanity sinful and wretched? the serpent which the Lord condemned to creep upon its belly and to eat dust? Yes, you creep upon the belly; you live upon the belly; and instead of manna you eat dust, you black adder!

"Poor, pitiable human race! You 'race of kings and priests,' to which the Lord would exalt you, how have you been trodden under foot! If the poor man should go forth out of his hut seeking food, and should kill a wild animal of the field, the master of the soil comes and says, 'Away; the game is mine!' If he should catch a fish out of the waters, another says to him, 'Away; the waters are mine!' If he would fetch a piece of wood out of the forest to warm himself, there would come yet another to say, 'Away; for to me belongs the forest!' If he finds under the floor of his hut a vein of precious metal, that might aid him, the lord of the soil is again there, and gives the order, 'Don't disturb it; it is mine. Mine is the soil upon which you stand; mine the treasure under your feet; mine the bird flying through the air over your head.' And then if the poor man, with his need and his misery, would flee for refuge to his Christ, then comes Frau Theology, the serpent, then comes the church, and says: 'The house of Christ is mine; mine are the mansions in the house of the Father; mine are all the favors of the Lord; and if you want any of them, then buy them from me! You have nothing upon the earth; it must be, then, that you buy it from your landlord. You have nothing in heaven; it must be, then, that you buy it from me! I have the keys to heaven. You cannot come in unless you give much gold for masses, offerings, indulgences, and all my goods!'

"And, finally, the soul of the poor man erects itself against this order of the world, and he begins to ask himself, in his thoughts, about all this compulsory right. Then Frau Theology calls out to him: 'Restrain yourself; your brains are mine, as your fields are those of your landlord, your forests those of your prince! If you think with your brain, draw conclusions with your intellect, you trespass upon my territory; and as the landlord puts you in irons for the wild stag you poach, so will I let you be burned if you think!' Merciful God! the lot of man has become dreadful; not, indeed, for them, for these priests who blaspheme in saying masses, for these great ones doing what they wish, for these cardinals like Rafael—they live in joy and pleasure, and yet know how to get into heaven! Heaven is for them a great, ever-enduring feast. In order to be let in they need only to have pressed a bit of gold into the hand of Peter, the gatekeeper. To them heaven is a great masked party, a mumming occasion; in order to be admitted, one needs only come in a mask: one draws on a priest's robe, or has himself buried in a monk's habit—then Peter lets him in."

Brother Martin threw his hands over his face in perfect despair; he groaned aloud, as if in the deepest, most crushing pain. It was to him as if the earth were giving way under him.

"It is a great and difficult task," he began again, after a long pause, "to find the truth. But the merciful God will assist me if I seek it, — seek, and keep on seeking to the end of my life! This, however, dawned clearly upon my soul to-day : with this creed can mankind not become noble, and good, and happy. And in regard to this creed, Lord Tommaso Inghirami was right when he said, 'Religion has no influence upon the morals, and the character, and actions of men.' Was not that what he maintained in Master Santi's house? He was right, — this belief cannot have it; this belief that his own innocent child must, by his death, have conciliated a wrathful, angry God in order to open the gate of heaven to mankind, and then give its doors to the care of the church, that she might open them to those who come with 'good works.' No, no; only the truth that Christ has come to us in the impulse of his divine love to make us good and noble through teaching and exhortation, and that we human beings have beaten him to death as a reward; that we must now conciliate him through love and a pure course of life according to his doctrine, — only that can save. Not the mere theology of the atoning death of Christ, but the teaching of the atoning life of man!"

With such thoughts the German monk walked up and down in his cell. He did not perceive how the night sank deeper and deeper; he did not hear, as, now far, now near, now in this, now in that cloister, the bells were rung for matins and nightly prayers. At length weariness compelled him to throw himself upon his hard bed; a feverish half-slumber, out of which he was startled from time to time, led past him dreamy visions. He saw the old man with the donkey, who had threatened him with the perniciosa; he sat now in the forest, and had taken upon his lap the bloody head of a boy, — a head with dark eye-sockets dreadful to behold. Over the forest arose a lofty, rich palace, and therein stretched out broad, stately rooms, in one of which stood the thorn-crowned Christ of the picture upon which Irmgard had looked, the entire form leaning upon the cross. This Christ followed, with painful glances and gentle turnings of the head, a weeping maiden who was hastening through the room; but the maiden did not see him, and hurried past.

CHAPTER XIV.

THE POPE GOES TO SLEEP.

Motto: *Eternal God, if thou didst not watch, how bad it would be for the world which we rule, I, a wretched hunter, and that drunken, wicked Julius!* — EMPEROR MAXIMILIAN I.

ONG before the hour in which these images, like an Alp, lay upon the breast of Brother Martin, had Pope Julius left the circle of those who surrounded him in the last evening hour, and with whom, after the troubles of the day, he had passed the time, till going to sleep, in gay conversation. Julius II., as well as no theologian, was also no learned man. Some one has said of him, that as he was once going out to war, he threw down from the Tiber bridge the keys of Peter into the river, that he might draw his polished sword. When Michael Angelo had finished his statue for the façade of San Petronio, in Bologna, Julius was angry that a book had been placed in his hand, and cried out, "I am no scholar; give me a sword in my hand!" But he liked to see around him people of culture and learning, and in those hours of recreation he often won the admiration of these men for his knowledge of the world, his knowledge of political relations, and his penetration in judging of them. At these times, in spite of his rough nature, his open honesty and frank manner of expression could give to him something amiable; a trait which stands forth more vividly when one compares him with his predecessors.

To-day, when he left his own attendants and betook himself to his bedroom, his step was tottering, and the head of the old man sank heavily forward. He had in the evening drunken the strong red Gradoli; at last he had felt it was time for him to betake himself to rest.

"Gennaro," he said, breathing heavily and leaning upon his body-servant, who was undressing him, "you must read to me, when I lie down, out of the book, there, the night prayer; I fear I could no longer bring the words together. Were you not down in the city to-day?"

"Yes, Holy Father."

"And what are they talking about in the city — of the death of Savelli?"

"Of the death of Savelli, and also of a feast in the Colonna Palace in the honor of Duke Alfonso."

"So, so — they were celebrating a feast there — Alfonso von Ferrara was having a feast!" murmured the Pope.

And then after a pause he added : —

"He has found that the supreme pontifex is a good-natured old man, with whom he lets himself live! Now let them rejoice and drink! In the Colonna Palace let them rejoice! The rejoicing will be past, Gennaro, I think even to-morrow, to-morrow morning. Lay the cushion upon my feet, and push the light out of my eyes; the light makes them ache!"

"What was Your Holiness going to say?" asked Gennaro, who knew that at this hour he might venture any question.

"What was I going to say? That I will take away from him his entire dukedom of Ferrara. That is what I will say, Gennaro. He shall hand it over to me entire, entire; he shall not keep back a rod of its tillable land. That is what I would say. To-morrow the cardinals will say it to him — to this Este!"

"And will he let it please him? He will ride home and begin war again!"

"Ride home? One will teach him that!"

"But, Holy Father, you have just granted him peace and pardoned him upon the condition that he humble himself, and acknowledge himself your vassal. He has had your promise, and it is wrong ——"

"Wrong — wrong," answered Julius, with a thick tongue. "You blockhead, will you restrain me from calling it right? Is it not right if I make it right? Has another to decide what is right or wrong, or have I? Am I the Pope, or are you, Gennaro? Gennaro, if you were the Pope, would you not wish Ferrara? Go and read out of the book the night prayer; we dare not neglect the night prayer. What would Father Anselmo say? I can bind and loose, Gennaro; I will loose Ferrara from this Este — loose from this Este — the Alfonso I will have bound — seized and bound ——"

The voice of the Pope went off into an unintelligible murmur. He had long before shut his eyes. He moved his lips still a few times, and then went to sleep.

Gennaro slipped out of the room on tiptoe.

CHAPTER XV.

CALLISTO'S NEWS.

T was on the following morning. Callisto had been led into the city by his business and by the desire to obtain information as to what they were saying down there in regard to the occurrences in the house of Savelli, also as to what else had happened. Donna Ottavia was sitting on the couch which, yesterday, Egino was still occupying. He himself, much stronger after a night of profound and healthful sleep, and almost restored to the feeling of perfect health, sat in an armchair at the open window, into which streamed a warm, odor-impregnated, ever salubrious breeze. His wound was in the act of healing over; what had kept him weak and feeble was only the fearful mental pain, the tormenting anxiety, about Irmgard, about Corradina's fate, the frightful images which had haunted him in the prison. The events of the night which had brought to him freedom, must, then, have agitated him anew most violently. Now, however, had his elastic, youthful strength begun again to permeate his being; and, breathing deep, he inhaled the mild air with the perfect delight of returning strength, though his breast could still heave so little free from the pressure of care. There was, on the contrary, sufficient ground for finding a condition such as his rather full of despair. The threatening danger swaying over him and over Corradina; the condition of Irmgard, upon which he dwelt with so much uneasiness; the danger into which he had brought his noble entertainers, and in which he was still keeping them; the certainty that he had thoroughly marred his brother's lawsuit, for the sake of which he had come hither; and, more than all, the future of Corradina, whom no one but just he had severed so violently from her relations, to lead her into a future lying before him like a chaotic dream, — all this was effective enough to cause him to say to Donna Ottavia, with painful emotion : —

"I feel myself strong enough in order to-day, as soon as night has come, to thank you for your noble hospitality, and to free you from my dangerous presence in your house. Signor Callisto will, of course, lend to me the means for the journey, for which he can repay himself out of my possessions, through my servant, so soon as there would no longer be any danger to him in seeking out my servant in my lodgings in the city. Believe me, I also now know enough of Rome to leave it without reluctance. I will go filled with your theory that there are two kinds of poesy, or, better even, three, and three kinds of flames which can blaze up in the human soul."

"Three flames, and all at once?" remarked Donna Ottavia, smiling. "I think one would be enough for one heart."

"I mean not all at once, but, as you also meant it then, fairly in succession, and as one becomes more mature: the first, for the great and sublime, for God in the phenomena; the second for truth and the eternal ideas, whose daughters the phenomena are, for God in the thoughts; finally, the third, for love and for goodness and for the human being, for God in the soul ——"

"And have I taught to you this new kind of a trinity, Conte Gino?" said Donna Ottavia, smilingly interrupting him.

"About that! Did you not say then that I need only fall in love a little unhappily to find that behind the poesy of Rome, which caused me to break out into such ecstasies in your presence, stands a higher?"

"I remember."

"Well, now, I have reflected over that. I have had some experiences since then."

"And you have very quickly followed my advice, and fallen in love, Don Gino! And that," she added, "has made a philosopher of you,— a discoverer of a new trinity? You Germans are a wonderful people!"

"Not so wonderful as you think; for although we rack our brains a great deal, especially when the Inquisition throws us into her dungeons, we conduct ourselves, at least, not differently from others, and are, perhaps, much more helpless than they. I am very much in need of advice at this moment, Donna Ottavia."

"Are you? And wherefore, Conte Gino?" asked Donna Ottavia.

"Are you not yourself aware? I have made no secret of the deep passion which has filled me for Corradina since the moment in which I saw her for the first time. I need not paint for you the depth of this passion, for you know to what length it has carried me; how it has caused me to defy every danger and consideration. And still I scarcely knew Corradina,—knew little of her mind and thoughts, and nothing at all of her past. Now, when she has related it all, when she has granted to me for whole hours the favor of her sweet presence, my heart, which in the beginning beat boldly for every venture, and considered nothing unattainable, is now filled with the deepest despondency. I feel myself so unfortunately needy, Donna Ottavia! Her name, her blood, her culture, and her mind would not overawe me, and restrain me from suing for her heart and hand. I am conscious of a pure nature, of a noble will, and of at least enough mind to vouchsafe to us sufficient insight and intellect to be able to act for the happiness of those who depend upon us. And what would I not do, sacrifice, give up, to make such a wife as Corradina happy! My whole life would I devote to this one thought!"

"And yet you dare not now woo her, Conte Gino?" asked Donna Ottavia, directing her glance thoughtfully, and as if half-abstractedly, upon Egino.

"It is so," responded Egino. "I feel myself too poor in the presence of her inner wealth; I become absorbed in all that she has experienced,— I live it over anew with her; I follow the thoughts, the feelings with which her soul is filled, her mind expanded, and how it must place her with her inner world toward the men and the world outside of her; and then, despairing, hopeless, I say to myself, What can I be to her? How can I remove the dark shadows her experiences have thrown over her soul? What am I, that I could be the price to purchase her back to happiness? Can I walk before her and say, Throw into one scale all the bitterness, the hardness, the dreadfulness of your life, throw me into the other, and I will outweigh it, and make you happy?"

If Count Egino had secretly entertained the hope that Donna Ottavia would contradict him, and pronounce his despair the result of groundless diffidence, he had erred, for she thoughtfully answered :—

"The mind of the countess must have become gloomy, through what she has experienced; in that you are right, Count Egino. Bitterness must have sunk to the bottom of her heart: this must have closed it against softer feelings; this must have taught her to hate all men; she must have come to the conclusion never to belong to any man,— all that is natural ——"

"So natural it would be a wonder if it were otherwise!" put in Egino.

"And so," continued Donna Ottavia, "I can only pronounce you right when you despair of wooing her. Of course you are a different man from the kind of men she has learned to know. What you and she have together passed through has of itself brought you nearer to her: besides, you could offer her a destiny that would remove her far from all the circle in which she was so unhappy; that would take her away into a sure, protecting distance; that would rescue her from the only remaining escape — that of going into a cloister. But, — I will speak to you candidly, as a true friend, Count Egino,— granted these reasons should move her to listen to your wooings and the entreaties of your love, and to give you her hand, would you both become happy, she as well as you? Would you not then be always asking yourself: Is she satisfied now with being and living in my rough northern land? Do not our customs repel her? Does she not ponder in secret whether I am worthy of her having, for my sake, become untrue to her sunny native land, the Ausonian earth, and to her vow of belonging to no man? Could two persons be happy who are of such entirely different blood, different race, different nature, and different character,— your open and warm German soul, shining so clear and innocent from your eyes, your unembittered young Gothic blood, and her earnest, gloomy spirit with all its wounds?"

"And still, and still," Egino broke out in perfect despair, "I would not know how to leave her, and my heart would break in two; my whole life would be destroyed, my future be a long grief, if I must relinquish the thought of her."

"Time is man's greatest benefactor, Conte Gino. Do not despair on that account. Time will transform your grief into melancholy, and the melancholy will give place to the satisfaction which you will hereafter feel that you are chained no longer by any kind of bond to Roman things and relations."

Count Egino was silent. He stared at the floor; his face became paler under the pressure with which the words of Donna Ottavia had still more afflicted his soul, losing itself in hopelessness.

"But she?" he asked, after a pause, with trembling lips. "What will become of Corradina?"

"Do not be uneasy about her," replied Donna Ottavia. "She will go into a cloister, and in its protection will easily feel happier than she was in the house of Savelli. The cloister will compel them to deliver up her possessions: cloisters have ways and means of helping those belonging to them to their rights, and they love heiresses. Her name and her riches will rapidly promote her. She will soon be the principal of such an order and its domains. Believe me, you need not fear for her future; and if after years you think of her, consoled, represent her to yourself as a commanding abbess, with a crucifix upon her breast and a silver staff!"

"She — she a nun! Never will this happen! What would a nun be without faith!" exclaimed Egino.

"What thousands of nuns are to-day out of the noblest races."

At this instant Callisto entered quickly, and overheated.

"You must flee, Count Egino, this very night!" he said. "The Savelli people have not yet discovered you, it is true, but I know they have had spies put around my house, while already, day before yesterday, two troops of horse have been sent out after you; one upon the road to Civitavecchia, the other upon the road to the north. They considered it most likely that you had fled in the direction of Viterbo, upon the road to your home. This troop have just now returned without having discovered any trace of you, and likewise the one pursuing you toward the sea; so they will conclude that you are still here, and will break in upon me; of that you may be certain."

"You are right," said Egino, rising, with a constrained tone; "I must flee — flee. And you, Donna Ottavia, say yourself whether I can do it. O my God, I cannot do it!" he added, with a cry of pain, clasping his hands together and then covering his face with them.

At this outcry, and this movement of his young friend, Callisto looked at his wife in astonishment. Donna Ottavia laid her hand upon Egino's shoulder, and said: —

"Courage, courage, Count Egino; what a man has found out to be the right thing, he must also have the strength to put into execution."

"I will arrange everything for your flight," added Callisto. "For your suit, leave me your power of attorney, and rely upon me to bring out of it whatever is to be brought out of it. As soon as it is night, my horse shall be saddled and ready for you. Donna Ottavia will take care that there is no lack of clothing, and I that there is no lack of money in the knapsack."

"I thank you a thousand times, Callisto, for all your kindness; I thank you from the profoundest depths of my heart; but ——"

"You dare not," continued the lawyer, "take the direct way over the Ponte Molle; that bridge, as well as the one in front of Porta Salara, is guarded. We must (for I will myself be your guide) go through Porta Sant Agnese to Ponte Mammolo, in order to pass over the Anio; and then down it to the left, to set you over the Tiber by ferry."

"But, my God! can I do it,—can I do it then?" exclaimed Egino, as if crushed. "Is it possible that I tear myself away, never to return, also without one hope ever to find out what has become of Corradina; that never again can a greeting or a word from her reach me; with the feeling that I am dead for her, — that she, and with her the world, is dead for me!"

Callisto looked at him in surprise, and then again, questioningly, at Donna Ottavia.

"*Dira necessitas!*" he said then, in a low tone. "In that, you will know how to submit. The proud Hohenstaufen blood will not become your wife, and cannot, Count Egino. You cannot plant a palm among your oaks and pines. If you love her you could not wish that; if you should ask it of her she would find out from that that you are an egotistic man, no better than all the rest!"

Egino was yet too much enfeebled by his illness, too excitable, to be able to maintain his self-control; he threw himself upon a chair, and pressing his hands before his face he broke into a flood of tears.

Donna Ottavia left the room and ascended to Corradina's chamber upstairs, while Signor Callisto resorted to everything possible in talking, to alleviate the grief of his young friend. After awhile Donna Ottavia came back.

"The countess," she whispered, "was very much startled at the news I just now brought her. She insists that Count Egino must flee ——"

"She sends me away — she also sends me away!" exclaimed Egino, who had heard the last words. "Then I will go — I will go. But I beg you let me not see her again; a leave-taking would break my heart. Only to Irmgard will I go. From her will I take leave. I will tell her ——"

"But I beg you, Count Egino, not to think of risking yourself again in the city!" broke in Callisto.

"What risk do I take?" said Egino, cutting short his speech. "For a duty, my life. That is something great, when my life has become so worthless and miserable."

"And yet you shall not," exclaimed Callisto, angrily aroused. "My God! you dare not ——"

Donna Ottavia laid her hand upon his shoulder.

"Be quiet, Callisto; he will not do it," she said. "The Countess Corradina asked after the German monk; we are to bid him come. She truly thinks he will best know how to console our friend. He will also know how to restrain Count Egino from executing such a foolhardy resolution."

"And I tell you," cried Egino, "that even he will assist me, and recognize the fact that I cannot go without having pressed the hand of the poor, brave girl who has done so great a thing for me."

At this moment the door of the room opened, and Corradina came in. Her face, with its finely chiseled features, which usually showed an unchangeable, faintly perceptible tinge of color, was overspread with a delicate flush, as if from inner agitation. Ottavia had never seen upon her countenance this expression of spiritual beauty. Before Egino stood again quite that daughter of the Hohenstaufens before whom he knelt when he had held that first interview with her, when she so proudly, and yet with so much emotion, had bowed her brow to his.

She threw a glance upon Egino, and then turned to Donna Ottavia.

"Did you have the goodness to send for Fra Martino?" she asked.

"I am going to have him bidden to come," said Donna Ottavia, and she left the room.

Callisto exclaimed:—

"You come at the right moment to help us, Countess. You must forbid our friend, there, to commit a boundless folly; he will surely heed your reasonable remonstrances ——"

"I will not spare them," broke in Corradina. "Will you leave me alone with Count Egino, Signor Callisto?"

The lawyer bowed and went out.

"Count Egino," she now said, approaching him and extending to him her hand, "Donna Ottavia tells me that the moment has come when you must flee,—the moment of separation for us, as she says. So I must talk to you and give expression to that which I have avoided, in order not to excite you when convalescing, and thus to prevent your recovery."

"Must you give expression to it?" rejoined Egino, with a bitter tone, and turning himself away. "Is it then necessary that it should be spoken,—that word of final separation, of blank-eyed hopelessness? Is it necessary that you lead me into this temptation to break out into a last storm of passion, and vainly throw myself at your feet to pour out my heart to you——"

"Count Egino," she interposed, "you know not what you say! I demand it of you to remain quiet,—to hear calmly what I have to say to you. Seat yourself there and hear the reasonable remonstrances which, as Signor Callisto says, I have to make to you. I beg of you not to show me in this hour that you are no better than the men whom I hate,—who can do nothing but torment and persecute us with their horrible passion. Show to me that in you rolls a different blood, a true warm blood; not one which now, wildly heated, seethes and rages, now turns to ice."

Count Egino had seated himself upon the couch; Corradina had seized his right hand and stood before him while she spoke further:—

"See, Count Egino, I do not love you—not with the feeling I have been obliged to hear called love by men, and before which I would dread myself, if I should feel myself seized by its consuming fire, its sense-destroying madness——"

"You are very kind to tell me!" stammered Egino, with pale lips.

"I owe it to you," she responded. "I owe it to you to place clearly before you my feeling for you. I see in you a friend, a brother. I hear your voice gladly; I rejoice in your presence; my whole soul clings to you; and I feel that you would be able to make me better than I am. Your open, kind, cheerful nature, which is like the cup of a white flower, upon which yet lies the dawn of life with a rosy shimmer and brightness—I feel that this nature could even powerfully influence mine, and extinguish my bitterness and the gloomy temper which is in me. With this you must now be content; I cannot grant you more; you dare not ask for more."

"Of course; I must be satisfied with it!" whispered Egino, cast down and bitter.

"And can you not do that? Is it not enough for your happiness?"

"No, no,—and again no!" added Egino, vehemently, aloud. "By the thought, by the hope of winning your heart, your love, I have lived all this time."

"Restrain yourself, restrain yourself," exclaimed Corradina; "no storm, no passion in this hour! You must reconcile yourself to that, Egino,— to speak to me only with calm reason ; and if you ——"

"But I cannot do it now ; this quiet renunciation of my happiness, of my life, of my earthly future, which will now become a place of torment to me ——"

"You are a fool, like all the men," said Corradina, indignantly cutting short his speech. "I can grant you no greater happiness!" she added, almost angrily. "And ask yourself what happiness you will afford me, if you are so foolish as to ask of me more than I can bestow,— at least, more than I can bestow now. A woman wishes to have the consciousness that she makes the man happy to whom she gives herself as his own. Therein consists her happiness,— only, exclusively therein. So, at least, I feel. And if I now tell you that I will become your wife, to go with you to your home ——"

"You—my wife?" cried Egino, hastily rising and seizing both her hands. "Yes, will you, then? You will become my wife?"

She looked at him with dilated eyes, in which Egino could read only surpise.

"Have you, then, doubted that?" she said. "That is strange, Count Egino. I think fate has united us more firmly than a priest's blessing can do! There are things which a noble woman can do only for her husband. To flee out of her house with a man ; to go up and down with him through the night alone ; to sit by the couch of a man nursing him, and to remain with him days at a time,— I can do this only when I belong to this man, and am his wife for time and eternity!"

"Corradina!" faltered Egino.

"And will you now still complain about your happiness? Well, then, if I cannot grant to you the happiness which lies in the confession of a passion for you such as you desire, I can yet afford to you that which another confession must produce ; that is, that I shall always see in you my rescuer, — the man who has wiped out relations unendurable to me, and who leads me into a better land, for which I have learned to long as after the land of liberty, as after the land of my nativity, — the land of my fathers and my own land."

"Hold, Corradina," exclaimed Egino, while he knelt down before her and pressed her hands upon his glowing face. "Oh! how little have I understood you! You give me so much joy that it might kill me!"

"Compose yourself, Egino," she said, withdrawing from him one of her hands and laying it upon his arm; "we have concluded that this hour should be devoted to reasonable deliberations. We need all our reason to escape the danger surrounding us. Let us consider our flight. I have had Brother Martin bidden to come. Your friend shall bless our betrothal in the presence of Signor Callisto, who, as a well-known legal personage, will give testimony that my marriage with Luca Savelli was an unreal appearance and a null action. Then, as your wedded bride, I can flee with you. If Callisto cannot provide you with means for the journey, I can help out; before I went with Livio Savelli to liberate you, I supplied myself with gold. When we shall have Rome and the Tiber behind us, we will buy either mules or horses."

They were interrupted, for already Brother Martin stepped into the room.

CHAPTER XVI.

THE LAST DROP.

ROTHER MARTIN, who, conducted by Callisto, now came in, was in the highest state of excitement. He threw himself upon a chair, wiped his brow, and, looking at Egino and Corradina, said: —

"You will up and away, Count Egino? You are obliged to do it, as Callisto says? Now may God guide your flight!"

"I will not be alone in it, Brother Martin," replied Egino, in his joy shaking both of Martin's hands. "See, here is my betrothed; she will accompany me. You are first to bless our vows. Callisto will tell you that you may do it."

"Oho!" exclaimed Brother Martin, "bless your vows? O? I am to bless to-day? Well, then, let it be so; I will bless, though, like Balaam, I came hither to curse — yes, to curse — although I am a priest, and a servant of blessing and peace. My heart would press it from me if I did not hurl a bold anathema against the whole Babel and the beast which sits upon its seven hills!"

"And what has happened to you — what has put you in such a passion, Brother Martin?"

"I will tell you what has thrown me into such a passion, Count Egino! Rome throws me into a passion! This wicked Rome, which has murdered our Christian life, and wishes to convert the free creatures of God to stupid praying-mills, such as they have in Thibet or in Mantchooria, as Marco Polo,— or is it Martin Behaim who describes them! These inquisitors in scarlet cardinal robes, for which red is the proper color, — for only take the garment and wring it, and there drops out the blood of a witness of the truth! This Pope puts me into a passion; for he is not an apostle of love, a guardian of the truth, but a false robber."

"What has our Holy Father done, that you fly out into such a passion against him?" said Callisto, smiling, but surprised at the passionate expressions of the German monk, whose speech he rather guessed at than understood.

"Listen!" replied Luther. "You may like to know that I have become sated and disgusted with the life here. I had formed my resolution. The Devil had begun with me such a disputation in my heart, that he had made me afraid of myself. And then I said to myself: Flee from here, you poor shote of a Martin, while it is yet time, and before you have yet suffered harm to your soul. If they have killed Christ in the world, and if they will bring it about that the churches stand empty, the altars deserted; that the sound of bells die out, and hearts apostatize from the faith,— do not suffer it that they extinguish the flames upon the altar of your heart; that they make dumb the bells resounding and chiming in your soul. You hold fast to your God, to your Christ, and to the faith in his Word. Go from hence before doubt becomes powerful in you, and the Devil obtains sway over you, and moves in you as in a swine of the Gergesene herd. Hasten from hence; shake the dust of Rome from your feet, and take in your hand the pilgrim-staff with which you came hither! Thus I spoke to myself. And so I went with it to my prior, that I might hand over to him my power of attorney intrusted to me by our congregation in Saxony — you know, on account of the process against you, Count von Ortenburg, at the Rota here. The prior is also willing to take it upon himself immediately; but he warned me first to go to Father Anselmo, and to take my leave of him. Of course, Father Anselmo is a powerful man, and he stands high in our order, and has been kind and of the best disposition toward me, as you yourself, indeed, saw and know, Count Egino. So I must walk to the Vatican — once more! I went, and went with heavy step, as if something held back my foot which was again treading this path. And when I arrived up there, Father Anselmo received me kindly and listened to what I had to say; but his countenance was gloomy, and he only half heard what I said, and at last he replied:—

"'The Holy Father did treat you rather roughly not long since, Brother Martin, but you brought it upon yourself, because you presented to him metaphysical things which he does not like, and then there still lay upon his mind this transaction with the Duke of Ferrara, which, I fear, will still take an evil turn for the Holy Chair and our poor Italy ——.'

"'The transaction with the Duke of Ferrara?' I asked thereupon.

'I hear, worthy Father, that this transaction was disposed of in the most beautiful peace; that the Holy Father promised to Fabricio Colonna that the duke should have peace, and the ban should be removed from him, in case he would come and beg for pardon and acknowledge the supremacy of the church over Ferrara. Since, now, all that has happened——''

"'That has happened,' remarked Father Anselmo; 'but do you know of nothing else? The Holy Father cannot be satisfied with such a mild settlement of the long strife; he has had it disclosed to Alfonso von Ferrara that he must make over to the church his dukedom of Ferrara. The duke has angrily refused; the Holy Father, however, will not let him withdraw until he has submitted. The Colonna Palace, where the duke is staying, is watched by armed men; all the gates will be guarded by a strong force; the duke will not be freed till he obeys. But then what will happen? The King of France is his old ally. Will he not find in this a call of honor to assist Alfonso? The Holy Father may become as angry as he will, I insist upon it we shall again have the French in Italy before two or three months go by !'

"Thus spoke Father Anselmo with gloomy, anxious mien; and I,—I stared the man in the face as if the lightning had struck before me.

"'By all the holy helpers in need,' I cried, 'that is a nefarious deed. A word is a word and a man is a man, and even Pope Julius——'

"Father Anselmo, however, hastily cut short my speech. I also saw that my words would be lost upon him There lay in his thoughts only the King of France and his gigantic subjects and his Swiss regiments, and how the Republic of Venice will stand in the matter; not a thought of truth, of faith, and of one's word; all that did not oppress his conscience. And that man is the Holy Father's father confessor! And so I left. Now, however, I pray you, Count Egino, is this to be endured? Has he not acted as a robber and a scoundrel? With friendly promise and a safe conduct has the duke been enticed hither, and now they will plunder him, and strip him to the shirt in this Italian fox-hole,— this Castle Malepartus! And he claims to be the father of Christendom, the guardian of its doctrine? Is it not enough that they have given to us a faith of dead works instead of the living faith of the heart? Now shall the world also receive from them another right? Must not the thoughts stand still in your brain according to this right? Truly, they wish even that! As at the command of Joshua the sun stood still in heaven, so at the command of the Pope must the thoughts of the world stand still! Signor Callisto, you, who are a lawyer, what do you do with your brains that such a deed may go into it? Do you get you another, for that which God has given you does not suit the Holy Father? Get you another!"

"I will guard myself against that, Fra Martino," answered Signor Callisto, quietly smiling and looking down upon the excited monk. "My brain is just right for me, for it says to me, If the Holy Father is a secular lord and prince, he must also act as the clever Florentine diplomatic writer, Signor Niccolo Macchiavelli, prescribes for secular princes. One is a consequence of the other, my brain says to me. And then it says, You are wrong, Fra Martino, with your zeal against the priests, as you find them and as they out there with you will become not much better. Or are they better? Then see: man creates his God after his own image, — the savage his fetish, the Hebrew his choleric Jehovah, and the Greek his Jupiter; and so he creates also for himself his priests suited to the image of his God. The people will that they be just so, and always whatever they do, they will not go so far as to seem unworthy of the people's God. Our illustrious pontiff, Alexander VI. of most glorious memory, was certainly a robust sinner. But is he not still to be considered a lamb in gentleness and mildness in comparison with the passionate God, the Thunderer from Sinai? Our courts of heresy have burned many poor human beings, racked them and caused them to pine to death; but what have you against them, since their God lets his millions burn in his hell throughout eternity?"

"Yes; there it lies!" said Brother Martin. "There is truth in what you say. They do not see the true God, who is only love and mercy, but only the angry God of the olden time. To them, Christ, the gentle, mild one, is the first heretic; therefore have they slain him."

"Brother Martin," here interposed Egino, whose thoughts in this moment had a direction so different from that of the two men, "will you pronounce our nuptial benediction?"

"Certainly I will," responded Brother Martin. "As I said to you, I will bless you as all of those who are of a good will and of a pure heart, but I will curse those who destroy the kingdom of God upon earth. I will go home to my poor German fatherland, and between these clean, honest hands of mine will I place my head, and day and night will I reflect how I shall begin to give testimony to the truth, so that the world may listen to the truth."

"Brother Martin," here said Corradina, stepping before him and placing her hand upon his shoulder, while she looked him searchingly in the eye, "you, honest brother, perhaps no longer need so much thought over it! Perhaps One greater than we all has found and pointed out the way by which the people may be led to the truth; but to walk upon this way is difficult. Prometheus brought fire from heaven, and for this was chained to the Atlas Mountains. You wish to do more; you wish to kindle for the world an inextinguishable sun. Do you believe you could do it unpunished?"

"No. But I am not afraid of punishment; for I know that if they burn me, as they did Girolamo Savonarola, and as Huss of Hussinecz, and as Hieronymus of Prague, and as Arnold of Brescia, and as so many others, they will, of course, cause me suffering, but they could not again darken and extinguish an enkindled sun."

"Yet," continued Corradina, "if you do not fear the enemies who will stand around you as numerous as the army of Pharaoh against Moses, will you never fear the enemy which will arise in yourself?"

"What enemy do you mean by that?"

"That which wakes up in every man who would walk upon a new way to a new, great, yet-unattained goal — doubt of yourself."

"No," responded Brother Martin, firmly and resolutely. "I can suffer, rack my brains, and let myself be agitated and be deeply unhappy thereby, till I have agreed with myself about a thing. Then, however, I hold fast to it in lasting fidelity. Thus I, originally a lawyer, have come into the order in spite of storm and weather, in spite of father and mother. Dissension has no power over my nature. I know that whatever in me would speak against the light, could be only the voice of darkness."

"And will not a worse voice be that of the spirit which whispers to you not to lay your hand upon that which is hallowed by time; not to take away from the faithful soul its pious consolation; not to destroy the relics, out of which the simple, pious nature creates its trust. Not to spill the holy water, out of which a blessing priestly hand once sprinkled hope and confidence upon the head of your praying mother? Will all that not hinder and stop you upon your way?"

"No," said Luther, firmly; "for the time is past for a blessing to burst forth upon humanity by the sprinkling of holy water. We have become men, and only from the truth can come to us pious thoughts, and trust, and hope, and confidence."

"Well, then," answered Corradina, "I trust to your word and your flashing eyes that you are firm in this avowal; and so I will place in your hands the heritage of my forefather, the great Frederic. May your hand scatter abroad the seed-thoughts of the most noble emperor; the world of to-day is a soil prepared to receive this crop. May God prosper it to a beautiful fruitage. You, however, will then be the benefactor of the human race, and with the inheritance of the Staufens avenge the overthrow of the Staufens upon their destroyer, the church!"

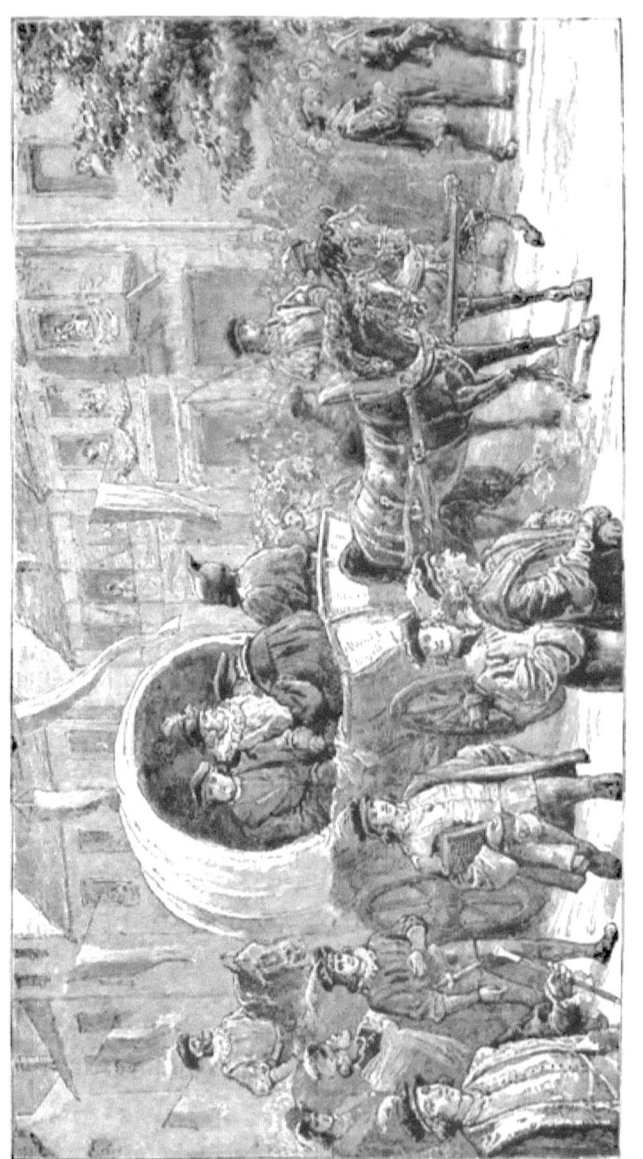

LUTHER'S ENTRY INTO ERFURT.

CHAPTER XVII.

THE BOOK OF FREDERIC II.

CORRADINA quickly left the chamber, and returned after a few minutes.

She carried in her hand a little book, which was bound in a thin covering overlaid with plate of gold; upon the gold was represented in embossed work all kinds of figures of flowers and animals; a clasp of gold filigree closed it.

"Here is this most noble legacy," said Corradina, when she handed over the book to the German monk. "I had hidden it in my girdle-pocket, in order not to be separated from it, when I entered upon my course with Livio Savelli; so I can give it to you."

Brother Martin took it from her and opened it. It contained a number of closely-written leaves of parchment written in Latin, in German, also in Greek, and in a writing which Martin was not able to read — it was Arabic, as Corradina explained. The words of the Apostle, "Do not quench the Spirit," was inscribed upon the inner side of the cover.

When Brother Martin would have immediately buried himself in the book, Egino, laying his hand upon it, said: —

"Not now, friend Martin; you still belong to us for awhile. Help and advise us for our flight, which must take place even this very night. And, above all, tell us about how Irmgard is, and how I can see her; for I cannot go away from here with my breast full of happiness and blessing without having thanked her, without having spoken to her, without having comforted her. That is impossible!"

"You will do that in spite of the mortal danger to which you would thereby be exposed?" asked Brother Martin.

"Certainly I will. I can even rejoice in the danger to which I thereby expose myself; for by that, Irmgard can measure how much and with what sacred duty I feel myself under obligation to her."

Brother Martin looked at him anxiously, and then turned his glance as if questioningly upon Corradina, while Callisto remarked:—

"Whoever is your friend must detain you by force from this venturesome undertaking. You know even now that my house is, perhaps, surrounded by spies and guarded on your account; that the gates are possessed by soldiers; exact descriptions of your person will be received by the watchmen. A crowd of people and clients of the Savelli and the Colonna are seeking for your track, not to think of the bailiffs which the monks will have bidden to search for you."

Egino shrugged his shoulders.

"I must!" he said. "There is something in me which bids me do it. I cannot resist it even if I must go through flames to reach Irmgard.

"And you, Countess,—you are silent, too? You do not assist me? Speak; forbid him to do it!" exclaimed Callisto, stirred up.

Corradina shook her head.

"I have nothing to forbid, my lord," she said in a low and subdued tone. "I know only one thing,—that where a mortal danger threatens him I must be at his side. I will go with him."

"Corradina, you would do that!" cried Egino. "That,—no, that I cannot suffer?"

"And yet you will be obliged to do so, Egino," she answered. "If there is something in you which bids you so powerfully to go, so there is something in me which bids me accompany you upon this course. Our fates are united from now on, for good and for evil days. Do not oppose it; it would avail nothing!"

Signor Callisto turned away indignant and angry. He washed his hands in innocency. Now had this clear-thinking Egino even yet changed himself into a crazy, stubborn-pated German! Callisto left the room, and left it to them to talk together over the way and manner in which they would pursue their course. It could only be risked in the darkness of the evening,—only in some kind of disguise. They could go as a pair of people from the peasantry. Callisto's old gardener had, without doubt, a costume to lend to Egino; Donna Ottavia's maid, who went clothed in the garb of the women of the Sabine Mountains, had one for Corradina. If Egino had been able to procure the costume of a common horseman, it would have suited him best; but whence to get it? One must take that which was most easily procured; and so Donna Ottavia was bidden to speak with the gardener and the maid. She did it, and after a short time she herself brought in the costume of the maid for Corradina.

At the time of the evening meal, between seven and nine o'clock according to our reckoning, the streets of Rome are least frequented and most quiet. It was this time, the hour of approaching night, which Egino and Corradina chose for their purpose. Brother Martin departed; he took it upon himself to inform Irmgard. He would himself be on the Quirinal in the evening and take leave of the friends, who, directly from there, would make their way to Sant Agnese, and enter into liberty, into the land of their nativity.

CHAPTER XVIII.

AT THE COUCH OF IRMGARD.

BROTHER MARTIN on his way home from Callisto's villa had arrived at his cloister at the hour of midday. He had gone in to partake of his meal with his comrades of the order. During the meal he had informed the prior, in a few words, of his visit to Padre Anselmo, just as he had previously informed him of his audience with Pope Julius II.,— in few words, and exactly what he considered sufficient for the comprehension of the honest, but wholly uncultivated man.

He had always, from the beginning, held himself aloof from these Roman order-brethren, who so thoroughly displeased him. He pretended in their presence that he did not understand how to express himself in Italian, and spoke only Latin with them. They did not like this kind of entertainment, and let him alone.

After the meal he had gone into his cell, there to rest during the hot noon hour, although it was contrary to his German nature to sleep at this hour of the day, as did the other monks. The eagerness to bury himself in the little book given to him by Corradina was, besides, too powerful in him for him not to forget everything else for that. With it he threw himself upon the bed in his cell and read it,— read till his head was hot, till his pulses throbbed in his temples, so that he forgot the world and time around him.

Finally, Luther sprang up. He must get air; he must take breath, and snatch himself from the whirlpool of thoughts which went through his brain,— which took deep hold upon his innermost being, and now threw as if a fearful, suffocating burden upon his soul; now again kindled as if a flaming fire in him, as an impulse to utter words of terrifying import,— an impulse to contest, to action, to blood, and to death for the deed. His whole combative nature was kindled to the highest degree by this book. And had Innocent IV., the destroyer of the Hohenstaufens, himself stood before him in this instant, he would have felt himself man enough to force him down, like Saint Michael.

He had sighed for a word, for a saving word for humanity, which seemed to him enticed by some evil magic from the path of truth into that of error. And now it seemed to him there lay not one, no, a whole stream of words upon his lips and in his heart; as if he need only walk out into the world, mount the nearest pulpit in every assembly of men, and there cry out what flashed up to him, in order to set free this poor beast of mankind which lay upon the ground and did not move, because some one had made a chalk-mark upon its neck in order to make clear to it that what bound it was only a chalk-mark. Was it then possible that this magic, which was no magic at all, which consisted, not in the enchanting power of the oppressor, but in the blindness of the oppressed, would not be dissolved if he should open the eyes of the blind? if he should pronounce the formula of exorcism, as this book taught it to him? if he should arouse his slumbering Germany with the thunder-cry of reason, with the full bell-chorus of the soul, with the alarm-peal of patriotism?

For it was this which pealed forth for himself out of this book that he held in his hands, out of this precious legacy of the great German emperor; this triple-note blending into one full chord, now roaring through his soul like the distinct crash of war, mighty and victory announcing, and moving his whole being so much the more powerfully because it had only awakened therein what had so long quietly slumbered there. The cry of intellect, of soul, of patriotism, when hurled crashing as a three-forked lightning among the German people, must be irresistible!

His heart filled to overflowing, his head dizzy with all these thoughts, Luther left the cloister.

Even if this had not driven him irresistibly out of his narrow cell into the open air, he would not have forgotten what he had promised,—to make his way to the Quirinal, to the sick-bed of Irmgard.

He now walked rapidly and energetically thither by the shortest way.

When he came near the Colonna Palace, he saw in the vestibule of the antiquated structure of the Pope's Pelagius, the Church of the Holy Apostles, which lay close to the palace, a host of armed men, who had their halberds and guns leaning against the walls, and were playing morris, or stooped over an antique sarcophagus, were throwing dice upon it. They had evidently quartered themselves there. Brother Martin could interpret the purpose of their being in this place; Father Anselmo had explained it to him: in the Colonna Palace dwelt the Duke of Ferrara; for this reason the exit from the palace was already guarded!

Brother Martin walked farther up the hill; he reached the little garden and house of Frau Giulietta; the door was locked. When he knocked, the widow herself opened it; she stuck her head through the crevice of the door, and in her countenance was to be read alarm and excitement. Quieted by the sight of the monk, she opened the door wider, and whispered:—

"Is it you, brother! You come into a house of mourning; step in quickly."

She hastily locked the door again behind him.

Brother Martin, walking into the kitchen, looked through the open door into Beppo's room, and saw Beppo standing there. He presented a strange appearance: he stood as if immovable, supporting himself with one hand upon the back of a chair and staring at the floor, with his features distorted by grief; besides, he had a long rapier with a heavy pocket-pistol in his other hand, and an iron helmet lay upon the chair, upon the back of which he was leaning.

"What is the matter with you, Mother Giulietta?" asked Brother Martin. "It appears as if your son must be going out armed and equipped into battle, and you are grieving over it — you make such a sorrowful face! Is it so? Or what then has happened?"

"Hush, hush!" whispered Frau Giulietta, in turn; "no one must find it out. The clients of the Colonna have been secretly called out. The poor youth, however faithfully he wished to stay with me, must now go, and that even to-day, when I need him so, and when he is so crushed and despairing about the death of the poor girl now lying so cold and still in there——"

"Irmgard is dead?" cried Brother Martin, startled and agitated.

"Truly she is dead; she died at midday. If you had come earlier she could have been confessed by you, and have received from you the holy eucharist also. As it is, however, she has gone hence without confession or sacrament; indeed, she would not hear to it that I should bring hither the curate from Sant Apostoli, and Beppo stood by her, and the dwarf would not permit it either. The dwarf said if the curate were brought he would be betrayed and sold out; and so it stands with the poor soul there now on the earth. And what will become of her up there in our Saviour's heaven, when she comes in without sacrament, or anointing, or absolution of sins, God only knows; but he will not call me to account for it, for I am innocent in the matter, — I am as innocent in it as the youngest of the children whom the cruel Herod had slain in Bethlehem!"

During this flow of speech on the part of his mother, Beppo had long since stepped forward and had mutely opened the door to Irmgard's room before Brother Martin. The latter stepped in softly.

He saw Irmgard's corpse lying upon the bed. The features of the young girl, pale as wax, appeared to him infinitely beautiful. It was as if the whole rich and noble angelic soul, before its departure, had entered into these features, and had given to this sleeping countenance its moving and peculiarly fascinating expression.

"Was she so beautiful?" asked Brother Martin, astonished, feeling the tears upon his lashes. "How beautiful is the human soul — the pure human soul!"

He wiped the moisture from his eyes and looked at Uncle Kraps. The latter sat upon his chair near the bed, stared at the floor, and muttered unintelligible words between his teeth: he appeared as if deprived of his senses.

Brother Martin seated himself upon a stool in the window-niche. He supported his head upon his hand, and thus gazed upon the features of the dead.

The sight of this countenance had for him something overpowering.

"How is the human soul so beautiful! And how infinitely sad is her lot! So sad that the best thing for her was death!"

She had passed over into eternal rest, — into the blessed beyond. She was with God. Could it be otherwise? She had not died in the faith of the church. She had not been provided with the baggage of the soul, — had died without sacrament or anointing, as Frau Giúlietta complained. But she had loved her brother in the spirit, her Christ, and had died in a deed of love. Should God thrust from himself this pure soul, because she came to him without the works of a priest? Could the Eternal, Infinite Spirit turn himself from her, because upon the brow of the corpse did not glisten a little fatty matter from an oil placed there by a priest? It was a fearful, a horrible idea, a boundless illusion, — a dreadful blasphemy!

Martin arose suddenly; it made him quake in all his members, — this fearful illusion that the pardon, the love of the great Creator of the universe, of the All-merciful, of the Father of the world, would be determined by such insignificant outer actions and works!

He kissed Irmgard's cold brow, and then hastened away; he was too much moved to take leave of Frau Giulietta and Beppo otherwise than with a pressure of the hand. The latter still seemed self-absorbed as his mother was cleansing from dust an old, leathern rider's doublet for his use.

"I will come again, — I will come again to help you about the burial and with the old man. Let me go now; something else presses me," he said, while he tore out for himself the bolt of the door and hastened outside.

To sit by the dead body of one who had become dear to him, and become absorbed in the quiet melancholy, in the tender sadness surrounding such a death, — was he allowed even that? No; if he heeded the mission whose call he felt within him, the time was past for him to do this. He must also be able to say, "Let the dead bury their dead!" That is a hard command! You shall sacrifice your feelings for the deed you have to accomplish. You shall, on its account, rend asunder a thousand bands of love enclasping and holding you back. You shall no more exercise the anxiety of love, no more be allowed to trouble yourself about the little circle surrounding you with tenderness. You shall rely upon yourself, and be entirely with and in yourself. You shall be spanned about with threefold brass, and with the inflexible egotism of the hero, speak the great, inexorable word, "Let the dead bury their dead."

When he stepped through the inclosing hedge of the little garden he struck against a monk, who came slipping along the hedge and stepped up to him. He was in the black-and-white habit of St. Dominicus, — a lean man, with an olive-hued face and small, blinking eyes.

"Eh, Fra Agostino," he whispered, "listen, now, listen! That is the house of Frau Giulietta, the widow, is it not? What were you doing there? Do two Germans dwell there, — an old, deformed man, and a girl who came in the disguise of a lad to the Hospizio dell' Anima? Do they really dwell there? You can tell me; I am from Santa Minerva, and the Sant Uffizio wishes to know whether ———"

"If the Sant Uffizio is hunting for the maiden," answered Brother Martin harshly, "it comes too late; the maiden is dead."

"Dead? Ah! is she dead? Is she really dead? Then the old man will wish to have masses read for her soul. The old man has brought money here with him. Has he already ordered the masses? Have you already taken them away from us? You Augustines — one encounters you everywhere! As if they would not have been better read in Santa Minerva than —— "

Martin listened no further. He turned his back. He made haste to get away from the neighborhood of the man. As out of a pestilential atmosphere, he was impelled to get away, as if there he must be seized by the *perniciosa*, with which the old man with the donkey had threatened him,—the *perniciosa* of the corroding, destroying poison which he then felt in his bones upon the road over the desolate height.

Even before that must Luther now flee. He must be entirely and undividedly to himself. He did not dare to allow himself barked at again by the dog of Doubt, which snarled upon him out of the olive-yellow face of the Dominican. Such a mass-reading priest was in the condition to throw him back into the despair of unbelief, into doubt about everything. He must do away with whatever could break in upon his strength of action. He must cling to his Christ, and give back to the world alive him whom the church had slain: the well-known God-man, the well-known Christ, as the Bible gave him, not as a doubtful thinking spiritualized him to a phantom. Had he not read to-day in his book, the book of the emperor: "The hand can lay hold of no puff of air; the senses of man can seize upon no phantom of an idea. One cannot pray to the 'creative idea' of Plato or Aristotle's 'universal power of formation.' Religion is the claim of a something eternal. The teaching of philosophy, however, is always changing. It is as the wave which seizes us, lifts us up or throws us under, and rushes away over us, in order to lose itself in the stream of the ages. Give to the world, also, no unknown God. As Paul preached to the Athenians the unknown God, they would not have listened to him if he had not spoken to them of a God long known to their hearts, whom they had unconsciously borne about and longed for in spirit. Man had need of the old, familiar fire that he might warm himself: the reflection imprisoned in the mirror may dazzle us, but it does not thaw out our limbs!"

The next thing lying in the way for Brother Martin to do was now to go out to Callisto's house, to bring thither the news of Irmgard's death. He dare not delay to make it known to Egino and Corradina, so they need no longer enter upon their course into the city, which might become so fatal to them.

Therefore he walked the shortest way to the Porta del Popolo again. As he came nearer to it he perceived that an unusually strong body of armed people lingered under the gate-arch and sat upon the stone benches at the sides. Was that also on account of the Duke of Ferrara? Certainly; and it could not trouble him, the poor monk. He quietly entered the crowd.

A Swiss soldier extended his halberd toward him.

"Whither, little monk? You cannot pass out!" he said.

"Is that the order?" asked Brother Martin, in German. "Why,— for what purpose?"

The Swiss replaced the halberd upon his shoulder, and when he perceived the sounds peculiar to his fatherland, he answered less harshly: —

"It is the order, so trudge back. Anyone may come in who will, but no one may go out."

"Not even a harmless monk like myself?"

"No; go!"

"Is it on account of the Duke of Ferrara? You see, countryman, that I am not the duke — and I also do not carry him in my gown!"

"In what strange tongue is that monk talking? Is it German?" here said a gray-bearded ruffian having the appearance of a bandit, with a long knife in his girdle. "Perhaps is hidden under his gown the fellow whom we seek. Come here, Fra Tedesco, and let us see you under the eyes."

The man stretched out his arm to lay it upon the shoulder of Brother Martin; the latter moved back, and the Swiss soldier interposed: —

"Go, Lanfranco; let him alone! He is a German countryman, and may go free whence he came."

Brother Martin found it advisable to withdraw himself quickly from the crowd, and get out of their sight. The servant of the Savelli did not pursue him. Lanfranco, indeed, had an eye for the gait of a monk; he could see that the gown was no disguise with Brother Martin.

But now, how begin? How warn Egino? The other neighboring gates were certainly guarded in the same manner. And the walls were no more to be leaped over, as Remus had once done; they were high, strong, and not to be scaled. Truly, quite near, at the Strasze Ripetta, one could be put across the river; beyond the river there was no wall. But as the gates were guarded, no doubt the bridges and ferries were also watched. There was nothing left except to walk up the Pincian Mountain to the city wall running along its precipice, to walk along this and seek a place where a fallen portion or a portion undergoing repair might present the possibility of getting out.

Brother Martin climbed the Pincian Hill, then turned to the city wall and walked along beside it without seeing his hopes fulfilled. He came farther and farther: he passed the Porta Salara, the Porta Agnese; both were watched by an unusually strong force of soldiers; the road was long and bad, full of obstacles, which he must mount or go around.

Thus it grew darker and darker while Brother Martin, in haste and anxiety, continued his walk. When he came to the Porta di Sant Agnese, he saw that his design must be relinquished. If he were to get out now, the road from here to Callisto's villa was too long for him still to arrive there at the right time, even supposing that he did not get lost in the neighborhood so entirely unknown to him.

So he gave up his intention. He decided to go home by the shortest road. Walking with weary step, his heart oppressed with uneasiness, he had reached the Baths of Diocletian, whose ruins then still stretched to the place where the Fountain Aqua Felice murmurs.

There a man met him, who went slowly past him covered with a mantle, with the rim of his hat drawn down low over his face. It was too dark to recognize the shaded features. But the form, the carriage, reminded Brother Martin so much of Signor Callisto, that he stopped and turned his head to look after him. The man had also stopped to look back at Brother Martin. Now he came back to the latter, and looking into his eyes, he said:—

"Eh, Brother Martin, is it you?" It was the voice of Callisto.

"It is I — and I meet you here, Signor Callisto? What has happened to lead you, in night and darkness, to this deserted neighborhood?"

"That is easily explained, good brother. I have yielded to the desire of our young friend, as we elders, in the end, are always obliged to do in the presence of passionate youth; and after what I have already done, am striving to help them further in every way, in order that he and Corradina may get away from here and out of Rome. The most needful articles for them both are packed upon my horse, and my gardener has been sent away with them out to

Baccano; there he is to await them at a quiet, out-of-the-way inn. They both are to be in disguise; I have myself seen how my Ottavia was assisting the Countess Corradina to transform herself into a most stately maiden of the common folk. Then I tore myself away, as the twilight was approaching, and have leisurely ridden hither in advance of them. When they come from Irmgard they will turn this way; we are to meet here; I am then to lead them through the nearest gate into the open air and upon circuitous paths so far as necessary——"

"You are to conduct them through the nearest gate, Signor Callisto? My God! so you do not know——"

"That the gates are more strongly guarded than usual? Certainly, I have noticed that, as I was coming in; but what is that to us? They are the Pope's Swiss; that has to do with the Duke of Ferrara."

"No; it has to do with all!"

"All?"

"So surely, that you will seek in vain to get out to pass the night under your own roof!"

"Ah!— how do you know that?"

"I have myself already tried to get out, and have been chased back!"

"That is a bad, a dreadfully bad cross-stroke. Then our plan of flight goes to the ground. What, then, shall we do?" exclaimed Callisto.

"I have tortured my brain with this question for more than an hour!"

"The unhappy Egino, with his German stubbornness!" said the lawyer.

"Do not chide him. He was right in his desire. The saddest thing about it is he has quite uselessly brought himself into this unfortunately dangerous situation, for he comes to Irmgard too late. She is dead."

"Dead?"

"She died to-day, at noon."

"Then it seems just as if a wicked demon has control over the poor young man!"

"Indeed it does; as if a real defiance of fate!" answered Brother Martin.

"What shall we undertake in order to help him?"

"I know now only one thing to advise. Let us hasten to the house of Frau Giulietta. There we shall perhaps find him, and advise together whither we shall bring him and the countess till this unfortunate closing of the gates comes to an end."

"Yes, yes," exclaimed Callisto; "let us hasten thither; let us hasten thither this moment!"

They both moved quickly away through the darkness. Callisto walked in advance, Brother Martin after him with weary feet. The road was not too long. They saw already the dark outline of Constantine's Baths emerge before them, also the high wall of the Colonna Gardens, when they suddenly perceived the sound of hoofs and the clatter of weapons. A troop of horsemen sprang toward them; they had scarcely time to throw themselves to one side. When they then hastened quickly forward they perceived a still stronger troop, a confusion of men and horses, and the loud rattling of weapons.

Before we set about explaining this, let us turn back to Egino and Corradina.

CHAPTER XIX.

THROUGH!

T was about Ave Maria when Egino and Corradina entered upon their venturesome undertaking. Signor Callisto, as he said, had already left the villa; Donna Ottavia, after having changed Corradina into a peasant-maid, had embraced her with moist eyes, had again drawn the green apron in folds over the heavy budget, and tied the heavy shoes more securely, and then had taken leave of her and Egino with most heartfelt and touching wishes for their happiness.

And so, some minutes after Callisto had left the villa, Egino and Corradina stepped through its gate out on the Flaminian Way and walked leisurely to the Porta del Popolo. They carried by turns a basket filled with vegetables and early fruit.

The city gate appeared free. Only when they had passed through did they see on the inside, right as well as left, upon the stone benches, a crowd of armed watchmen, perhaps thirty or forty men, soldiers and bandits, whose long guns leaned against the wall.

The guards had taken no notice of those coming in. Only when they were some steps beyond them, one of the bandits, a gray-bearded man, looking after them, said:—

"Who are those two?"

"Who should they be, Lanfranco? Gardeners, who bring vegetables to a palace," responded another in the same bandit costume.

Lanfranco shook his head.

"They have not the gait or the crooked backs of gardening people," he said, and got up, while he added:—

"Run after them and look into their faces, Niccolo; you must know your Countess Corradina."

"Oh bah!" said Niccolo; "I will take care not to run needlessly. We are to see that they do not come out of the city, if they are still in there. If they are outside, they will certainly not come in, comrade."

"Who knows?" muttered Lanfranco, sullenly, between his teeth. Then he cried out:—

"Hey, you there,—people! Here now!"

Egino turned his head. Corradina quickened her step, and then Egino also walked on more rapidly.

"The lass has no desire to allow herself chucked under the chin by you; you are too ugly to her with your uncombed beard, comrade Lanfranco!" exclaimed Niccolo, and the other guards laughed.

Comrade Lanfranco, however, had now for once had his suspicion aroused, and he did not allow himself moved from it by his companions. He pursued the pair.

His sandals were soft, the street unpaved, so his step remained inaudible. Soon they also reached an inhabited street, where traffic, though now less, had not yet died out, and this made it more difficult to notice such pursuit.

Egino and Corradina moved on rapidly. At length they reached the foot of the Quirinal Hill, and climbed with slower pace. Two fellows having the appearance of bandits met them; the two were chatting together in an animated way, and did not notice the fugitives. The latter soon beheld the ruins of the Baths of Constantine close before them. Suddenly, however, they heard a cry behind them.

Egino looked around in surprise, since he thought he recognized the same voice which had already called to him before at the gate. He saw the two bandits who had just passed him, in company with a third, hastening after him; what they were calling out he did not understand.

"Let us flee,—let us flee!" whispered Corradina, in alarm.

"No, no," said Egino; "not that! They would overtake us, and then it would be so much worse for us. We must remain calm, and try to deceive them; but you must talk with them, because I might betray myself by the strikingly foreign accent of my speech."

Seemingly calm they continued their way, and came almost to a high-towering, black corner of the wall of the baths, which here projected to the road. Still, before they had quite reached the spot where the road ran around this corner of the wall, the three men, calling and abusing them, had caught up. Corradina, turning to them, while Egino seized the handle of a dagger in his breast-pocket, said:—

"What do you wish, people? If you are gentlemen, let us go and bring these fruits to the Colonna palace; we are poor gardeners, that you see truly——"

"The Devil!" exclaimed one of the three, no one else but Lanfranco, who had found in the two others good friends, and appeared to have had them join him in order to end the wearisome pursuit, and to assure himself whether or not his suspicion had grounds; "the Devil! I will swallow your vegetables there uncooked and the basket thrown in, if that is true!"

With that he laid his fist upon Corradina's shoulder, and stepping close before her looked into her face, while the other two seized Egino's two arms, in order at once to make defense impossible to him. Egino tore himself loose from them, while Lanfranco added:—

"Do you think I don't know you, Donna Corradina? Do you think old Lanfranco is so stupid——"

Lanfranco could not end, for he already, at this moment, felt upon his neck the hand of Egino, who hurled him back from Corradina, and with the other hand drew forth the dagger and raised it, in order therewith to keep from his person the two other bandits, who now, uttering half-audible curses, again pressed upon him.

Corradina uttered a cry of alarm. She threw herself upon Lanfranco, who, the instant Egino turned against the others, tried to seize his lower arm, in order to make him defenseless and to wrest from him the dagger. Mutely pressing his teeth together Egino struggled against this with a tenacious strength, which would have been fully a match for that of the old bandit; the two others, however, rushed upon him so violently, that they forced him down on his knees. Corradina saw that they must have overpowered him before many seconds would pass.

At this instant, though, two entirely unexpected apparitions approached the group wrestling in the darkness and wound in a tangle. There suddenly sounded in close proximity to them the strokes of horses' feet, and the clinking of weapons, and an outcry; two snorting horses as suddenly threw a dark shadow upon those contending, and a suppressed voice cried:—

"*Accidente!* what is going on here? Disperse, there, or I will hew your pates, mob!"

The man who called this down from his horse brandished at the same time a broad and long sword over the heads of the bandits, and came down with a flat stroke upon Lanfranco's back.

Corradina had already rushed toward them, and seizing the knee of the rider, she cried: —

"Sir, save us from these bandits. In the Redeemer's name, save us!"

"Body of the Madonna! Go to the hangman!" cried Lanfranco, on the contrary. "What business have you to meddle with it? We are no bandits; we are subjects of the Savelli, and these are our prisoners. Help us to make them fast!"

"Who are they?" asked the horseman, as if in surprise.

"Does that concern you? They are those whom we seek, whom——"

"But you know us!" now exclaimed Egino, aloud, for he had looked searchingly into the countenance of the horseman, whose voice had a sound familiar to him.

The horseman stooped over to look as well as possible into the face of Egino, and then into that of Corradina, and, startled thereby, he said: —

"You—is it you? And this," he added, quickly rising erect, and after that whispering a few words to the other horseman near him, —"this pretends to be a servant of the Savelli? You are bandits, gallows-birds, cutthroats, scabby dogs, rabble, that belong to the galleys! Cut among them, Gregorio, if they do not act as if they will get away!"

With that he brought out his long sword as if he would bring it down upon Lanfranco's skull. The bandits bounded back.

Lanfranco uttered an oath; the other horseman, however, crowded upon him likewise with his horse and drawn sword: if he would not be trodden down he must turn and flee, and the other bandits followed him, stumbling down the steep path.

"But, for God's sake," said Egino, taking a deep breath, "how did you come here just at the right moment to be our rescuer, Beppo? More than that, how have you become a horseman?"

"Follow me, follow me," hastily replied Beppo, transformed into a horseman, and he turned his horse around. "I will save you, you and the lady there; for Irmgard's sake I will save you,—but make haste!"

Egino and Corradina followed him, while the other horseman remained near them.

When, after a few steps, they came around the corner of the ruined walls, they saw a whole group of horsemen, perhaps ten or fifteen, keeping themselves in the dark shadow of the ruin. Beppo spoke some words with the first of them, then he beckoned to Egino with his hand; and while the second horseman remained with the troop, Beppo rode farther over the dry, grassy surface. Egino and Corradina had trouble to keep up with him.

They came past the hedge inclosing Frau Giulietta's little garden.

"Beppo," here exclaimed Egino, "is not that your mother's house, the dwelling of Irmgard? Whither are you conducting us? We came to see Irmgard. We are on our flight; before going, we wish to see Irmgard!"

"Irmgard is dead!" answered Beppo, in a subdued undertone. "There in the room you see the light shimmer through the shutters; there she lies!"

"Dead? O my God!"

"She died a few hours ago."

Corradina seized Egino's arm, as if to support him or as if in a violent emotion.

Egino had stopped; a sudden pang convulsed him. He stood as if rooted to the earth.

"Forward, forward!" cried Beppo, turning back and looking down from his horse, walking in advance of them. "I will save you, both of you, for her sake! Otherwise she would have died in vain, if you were not saved. But you must hasten!"

"Whither, then, do you lead us?" asked Corradina now, dragging Egino after her.

Beppo pointed with his hand to a strong troop, which at this moment became visible to them, as they turned around a corner of the high wall of the Colonna gardens. Before the gate which still to-day leads out of these gardens upon the Monte Cavallo, the ridge of the Quirinal Hill, tarried perhaps fifty horsemen, part high on horseback, part standing near the horses. When they came nearer they perceived that all these men were armed, many as regular warriors, with breastplates and helmets, pistols and swords, many only with helmets and long daggers. Still, almost all the last wore also strong doublets of buffalo-skin and cavalry-boots drawn high up to the knee,—the same costume in which Beppo also sat upon his black warhorse.

"There are led-horses and horses of burden there," continued Beppo. "To provide for the accident that some of our horses are shot or stabbed, we have taken along horses as substitutes. Come, now; I will get one for each of you."

He rode farther, and led Egino and Corradina into the midst of the crowd of horsemen. Here took place a brief interchange of words between Beppo and a tall, strongly built man, who wore a black cap upon his bearded head, while his helmet hung down from the horn of his saddle. The man appeared to make objections.

"What help to us is a man who has no sword, but, instead of that, takes a wife with him?" Egino heard him say.

Beppo grew angry.

"But he is a warrior, and a sword will also be found; and if you people of Ferrara are not willing to help us who are clients of the Colonna, you have only to say so; we will then go home, and let you see how you come through!"

The other muttered something in his beard; Beppo, however, had already sprung away and handed over his animal to a horseman. He brought from the circle a riderless horse, upon which he lifted Corradina, then quickly a second for Egino. Corradina was too much accustomed to riding not to feel soon comfortable and firm in the saddle; Egino had swung himself up in an instant without stirrups. Beppo now hastened back to his horse, and was just loosing his pistol from his saddle, where it hung, in order to reach it over to Egino, while the latter was grasping with his right hand for the reins of Corradina's horse, in order to draw it closer to his side.

At this instant, however, sounded forth a short, shrill whistle from the garden; immediately afterward appeared at its gate several armed men, who, coming out, seemed to issue orders, and, as well as the darkness enabled one to make out, to throw themselves upon richly equipped horses, which were led out before them. From a short distance beyond, the sound of hoofs reached them; this indicated that the troop halting behind the angle of the wall, to which Beppo had first led Egino, had darted away as advance force. The man in the cap, with whom Beppo had contended, cried out, "Advance!" And the whole crowd put themselves in motion, — at first in a walk, then in a very fast trot. They went over the ridge of the Quirinal, over the same road which Brother Martin traversed when he, coming from Frau Giulietta's house, had gone to the Porta del Popolo, with the baying dog continuously at his side.

While the tall and heavy horses were now rushing forward, their violent movements prevented all conversation, even if it had been possible, in spite of the clatter of harness and weapons and the strokes of hoofs upon the hard, dry ground, to make one's self understood. But they had soon reached the part of the road where it descended to the lower city, and where, with shortened reins, they must ride in a walk. Egino now saw Beppo at his side, and catching his breath he exclaimed : —

"But I beg you, Beppo, now explain to us among what people we are, who are thus bearing us away, as if we are held captive by a dream."

"Among what people you are!" remarked Beppo, breathing as heavily from the quick ride. "Are you not aware ? The lords there behind us are the Duke of Ferrara and the illustrious Fabricio Colonna ; the host of warriors around us are the Duke Alfonso's colossal people, in whose attendance he has come hither ; we others, — we are the clients of the Colonna, called out to their support. We have fallen upon the *bargello* with his deputies, who were guarding the palace over at the Holy Apostles, and have gagged him and dragged him to the court of the palace. Our way now leads to the Porta del Popolo, at which we must cut ourselves a way through, and to the Ponte Molle, which we must, likewise, take by storm. The object is to bring the Duke of Ferrara into liberty and safety. The Holy Father wishes to have him brought early in the morning to the Castle of St. Angelo, and we are bringing him to-night into liberty. The master of the house of our Lord Fabricio has secretly called out to-day those of his clients skilled in arms and all of us who can ride, and he has provided for us horses and weapons. It has been done quite in secret, so there are of our men altogether not more than sixty ; but I think we will be enough to make our way through. Now you know all about it."

"And that you previously came to us just at the right moment to give us help against the brigands —— "

"I was with the advance troop," interposed Beppo. "We were keeping quiet behind the old wall, when we perceived the cries and your struggling with the brigands close in our vicinity, and so I came just at the right moment to rescue you."

"And how shall we thank you," here remarked Corradina, "that you have taken us with you, and now lead us away in such stately, certain protection ?"

"You need not thank me, noble lady," responded Beppo. "I save you, because the poor Irmgard would have seen you saved, who is now up yonder with the angels. Poor Irmgard! From this dark, star-sprinkled heaven she will look down upon us! She will see you and also me. She will be as a saint who sees everything and hears every prayer that a poor mortal may direct to her — will she not?"

"Certainly," said Egino; "and she will also see how full of gratitude our heart is for you, Beppo!"

"Oh, thank you!" exclaimed Beppo, almost involuntarily. "Should I have let you be captured here by these people of the Savelli? They would have tortured you, and put you to the rack till you would confess everything to the very last: how your escape out of the cloister of Santa Sabina was set on foot; who had aided you in your flight; how Irmgard had found you, and how Beppo had guided the poor maiden; and how he, again, then conducted you out of the vaults; and then it would have gone hard with Beppo! So, if I did not do it for the sake of the dead Irmgard, and if I had not been anxious for her friends to escape unhurt, I must yet have done it for my own sake! But what happens to-night must Lord Fabricio Colonna settle later with the Holy Father; we do only what is commanded by our patron, and nothing beyond that concerns us who are dependent upon his protection, and must follow when he wishes our attendance. Therefore do not talk to me of thanks, but rather seat yourself firmly in the stirrups; you hear how they have just fallen upon each other at the gate."

In fact, from there resounded cries and noise of weapons; the advance troop must, at this moment, have encountered the watch at gate.

"Forward!" again cried aloud the leader of the cavalry host.

The horses were spurred up; the whole crowd, closely balled together, sprang to the gate; one could hear thence cries and shrieks amid the rattling of weapons clashing together. Above the dark bodies of prancing horses could be perceived the blades of swords drawn out for a stroke, brandished partisans and halberds. Now, also, firearms flashed; the crash of the heavy discharge echoed from the front of the Church of Santa Maria and the nearest walls. Still, the guard, surprised and thrown into consternation by the suddenness of the attack, seemed ready to yield, when the chief troop came to the spot and swung their weapons in order, pressing forward to enter into the contest.

Those in advance already were shouting aloud the battle-cry: "A noble Este! A noble Colonna!"

The gate was taken; the guards were scattered in flight except a half-dozen men, who were surrounded, and compelled by swords held before them and by flat strokes to draw up again the falling-gate, which had been let down by them at the first alarm.

When this had been done the whole crowd, like a storm-wind, rushed farther down the Flaminian Way, past the Villa of Callisto lying there in the dark. The space of a quarter of an hour later and the Tiber bridge, more feebly guarded than the gate, was won with less effort : with the far bank liberty was attained — liberty for the Duke of Ferrara, as well as for Egino and the woman of his love.

LUTHER BURNING THE POPE'S BULLS

CHAPTER XX.

THE MORTARA CHILD OF THE WORLD.*

E have left Brother Martin and the lawyer upon the height of the Quirinal, at the spot which one to-day calls Monte Cavallo, from the prancing, colossal horses, ascribed to the chisels of Phidias and Praxiteles, and formerly erected here as an ornament to the adjacent Baths of Sixtus V.

The two men had seen how also the second, larger troop of horsemen set themselves in motion, and had again fled to one side to get out of their way. Since they moved at first less rapidly than the advance troop, and passed the two men in a walk, this gave the latter time to perceive the two forms riding in the midst of the procession, who, from their dress and appearance, presented a strange aspect among the martial folk.

Although it was already far too dark for certain recognition, still, Callisto exclaimed in surprise: —

"Do you see those two, the man and the maiden in the peasant garb, Brother Martin? If they were our friends!"

"You must know better than I," said Brother Martin, cutting short his speech, "how you have disguised Egino and his countess to make them unrecognizable, and whether or not it could be they."

"It was certainly they; I could swear to it!" added Callisto.

"But what, then, can all this mean? Who are these horsemen; how come our friends among them? Are they discovered? Are they carried away as prisoners? For what purpose, then, this crowd of giant-like people? Have you any idea, Signor Callisto?"

"Not the least; we can do nothing to solve this riddle except to

---

* "Reference is here made to a child of the Mortara family, which was stolen and brought up as a devotee to the Catholic faith, though his parents had chosen for their child a career entirely different."— *Professor Helveti*, of State College, Lexington, Ky.

go to the house of Frau Giulietta, lying here before us ; perhaps we may receive information there."

"God grant it!" said Brother Martin, excited, and walking with redoubled haste to the house indicated by Callisto. They came into the garden of Frau Giulietta, and saw, standing immovable, a woman of her size and form close to the hedge-opening which served as an entrance. It seemed as if she were listening to the hoof-strokes of the horses dying away in the distance.

"Is it you, Donna Giulietta — yes, it is you; and you recognize us?" whispered Callisto.

"Certainly, certainly, Signor Callisto," answered Frau Giulietta, quickly. "Had I not already, long since, recognized your voice, do you think I would have so quietly waited here your approach — in this dreadful night, when I have the dead there behind me in the house, and am now still more desolate and lonely with her in the still house where only the old, bewitched man sits by her bed and does not stir or move, and will not take a bit of food in his mouth, and only mutters words which no Christian man can understand, and which are, in the end, only witchcraft, with which the old wizard makes my whole house and possessions and all of us unhappy? Oh! walk in, Signor Callisto, and see ——"

"Stop, only stop, Frau Giulietta," said Callisto, interrupting her words. "Only tell us quickly, were Count Egino and the Countess Corradina here? And what signifies the crowd of horsemen passing us just now? and who were the people of the peasantry who were being borne away so swiftly in their midst?"

"Who the horsemen were I can tell you, Signor Callisto," responded Frau Giulietta, eagerly; "for now, since they have carried it out and are up and away, it is not necessary to be silent any longer, — so full of secrecy as Beppo, the poor youth, has been over it all day; for he is with them, you must know, Signor Callisto, — Beppo; and he is so clever and quick, and also firm in the saddle as an old rider, and, in truth, useful in every way. They have given him a part to command, — him and Gregorio Benvieni, our cousin. May God now have them all in his protection, and guard them from misfortune; for if anything should happen to Beppo, you see, Signor Callisto, it would just be my death. I don't know what I ——"

"But, Donna Giulietta," said Callisto, breaking in upon her speech, "you were going to tell us what all this means. I pray you come to the point; who were these horsemen?"

"Didn't I tell you, Signor Callisto, that they are the subjects of the Colonna and the horsemen of Este. Our lord and patron, Fabricio Colonna, has received promises from the Holy Father that Alfonso should have kindness and peace from him; and now that he has come, the illustrious Alfonso, the Holy Father wishes to force him to leave his land and to withdraw to Asti, from this on to dwell as a beggar; and Fabricio Colonna will not suffer that one should thus deceive his friend and guest, and therefore they are conducting him with an armed force out of the city."

"God be with us!" broke in Brother Martin, with a deep breath of relief.

"But the two,—the young man and the maiden, who were being carried away?"

"I know nothing of a young man and a maiden," answered Frau Giulietta.

"Perhaps honest Beppo has recognized them, and now rescues them," said Callisto.

"Certainly it is so! At least, we can do nothing else but hope that it is so!" exclaimed Brother Martin.

"And perhaps this turn of affairs will be for my good," added Callisto. "If the Colonna break through the gate-guards and disperse them, the way will also be opened to me to get home and quiet Donna Ottavia's fears. Come, Brother Martin, there is nothing left us but to bid Frau Giulietta good-night and walk home."

Frau Giulietta would gladly have broken out again into complaints about how lonely she was now without Beppo, and about how she was afraid to go back into her house, with the still corpse and the wizard muttering his incantations; but the two men withdrew from her, and instantly disappeared in the darkness. After walking a quarter of an hour, they were at the cloister of Santa Maria and the Porta del Popolo.

Callisto had cherished a deceptive hope when he thought they would now let him out; the surprised guard had now recovered from their fright and their overthrow, and were again assembled, and shoved him back angrily and with curses. Perhaps it was the military order to which they held, in spite of the fact that the reason for it had now ceased to exist, and the closing of the gate had become aimless. Perhaps, also, they were too lazy to draw up the heavy falling-gate, now again let down. Signor Callisto must reconcile himself to seeking a shelter for the night with one of his acquaintances dwelling near by. Brother Martin went to seek out his cloister and his cell, and there, tired to death, let himself drop down upon his couch.

It was late the next morning when he awoke out of an invigorating slumber; he had slept through the matin service of the monks, as well as the morning masses and the breakfast-time. He was obliged to beg of the lay brother appointed to his service a little milk and bread; and when this had been brought to him he began to tie up his bundles. It was little that he had brought hither; what he was taking away was not much more,— a little linen, so much as a traveling monk needed, and some legal documents from the process which he had been sent here to carry on, and several books which he had found opportunity to buy in Rome, and partly also in Verona and Bologna, on his way hither. Fastened together, all these now made a burden too heavy for a pedestrian to carry. Some other means of bearing them away must be devised. Treasures of this kind, such as, for the most part, were scarcely to be had at home in Germany, could not be left behind.

Then he devoted the day to taking leave of Rome. It was a mute leave-taking: first, from some sacred places where he had prayed and meditated when he first made a pilgrimage through the "Eternal City"; from the finest of the basilicas, in whose great and magnificent naves wherein Christians of remote centuries had knelt, the spirit of the pure, primitive times of the faith had blown upon him,— the spirit of the Apostles, and of those who had died as martyrs to the evangelical truth. He went to take leave of the graves of the Apostles; and coming home from there, he stepped once more into the Pantheon of Agrippa, into the silent domain of beautiful paganism which here still extended its arches over him, so great, so bright, so illumined by thought; he mounted once more to the Capitol, from which Rome had plundered the world; he let his glance sweep over the ruins of the Palaces of the Cæsars and the high walls of the Flavian Amphitheater, and fixed it then, for the last time, upon the world of ruins at his feet,— upon the spot where once upon the Forum fell the dice for the destinies of the earth.

At last he stepped into a restaurant lying upon his way, and allowed himself helped to wine and something to eat. They brought to him food, and a bottle woven around with a bright straw, and a little tin cup, out upon a table nailed together out of rough planks, which stood before the house under a great mulberry tree. In the shade of the tree he seated himself upon a piece of red marble,—a block of that *antico rosso* which Africa had paid as tribute to Rome, the mistress of the world, which fifteen hundred or two thousand years before had perhaps formed the altar of a god or the socle of a hero's statue, and which now served for the seat of the German monk Martin with his thought-laden brain.

The restaurant lay high; one overlooked from the place under the mulberry tree a good bit of the "Eternal City" and the Campagna, and behind them the pure, beautifully sweeping lines of the two mountains with the little cities, castles, and settlements of the primitive Latin times on their cliffs. In his farewell wanderings and ramblings through the city, the whole day had almost disappeared before Brother Martin was aware.

Now, the sun already sunk, the air was so clear and transparent that all distances became near, and every point of the landscape seemed attainable in the shortest space. Was it not as if one could count the windows in the houses of Frascati? But still, the distance bore a wonderfully fine shimmer of violet, and the sky above the heights and above the Campagna began to glow in rosy tints; the light of dying day heralded its approach with all the magic of a southern sunset.

It came with all the deeply moving beauty with which the golden flames and the purple tints of evening gleamed above the heights of this wonder-land, diffused themselves, and blended into ravishing hues; with that beauty which Dante felt when he sang so proudly his father-land, "*Il bel paesa, che il mar circonda;*" which filled the heart of Filicaja with such deep melancholy when he expressed pity for this "*Dono infelice di belleza,*" and which influenced in Lord Byron that sadness, placing upon his lips that winged word of the "Niobe of the Nations."

The German cloister brother, however, when he looked upon the Eternal City, woven about with the eternal beauty of enchanting nature, thought of Horace's celebrated stanza:—

> "Alme Sol, curru nitido diem qui
> Promis et celas, aliusque et idem
> Nasceris; possis nihil urbe Roma
> Visere majus!"

"In truth," he said to himself, "the world has nothing greater! She is the creature, the child, the heiress of the world, this Rome! The generations of men, as they have succeeded each other, have built her; the nations have created their best for her. Egyptians, Greeks, Etruscans, Latins — they all have left their treasures for her culture, and the great spirits of mankind, the creative geniuses, their best works. From the upper Nile, out of the city of a hundred palaces, came this marble; out of Greece came the artists who, out of such blocks, created the magnificence of statuary. Thus the world adorns her creature; she belongs to the world, — she is the eternal possession of the nations. But the priests came and took this child of the world to bring it up in their faith, to fill it with their superstition, to put upon it a monk's gown."

If this German critic had lived in our days, he would have broken out in the cry : —

"In truth, this child of the world, this rich heiress of the nations, whom they have won for the cloister, is the Mortara child of the world's history."

As it was, however, only a great aching, a great pain of farewell, passed through his heart, while he said to himself that he must go, never to return. The hands which had taken possession of the heiress of history, had risen in hostility against men of his spirit. They drove him out, — away out of this beautiful world; away from the Ausonian soil; from the soft and gentle breezes of evergreen gardens; from the neighborhood of the sublime monuments of antiquity; from the circle of a life refined by manners, ennobled by art and poesy; from this atmosphere of a care-free enjoyment of existence, where it would cost nothing but a little mute subjection, nothing but a little treachery to an inner fidelity to self, to the feeling of truth, and to living testimony, in order to become led easily and smoothly past sin and vice, and through death into the luminous gate of heaven, — into the eternal continuation of the care-free life here below. From all this Brother Martin felt himself shut out, banished, driven away.

The bridge was broken down between them and him, and a deep abyss yawned between the men of works and the men of faith, as he called his love. Rome thrust him from her forever. He turned upon her his back as did Tannhäuser, who had come thirsting for reconciliation, and whose German impulse of soul had also not understood Rome. He went home over the Alps into the German father-land, the cradle of the human thought of the future. Upon his breast rested the gospel of this future.

There were the leaves of the great Hohenstaufen emperor. Once had the kingdom been overthrown because these Hohenstaufens had united their political destinies with the destiny of Italy. Now, the greatest of these would avenge the overthrow ; he punished the rebellion and the tearing loose of rebellious powers from the kingdom, while he with sharp sword-stroke divided, also, the religious destinies of the two peoples, and tore loose the faith of the native land from the faith of that beyond the Alps.

Such a sword-stroke this doctrine contained by his book would, indeed, become, so soon as this book was placed in the hand of the proper champion chosen by God.

When Brother Martin came home to his cloister, the gate-keeper gave to him a sealed note. The porter said a man from the villa of Signor Callisto Minucci had brought it. When Martin had broken the seal he read the words : —

"Callisto's gardener, who brings home with him this note, will tell you that we are safe. We await you, Brother Martin, beyond the boundary, in Sienna."

CHAPTER XXI.

THOUGHTS OF THE EMPEROR.

*"The real Pope, that is the righteous will;
And not in Rome this dwells, but in ourselves."*
— Z. WERNER, "The Consecration of Power."

T was five days later. A quarter of an hour distant from the city of Sienna, on the road leading to Rome, at a well placed there for the refreshing of travelers, two men had laid themselves down, rejoicing, as it seemed, in the rest under the thick shade of the plane trees surrounding this repose-inviting place.

One of them, a little, oldish, deformed man, lay stretched out upon the hard ground covered with short grass. He had his two elbows propped up, let his capacious jaws rest upon his fists, and stared, apparently without thought, at the fresh, bubbling water which was rushing down out of the stone-hewn lion's mouth into a sarcophagus, thus converted into a trough.

The other was a white-clad monk, who sat reading upon a seat at the side of the well. He had, in truth, on account of the heat, thrown off the black cape, which hung half out of the hamper of a donkey standing still, with sunken head, near the man stretched out on the grass. This animal betrayed life only by the oscillations of his tail, with which he drove from himself the dense swarm of flies buzzing about him.

In the hampers of the donkey one perceived all kinds of effects, above all, a package of heavy books. The monk was absorbed in the little book held in his hand.

The book of the Emperor Frederick II. had been written by him about the time of the Council of Lyons, in the days when Innocent IV., with only one hundred and forty French and Spanish bishops, had excommunicated the emperor, declared his crown forfeited, formally displaced him from his kingdom, and, in the fullness of spiritual power, had taken from the German nation her anointed and crowned head. This had been the great death-stroke for the old Germanic empire. Frederick had called upon the kings and princes to conquer this hierarchy, which, with open violence, snatched for itself the mastery of the world. But the kings and princes had deserted him, and submitted. The people bowed themselves to the yoke of the priesthood, and the deserted emperor, who, with broad view, saw in the future the wretchedness and inner ruin which must enter into Germany, if the "German individuality," the tendency to divide and separate and struggle apart in a thousand directions, thus received the consecration and blessing of the church, which tore away the uniting band of the nation — the abandoned emperor could do nothing but hold his banner laboriously aloft with his remaining strength, till it should fall from his dying hand; and then, dying, to bequeath the expression of his own inner spiritual freedom to him whom the future would send to avenge him.

He thought of this: —

"*Exoriare aliquis nostris ex ossibus ultor.*"

But what he wrote down for this avenger were far less the oracles of a philosopher, who, in seclusion from the world, sought treasures in the still mine of his thoughts, than the practical hints, counsels, and warnings of a man who had grown up in worldly pursuits, had been educated to human shrewdness, and had learned to reckon with the real.

"Men as they are," he had written, "need still a supernatural, divine warrant for the law according to which they are to act. The authority of the reason and of thought will always lead only the wise and good; the power of beauty will extend over only beautiful hearts. The great mass, in order that the law may have authority over them, need the seal of wonder and the signature of a hand coming out of the clouds.

"Let us not contend with the masses about this. Do not waste your strength in struggles over their dogmas. If they need to consider the Holy Spirit a white dove, then do not think it will be much advantage if you pluck out of this white dove a part of its feathers. Do not think when you have broken to pieces the dogmas in the hand of the priests, that the priests have been won to the service of the truth. You are not to take away the dogmas from the priests;

no, but the priests from the dogmas. By this course alone will you see minds gradually make themselves free.

"And you will be able to do it, if you place mankind and their God in the proper relation to each other, which relation was hidden from the ancients, and which Christ has revealed; for the ancients did not find it out: with one people of them, mankind was made too subordinate, and became as nothing, and was overwhelmed under the weight of its representation of God, as with the Indians and the Jews; mankind became the slave of their God; with another race, God became the servant of man; the human crushed out the divine nature, and finally made sport of it, as with the Greeks and Romans. God, however, is not the servant of man, nor is man the slave of God; we are sons of the Great Father, and between father and son no priest need thrust himself. The priest knows that '*divide et impera*,' and acts accordingly. Since, however, the Deity does not allow himself stirred up against man by the priest, the priest instills into man a dread of the Deity.

"Others before you have wished to give to the world a better, a more worthy priesthood. You give to each one the pure, higher man in himself as his priest; for in each one there are two men,— the one which errs, makes mistakes, grows diseased, and sins, and the other which repents, makes atonement, and loves. Give to each one this higher man for a priest, for an intercessor between him and the Eternal. This inner priesthood will bring to the world the doctrine of the liberty of faith and of thought, and it will also bring the doctrine of the freedom of natures and characters.

"For the natures of men are different; the weak and mild seek a road upon which to walk gently forward, different from that over which the strong and impetuous rush ahead. Only one way leads to Rome, but a thousand lead to Jerusalem. Whoever hears God in the beating of his heart needs not the thunder of a Sinai, which no more fills him with alarm.

"Also the races differ in nature. You cannot span together the bear, the lion, and the horse in the same yoke, nor nourish them all with the same food. You will never teach the German to think of his God as the Chaldean or the Scandinavian, nor that he pray to him as the Indian. As each one has in his higher self his priest, so each race has its high-priest, according to the genius of the nation.

"Teach the princes to hear the voice of their reason, of their soul, and of their poor subjects, and force into their ear the cry of complaint from the disturbed, severed kingdom. Cause them to blush for shame that the crown of the great Emperor Karl and of the Ottos has become a plaything in the hand of the priest, with which he rewards an obedient child. Show to them yourself a reward. There is sufficient for this in the booty of the conflict; for will there not fall to them what you take back of the unrighteous mammon, in which the church is suffocated? Truly, the word of Christ, 'My kingdom is not of this world,' points the princes to a rich inheritance, and calls them to share the treasures of more than the Indies.

"In one thing, however, above all, be shrewd. Work by means of the word, less by means of the deed. Be courageous with the word, but timid about the deed, for the deed draws you to things incalculable. Not for your word, but for your deed, will the enemies punish you. Call the believers away from the temples,—call them to you; the temple, however, and the image therein, leave standing, or its watchmen will slay you.

"Whoever goes into the field against the whole world at once, is beaten before the slaughter has begun. No prophet has the power, by one and the same sermon, to take away from the priests their benefices and tithes; from the princes their bondmen and their revenues; from the citizens their superstitions; and from men all their vices. Therefore do not call your congregation to you by an alarm of bells, and do not stride along as a preacher of penitence who threatens, and punishes, and curses. The world has had more than enough of them. It is folly to think, because the Pope revels at a luxurious table, a man can be of use to humanity if he eats locusts in a hairy garment. The truth is the same, whether it is made known in a velvet mantle or in the skin of a beast.

"If you wish to bring liberty, remember her foster-mother is culture. An unbelieving, but cultivated man, stands nearer God than the savage who is full of faith; for the former can have love, the latter cannot.

"Before all, do not force yourself to martyrdom. Those who fall in battle only swell the triumph of the victor, and every one overcome increases his pride. To preserve one's self for a good business is wiser than to be killed for it, and a living witness to the truth is of more value than the ashes of a thousand dead ones. Do not forget that you stand in the midst of life, and of earthly human things as they are. Bring the spirit down into this life, but do not wish in vain to bring this life up to the spirit. The soil of man is this earth; do not wish to place him upon the pillar of Simeon Stylites. Whoever will lift men up above their nature is only a fanatic. The lifting up by the fanatic, however, will always be like the great crusade of the children to the grave of the saints. They are scattered as chaff in the wind.

"Fire testifies the presence of wind. With the flame of fanaticism you may make evident a storm; but the storms pass away over the heads of men, the flame dies out, and what follows is stillness and the old night.

"It is easier to reach a great aim, than, when it has been reached, to stand by it. To the former only courage is needed; to the latter, self-control. When you have done a great thing, then come those who desire of you a greater,— and require that which lies beyond your aim and for which your time is not ripe. With the reproaches of cowardice and incompleteness they will spur you on to strive for the unattainable; and this struggle will deprive you of that which you have attained.

"Therefore stand fast by your judgment. Do not take from man his faith in the ruling, omnipotent God, and his purest revelation in Christ and in Christ's Word. Do not take from him his faith: faith places there the petals of the flower whose fragrance is the love of God, which alone sanctifies us. But give to man a new priesthood,— that for which the human soul is itself calling. Only unclasp from the reason the goading girdle of illusion; loose the screws of inconsistency under which the growth of his spirit is restrained, and arouse him to reflection, in order that his soul-life no longer endure the violence of the strait-jacket about his spirit."

Brother Martin had come to this place in the book of the first reformer who here, in such detached thoughts, near a mass of other utterances taken from the writings of the ancients and of his own time, had laid down an entire policy of a reformation, when, looking up, he saw two forms approaching him from the city: a young man, a female form, whom a servant followed at some distance. They came nearer; they had already taken into their view the group resting at the well, when Brother Martin recognized them. He sprang up and went briskly to meet them.

"Count Egino," he exclaimed, joyously, "and you, noble lady, receive my salutations! What joy to see you well preserved before me!"

"And we have the same joy to be, at last, able to conduct you into the good city of Sienna," said Egino, shaking the hand of his countryman. "We have been awaiting you here in the inn for two days, since we have fortunately arrived here and have let Duke Alfonso continue his journey.

"You also came walking this way for my sake?" asked Brother Martin. "Then I can bless Rome for one thing,— that it gives to me a noble friend to take home with me!"

During these remarks Corradina had taken some steps forward, and had observed Martin's traveling companion still lying quiet upon the sod. He turned to her his face, stared at her awhile, then he said:—

"Ah! is it you — you? And I know him, there, too!"

After a pause he continued in a whisper:—

"I have made way with him,— entirely made way with him! It is still a good thing, now, that I have made way with him. Is it not? The monk there has absolved me. Now, since Irmgard is dead, it is a good thing that he had his share. He never moved any more; didn't you notice that?"

Corradina shrank back before the ugly man, who seemed to be able to do nothing but brood over his murder. Brother Martin stepped near him, and said:—

"You know him; he is now our traveling companion. You must also receive him in that capacity, Countess, the poor Uncle Kraps——"

"Oh certainly!" she put in; "we are thankful to you for thinking of him."

"I helped bury Irmgard at the Campo Santo," continued Martin, "and her uncle then followed me, as if involuntarily. We have together bought a donkey, and then started together upon our pilgrimage."

"This poor man is to me as a fortune to which you lead me, Brother Martin," said Egino. "What consolation it will be for me that I can care for his future, you may feel with me."

"But there is also Götz, your trusty follower," exclaimed Brother Martin, espying the servant following Egino.

"I owe that to Callisto, my brave friend. He has brought it about that Götz might be allowed to leave the city; and since Callisto's gardener, whom we found at Baccano, knew that we had turned toward Sienna, Gotz has overtaken us here yesterday, and upon my good steed at that."

During this they had betaken themselves to the shade of the well. Egino and Corradina seated themselves upon the stone bench to rest.

"So we can go farther, then, to-morrow, with good courage," said Brother Martin, standing before them, "homeward, over the Alps. If we leave a dear soul behind us, let us comfort ourselves that she ever lives in our thoughts, and thus remains with us and goes with us. The happiness of the future should build itself now upon such an offering. That is the law of life. Every happiness demands its price, which we must pay for it; now a lighter one, now one more weighty. The lighter spirit comes from an easier purchase; from the more earnest and profound, a harder one is required."

"That is so," responded Egino; "and you, Brother Martin, can utter that from the depths of your own soul; for Rome has also demanded of you a sacrifice."

"Yes, a great one: the inner peace with which I came; the faithful simplicity of my German nature; and it has given one in its place, — the urgent impulse to the struggle for truth and the pure Word of God. I came in the light gown of a mendicant monk, and go home laden with the heavy armor of a warrior for Christ, with your book in my hand, noble lady, as a sharp, victorious sword!"

She was silent. Egino then arose.

"Let us go back to prepare ourselves for our departure at the earliest hour to-morrow," he said.

But Corradina laid her hand upon his and interrupted him, turning to Brother Martin: —

"Do you know you have still a promise to us to redeem? You were to give to our betrothal the consecration of a priest, and, in the pressure of events, you have omitted it. It is, indeed, the custom that one also blesses betrothals; and I wish it, because I follow your young friend alone into his land."

Brother Martin looked at her awhile in silence, then he answered: —

"God dwells as well under the shady roof of this treetop, as in a church of stone. Let yourselves, also, be immediately blessed here in his presence with the purest intentions and the best emotion which lies in your souls. Is it not written in your own book, in that of your grandfather, 'Give to each one as his priest the higher man in himself'? Well, then, call upon this priest in yourselves and let him bless your united hands; let him pronounce over you the word that binds you forever. It will be a more spiritual, a more holy act than I, the weak, sinful cloister-brother, can make of it with holy water and formulæ of prayer."

He placed their hands together, and while each became absorbed in the glance of the other, he added with a mournful smile: —

"See, that is the first act of the new priesthood which we will give the world. I, the monk, can do nothing more than bless it, give testimony to it. And now away to our native land, — to Wittenberg."

www.ingramcontent.com/pod-product-compliance
Lightning Source LLC
Chambersburg PA
CBHW020101020526
44112CB00032B/721